Advancing the Right to Health Care in China: Towards Accountability

Human Rights Research Series, Volume 83.
The titles published in this series are listed at the end of this volume.

Advancing the Right to Health Care in China: Towards Accountability

Intersentia Ltd
Sheraton House | Castle Park
Cambridge | CB3 0AX | United Kingdom
Tel.: +44 1223 370 170 | Fax: +44 1223 370 169 Email: mail@intersentia.co.uk
www.intersentia.com | www.intersentia.co.uk

Distribution for the UK and Ireland:
NBN International
Airport Business Centre, 10 Th ornbury Road
Plymouth, PL6 7 PP
United Kingdom
Tel.: +44 1752 202 301 | Fax: +44 1752 202 331
Email: orders@nbninternational.com

Distribution for Europe and all other countries:
Intersentia Publishing nv Groenstraat 31
2640 Mortsel
Belgium
Tel.: +32 3 680 15 50 | Fax: +32 3 658 71 21
Email: mail@intersentia.be

Distribution for the USA and Canada:
Independent Publishers Group
Order Department
814 North Franklin Street
Chicago, IL 60610
USA
Tel.: +1 800 888 4741 (toll free) | Fax: +1312 337 5985
Email: orders@ipgbook. com

Advancing the Right to Health Care in China: Towards Accountability

ISBN 978-1-78068-677-6 (paperback)
ISBN 978-1-78068-678-3 (PDF)
D/2019/7849/10
NUR 828

British Library Cataloguing in Publication Data. A catalogue record for this book is available from the British Library.

ACKNOWLEDGEMENTS

To my family

I sometimes hear that doing a PhD can be as tough as training for a marathon. I abandoned jogging many years ago and I would not have finished this lonely and tough PhD journey if I did not meet and work with these amazing people, to whom I am deeply grateful for their trust, encouragement, support, friendship and love.

First and foremost, I would like to extend my heartfelt gratitude to my supervisors Prof. Brigit Toebes and Prof. Marcel Brus for their excellent guidance throughout the entire process of my PhD. Being given the opportunity to do a PhD at the University of Groningen was definitely one of the best opportunities of my academic career.

My sincere appreciation also goes to the members of my reading committee, Prof. Aart Hendriks, Prof. Chenguang Wang and Prof. Hans Hogezeil for their thoughtful review and their approval of this thesis.

A special thank you to my colleagues at the International Law Department. It has been a great pleasure and privilege to be part of the team over the years.

I am endlessly grateful to my officemate, my language editor, my paranymph and most importantly, my best friend, Lottie Lane. I cannot imagine that I could have completed this project without her. My deep gratitude goes to Erna, Ira, Katrina, Lucia, Marlies, Marie Elske and Veronika, not only for the interesting academic discussions, but also for their company. I am also grateful for the time spent with my Chinese friends, especially Huanlin Lang, Bin Jiang, Yu Sun and Hao Cui. I will cherish all the fun and adventures we have had in Groningen.

I gratefully acknowledge the Chinese Scholarship Council for funding me to do this PhD project.

Last but certainly not least, I would like to express my deepest gratitude to my family for their unconditional support. I dedicate this book to them.

Yi Zhang
April 2018
Groningen

Contents

List of Abbreviations

AAAQ-AP	Availability Accessibility Acceptability Quality Accountability Participation
AIDS	Acquired Immune Deficiency Syndrome
APL	Administrative Procedure Law of the People's Republic of China
Art	Article
BMI	Basic Medical Insurance
CDC	Centre for Disease Control and Prevention
CEDAW	Convention on the Elimination of All Forms of Discrimination against Women
CERD	International Convention on the Elimination of All Forms of Racial Discrimination
CFDA	Chinese Food and Drug Administration
CPC	Communist Party of China
CRC	Convention on the Rights of the Child
CRMW	International Convention on the Protection of the Rights of All Migrant Workers and Members of Their Families
CRPD	Convention on the Rights of Persons with Disabilities
CSOs	Civil Society Organisations
CteeEDAW	United Nations Committee on the Elimination of Discrimination against Women
CteeESCR	United Nations Committee on Economic, Social and Cultural Rights
CteeRC	United Nations Committee on the Rights of the Child
ECHR	Convention for the Protection of Human Rights and Fundamental Freedoms
ECOSOC	Economic and Social Council
ECtHR	European Court of Human Rights
Eg	Exempli gratia (for example)
ESCR	Economic, Social and Cultural Rights
EU	European Union
GP	General Practitioner
GPCL	General Principles of Civil Law of the People's Republic of China
HIV	Human Immunodeficiency Virus
ICCPR	International Covenant on Civil and Political Rights
ICESCR	International Covenant on Economic, Social and Cultural Rights
IPCD	Insurance Programme for Catastrophic Diseases

MFA	Medical Financial Assistance
MOCA	Ministry of Civil Affairs
MOF	Ministry of Finance
MOH	Ministry of Health
MOHRSS	Ministry of Human Resources and Social Security
NDRC	National Development and Reform Commission
NHFPC	National Health and Family Planning Commission
NHR	New Round of Health Care Reform
NHRI	National Human Rights Institution
NGOs	Non-governmental Organisations
NPC	National People's Congress
NPCSC	Standing Committee of the National People's Congress
NRCMS	New Rural Cooperative Medical Scheme
OECD	Organisation for Economic Cooperation and Development
OHCHR	Office of the United Nations High Commissioner for Human Rights
OOP	Out-of-pocket
OP	Optional Protocol
PHC	Primary Health Care
SARS	Severe Acute Respiratory Syndrome
SDGs	Sustainable Development Goals
TCM	Traditional Chinese Medicine
UDHR	Universal Declaration of Human Rights
UEBMI	Urban Employees' Basic Medical Insurance
UHC	Universal Health Coverage
UK	United Kingdom
UN	United Nations
UNAIDs	United Nations Programme on HIV/AIDS
UNDP	United Nations Development Programme
UNGA	United Nations General Assembly
UNICEF	United Nations Children's Fund
URBMI	Urban Residents' Basic Medical Insurance
USA	United States of America
VCLT	Vienna Convention on the Law of Treaties
WHA	World Health Assembly
WHO	World Health Organisation

Chapter 1
General Introduction

1.1 Background and problem

Health is indispensable for living a life of dignity.[1] As a matter of necessity, health, and in particular access to health care, are among the top concerns of every human being. As a result, there is a broad consensus that the right to the enjoyment of the highest attainable standard of physical and mental health (the right to health) is a fundamental human right.[2] The right to health encompasses access to timely and appropriate health care, as well as access to safe drinking water, adequate sanitation, education, health-related information, and other underlying determinants of health.[3] The right to health care, as one of the key aspects of the broader framework of the right to health, has been enshrined in a wide range of human rights treaties and has obtained considerable legal weight over the past decades.[4]

Currently, there is an almost universal commitment to the right to health (care), as the core conventions incorporating the right to health (care) have been ratified by

---

1 United Nations Committee on Economic, Social and Cultural Rights (CteeESCR), 'General Comment No. 14: The Right to the Highest Attainable Standard of Health (Art. 12 of the Covenant)' (General Comment 14) (11 August 2000) UN Doc E/C12/2000/4, para 1.

2 ibid; Brigit Toebes, *The Right to Health as a Human Right in International Law* (Intersentia/Hart 1999) 4; John Harrington and Maria Stuttaford, 'Introduction' in John Harrington and Maria Stuttaford (eds), *Global Health and Human Rights: Legal and Philosophical Perspectives* (Routledge 2010) 1.

3 CteeESCR, General Comment 14 (n 1) para 11.

4 The right to health care, as an essential aspect of the right to health, is recognised in numerous international instruments, for example the International Covenant on Economic, Social and Cultural Rights. United Nations General Assembly (UNGA), International Covenant on Economic, Social and Cultural Rights (ICESCR) (adopted 16 December 1966, entered into force 3 January 1976) 993 UNTS 3, art 12. The provisions regarding the right to health care will be discussed in more detail in the following sections. See also Paul Schoukens, 'The Right to Access Health Care: Health Care According to International and European Social Security Law Instruments' in Andre den Exter (ed), *International Health Law: Solidarity and Justice in Health Care* (Maklu 2008) 19-32; Maite San Giorgi, *The Human Right to Equal Access to Health Care* (Intersentia 2012) 3-4.

up to 99% of Member States of the United Nations (UN):[5] of 194 Member States, 166 have ratified or acceded to the International Covenant on Economic, Social and Cultural Rights (ICESCR) (85%); 174 States are party to the Convention on the Rights of Persons with Disabilities (CRPD) (88%); 178 States are party to the International Convention on the Elimination of All Forms of Racial Discrimination (CERD) (90%); 189 States have ratified or acceded to the Convention on the Elimination of All Forms of Discrimination against Women (CEDAW) (96%); and all States but one (the United States of America) are party to the Convention on the Rights of the Child (CRC) (99%).[6] Therefore, it can be concluded that all countries in the world have ratified at least one binding treaty that includes the provision of the right to health (care) and it can be stated that the recognition of the right to health (care) has reached near universality.[7]

Furthermore, the growing legal recognition of health as a human right in international law has led to the development of normative frameworks for realising this right, including through General Comment 14, which is an explanatory document to Article 12 of the ICESCR. Although not legally binding, General Comment 14 provides authoritative guidance on how the right to health (care) can be implemented at the domestic level.[8] In addition to general comments, there has been a burgeoning stream of legal reports and publications clarifying the normative content of the right to health (care) in the past two decades.[9] As a result of these key developments, the right to health (care) is rather well-defined under international human rights law.

5 Linda Keith, 'Human Rights Instruments' in Peter Cane and Herbert Kritzer (eds), *The Oxford Handbook of Empirical Legal Research* (Oxford University Press 2010) 354.

6 Office of the United Nations High Commissioner for Human Rights (OHCHR), 'Status of Ratification Interactive Dashboard' <http://indicators.ohchr.org/> accessed 19 November 2017.

7 Although the United States of America (US) has not ratified the Convention on the Rights of the Child (CRC), it is party to the International Convention on the Elimination of All Forms of Racial Discrimination (CERD). Therefore, all countries have ratified at least one binding treaty that includes the provision of the right to health (care).

8 UNGA, 'Report of the Special Rapporteur on the Right of Everyone to the Enjoyment of the Highest Attainable Standard of Physical and Mental Health, Paul Hunt' (17 Janauary 2007) UN Doc A/HRC/4/28, para 9; Gunilla Backman and others, 'Health Systems and the Right to Health: An Assessment of 194 Countries' (2008) 372 The Lancet 2047, 2048.

9 See eg United Nations Economic and Social Council, 'Report of the Special Rapporteur on the Right of Everyone to the Enjoyment of the Highest Attainable Standard of Physical and Mental Health, Paul Hunt' (13 February 2003) UN Doc E/CN.4/2003/58, paras 23-26; Lawrence Gostin, *Global Health Law* (Harvard University Press 2014) 243-269; Paul Hunt and Gunilla Backman, 'Health Systems and the Right to the Highest Attainable Standard of Health' (2008) 10 Health and Human Rights 81; Toebes (n 2).

Given that the ICESCR is widely recognised as the core instrument for the protection of the right to health (care),[10] and that China is party to this treaty, the analyses in this thesis mainly focus on the ICESCR. Pursuant to Article 12 of the ICESCR, States parties should 'take steps' to meet their obligations arising from the right to health by 'all appropriate means, including in particular the adoption of legislative measures'. The United Nations Committee on Economic, Social and Cultural Rights (CteeESCR) also mentions other appropriate measures for the purpose of Article 12 of the ICESCR, including administrative, financial, educational and social measures.[11] Such measures often take the form of policy. Furthermore, in General Comment 14 the CteeESCR emphasises the obligation of States parties to provide judicial remedies with regard to the rights within the ICESCR which may be deemed justiciable in domestic legal systems.[12] While the right to health is not mentioned as one of the 'justiciable rights', which can be directly invoked by national judicial organs,[13] the CteeESCR notes that, 'any person or group victim of a violation of the right to health should have access to effective judicial or other appropriate remedies at both national and international levels'.[14] Thus, all victims of violations of the right to health (care) should be provided with an avenue for claiming reparation, in the form of restitution, compensation, satisfaction or guarantees of non-repetition.[15]

Many States have now recognised the right to health or the more specific right to health care in their national constitutions and other statutes.[16] This is supported by the substantial number of empirical analyses that have been conducted to address the domestic implementation and protection of the right to health (care). Some of these studies have focused on the State's commitments to and compliance with the right to health (care), for example whether domestic laws and policies have been enacted, formulated or amended so as to give effect to the right to health (care), or to what extent a State's health care system includes the necessary features that arise from the

10 OHCHR and World Health Organization (WHO), 'Fact Sheet No. 31: The Right to Health' (June 2008) 9.

11 CteeESCR, 'General Comment No. 3: The Nature of State Parties' Obligations (Art.2 Para. 1 of the Covenant)' (General Comment 3) (14 December 1990) UN Doc E/1991/23, para 7.

12 ibid, para 5; CteeESCR, 'General Comment No. 9: The Domestic Application of the Covenant' (General Comment 9) (3 December 1998) UN Doc E/C12/1998/24, para 5.

13 CteeESCR, General Comment 3 (n 11) para 7.

14 CteeESCR, General Comment 14 (n 1) para 59.

15 ibid.

16 Backman and others (n 8) 2059.

right to health (care).[17] For instance, in a 2008 analysis of 186 accessible constitutions, Perehudoff identified that 135 countries have entrenched health or health care-related rights in their constitutions.[18] In addition, we have already witnessed a steady development of the right to health (care) in national jurisprudence over the past two decades, in particular in Latin American countries and in South Africa.[19]

Currently, academic debate on the domestic implementation of the right to health (care) has moved beyond judicial accountability (or *justiciabililty*).[20] A broader approach is being taken to addressing violations of the right to health (care), along the lines of 'accountability'. In this context, judicial accountability is seen as just one form of accountability, while others include quasi-judicial, political, administrative and social accountability. These various forms of accountability reinforce the realisation of the right to health (care) by providing right-holders with an opportunity to call into question how State (and other relevant) actors (i.e. duty-bearers) have discharged their obligations under the right to health (care).[21] In a similar fashion, accountability in each form provides State actors with right to health obligations with the opportunity to inform right-holders about what they have done to achieve the full realisation of the right to health (care), and to explain and justify their reasons for it.[22] Where violations occur, responsible State actors are to be held accountable for their failures and face negative consequences, including eventual sanctions.[23] Without accountability, the right to health (care) runs the risk of becoming an empty promise.[24] As such, Paul Hunt, one of the former UN Special Rapporteurs on the

17 ibid 2053; Keith (n 5) 354.

18 Katrina Perehudoff, 'Health, Human Rights and National Constitutions' (WHO 2008) 20.

19 Aart Hendriks, 'The Right to Health in National and International Jurisprudence' (1998) 5 European Journal of Health Law 389, 394–402. Cases see eg *Minister of Health* v *Treatment Action Campaign* (TAC) (2002) 5 SA 721 (CC); Hans Hogerzeil, Melanie Samson and Jaume Casanova, 'Ruling for Access: Leading Court Cases in Developing Countries on Access to Essential Medicines as Part of the Fulfilment of the Right to Health' (WHO 2004) 17-35; Daniel Wei Wang, 'Right to Health Litigation in Brazil: The Problem and the Institutional Responses' (2015) 15 Human Rights Law Review 617.

20 Paul Hunt and others, 'Implementation of Economic, Social and Cultural Rights' in Scott Sheeran and Nigel Rodley (eds), *Routledge Handbook of International Human Rights Law* (Routledge 2013) 550.

21 UNGA, 'Report of the Special Rapporteur on the Right of Everyone to the Enjoyment of the Highest Attainable Standard of Physical and Mental Health, Paul Hunt' (31 Janauary 2008) UN Doc A/HRC/7/11, para 51 (d).

22 ibid.

23 ibid.

24 ibid, paras 8 -18.

Right to Health, has mentioned on several occasions within various reports that accountability is a fundamental component of the right to health (care) and that States parties to the ICESCR undertake a core obligation to establish effective, transparent, accessible and independent accountability mechanisms for the implementation of the right to health (care) at the domestic level.[25]

However, irrespective of the constitutional recognition of this right, empirical evidence suggests that as a whole, the implementation of the right to health (care) remains largely rhetorical at the domestic level.[26] For example, China has ratified most of the international human rights treaties recognising the right to health (care) and is considered to have a monist system in terms of the domestic implementation of international law. Theoretically, this means that international (human rights) treaties are automatically incorporated into China's legal system when it becomes party to them. However, this does not mean that provisions of international (human rights) treaties are directly applicable in China's domestic courts. In fact, when it comes to international human rights treaties, a conventional understanding suggests that provisions of human rights treaties cannot be directly applied by the domestic courts (see chapter 3). Therefore, a prerequisite for invoking the right to health (care) within China's jurisdiction is that this right be (entirely or partially) transformed into China's domestic legal system through legislative acts amending or supplementing pre-existing laws. To fully comply with its binding international obligations, China must indeed fulfil an obligation under the ICESCR to give effect to the rights enshrined therein (including the right to health) in its domestic legal order.

As noted in the periodic reports submitted to the CteeESCR, China has enacted a handful of laws that provide important legal ground for the promotion and protection of the right to health (care) (see more detail in chpater 3).[27] However, as of November

25 See eg ibid, para 11; UNGA, 'Report of the Special Rapporteur on the Right of Everyone to the Enjoyment of the Highest Attainable Standard of Physical and Mental Health, Paul Hunt' (11 August 2008) UN Doc A/63/263, para 8.

26 See eg Backman and others (n 8) 2059–2082.

27 See generally United Nations Economic and Social Council, 'Implementation of the International Covenant on Economic, Social and Cultural Rights: Intial Reports submitted by States Parties under Articles 16 and 17 of the Covenant, Addendum, People's Republic of China' (4 March 2004) UN Doc E/1990/5/Add.59, paras 14, 145-209; United Nations Economic and Social Council, 'Implementation of the International Covenant on Economic, Social and Cultural Rights: Second Periodic Reports submitted by States Parties under Articles 16 and 17 of the Covenant, China' (6 July 2012) UN Doc E/C.12/CHN/2, ch 10 paras 1-9.

2017, neither constitutional nor other legal provisions exist that explicitly address the right to health (care). Nonetheless, clear references to non-discrimination and equality, which constitute key principles (and obligations) under the right to health (care), and human rights more generally, are made in the Chinese Constitution and several domestic laws (see sections 3.4.2 and 3.4.3 of chapter 3). Additionally, provisions containing elements of the right to health (care) can also be found in a wide variety of health-related laws (see section 3.4.3 of chapter 3). Moreover, although they are not entirely equivalent to the right to health care as such, provisions concerning judicial remedies to redress violations of health-related rights can also be found in several laws. However, as will be explained in chapter 3, gaps exist between *de jure* and *de facto* implementation of the right to health (care). Generally speaking, China's current legal framework is ill-equipped to regulate the health care system and no law explicitly stipulates what the government should provide in terms of essential health care.

When it comes to health policies, China has issued a variety of human rights-related documents (eg Human Rights White Papers and National Human Rights Action Plans) that set clear and concrete goals for the promotion and protection of human rights, including the right to health care (see chapter 4). These documents not only reaffirm China's international and constitutional commitments to human rights, but more importantly, they transformed the human rights cause in China into the realm of practice and routine.[28] It is also evident in many of its health-related documents that priority has been given to achieving universal access to basic health care in China's policy-making. However, it is much less apparent whether the efforts that China has made towards achieving universal access to basic health care or Universal Health Coverage (UHC) are in line with its commitments under the right to health (care). Arguably, China has already made remarkable progress towards basic UHC since the launch of its new round of health care reform (NHR) in 2006. In order to extend its basic health safety net to every citizen and to guarantee access to health care, China established three basic medical insurance (BMI) schemes and by the end of 2014 had managed to expand the insurance coverage to nearly 95%

28 OHCHR, 'Handbook on National Human Rights Plans of Action' (UN 2002) 9 <www.ohchr.org/Documents/Publications/training10en.pdf> accessed 28 November 2017

of the entire population.[29] This means that over 1.3 billion Chinese citizens are now covered by one of the BMI schemes.[30] Despite China's impressive achievements over the past decade, key challenges remain. For example, the inappropriate use or over-prescription of (essential) medicines, unequal treatment of individuals based on their social-economic status and lack of transparent and participatory processes, among others, may continue to undermine efforts to progressively realise the right to health (care) in China.

Another critical challenge that China faces in its implementation of the right to health (care) is the lack of accountability. While scholars acknowledge that accountability is a fundamental component of human rights,[31] doubts have been voiced regarding the (limited) role that accountability, as a Western concept that has recently been introduced to China, can play in advancing the right to health (care).[32] In light of the lack of competitive elections in China, some scholars even question whether accountability could exist at all under China's current political system.[33] Furthermore, as Philip Alston, the UN Special Rapporteur on Extreme Poverty and Human Rights, observes, there are top-down accountability mechanisms to exert control over public officials in China; however, although theoretically there are many mechanisms for Chinese citizens to complain and seek remedies for human rights violations, they are difficult to use in practice (see more detail in chapter 7).[34]

Considering that China's health care reform is entering the so-called 'deep-water zone', it is vital for the Chinese government to investigate how to guarantee

29 United Nations Economic and Social Council, 'Implementation of the International Covenant on Economic, Social and Cultural Rights: Second Periodic Reports submitted by States Parties under Articles 16 and 17 of the Covenant, China' (6 July 2012) UN Doc E/C.12/CHN/2, ch 10 paras 1-9.

30 Information Office of the State Council of the People's Republic of China, 'Progress in China's Human Rights in 2014' (2015) ch 1 <http://english.gov.cn/archive/white_paper/2015/06/08/content_281475123202380.htm> accessed 28 November 2017. The English version was obtained from the official website of the State Council.

31 UNGA, 'Report of the Special Rapporteur on the Right of Everyone to the Enjoyment of the Highest Attainable Standard of Physical and Mental Health, Paul Hunt' (n 25) para 8.

32 Shengnan Qiu and Gillian MacNaughton, 'Mechanisms of Accountability for the Realization of the Right to Health in China' (2017) 19 Health and Human Rights Journal 279, 281.

33 Yuko Kasuya and Yuriko Takahashi, 'Streamlining Accountability: Concepts, Subtypes, and Empirical Analyses' (2012) 23 <http://ssrn.com/abstract=2493654> accessed 28 November 2017.

34 UNGA, 'Report of the Special Rapporteur on Extreme Poverty and Human Rights on His Mission to China, Philip Alston' (28 March 2017) UN Doc A/HRC/35/26/Add.2, paras 68-69.

everyone equal access to health care.[35] The publication of the 'Healthy China 2030' Plan (2016) and the Basic Health Law (draft) provide great opportunities to place the implementation of the right to health (care) squarely within China's overall policy-making agenda.[36] The 'Healthy China 2030' Plan was the first medium- to long-term national strategic plan regarding the health sector since the foundation of the People's Republic of China.[37] In 2016, top Chinese leaders announced that health would be placed at the centre of the country's entire policy-making machinery and become an explicit national political priority.[38] The 'Healthy China 2030' Plan officially recognises the 'health-in-all-policies' approach and stresses that the government has a leading role to play in developing a healthy China.[39] Most importantly, this plan emphasises that health care reform should adhere to the principles of justice and fairness and calls for the legal foundation for the health care system to be strengthened, in particular through the drafting of a Basic Health Law as well as the review and revision of health-related laws and regulations.[40]

The emphasis on the legal foundation for the current NHR is unprecedented in China. Although the Chinese government invited scholars to design 'an overall conception and framework of the healthcare reform' during the 2006 NHR, the debate focused more on whether China should take a market-oriented or government-

35 This term refers to the fact that many of the easier reform tasks have been accomplished in China, leaving the more difficult ones still to be discharged. See Zhanhui Zhao, Ke Wu and Siqi Wang, 'Xinyigai: Zai Shengshuiqu Li Youyong (Guancha) [New Health Care Reform: Swim in the Deep-Water Zone (Observation)]' People's Daily (Overseas) (19 April 2012) 5 <http://paper.people.com.cn/rmrbhwb/html/2012-04/19/content_1038086.htm> accessed 28 November 2017. Author's translation.

36 At the time of writing, China is drafting its national health law which is entitled 'Jiben Yiliao Weisheng Fa'. However, as will be explained in detail in section 1.4, there are various English translations of the draft of the new law. In the remainder of this study, this new draft law will be referred to as the Basic Health Law.

37 National Health and Family Planning Commission of the People's Republic of China (NHFPC), 'Jiedu: "Jiankang Zhongguo 2030" Guihua Gangyao [Intepretation: the 'Healthy China 2030' Plan]' (2016) <www.moh.gov.cn/guihuaxxs/s3586s/201610/a2325a1198694bd6ba42d6e47567daa8.shtml> accessed 28 November 2017. Author's translation.

38 President Xi, Jinping presided at the National Health Conference (August 2016) <www.who.int/healthpromotion/conferences/9gchp/healthy-china/en/> accessed 28 November 2017.

39 Central Committee of the Communist Party of China and the State Council, '"Healthy China 2030" Plan' (25 October 2016) <www.gov.cn/zhengce/2016-10/25/content_5124174.htm> accessed 28 November 2017. Author's translation.

40 ibid.

led approach towards health care reform;[41] little attention was paid to the domestic implementation of the right to health (care), although China ratified the ICESCR in 2001. In addition, as most of the scholars involved in the 2006 reform were health economists or public health experts,[42] the voice of legal scholars was largely neglected. The Basic Health Law (draft) makes it possible to formally recognise the right to health (care) in China's domestic legal system and provides an opportunity to improve the implementation of this right through various forms of accountability.

With this in mind, the major challenges this study seeks to address are, inter alia, the use of essential medicines, unequal access to health care and the lack of accountability (mechanisms), most of which fall within the ambit of the right to health care. Due to the focus on the right to health (care), the underlying determinants of health fall outside the scope of the present study.

1.2 Research questions and structure

1.2.1 Research questions

The primary research question of this study is whether and how accountability could advance the right to health care in light of China's unique legal, political and social background. This question can encompass the following sub-questions:

- What is meant by 'the right to health care'? What does the right to health care entail?
- What are the core obligations under the right to health care that States have to discharge irrespective of resource constraints?
- To what extent has the right to health care been given effect in China through legislative or policy measures?
- What is meant by accountability? What is meant by right to health-based accountability?
- Is accountability a regime-specific concept? Does accountability also exist in non-electoral regimes such as China?
- Who is accountable, for what are these actors accountable, to whom are these actors accountable, and how are these actors to be held accountable?

41 Changshan Ma, 'Gonggong Zhengce Hefaxing Gongji Jizhi Yu Zouxiang - Yi Yigai Jincheng Wei Zhongxin de Kaocha [The Formulation and the Legitimacy Supply Mechanism of Public Policies - Review of the Health Care Reform]' (2012) Faxue Yanjiu [Legal Research] 20, 30-31.
42 ibid.

- What is the difference between accountability and accountability mechanisms? What types of accountability mechanisms are available for advancing the right to health care?
- What are China's existing accountability mechanisms for generating right to health-based accountability? What types of accountability mechanisms should be established for generating accountability, with the ultimate purpose of advancing the right to health care in China?

The primary goal of this study is to examine what role 'accountability' can play in advancing the right to health care in China. In doing so, this study synthesises two different concepts: (1) the right to health; and (2) accountability, and integrates them into an analytical framework for 'right to health-based accountability'. By answering the above questions through both theoretical and empirical analyses (see section 1.3 on the methodology), this study further provides a greater understanding of accountability and the various forms of accountability mechanisms that should be established by States. More specifically, the research is expected to establish a constructive accountability model that can be applied to specific health concerns in China, as well as in other countries, particularly those with non-electoral regimes.

1.2.2 Research structure

Part 1 of this thesis lays the foundations for the entire study – the implementation of the right to health care in China. It maps and analyses various measures, including in particular the legislative and policy measures that China has taken to give effect to its obligations arising from the right to health care. By doing so, this part identifies the gaps that exist between *de jure* and *de facto* implementation of the right to health care in China.

Before examining the degree to which China complies with its obligations arising from the right to health care, based on existing literature chapter 2 identifies the normative content of the right to health care. The chapter answers two questions: what does the international human right to health care mean and what does this right entail? Subsequently, the research moves to examine the domestic implementation of the right to health care in China. As a party to the ICESCR, China undertakes a legal obligation to 'take steps', 'to the maximum of its available resources' to achieve progressively the realisation of the right to health care 'by all appropriate means'.[43] Therefore, chapter 3 explores whether domestic laws have been enacted or amended to give effect to the right to health care in China's legal order. Subsequently, chapter 4 moves beyond the legal perspective by evaluating the extent to which China has committed to realise the right to health care through the adoption of other measures, including in particular health policies. This chapter also considers whether the efforts that China has taken to achieve UHC are in line with its obligations under the right to health care. Part 1 concludes with the identification of a number of remaining challenges and of the next steps to be taken for promoting the realisation of this right in China.

Part 2 offers a possible solution to the remaining challenges confronting China in its realisation of the right to health care – the exertion of accountability. A unique contribution of the right to health framework is that it provides a rather comprehensive and objective framework for accountability.[44] Hunt has repeatedly mentioned that States have a core obligation to establish a range of (domestic) accountability mechanisms so as to ensure the full enjoyment of the right to health.[45] The right to health norms and standards provide a compelling normative framework for defining right to health-based accountability and for developing effective accountability mechanisms to advance the right to health (care) at the domestic level.[46] Conversely, accountability reinforces the realisation of the right to health (care) by providing right-holders with the opportunity to question how State (and other relevant) actors have discharged their obligations under the right to health (care). In addition, it enables right-holders to hold State actors to account for failing to comply with their obligations. Therefore, part 2 of this study proposes an analytical framework for right to health-based accountability (which can also be applied to more human rights contexts), so as to lay the foundations for the discussion of accountability in the Chinese context in chapter 7. The purpose of chapter 5 is twofold. First, it aims

43 UNGA, ICESCR (n 4) art 12.
44 OHCHR, 'Claiming the Millennium Development Goals : A Human Rights Approach' (2008) vii, 7 <www.ohchr.org/Documents/Publications/Claiming_MDGs_en.pdf> accessed 28 November 2017.
45 See eg UNGA, 'Report of the Special Rapporteur on the Right of Everyone to the Enjoyment of the Highest Attainable Standard of Physical and Mental Health, Paul Hunt' (n 21) para 51 (d); UNGA, 'Report of the Special Rapporteur on the Right of Everyone to the Enjoyment of the Highest Attainable Standard of Physical and Mental Health, Paul Hunt' (n 25) para 11.
46 OHCHR and Center for Economic and Social Rights, 'Who Will Be Accountable? Human Rights and the Post-2015 Development Agenda' (2013) 10.

to refine the concept of accountability (which remains a rather elusive concept in several disciplines) from a human rights perspective. Second, it seeks to explore how accountability can advance the right to health (care) at the domestic level. Chapter 6 further explores the nature and scope of accountability mechanisms that can hold State actors to account at various levels, with a particular focus on judicial, quasi-judicial, political, administrative, and social accountability mechanisms.

For many scholars, the first and foremost form of accountability within democracies is political accountability, where societies select their leaders through elections.[47] There is a considerable body of literature focusing on accountability in democratic countries with competitive, free and fair elections, whereas little attention has been paid to accountability in non-electoral regimes. This gives rise to the question of whether the Western concept of accountability can be applied in the same fashion in non-electoral regimes, thus enhancing our understanding of accountability through the identification of accountability in different political regimes.[48] One contribution of this study is thus the discussion of 'accountability' within non-electoral regimes, taking China as a case study. Accountability is undoubtedly a complicated issue for non-electoral regimes, but there is no reason to assume that the basic principles of accountability cannot be applied within them. Some scholars have already noted the emergence of 'accountability without democracy' or 'accountability without elections' in existing non-electoral, single-party countries such as Vietnam and China. [49] In fact, given the lengthy process of holding an election, criticism of the effectiveness of elections to ensure political accountability is increasing. There is a growing consensus that the existence of elections alone cannot ensure all forms of accountability. Indeed, this study recognises that in addition to political accountability,

47 See eg Mark Bovens, 'Analysing and Assessing Accountability: A Conceptual Framework' (2007) 13 European Law Journal 447, 455; Derick Brinkerhoff, 'Taking Account of Accountability: A Conceptual Overview and Strategic Options' (US Agency for International Development 2001) 1 <http://1qswp72wn11q9smtq15ccbuo.wpengine.netdna-cdn.com/wp-content/uploads/2011/07/IPC_Taking_Account_of_Accountability.pdf> accessed 28 November 2017.

48 Kasuya and Takahashi (n 33) 2.

49 Jun Ma, 'The Dilemma of Developing Financial Accountability without Election - A Study of China's Recent Budget Reforms' (2009) 68 The Australian Journal of Public Administration s62 - s72; Regina Abrami, Edmund Malesky and Yu Zheng, 'Accountability and Inequality in Single-Party Regimes: A Comparative Analysis of Vietnam and China' (2008) Harvard Business School Working Paper 08-099 <https://wcfia.harvard.edu/files/wcfia/files/abrami_accountability.pdf> accessed 28 November 2017.

other forms of accountability (eg judicial, quasi-judicial, administrative and social accountability) may be found in non-electoral regimes.

As a result, part 3 is based on the hypothesis that accountability could exist with the absence of competitive elections. To come to a greater understanding of accountability for advancing the right to health care, part 3 conducts in-depth research into one selected country (China). Previous research has either focused on the right to health framework or on the concept of accountability in a more general and abstract fashion. In comparison, chapter 7 adopts the analytical framework for right to health-based accountability (developed in chapter 6) to assess China's idiosyncratic realities. Particular attention is paid to a number of health-related concerns, including people living with HIV/AIDS and Hepatitis B and maternal mortality. Through extensive case analyses, this chapter explores the extent to which accountability could advance the right to health care against the backdrop of China's unique legal, political and social background.

Chapter 8 summarises the main findings in this study and identifies a number of overall conclusions. It also offers a handful of recommendations for Chinese law- and policy-makers for implementing China's core obligations under the right to health care and for establishing accountability mechanisms through enacting the Basic Health Law.

1.3 Methodology

In order to answer the aforementioned research questions, this study adopts descriptive, normative and empirical research methods.[50]

To delineate the normative content of the right to health care in chapter 2 of part 1, this study takes a normative approach and stays within the limits of doctrinal analysis. A secondary data analysis of primary legal documents, reports and publications addressing the right to health (care) is conducted in this chapter. To a large extent the analysis depends on the key concepts and components derived from Article 12 of the ICESCR as well as General Comment 14. Other general comments, the reports of the

50 Maria Stuttaford, 'Methods in Health and Human Rights Research' in Fons Coomans, Fred Grünfeld and Menno Kamminga (eds), *Methods of Human Rights Research* (Intersentia 2009) 135–157; Keith (n 5) 353–375.

UN Special Rapporteurs on the Right to Health and academic publications are also included in the analysis.

Regarding the analysis of China's domestic implementation of the right to health care in chapters 3 and 4 of part 1, I conducted a normative analysis of existing national health-related laws and policies for the purposes of identifying China's practice. The indicators and benchmarks for evaluating progress towards the realisation of the right to health care were selected on the basis of the 'OPERA framework' developed by the Center for Economic and Social Rights.[51] Given that the framework was developed for all economic, social and cultural rights, and not for the right to health (care) in particular, I adapted the indicators and benchmarks on the basis of the framework developed both by Ooms and others for the WHO policy brief and Backman and others for the 'Health Systems and the Right to Health: An Assessment of 194 Countries' (see Annex 1).[52]

Chapters 3 and 4 investigate China's (pre-existing health-related) laws and policies for assessing its implementation of the right to health (care) at the domestic level. To ensure the accuracy of my analysis, I searched not only key words in the English-language versions of relevant laws, but also the official Chinese-language versions. Furthermore, to prevent errors in English translation, I obtained the official English versions of the legal documents published on the databases on the official Chinese websites, including, in particular, the websites of the National People's Congress and the State Council.[53] If the official version was not available, I turned to the academic database of authority – the pkulaw (*'beida fabao'*)[54] and verified the accuracy of its translation by reference to the original Chinese-language version. If there was no English translation available, I provided the translation myself.

The keywords selected include: 'discrimination (*qishi*)', 'equal/equality (*pingdeng*)', 'equity/equitable (*pingjun/gongzheng/jundeng/henping*)', 'medical

51 The so-called OPERA Framework triangulates outcomes, policy efforts and resources for making an overall assessment. See Center for Economic and Social Rights, 'The OPERA Framework: Assessing Compliance with the Obligation to Fulfill Economic, Social and Cultural Rights' (2012) 1 < http://cesr.org/sites/default/files/the.opera_.framework.pdf > accessed 28 November 2017.

52 ibid; Backman and others (n 8) 2053-2059; WHO, 'Anchoring Universal Health Coverage in the Right to Health: What Difference Would It Make? ' (WHO 2015) 26-28 <http://apps.who.int/iris/bitstream/10665/199548/1/9789241509770_eng.pdf> accessed 28 November 2017.

53 See generally 'The Database of Laws and Regulations' <www.npc.gov.cn/englishnpc/Law/Integrated_index.html> accessed 28 November 2017.

54 All translations of the legal documents on this online database are provided by the Legal Translation Research Centre of Peking University <http://en.pkulaw.cn> accessed 28 November 2017.

(*yiliao*)', 'health/health care (*jiankang/weisheng*)', 'disabled (*canji*)', 'women (*funv/nvxing*)', 'ethnic minority (*shaoshu minzu*)', 'minor (*ertong*)', 'the elderly (*lao*)', 'insurance (*baoxian*)', 'affordability (*fudan*)', 'out-of-pocket cost/expenditure (*geren huafei/zhifu*)' 'primary (*jichu/chuji*)', 'basic/essential (*jiben*)', 'medicines/drugs (*yaowu/yaopin*)', 'availability/available (*kede/huode*)', 'accessibility/accessible (*keji*)', 'resource (*ziyuan*)', distribution/allocation (*fenpei*)', 'participation (*canyu*)', and 'policy/plan/strategy (*zhengce/jihua/celue*)'. The reasons for selecting these key words will be explained in detail in chapter 3.

Concerning the health policies selected for analysis, I obtained data from public sources, including (pre-existing) health-related policies and journal articles. Both health-related and human rights-related documents were obtained from the databases on the official Chinese websites of, in particular, the State Council and the National Health and Family Planning Commission (NHFPC). The primary source of health statistics is the database managed by the Centre for Health Statistics and Information of the NHFPC, together with the annual China Statistical Year Books, the China Health Statistical Yearbooks and the websites of the Organisation for Economic Co-operation and Development (OECD) and the WHO.[55] The aforementioned key words were also used in my search for relevant documents and data in a wide variety of health-related commitments and statistics.

Subsequently, this research takes a descriptive approach in the analysis of right to health-based accountability in chapters 5 and 6 of part 2. Given that accountability is a concept recognised in different disciplines, this part is mainly based on the study of secondary sources across the disciplines of political science, public administration, law and human rights.

Part 3 adopts both descriptive and empirical approaches. To better understand the application of accountability mechanisms in China, bearing in mind its unique legal, political and social background, chapter 7 not only examines existing accountability mechanisms in China but also investigates their practical application. This data was obtained through interviews with judges, officials from the health sector and people

55 National Bureau of Statistics of the People's Republic of China, 'China Statistical Year Books' <www.stats.gov.cn/english/Statisticaldata/AnnualData/ >; NHFPC, 'China Health Statistical Year Books' <www.nhfpc.gov.cn/zwgkzt/tjnj/list.shtml>; Health, the official website of the Organisation for Economic Co-operation and Development (OECD) <www.oecd.org/health/> accessed 28 November 2017.

from civil society organisations (CSOs). The results of the interviews fed directly into the recommendations for the effective operation of accountability mechanisms, which have the ultimate aim of advancing the right to health care in China.

1.4 Terminology

This section pays attention to the translation of the right to health terminology into the Chinese language. This is important because there are considerable inconsistencies in the translations of the vocabulary into Chinese, leading to terminological confusion. For example, there are various English translations of the draft of China's new fundamental health law – the 'Jiben Yiliao Weisheng Fa' (in Chinese) – including 'basic medical and healthcare law', 'basic medical and health law', and 'basic health law'. Vice versa, the Chinese translations of the term 'right to health' also vary. In mainland China, the right to health is generally translated as *'jiankang quan'*; while in Taiwan it is (also) called *'yiliao renquan'*, which literally means the human right to access medical care.[56] Moreover, there is no clear distinction between the Chinese translations of the right to health and the right to health care. For a proper understanding of the implementation of the right to health care in China, it is therefore of the utmost importance to be more specific about the terminology used in the Chinese context.

In Chinese, the term health is translated in at least three different ways, as: *'weisheng'*, *'yiliao'* and *'jiankang'*. One reason for this terminological confusion is the deficit in language translation. More importantly, however, this ambiguity is attributed to a lack of conceptual clarification among Chinese translations of Western concepts. The terms *weisheng*, *yiliao* and *jiankang* each have a distinct meaning in Chinese and convey different content. To some extent, these Chinese translations reflect how government and academia perceive Western concepts of health, medical care, and the right to health in particular. As will be discussed in more detail in Annex 2, sometimes the Chinese translations even go beyond the scope of the original Western concepts and convey unique content. Therefore, before evaluating whether China has recognised the right to health norms and standards in its domestic laws and policies, it is important to revisit the Chinese translations of the relevant Western concepts and to clarify their meaning.

56 Chuan-feng Wu, 'Yiliao Renquan zhi Fazhan yu Quanli Tixi [The Development of the Right to Health and its Right System]' (2007) 148 Taiwan Law Review 128, 128. Author's translation.

Annex 2 extensively discusses the evolving conceptions of the terms *weisheng*, *yiliao* and *jiankang*. In general, (1) *weisheng* has two English translations: hygiene and health; (2) health has two Chinese translations: *weisheng* and *jiankang*; and (3) *weisheng* and *yiliao* have one overlapping element: the administration of medical practices. I perceive *'jiankang quan'* as the correct translation of the right to health. In light of the lengthy evolution of the conception of *weisheng*, with meanings having included the preservation of health and to some extent the preservation of life, individuals' self-protection, and the administration of health, it is better to use *weisheng* as the translation of most health laws and policies. The question then arises: how can the right to health care be specifically translated in a way that encompasses access to timely, acceptable, and affordable health care of appropriate quality? According to the WHO, health care 'embraces a full range of services covering health promotion and protection, disease prevention, diagnosis, treatment, care and rehabilitation.'[57] It also refers to 'the prevention, treatment, and management of illness and the preservation of mental and physical well-being through the services offered by the medical, nursing, and allied health professions.'[58] In this sense, health care is a broader concept than medical care (*yiliao*), given that the latter is merely provided by medical professionals,[59] and that health care also covers preventative care.[60] Notably, in some English speaking countries such as the United States of America, scholars tend to perceive health care as equivalent to medical care.[61]

In this study, I contend that health care as a concept is broader than medical care. The right to health care is a general term used to refer to a variety of techniques for the preservation of health, which can best be literally translated as *'baojian quan'* in Chinese.

---

57 WHO, 'A Declaration of the Promotion of Patients' Rights in Europe' (28 June 1994) 6 <www.who.int/genomics/public/eu_declaration1994.pdf> accessed 28 November 2017.

58 FXB Center for Health and Human Rights and Open Society Foundation, *Health and Human rights Resource Guide* (5th Edn 2013) 1.50 <https://cdn2.sph.harvard.edu/wp-content/uploads/sites/25/2014/03/HHRRG_Chapter-1.pdf> accessed 28 November 2017.

59 Toebes (n 2) 246-247.

60 ibid 246.

61 Puneet Sandhu, 'A Legal Right to Health Care: What Can the United States Learn from Foreign Models of Health Rights Jurisprudence?' (2007) 95 California Law Review 1151, 1160.

1.5 Concluding summary

This study seeks to contribute to China's new round of health care reform by proposing a right to health approach. As mentioned above, although significant progress has been made over the past two decades, challenges remain in deepening China's health care reform. The key fields that influence health care reform are health economics, public health, medicine and health care administration, within which different approaches are taken to address the same health problems.[62] Nevertheless, such disciplines do not necessarily focus on the protection of vulnerable and marginalised groups within society when scaling up health care reform. The added value of a rights-based approach is that it highlights that States have a legally binding obligation to ensure everyone's right to health care, paying particular attention to vulnerable and marginalised groups. Furthermore, a rights-based approach enables and facilitates the participation of the entire population, including in particular vulnerable and marginalised groups, in all health-related decision-making processes,[63] thus enhancing their ability to claim their health-related rights and making their prioritised health needs clear to the State.

However, the full enjoyment of the right to health care remains a distant goal world-wide, including in China.[64] While numerous approaches to this issue are possible, this study chooses to focus, through the lens of accountability, on advancing the right to health care in China, bearing in mind its unique legal, political and social background. The rationale for this approach is that accountability is a vital component of human rights, without which the right to health care may become toothless. This study seeks to identify whether and how accountability can be applied to advance the right to health care in China. It also offers a set of recommendations for Chinese law- and policy-makers to incorporate right to health norms and standards domestically, and makes suggestions for better embedding accountability mechanisms in the draft Basic Health Law. Moreover, the successful synthesis of the concepts of the right to health and accountability may also inform other non-electoral countries with high-cost and/or low-quality health care services as to how they could ensure the progressive realisation of the right to health (care).

62 Gilbert Abiiro and Manuela De Allegri, 'Universal Health Coverage from Multiple Perspectives: A Synthesis of Conceptual Literature and Global Debates' (2015) 15 BMC International Health and Human Rights 1, 3-5.
63 CteeESCR, General Comment 14 (n 1) para 11.
64 ibid, para 5.

Part 1

The Implementation of the Right to Health (Care) – An Analysis of China's Practice

Chapter 2
The Right to Health Care as a Human Right

2.1 Introduction

Part 1 of this thesis lays the foundation for the implementation of the right to health care in China. As discussed in chapter 1, the right to health care, as one of the key aspects of the broader framework of the right to health, has been firmly established under various international and regional human rights treaties as well as national constitutions.[1] A wide range of legal documents and reports clarifying the normative content of the right to health care has also been adopted over the past two decades.[2] These key developments have made the right to health care a rather well-defined norm under international human rights law. This has, however, not resulted in the effective and full implementation of the right to health care at the domestic level.[3] To address this lacuna, the main focus of this study is on the effective domestic implementation of the right to health care.

A first step towards enhancing the effective implementation of this right concerns the legal recognition of the right to health care in national constitutions and in other

1 See generally, United Nations General Assembly (UNGA), International Covenant on Economic, Social and Cultural Rights (ICESCR) (adopted 16 December 1966, entered into force 3 January 1976) 993 UNTS 3, art 12; United Nations Committee on Economic, Social and Cultural Rights (CteeESCR), 'General Comment No. 14: The Right to the Highest Attainable Standard of Health (Art. 12 of the Covenant)' (General Comment 14) (11 August 2000) UN Doc E/C12/2000/4, para 11; Eleano Kinney and Brian Clark, 'Provisions for Health and Health Care in the Constitutions of the Countries of the World' (2004) 37 Cornell International Law Journal 285, 287; Maite San Giorgi, *The Human Right to Equal Access to Health Care* (Intersentia 2012) 3-4; Gunilla Backman and others, 'Health Systems and the Right to Health: An Assessment of 194 Countries' (2008) 372 The Lancet 2047, 2047-2048.

2 See eg UNGA, 'Report of the Special Rapporteur on the Right of Everyone to the Enjoyment of the Highest Attainable Standard of Physical and Mental Health, Paul Hunt' (17 Janauary 2007) UN Doc A/HRC/4/28, para 9; United Nations Economic and Social Council, 'Report of the Special Rapporteur on the Right of Everyone to the Enjoyment of the Highest Attainable Standard of Physical and Mental Health, Paul Hunt' (13 February 2003) UN Doc E/CN.4/2003/58, paras 23-26; Lawrence Gostin, *Global Health Law* (Harvard University Press 2014) 243-269; Paul Hunt and Gunilla Backman, 'Health Systems and the Right to the Highest Attainable Standard of Health' (2008) 10 Health and Human Rights 81, 81-90.

3 Backman and others (n 1) 2050.

domestic legislation.[4] In addition to taking legislative measures, other administrative, financial, educational and social measures, which often have the nature of policy, are also sought-after.[5] Therefore, part 1 of this thesis first delineates the obligations that States parties undertake to give effect to the right to health care and evaluates the status quo of the legislative and policy measures China has taken to realise this right. By doing so, this part can identify the gaps between *de jure* and *de facto* implementation of the right to health care in China.

Chapter 2 does not aim to provide an exhaustive analysis of all contentious issues involved in the debate surrounding the definition of the right to health. Rather, the aim of this chapter is to set the stage for the analysis of the implementation of the right to health care in China. It does so by answering two simple questions: *what does the right to health care mean* and *what does this right entail*?

To answer these questions, it is necessary to have a clear picture of the various components of the right to health care, and of its underlying normative tools. To identify these elements, I have made a secondary data analysis of primary legal documents, reports and publications addressing the right to health (care). This analysis depends largely on the key concepts and components derived from Article 12 of the International Covenant on Economic, Social and Cultural Rights (ICESCR) as well as General Comment 14 of the Committee on Economic, Social and Cultural Rights (CteeESCR), which serves as the most authoritative interpretation of the right to health (care) as provided for in Article 12 of the ICESCR.

This chapter is divided into five sections. Section 2.2 first offers an introduction to the origins of health as a human right and the primary human rights instruments addressing the right to health (care). This section also clarifies the meaning of the right to health care. Subsequently, section 2.3 delineates the normative content of the right to health care. Before drawing some conclusions, section 2.4 sheds light on States parties' (core) obligations arising from the right to health care.

---

4 CteeESCR, 'General Comment No. 3: The Nature of State Parties' obligations (Art.2 Para. 1 of the Covenant)' (General Comment 3) (14 December 1990) UN Doc E/1991/23, para 3; Backman and others (n 1) 2059.

5 CteeESCR, General Comment 3 (n 4) para 7.

2.2 Defining the right to health care

2.2.1 The meaning of the terms 'health' and 'health care'

2.2.1.1 Definition of 'health'

While many attempts have been made to define 'health' and 'health care', the definitions of these two terms remain controversial.[6] Health can either be a subjective experience or an objective standard.[7] Based on my individual assessment, I may consider myself healthy, while for doctors applying objective health standards, the answer as to what health is may be as simple as 'the absence of disease', from a pure biomedical perspective.[8] Nevertheless, a pure biomedical definition of health has been criticised for not capturing the full dimensions of health.[9] For example, Daniels points out that disease is not a broad enough concept to cover either our daily usage or the theoretical concept of pathology.[10]

In the 1946 World Health Organisation Constitution, health was defined as 'a state of complete physical, mental and social well-being and not merely the absence of disease or infirmity.'[11] This authoritative definition broadens the negative definition of health from the absence of disease to include many positive aspects.[12] It also covers physical, mental and social domains.[13] However, many scholars have asserted that this definition is too absolute and broad.[14] For example, Daniels notes that the World

6 Brigit Toebes, *The Right to Health as a Human Right in International Law* (Intersentia/Hart 1999) 16-25; Norman Daniels, *Just Health : Meeting Health Needs Fairly* (Cambridge University Press 2008) 36; Puneet Sandhu, 'A Legal Right to Health Care: What Can the United States Learn from Foreign Models of Health Rights Jurisprudence?' (2007) 95 California Law Review 1155, 1155–1161; Kinney and Clark (n 1) 288.

7 Toebes (n 6) 20.

8 Daniels (n 6) 36; Richard Smith, 'The End of Disease and the Beginning of Health' (The BMJ Opinion 2008) <http://blogs.bmj.com/bmj/2008/07/08/richard-smith-the-end-of-disease-and-the-beginning-of-health/> accessed 28 November 2017.

9 Daniels (n 6) 36.

10 ibid 36-37.

11 Constitution of the World Health Organisation ('WHO Constitution') (adopted 22 July 1946, entered into force 7 April 1948) 14 UNTS 185, preamble.

12 Benjamin Meier, 'Global Health Governance and the Contentious Politics of Human Rights: Mainstreaming the Right to Health for Public Health Advancement' (2010) 46 Stanford Journal of International Law 1, 6; Machteld Huber and others, 'How Should We Define Health?' (2011) 343 BMJ 1–3 <http://www.bmj.com/content/343/bmj.d4163> accessed 28 November 2017.

13 Meier (n 12) 6; Huber and others (n 12) 1-3.

14 See generally Toebes (n 6) 23; Daniels (n 6) 37.

Health Organisation (WHO) definition would potentially lead to the misconception that health is 'all there is to well-being or happiness' and turn 'all of social philosophy and social policy into health care'.[15] As such, he proposes that we define health as

> normal functioning for our species' and argues that we can 'rely on the scientific methods of the biomedical sciences to characterize pathology, as well as on our growing understanding of epidemiology [...] to clarify what we need to function normally.[16]

In turn, this alternative definition has been criticised for being of limited value to advancing the human right to health.[17] Admittedly, the bio-statistical concept of health contributes to the measurement of an individual's health and is useful for monitoring bodies that are responsible for evaluating the compliance of the right to health.[18] However, as Marks correctly notes, this concept does not clarify 'what a human rights-inspired health policy should strive to achieve for the population' and may have the risk of resulting in positions being taken that are contradictory to human rights.[19] Although there is still no consensus as to what health is, a more recent approach is to regard health as a person's ability to adapt and self-manage, or as 'a person's ability to achieve or exercise a cluster of basic human activities'.[20]

Compared to the evolving understanding of the concept of health in the West, the Chinese definitions of health have not changed much over the past decades. As explained in chapter 1, health has two Chinese translations: *weisheng* and *jiankang*. *Weisheng* was initially a term applied in the Chinese cosmology as an expression of 'guarding life'.[21] It was not until the late Qing period (1875-1908) that *weisheng* was given a modern meaning of hygiene. The term *weisheng* now encompasses two dimensions: (1) the science and art of promoting health; and (2) the State administration of a national health system. When mentioning health as a legal right, most Chinese

---

15 ibid.
16 ibid.
17 Stephen Marks, 'The Emergence and Scope of the Human Right to Health' in José Zuniga, Stephen Marks and Lawrence Gostin (eds), *Advancing the Human Right to Health* (Oxford University Press 2013) 6.
18 ibid.
19 ibid 6-7.
20 Huber and others (n 12) 1–3; Sridhar Venkatapuram, 'Health, Vital Goals, and Central Human Capabilities' (2013) 27 Bioethics 271, 279.
21 Ruth Rogaski, *Hygienic Modernity: Meanings of Health and Disease in Treaty-Port China* (University of California Press 2004) 1, 22, 25.

legal scholars tend to use the term *jiankang* rather than *weisheng*.[22] The Chinese legal definition of the term health is also similar to the WHO definition – *jiankang* is both physical and mental well-functioning.[23] However, most Chinese scholars discuss *jiankang* in the realm of civil law, i.e. perceiving health as a personality right, and doubt whether mental well-being can be the subject of this right.[24] As such, health as a personality right in Chinese civil law theory is different from the right to health theory. This will be discussed in more detail in chapter 3.

2.2.1.2 Definition of 'health care'

There is also no standard definition of the term 'health care'.[25] In English-speaking countries such as the United States of America (USA), sometimes health care is also regarded as equivalent to medical care, whether preventative, primary or specialised.[26] In addition, in one of the reports of the Special Rapporteur on the Right to Health in 2008, Hunt used the term 'timely and appropriate medical care' rather than health care.[27] According to this approach, health care can be equated to medical care.

However, the WHO takes a broader approach to health care, defining it as 'medical, nursing or allied services dispensed by health care providers and health care establishments'.[28] The WHO defines health care as 'a full range of services covering health promotion and protection, disease prevention, diagnosis, treatment, care and rehabilitation'.[29] As such, health care is considered to be a broader concept than medical care, since the latter is merely provided by medical professionals,[30]

22 See eg Liming Wang, 'Rengequanfa de Fazhan yu Wanshan - Yi Renge Zunyan de Baohu wei Shijiao [Developing and Improving the Law of Personality - From the Perspective of Human Dignity Protection] (2012) 4 Science of Law 166; Lixin Yang, *Rengequanfa [Law of Personality]* (China Legal Publishing House 2006) 145-161.

23 Yang (n 22) 146.

24 ibid 146-149.

25 Toebes (n 6) 246-247.

26 Sandhu (n 6) 1160.

27 UNGA, 'Report of the Special Rapporteur on the Right of Everyone to the Enjoyment of the Highest Attainable Standard of Physical and Mental Health, Paul Hunt' (31 Janauary 2008) UN Doc A/HRC/7/11, para 45.

28 World Health Organisation ('WHO') 'A Declaration of the Promotion of Patients' Rights in Europe' (28 June 1994) 6 <www.who.int/genomics/public/eu_declaration1994.pdf> accessed 28 November 2017.

29 ibid.

30 Toebes (n 6) 246-247.

and because health care covers preventative care as well.[31] In this study, I follow the WHO's definition, perceiving health care as a concept covering medical care as well as other care such as preventative health care and family planning services.[32]

Another term closely related to 'health care' is 'health service', which generally refers to 'any service which can contribute to improved health, or the diagnosis, treatment and rehabilitation of sick people, and is not necessarily limited to medical or health-care services.'[33] Health services also cover 'health education, health promotion, and environmental services such as housing, sanitation, etc., which have a known health benefit.'[34] Accordingly, health care service is the point at which health care and health service overlap.

In sum, health care, as the subject of this study, can be understood as a broad range of services, goods and facilities offered by the medical, nursing, and allied health professionals for the purpose of maintaining, promoting or restoring health.

2.2.2 The emergence of health as a human right

The emergence of health as a human right can be traced back to the 19th century, arising from the public health movement in Europe.[35] A consecutive historical development concerns the recognition of economic, social and cultural rights, including the right to health throughout the 20th century.[36] During the course of World War II, President Franklin Roosevelt of the USA delivered a speech known as the 'Four Essential Freedoms'.[37] Among these freedoms, Roosevelt explained that the 'freedom from want' entails 'economic understandings which will secure to every nation a healthy peacetime life for its inhabitants - everywhere in the world'. Arguably, this freedom

31 ibid 246.
32 ibid 248.
33 WHO Regional Office for Europe, 'Terminology - A Glossary of Technical Terms on the Economics and Finance of Health Services' (17 July 1998) EUR/ICP/CARE 94 01/CN01, 45 <www.euro.who.int/__data/assets/pdf_file/0014/102173/E69927.pdf> accessed 28 November 2017.
34 ibid.
35 John Tobin, *The Right to Health in International Law* (Oxford University Press 2012) 8; Toebes (n 6) 10-11.
36 Toebes (n 6) 14-15.
37 Roosevelt claimed that a secure world would be founded upon the 'freedom of speech and expression, freedom of every person to worship God in his way, freedom from want, and freedom from fear'. Franklin Roosevelt, 'The Annual Message to Congress' (6 January 1941). <http://avalon.law.yale.edu/20th_century/decade01.asp> accessed 28 November 2017.

also embraces an obligation on the part of the State to provide for the health of its population.[38] These developments laid the foundation for the formulation of the right to health under the new United Nations (UN) system.

2.2.2.1 The right to health in international human rights law

The first formal articulation of health as a human right can be found in the 1946 WHO Constitution. The preamble to the Constitution affirms that 'the enjoyment of the highest attainable standard of health is one of the fundamental rights of every human being without distinction of race, religion, political belief, economic or social condition' and that 'governments have a responsibility for the health of their peoples which can be fulfilled only by the provision of adequate health and social measures.'[39] However, the Constitution does not provide further clarification as to what constitute 'adequate' measures.[40]

Two years later, the UN formally recognised health as a human right in its 1948 Universal Declaration of Human Rights (UDHR).[41] The UDHR articulates a wide range of civil and political rights as well as economic, social and cultural rights. Article 25(1) of the Declaration enunciates that 'everyone has the right to a standard of living adequate for the health and well-being of himself and of his family, including [...] medical care and necessary social services.'[42] This provision associates health and well-being with other social rights, making health just one component of 'the right to an adequate standard of living'.[43] This begs the question of what standard of living is 'adequate' for health and well-being.[44] In addition, as Toebes rightly notes, the lack of a clarification of the meaning of the term 'health' would likely reduce the

38 Meier (n 12) 3.
39 WHO Constitution, preamble. As Meier explained, despite this statement in the Constitution, the 'WHO intentionally neglected human rights discourse during crucial years in the development and implementation of the right to health, projecting itself as a technical organization above "legal rights".' See Meier (n 12) 2.
40 Lisa Forman and Sivan Bomze, 'International Human Rights Law and the Right to Health: An Overview of Legal Standards and Accountability Mechanisms' in Gunilla Backman (ed), *The Right to Health: Theory and Practice* (Studentlitteratur 2012) 37.
41 UNGA, Universal Declaration of Human Rights (UDHR) (10 December 1948) UNGA RES 217A (III).
42 ibid, art 25 (1).
43 Toebes (n 6) 40.
44 Elizabeth Tyler, '"Small Places Close to Home": Toward a Health and Human Rights Strategy for the US' (2013) 15 (2) Health and Human Rights 80, 81.

wording in Article 25 to 'a right to medical care and sickness benefits' rather than a right to health.[45] As such, this article is generally considered as broad and vague.[46] It is also worth noting that as a declaration, the UDHR is in principle not legally binding upon States, although some rights in the UDHR can now be considered customary international law.[47]

In 1966, provisions in the UDHR were further codified in two human rights treaties: the International Covenant on Civil and Political Rights (ICCPR) and the ICESCR. These two treaties reflect a distinction between two categories of human rights: civil and political rights on the one hand and economic, social and cultural rights on the other hand.[48] Health was recognised as one of the economic, social and cultural rights in the ICESCR.[49] Since then, the right to health has been further codified by a considerable number of international human rights instruments, and as discussed in chapter 1, all countries have already ratified at least one legally binding treaty that recognises this right (see more details in Table 2.1).

Of all the human rights treaties addressing the right to health, the ICESCR is considered as the central instrument of protection for the right to health care.[50] The ICESCR is legally binding upon all 166 ratifying States.[51] Article 12(1) of the ICESCR defines the right as 'the right of everyone to the enjoyment of the highest attainable standard of physical and mental health'. Article 12 (2) contains a non-exhaustive enumeration of specific State obligations to be taken for the realisation of this right, including 'the creation of conditions which would assure to all medical service and medical attention in the event of sickness.'[52] Furthermore, the ICESCR also obliges States parties to 'take steps, individually and through international assistance and cooperation [...] to the maximum of available resources, with a view

45 Toebes (n 6) 40.
46 ibid.
47 ibid.
48 ibid.
49 See Forman and Bomze (n 40) 38; Paul Hunt and others, 'Implementation of Economic, Social and Cultural Rights' in Scott Sheeran and Nigel Rodley (eds), *Routledge Handbook of International Human Rights Law* (Routledge 2013) 546-550.
50 Forman and Bomze (n 40) 38; San Giorgi (n 1) 11; Helena Nygren-Krug, 'The Right to Health: From Concept to Practice' in in José Zuniga, Stephen Marks and Lawrence Gostin (eds), *Advancing the Human Right to Health* (Oxford University Press 2013) 41.
51 As of 28 November 2017, 166 states have ratified (accessed) to the ICESCR. The ratification data was collected via <http://indicators.ohchr.org/> accessed 28 November 2017.
52 UNGA, ICESCR (n1) art 12.

to achieving progressively the full realization' of the right to health.[53] However, as will be discussed below, critics argue that the terms 'highest attainable', 'maximum of available' and 'progressively' make the right to health vague and difficult to implement and to enforce in reality.[54] In addition to the ICESCR, although the ICCPR does not contain the right to health, it protects various interests that are closely related to the right to health, such as the right to life (art 6), equality (art 26) and the protection of minorities (art 27).[55]

Similar to the ICESCR, other international human rights instruments also address the right to health (as shown in Table 2.1). While some of the treaties provide for general protection of the right to health, others focus on the protection of a specific vulnerable or marginalised group, such as racial and ethnic groups, women and children.[56] For example, the International Convention on the Elimination of All Forms of Racial Discrimination (CERD) prescribes the right to equal treatment and non-discrimination.[57] It also obliges States parties to guarantee the right to public health and medical care to everyone, without distinction as to race, colour, or national or ethnic origin.[58] According to Forman and Bomze, this article not only recognises an individual right to medical care, but also identifies a collective right to public health.[59] Furthermore, the Convention on the Elimination of All Forms of Discrimination against Women (CEDAW) provides for the protection of women in relation to health.[60] Unlike the ICESCR, which refers to 'physical and mental health' more generally, this treaty focuses specifically on the protection of the health of women on a basis of equality of men and women.[61] Thirdly, the Convention on the Rights of the Child (CRC) contains elaborate provisions for the protection of

53 ibid
54 Tyler (n 44) 82.
55 UNGA, International Covenant on Civil and Political Rights (adopted 16 December 1966, entered into force 23 March 1976) 999 UNTS 171, arts. 6, 26-27. See also Forman and Bomze (n 40) 39.
56 Office of the United Nations High Commissioner for Human Rights (OHCHR) and WHO, 'Fact Sheet No. 31: The Right to Health' (June 2008) 9; United Nations Economic and Social Council, 'Report of the Special Rapporteur on the Right of Everyone to the Enjoyment of the Highest Attainable Standard of Physical and Mental Health, Paul Hunt' (n 2) para 11.
57 UNGA, International Convention on the Elimination of All Forms of Racial Discrimination (adopted 21 December 1965, entered into force 4 January 1969) 660 UNTS 195, art 5.
58 ibid.
59 Forman and Bomze (n 40) 40.
60 UNGA, Convention on the Elimination of All Forms of Discrimination against Women (adopted 18 December 1979, entered into force 3 September 1981) 1249 UNTS 13, arts 11-12.
61 ibid; Toebes (n 6) 55.

children's health, with a broader coverage of a right of access to health care services as well as other determinants such as rights to adequate food and drinking water.[62] Fourthly, the International Convention on the Protection of the Rights of All Migrant Workers and Members of Their Families (CRMW) focuses on the legal protection of the right to health of migrant workers and their families. Like the CERD, it identifies the right to medical care and the right to equal treatment with nationals of the State of employment in relation to access to health services.[63] Lastly, the Convention on the Rights of Persons with Disabilities (CRPD) aims to protect persons with disabilities. It emphasises the enjoyment of the right to health without discrimination on the basis of disability.[64]

62 UNGA, Convention on the Rights of the Child (adopted 20 November 1989, entered into force 2 September 1990) 1577 UNTS 3, art 24; Toebes (n 6) 59.

63 UNGA, International Convention on the Protection of the Rights of All Migrant Workers and Members of Their Families (adopted 18 December 1990, entered into force 1 July 2003) 2220 UNTS 3, arts 28, 43 and 45.

64 UNGA, Convention on the Rights of Persons with Disabilities (adopted 13 December 2006, entered into force 3 May 2008) 2515 UNTS 3, art 25.

Table 2.1 Major human rights treaties recognising the right to health

Treaty	Provision
CERD	'The right to public health, medical care, social security and social services (art 5 (e) (iv))'.
ICESCR	'[T]he right of everyone to the enjoyment of the highest attainable standard of physical and mental health', followed by five 'steps to be taken by the States Parties to the present Covenant to achieve the full realization of this right (art 12 (1) (2))'.
CEDAW	'The right to protection of health and to safety in working conditions, including the safeguarding of the function of reproduction (art 11 (1) (f))'; 'States parties shall take all appropriate measures to eliminate discrimination against women in the field of health care in order to ensure, on a basis of equality of men and women, access to health care services, including those related to family planning' [and] 'States parties shall ensure to women appropriate services in connection with pregnancy, confinement and the post-natal period, granting free services where necessary, as well as adequate nutrition during pregnancy and lactation (art12 (1)(2))'.
CRC	'[T]he right of the child to the enjoyment of the highest attainable standard of health and to facilities for the treatment of illness and rehabilitation of health. States Parties shall strive to ensure that no child is deprived of his or her right of access to such health care services', followed by six appropriate measures to be taken to 'pursue full implementation of this right (art 24 (1) (2))'.
CRMW	'The right to receive any medical care that is urgently required for the preservation of their life or the avoidance of irreparable harm to their health on the basis of equality of treatment with nationals of the State concerned (art 28)'; 'Migrant workers shall enjoy equality of treatment with nationals of the State of employment in relation to: [a]ccess to social and health services, provided that the requirements for participation in the respective schemes are met (art 43 (1)(e))'; 'Members of the families of migrant workers shall, in the State of employment, enjoy equality of treatment with nationals of that State in relation to: [a]ccess to social and health services, provided that requirements for participation in the respective schemes are met (art 45 (1) (c))'.
CRPD	'[P]ersons with disabilities have the right to the enjoyment of the highest attainable standard of health without discrimination on the basis of disability', followed by six measures to be taken 'to ensure access for persons with disabilities to health services that are gender-sensitive, including health-related rehabilitation (art 25)'.

2.2.2.2 *The right to health in regional human rights law*

The right to health is also recognised in a range of regional human rights treaties, including: the European Social Charter (Revised),[65] the African Charter on Human and Peoples' Rights,[66] and the Additional Protocol to the American Convention on Human Rights in the Area of Economic, Social and Cultural Rights.[67] While some provisions in the regional human rights treaties directly affirm the right to health,[68] others contain health-related rights such as the right to life and the prohibition on torture and other cruel, inhuman and degrading treatment.[69] However, as China is not a State party to any regional human rights treaties, this section will not offer an in-depth analysis of these treaties.

2.2.2.3 *The right to health in national constitutions*

As well as international and regional human rights law, many countries also provide for the constitutional protection of health.[70] For example, South Africa has a very renowned constitution that explicitly recognises the right to health. Chapter II, Section 27 of its 1996 Constitution sets out a number of rights, including the right to access to health care, *inter alia* '(a) health care services, including reproductive health care; […]; (c) social security, including if they are unable to support themselves and

65 Council of Europe, European Social Charter (Revised) (adopted 3 May 1996, entered into force 1 July 1999) ETS 163.
66 Organization of African Unity, African Charter on Human and Peoples' Rights ('Banjul Charter') (adopted 27 June 1981, entered into force 21 October 1986) 1520 UNTS 271.
67 Organization of American States, Additional Protocol to the American Convention on Human Rights in the Area of Economic, Social and Cultural Rights ('Protocol of San Salvador') (adopted 17 November 1988, entered into force 16 November 1999) OASTS 67.
68 For example, Article 2 of the European Social Charter (Revised) stipulates that 'everyone has the right to benefit from any measures enabling him to enjoy the highest possible standard of health attainable'; Article 16 of the African Charter on Human and Peoples' Rights prescribes that 'the right to enjoy the best attainable state of physical and mental health'; Article 10 of the Additional Protocol to the American Convention on Human Rights in the Area of Economic, Social and Cultural Rights mandates that 'everyone shall have the right to health, understood to mean the enjoyment of the highest level of physical, mental and social well-being'.
69 OHCHR and WHO (n 56) 10.
70 Eleanor Kinney, 'The International Human Right to Health: What Does This Mean for Our Nation and World' (2001) 1457 (34) Indian Law Review 1457, 1464-1465; Kinney and Clark (n 1) 288.

their dependants, appropriate social assistance.'[71] It also obliges the State to adopt reasonable legislative and other measures, within its available resources, to achieve the progressive realisation of the foregoing rights.[72] The Constitution further prescribes that 'no one may be refused emergency medical treatment.'[73] The Dutch Constitution addresses health in a different way. Article 22 (1) of the Constitution stipulates that '[t]he authorities shall take steps to promote the health of the population.'[74] Instead of granting an individual 'right' or entitlement to health, the Dutch Constitution imposes a duty on the government to promote the health of its population.[75]

Kinney and Clark conducted a survey in 2004, which suggested that 67.5% of the constitutions of all nations have provisions addressing health or health care.[76] They further categorised these constitutional provisions into five types:

- A statement of aspiration, setting a goal with regard to the health of its people;
- A statement of entitlement, recognising a right to health or health care or public health services;
- A statement of duty, obligating the State to provide health care or public health services;
- A programmatic statement, stating specific approaches for the financing, delivery or regulation of health care and public health services;
- A referential statement, incorporating specific reference to any international or regional human rights treaty that recognises the right to health or health care.[77]

This classification indicates that the entitlement statement has an explicit recognition of the right to health or the right to health care while the referential statement implicitly recognises this right.[78] Their data suggest that 74 countries

71 Constitution of the Republic of South Africa (1996) (as amended in 2003), chap 2 section 27 (1). <www.justice.gov.za/legislation/constitution/SAConstitution-web-eng.pdf> accessed 28 November 2017.
72 ibid, chap 2 section 27 (2).
73 ibid, chap 2 section 27 (3).
74 Constitution of the Kingdom of the Netherlands (2002), art 22 (1). <www.rechtspraak.nl/SiteCollectionDocuments/Constitution-NL.pdf> accessed 28 November 2017.
75 Brigit Toebes and Maite San Giorgi, 'Dutch Realities: Evaluating Health Care Reform in the Netherlands from a Human Rights Perspective' in Brigit Toebes and others (eds), *The Right to Health: A Multi-Country Study of Law, Policy and Practice* (Springer 2014) 414.
76 Kinney and Clark (n 1) 287-298.
77 ibid 290-291.
78 ibid.

include the right to health or the right to health care in their constitutions.[79] However, in another article published in 2001, Kinney had claimed that 109 countries have provisions establishing a right to health in their national constitutions.[80]

Interestingly, the statistics regarding the number of nations that recognise a right to health (care) in their constitution varies in different publications. For example, the WHO suggested in 2008 that the right to health or the right to health care has been recognised in at least 115 constitutions,[81] while Backman and others in the same year found that only 56 States parties to the ICESCR included the right to health in their constitution or other statute.[82] In another 2008 analysis of 186 accessible constitutions, Perehudoff identified that 135 countries have entrenched health or the right to health in their constitutions.[83] Gostin also noted in 2014 that over 130 countries guarantee health rights in their national constitutions and that most of them 'grant an explicit right to health, such as "the highest attainable standard of physical and mental health", "health protection", "health care", "health security", or "health and medical care"'.[84]

Moreover, in one of the reports of the Special Rapporteur on the Right to Health in 2003, Hunt refers to 'a survey of national constitutions that enshrine the right to health and health-related rights', which shows that,

> over 60 constitutional provisions include the right to health or the right to health care, while over 40 constitutional provisions include health-related rights, such as the right to reproductive health care, the right of the disabled to material assistance, and the right to a healthy environment.[85]

It is apparent that Hunt made a distinction between the right to health and health-related rights, distinguishing the right to reproductive health care or the right to a healthy environment from the right to health.

---

79 ibid 298. This statistic was calculated on the basis of the data provided in Table 2 of their paper, i.e. 38.7% of the 193 countries have constitutions classified as entitlement statements.
80 Kinney (n 70) 1465.
81 OHCHR and WHO (n 56) 10.
82 Backman and others (n 1) 2059.
83 Katrina Perehudoff, 'Health, Human Rights and National Constitutions' (WHO 2008) 20.
84 Gostin (n 2) 263.
85 International Court of Justice, 'Rights to Health Database, Preliminary Proposal' (2002). Quoted in United Nations Economic and Social Council, 'Report of the Special Rapporteur on the Right of Everyone to the Enjoyment of the Highest Attainable Standard of Physical and Mental Health, Paul Hunt' (n 2) para 20.

These different statistics are due to the various definitions of the right to health (care). They also give rise to the question of whether constitutional provisions that impose an obligation on a State to provide for health care or set aspirational goals regarding the health of the population constitute a recognition of the right to health or the right to health care. To avoid conceptual confusion when evaluating the legislative measures China has taken in order to implement the right to health care, the following section first clarifies the different meanings of the right to health and the right to health care on the basis of the key notions elaborated in General Comment 14.

2.2.3 The meaning of the right to health care

A brief review of the language employed in international or regional human rights treaties as well as national constitutions shows that these legal instruments use different terms to refer to a human right to health, ranging from the term 'right to health' to narrower and more precise terms such as the 'right to health care', 'right to medical care', or 'right to public health'. Generally, the term 'right to health' is considered to be the most appropriate term to describe a human right to health at both the international and regional levels.[86] The main reason is that the right to health corresponds best to the international treaty provisions that do not only encompass access to health care but also the underlying determinants of health.[87]

However, the term 'right to health' has also been criticised for being too vague and broad, as it covers many areas related to social well-being that extend beyond the scope of health care.[88] Some scholars have also argued that the 'right to health' implies that people are entitled to something that cannot be guaranteed, namely 'perfect health' or 'to be healthy'. Consequently, it would impose a duty on governments that is impossible to fulfil.[89] Based on this idea, they have asserted that the choice of the

86 Toebes (n 6) 16, 79-84.

87 ibid 16-18.

88 Abdellah Boudahrain, Le Droit de la Santé au Maroc, Plaidoyer pour une Santé Humaine [Health Law in Morocco, a Plea for Humane Health] (Editions L' Harmattan 1996) 25. Cited in Toebes (n 6) 17.

89 Roscam Abbing, *International Organizations in Europe and the Right to Health Care* (Kluwer 1979) 104-105; Ruth Roemer, 'The Right to Health Care' in Hernan Fuenzalida-Puelma and Susan Connor (eds), *The Right to Health in the Americas: A Comparative Constitutional Study* (Pan American Health Organization, 1989) 17. Cited in Toebes (n 6) 16.

term 'right to health care' is more realistic.[90] Another reason for preferring the term 'right to health care' was to prevent indeterminacy.[91] As Sandhu claims, although international and regional human rights treaties acknowledge health as a human right, none of them impose concrete obligations on ratifying States.[92] However, by granting a right to health care, the government holds a precise legal duty to provide health services, goods and facilities other than guaranteeing good health.[93] Thus, Sandhu asserts that a right to health care, which entitles individuals to health services, goods and facilities, would be more suitable for adjudication.[94] However, as Hendriks points out, although the right to health care has the advantage of conveying much more clarity and specificity, reducing the right to health to a right to health care runs the risk of being inconsistent with the object and purpose of the various international and regional instruments guaranteeing health as a human right.[95]

I agree with Toebes and Hendriks that the term 'right to health' is a more appropriate term to refer to this right. In my view, the disagreement among scholars was attributed to the different understanding of the meanings of the right to health and the right to health care. In fact, early discussions on the right to health often focused on its moral and aspirational components, in which 'a right to health' is a declarative goal, without identifying the concrete implications.[96] It was not until the adoption of General Comment 14 in 2000 that we had a comprehensive interpretation of the right to health.[97] Although not legally binding, this general comment is highly authoritative and enhances our understanding of the right to health considerably. First of all, General Comment 14 confirms that the right to health is not a right to be healthy.[98] This rebuts the argument that the right to health implies a claim to good health. Indeed, as health is influenced by many aspects which are out of the control of the State, it is not possible for the State to guarantee good health or provide protection

90 ibid.
91 Sandhu (n 6) 1159.
92 ibid.
93 ibid.
94 ibid 1160; See also Roscam Abbing, *International Organizations in Europe and the Right to Health Care* (Kluwer 1979) 104-105. Cited in Toebes (n 6) 16.
95 Aart Hendriks, 'The Right to Health in National and International Jurisprudence' (1998) 5 European Journal of Health Law 389, 390–391.
96 Sandhu (n 6) 1158.
97 Backman and others (n 1) 2048.
98 CteeESCR, General Comment 14 (n 1) para 8.

against every possible cause of human ill-health.[99] It is therefore more accurate to describe the human right to health as the right to *the highest attainable standard* of physical and mental health.[100]

In addition, the CteeESCR interprets the right to health as an inclusive right, encompassing not only access to 'timely and appropriate health care' but also the underlying determinants that are essential to people's health.[101] The underlying determinants include: access to safe and portable water and adequate sanitation, adequate nutrition and housing, healthy occupational and environmental conditions, an adequate supply of food and access to health-related education and information.[102] It is now widely acknowledged that the underlying determinants are decisive factors for people's health.[103] However, as explained, the focus of this study is the reform of the Chinese health care system; therefore, the following sections are confined to an analysis of the right to access to timely and appropriate health care and answer two simple questions: what does the right to health care mean and what does the right to health care entail?

2.3 Normative content of the right to health care

The right to health care refers to the right to access to timely and appropriate health facilities, goods and services that are essential for the realisation of the highest attainable standard of health. It is an inclusive right to various freedoms and entitlements. It can be broken down into more specific freedoms such as the right to control one's health and body (eg sexual and reproductive freedom) and the right to be free from interference (eg the right to be free from non-consensual medical treatment and experimentation).[104] With regard to more specific entitlements, it is noteworthy that the right to health care consists of various entitlements (as shown in Table 2.2) that overlap with other underlying determinants of health. For example, as Toebes points out, health protection and disease prevention go beyond the narrow

99 ibid, para 9.
100 ibid, paras 9-11.
101 ibid, para 11.
102 ibid.
103 Toebes and San Giorgi (n 75) 414.
104 CteeESCR, General Comment 14 (n 1) para 8.

scope of the right to health care and may extend to other underlying determinants.[105] This is because health protection and disease prevention also include issues such as health education, improved nutrition and the improvement of sanitation and working conditions.[106] Toebes thereby further distinguishes the scope, core content and overlapping elements of the right to health to provide for more conceptual clarification.[107] Along the same line, San Giorgi also provides a comprehensive overview of the scope and core content of both the right to health and the right to health care.[108] Based on their work, the following sections delineate the normative content of the right to health care for answering the question as to what the right to health care entails.

2.3.1 The scope of the right to health care

To outline the normative content of the right to health care, it is useful to first identify all elements embedded in the aforementioned treaty provisions affirming the right to health. As a point of departure, this section uses the classification of different elements of the right to health set out by Toebes, namely the scope, core content and overlapping elements of the right to health.[109] According to Toebes, the scope is the general content of the right to health; the core content contains the minimum elements of the scope of the right to health.[110] The overlapping elements are the elements of other human rights that permeate the scope of the right to health or vice versa.[111] Examples of overlapping elements of the right to health include the right to life and the prohibition on torture and other cruel, inhuman and degrading treatment. However, as the focus of this study is the right to health care, the analysis will not extend to these overlapping elements.

Read in conjunction with the aforementioned human rights treaties (see more detail in Table 2.1) to which China is a State party[112] and General Comment 14, as well as the overview provided by San Giorgi, the scope of the right to health is

105 Toebes (n 6) 247.
106 ibid.
107 ibid 243-246.
108 San Giorgi (n 1) 15-16.
109 Toebes (n 6) 243.
110 ibid.
111 ibid 243-244.
112 As of 2017, China has become a State party to the CERD, ICESCR, CEDAW, CRC and CRPD.

summarised as visualised in Table 2.2. Generally, the following elements are derived from the elements embedded in Article 5 CERD, Article 12 ICESCR, Article 12 CEDAW, Article 24 CRC, Article 25 CRPD and Articles 28, 43 and 45 CRMW. Here, I briefly summarise the elements regarding the right to health care. First of all, most of the aforementioned treaty provisions identify medical care. Secondly, according to General Comment 14, Article 12(2)(d) ICESCR proclaims the right to health facilities, goods and services, including in particular 'the provision of equal and timely access to basic preventive, curative, rehabilitative health services'; 'appropriate treatment of prevalent diseases'; 'the provision of essential drugs'; and 'appropriate mental health treatment and care'.[113] In addition, General Comment 14 mentions the provision of primary health care.[114] Article 24 CRC also explicitly enunciates primary health care. Moreover, both the ICESCR and the CRC provide for the protection of child health care.[115] Furthermore, according to General Comment 14, States parties are required to refrain from 'denying or limiting equal access for all persons, [...], to preventive, curative and palliative health services'.[116] The scope of the right to health care also covers sexual and reproductive (health) services, on which the CEDAW has a more or less exclusive focus.[117] Article 12(1) CEDAW especially mentions family planning services as part of health care services. Article 12(2) (a) ICESCR also articulates the right to maternal, child and reproductive health. According to General Comment 14, this subparagraph can be understood as 'requiring measures to improve [...] sexual and reproductive health services, including access to family planning, pre-and post-natal care [...], as well as to resources necessary to act on that information'.[118] Additionally, pre-and post-natal health care is also explicitly mentioned in Article 24 (2) (d) CRC. Lastly, as mentioned in the previous section, the right to health care also includes the right to be free from interference, including the rights to be free from involuntary medical treatment and from harmful traditional practices.[119]

113 CteeESCR, General Comment 14 (n 1) para 17.
114 ibid, para 43; San Giorgi (n 1) 17.
115 UNGA, ICESCR (n 1) art 12(2); UNGA, CRC (n 62) art 24.
116 CteeESCR, General Comment 14 (n 1) para 34.
117 Toebes (n 6) 247.
118 CteeESCR, General Comment 14 (n 1) para 14.
119 ibid, para 8; UNGA, CRC (n 62) art 24 (3).

Table 2.2 The scope of the right to health

General content	Treaty
Health care	
Medical care	All
Preventative health care	All
Curative health care	ICESCR, CRC, WHO Preamble
Rehabilitative health care	ICESCR, CRC, CRPD
Mental health care	ICESCR, CRMW, WHO Preamble
Child health care	ICESCR, CRC, UDHR, WHO Preamble
Primary health care	ICESCR, CRC
Palliative health care	ICESCR
Provision of essential drugs	ICESCR
Family planning services	ICESCR, CEDAW, CRC, CRPD
Pre-and post-natal health care	ICESCR, CEDAW, CRC, CRPD, UDHR
Public health (Prevention, treatment and control of epidemic, endemic, occupational and other diseases)	ICESCR, CERD
Freedom from interference[120]	ICESCR, CRC
Underlying determinants	
Safe and portable water	ICESCR, CRC
Adequate nutrition	ICESCR, CEDAW, CRC, UDHR
Adequate sanitation	ICESCR, CRC
Housing	ICESCR, CRC, UDHR
Social services	CEDAW, CERD, CRMW, UDHR
Social Security	CEDAW, CRC, CERD, CRMW, UDHR
Safe and healthy occupational conditions	ICESCR, CEDAW
Healthy environment	ICESCR, CRC
Health-related information and education	ICESCR, CRC, CEDAW, WHO Preamble

120 San Giorgi listed the element 'freedom from interference' as the underlying determinants of the right to health. However, I argue that the right to health care also contains both entitlements and freedoms, given that it is an essential component of the broader right to health framework. Therefore, freedom from interference, such as the right to be free from non-consensual medical treatment, is also an element of the right to health care.

Overall, we may conclude that the scope of the right to health care covers access to medical care, preventative health care, curative health care, rehabilitative health care, mental health care, child health care, primary health care, palliative health care, the provision of essential drugs, and sexual and reproductive services, including family planning services and pre-and post-natal health care, and the prevention, treatment and control of epidemic, endemic, occupational and other diseases. However, in light of resource limitations in each country, it is arguable that a State may not be able to guarantee everyone access to each type of health care mentioned earlier.

2.3.2 The core content of the right to health care

As Toebes notes, the obligations arising from economic, social and cultural rights are very often vague and open-ended, leaving it unclear as to what extent and how these rights should be realised.[121] Article 2(1) of the ICESCR, for example, acknowledges resource constraints and allows each State party to *progressively* realise the rights recognised in the Covenant 'to the maximum of its available resources'.[122] Critics argue that this provision creates 'a loophole large enough in practical terms to nullify the Covenant's guarantees' – namely, the possibility that States parties will claim resource scarcity as the reason they have not complied with their obligations.[123]

The limitations of obligations regarding economic, social and cultural rights in Article 2(1) of the ICESCR have prompted a debate about the 'core' of the right to health (care), which is one of the most difficult concepts in the context of economic, social and cultural rights.[124] More specifically, in an effort to prevent progressive realisation from undermining States parties' obligations under the right to health (care), human rights treaty monitoring bodies and scholars have developed the notion that the right to health (care) has 'an inviolable "core" equivalent to essential health needs'.[125] In other words, States parties to the ICESCR have to ensure the minimum

121 Toebes (n 6) 276.
122 UNGA, ICESCR (n 1) art 2(1).
123 Audrey Chapman and Sage Russell, 'Introduction' in Audrey Chapman and Sage Russell (eds), *Core Obligations: Building a Framework for Economic, Social and Cultural Rights* (Intersentia 2002) 9.
124 ibid.
125 CteeESCR, General Comment 14 (n 1) paras 30, 43; Toebes (n 6) 276; San Giorgi (n 1) 25-28; Lisa Forman and others, 'Conceptualising Minimum Core Obligations Under the Right to Health: How Should We Define and Implement the "Morality of the Depths"' (2016) 20 International Journal of Human Rights 531, 531-532.

essential level of the right to health (care) under all circumstances, regardless of resource scarcity.[126] However, it deserves pointing out that States parties should continuously strive to realise the full spectrum of the right to health (care) to the maximum extent of their available resources.[127]

A great deal of scholarly debate has centred on the concept and content of the 'core' of economic, social and cultural rights, including the right to health (care).[128] This 'core' concept is generally referred to as 'minimum core content', 'minimum core obligations', 'essential elements', 'core entitlement', and other variations.[129] Nevertheless, these terms are not synonymous. Forman and others, for example, have provided a comprehensive examination of the development of the 'core' concept in human rights scholarship.[130] This section does not intend to repeat their findings in great detail, other than to mention that the ideas, such as 'basic rights to subsistence',[131] a 'minimal floor of well-being',[132] and an 'absolute minimum entitlement',[133] have played a significant role in the genesis of the core concept. German and Turkish constitutional laws, entrenching 'core' and 'essential' rights, have also contributed to the understanding of rights having a 'core' content.[134] These shifts in terminology actually reflect the development of the core concept.

126 CteeESCR, General Comment 14 (n 1) paras 30, 43.

127 ibid, paras 30-33; CteeESCR, General Comment 3 (n 4) para 10; Toebes (n 6) 276.

128 See generally, UNGA, 'Report of the Special Rapporteur on the Right of Everyone to the Enjoyment of the Highest Attainable Standard of Physical and Mental Health, Paul Hunt' (8 August 2007) UN Doc A/62/214, para 28; Lisa Forman and others, 'What Do Core Obligations under the Right to Health Bring to Universal Health Coverage' (2016) 18 Health and Human Rights 23, 28-29; San Giorgi (n 1) 25-28; Forman and others (n 125) 531-540; Tobin (n 35) 243-251.

129 Chapman and Russell (n 123) 9.

130 Forman and others (n 125) 531-540.

131 Shue defines basic rights as 'everyone's minimum reasonable demands upon the rest of humanity', including 'minimal preventative public health care'. See Henry Shue, *Basic Rights: Subsistence, Affluence and US Foreign Policy* (2nd Edn Princeton University Press 1996) 19. Cited in Forman and others (n 125) 533.

132 Bard-Anders Andreassen and others, 'Assessing Human Rights Performance in Developing Countries: The Case for a Minimal Threshold Approach to the Economic and Social Rights' in *Yearbook of Human Rights in Developing Countries* (1987–1988) 334. Cited in Forman and others (n 125) 533.

133 Phillip Alston, 'Out of the Abyss: The Challenges Confronting the New U.N. Committee on Economic, Social and Cultural Rights' (1987) 9 Human Rights Quarterly 332, 352-353. Cited in Forman and others (n 125) 533.

134 Esin Orucu, 'The Core of Rights and Freedoms: The Limits of Limits' in Tom Campbell and others (eds), *Human Rights: From Rhetoric to Reality* (Blackwell 1986) 47. Cited in Forman and others (n 125) 533.

This section starts with the evolution of the core concept in international human rights law interpretations, paying particular attention to the General Comments of the CteeESCR. It then explores the limitations of the CteeESCR's interpretation of the core obligations. Lastly, it sheds light on some conceptual questions concerning the core concept: what kinds of essential health services should fall within the scope of the core? Is the core intended to apply universally or to be tailored to national settings given their different levels of development and health conditions?[135]

2.3.2.1 The evolution of the 'core' concept

In the beginning of the 1990's, the CteeESCR began to adopt and develop the concept of the 'core' in its clarification of Covenant norms.[136] First of all, in General Comment 3, adopted in 1990, the Committee suggested that resource scarcity does not exonerate any State party, including the least developed States, from a *minimum core obligation* 'to ensure the satisfaction of, at the very least, minimum essential levels of each of the rights is incumbent upon every State party'.[137] Here, the Committee noted the connection between the 'minimum core obligations' and the 'minimum essential levels' of human rights.[138] Nevertheless, the Committee did not provide any guidance in General Comment 3 as how to determine minimum core obligations, but only provided a handful of examples, including essential foodstuffs, essential primary health care, basic shelter and housing and the most basic forms of education.[139] Thus, for instance, a State party in which a significant number of individuals are deprived of essential primary health care is 'prima facie failing to discharge its obligations under the Covenant'.[140]

Notably, according to General Comment 3, minimum core obligations are subject to resource constraints;[141] a State party may attribute a failure to meet its minimum core obligations to resource constraints by demonstrating that 'every effort has been made to use all resources that are at its disposition in an effort to satisfy, as a matter

135 Forman and others (n 125) 532.
136 ibid 533.
137 CteeESCR, General Comment 3 (n 4) para 10.
138 Chapman and Russell (n 123) 9.
139 CteeESCR, General Comment 3 (n 4) para 10.
140 ibid.
141 Forman and others (n 125) 534.

of priority, those minimum obligations'.[142] This implies that States parties should prioritise the provision of essential primary health care in the allocation of resources so as to ensure the satisfaction of the minimum essential levels of the right to health.[143]

In 1993, the CteeESCR organised a day of general discussion on the right to health and urged participants to explore the implication of the idea that 'there is a minimum core content of each right which constitutes a "floor" below which the conditions should not be permitted to fall in any State party.'[144] The Vice-Chairperson of the Committee, Alvarez Vita, noted at the discussion that it was not possible to set a minimum limit for the enjoyment of the right to health, given 'the ideal of the individual is to achieve the highest possible level of life'. [145] However, he asserted that it was feasible to monitor the 'progress, regression or stagnation in the enjoyment of the right to health', although he refrained from providing any specific benchmarks and indicators for the assessment.[146] He also argued against setting varying limits on the basis of each State party's level of development, considering that 'all human beings have a right to enjoy the same level of health'.[147]

Instead of considering the core as a 'floor', Chapman, who has also contributed actively to the discussion, defined the minimum core content as 'the minimum duties all States parties set for themselves regardless of the resources available'.[148] Chapman proposed a conduct-oriented interpretation of the core and argued that such an approach 'has the benefit of focusing on public policy and implementation, both of which are under the control of States parties', regardless of 'health development

142 CteeESCR, General Comment 3 (n 4) para 10.

143 Lisa Forman and others, 'What Could a Strengthened Right to Health Bring to the Post-2015 Health Development Agenda? Interrogating the Role of Minimum Core Concept in Advancing Essential Global Health Needs' (2013) 13 BMC International Health and Human Rights 1, 6.

144 CteeESCR, 'Provisional Agenda and Annotations: Note by the Secretary-General', UN Doc E/C.12/1993/11, para 5; See also CteeESCR, General Comment 14 (n 1) paras 30, 43; CteeESCR, General Comment 3 (n 4) para 9.

145 CteeESCR, 'Report on the Eighth and Ninth Sessions' (UN Economic and Social Council Official Records Supp. 3 1994) UN Doc E/1994/23 and E/C.12/1993/19, para 292.9.

146 ibid.

147 ibid, para 292.8.

148 ibid para 332; United Nations Economic and Social Council, 'Summary Record of the Forty-Second Meeting' (6 December 1993) UN Doc E/C.12/1993/SR.42, para 62; Audrey Chapman, 'Core Obligations Related to the Right to Health' in Audrey Chapman and Sage Russell (eds), *Core Obligations: Building a Framework for Economic, Social and Cultural Rights* (Intersentia 2002) 201.

standards', 'including levels of economic development.'[149] She then identified a number of obligations of conduct that constitute the minimum core content of the right to health.[150]

However, PROVEA, a Venezuelan human rights organisation, criticised Chapman's approach, asserting that 'the minimum core content of a right is not exhausted in the minimum obligations of the State, although the former may be useful to provide the latter with the institutional action framework required for the achievement of the right to health.'[151] PROVEA also argued for the understanding of the core as a 'floor' as it considered the minimum content 'as a starting point and not as the arrival point'.[152] They then suggested that the minimum core content includes a set of indicators and goals to be achieved by the State.[153]

Critics argue in general that viewing the core as a 'floor' runs the risk that 'the "floor" will become a "ceiling"'.[154] The identification of minimum core content reflects how little a State party has to do to comply with its obligations – it is likely that a State will only do the minimum required of it and nothing more.[155] Furthermore, as Forman and others suggest, understandings of the core as the 'floor' (i.e. the beginning point) and the 'minimum' (i.e. the very least a State should do) seem to conflict with each other.[156] Together with Russell, Chapman also argues against 'ranking the various components of a human right in some sort of hierarchy according to relative worth' and proposes an alternative approach by considering what a State party must do immediately after ratifying the ICESCR to realise the right to health.[157] In light of these arguments, and also considering that the 'raison d'être' of the Covenant is to 'establish clear obligations for States parties' to fully realise the right to health,[158] it is not surprising to see the discussions of the core concept shift from the *minimum*

149 United Nations Economic and Social Council, 'Summary Record of the Forty-Second Meeting' (n 148) paras 62-66; Chapman (n 148) 201.
150 ibid.
151 PROVEA, Health as a Right: Framework for National and International Protection of the Human rights of Health (Caracas 1996) V, 41. Cited in Chapman (n 148) 201.
152 ibid.
153 ibid.
154 Chapman and Russell (n 123) 9.
155 ibid.
156 Forman and others (n 125) 536.
157 Chapman and Russell (n 123) 9.
158 CteeESCR, 'General Comment No. 9: The Domestic Application of the Covenant' (General Comment 9) (3 December 1998) UN Doc E/C12/1998/24, para 9.

core content to an exclusive focus on *core obligations* in the Committee's subsequent interpretation of this right.[159]

The CteeESCR has done little to further develop the core concept since 1993. It was not until 1999 that the Committee began drafting and adopting new general comments in relation to individual rights under the ICESCR, including the right to health. At a meeting discussing the proposed General Comment 14 in 2000, acting as the Special Rapporteur of the Right to Health, Hunt explained that the CteeESCR had struggled with how to incorporate the idea of a core content in General Comment 3 into new general comments. Hunt stated that the CteeESCR had ultimately decided to adopt 'the pragmatic approach of defining not the core content but the core obligations incumbent upon States parties'.[160] He further noted the importance of richer countries fulfilling their obligations of international cooperation. Hunt regarded the core obligations and the obligations of international assistance and cooperation as 'two halves of a package'.[161] Another participant in the meeting, Riedel, suggested that 'the Committee had to make a policy decision on whether or not to include a demanding list of those obligations which all States, rich or poor, should fulfil as a bare minimum'.[162] The Chairperson, Mendonça e Moura concluded that 'it was not possible or appropriate for the general comment to refer individually to every health problem that might need to be addressed', 'the purpose of the general comment was to define States parties' core obligations.'[163] She also emphasised the obligations of wealthier countries to assist poorer countries in fulfilling out the core obligations.[164]

It can be deduced from this meeting that the CteeESCR was fully aware of the different levels of development between rich and poor countries. Therefore, in General Comment 14 the Committee presumably did not intend to 'list all the obligations that were considered important but to list only those that were absolutely essential'.[165] In addition, to make the core obligations more financially realistic for poor countries

159 Forman and others (n 125) 536.
160 CteeESCR, 'Twenty-Second Session, Summary Record of the 10th Meeting Held at the Palais Wilson, Geneva' (4 May 2000) UN Doc E/C. 12/2000/SR.10, para 27; Forman and others (n 125) 537.
161 CteeESCR, 'Twenty-Second Session, Summary Record of the 10th Meeting Held at the Palais Wilson, Geneva' (n 160) para 27.
162 ibid, para 24.
163 ibid, para 29.
164 ibid.
165 ibid, para 32.

with limited resources, the Committee also attached great importance to obligations of international assistance and cooperation.

The CteeESCR reaffirms in its General Comment 14 (adopted in 2000) that States parties have a core obligation to ensure the satisfaction of the minimum essential levels of rights recognised in the Covenant, including essential primary health care.[166] The Committee further notes that the 1978 Alma-Ata Declaration on primary health care and the 1994 Programme of Action of the International Conference on Population and Development (ICPD) provide 'compelling guidance' on the core obligations of the right to health.[167] In paragraph 43 of General Comment 14, the Committee outlines a relatively small but fundamental number of core obligations. Moreover, in contrast with its interpretation in General Comment 3 that minimum core obligations are subject to resources constraints, the Committee holds in General Comment 14 that 'a State party, cannot, under any circumstances whatsoever, justify its non-compliance with the core obligations set out in paragraph 43'.[168] Specifically, as shown in Table 2.3, States parties without exception are obliged to:[169]

Table 2.3 Core obligations under the right to health

Health care	• ensure the right of access to health facilities, goods and services, on a non-discriminatory basis, especially for vulnerable or marginalised groups; • provide essential drugs, as from time to time defined under the WHO Action Programme on Essential Drugs; • ensure equitable distribution of all health facilities, goods and services; • adopt and implement a national public health strategy and plan of action, on the basis of epidemiological evidence [...] give particular attention to all vulnerable or marginalised groups.
Underlying determinants	• ensure access to the minimum essential food which is nutritionally adequate and safe, to ensure freedom from hunger to everyone; • ensure access to basic shelter, housing and sanitation, and an adequate supply of safe and potable water.

166 CteeESCR, General Comment 14 (n 1) para 43.
167 ibid; WHO, Declaration of Alma-Ata (International Conference on Primary Health Care, Alma-Ata, USSR, 6-12 September 1978); United Nations (UN), Programme of Action adopted at the International Conference on Population and Development (5-13 September 1994) (Declaration of Alma-Ata) <www.unfpa.org/sites/default/files/event-pdf/PoA_en.pdf> accessed 28 November 2017.
168 CteeESCR, General Comment 14 (n 1) paras 43, 47.
169 ibid, para 43.

In addition to the core obligations specified in paragraph 43, the Committee further identifies a set of obligations of 'comparable priority' in paragraph 44 of General Comment 14. These obligations include the provision of 'reproductive, maternal (pre-natal as well as post-natal) and child health care'; the provision of 'immunization against the major infectious diseases occurring in the community'; the prevention, treatment and control of epidemic and endemic disease; the provision of health education and information related to major health problems at the community level; and the provision of 'appropriate training for health personnel, including education on health and human rights and health education'.[170]

2.3.2.2 Limitations of the Committee on Economic, Social and Cultural Rights' interpretation of 'core obligations'

Although the core obligations regarding the right to health (care) have the potential to void governmental claims of resource constraints by providing normative priority of essential health needs, several deficiencies in the Committee's interpretation of this concept have been identified in human rights scholarship.[171] Firstly, the relationship between *core obligations* and *obligations of comparable priority* remains ambiguous. The CteeESCR implies in paragraph 45 of General Comment 14 that obligations of comparable priority are *not* part of core obligations, by stating that,

> it is particularly incumbent on State parties and other actors in a position to assist, to provide 'international assistance and cooperation [...]' which enable developing countries to fulfil their core and other obligations indicated in paragraphs 43 and 44 above.[172]

It is therefore apparent that the Committee recognises obligations of comparable priority as distinct from core obligations, even though both paragraphs are listed under the section of 'Core obligations' in General Comment 14.

However, some content of the obligations of comparable priority actually fall within the scope of primary health care. According to the 1978 Alma-Ata Declaration, primary health care includes at least:

---

170 ibid, para 44.
171 See generally Chapman (n 148) 187-202, Forman and others (n 143) 1-11, Forman and others (n 128) 28-29, Tobin (n 35) 239-253.
172 CteeESCR, General Comment 14 (n 1) para 45.

> education concerning prevailing health problems and the methods of preventing and controlling them; promotion of food supply and proper nutrition; an adequate supply of safe water and basic sanitation; maternal and child health care, including family planning; immunization against the major infectious diseases; prevention and control of locally endemic diseases; appropriate treatment of common diseases and injuries; and provision of essential drugs.[173]

Apparently, many of the duties outlined in paragraph 44 overlap with primary health care.

If both paragraphs 43 and 44 are concerned with primary health care, the question then arises: why does the CteeESCR differentiate between core obligations and obligations of comparable priority? A possible explanation may be that primary health care as a whole is not explicitly recognised as a core obligation, given that the precise term used in paragraph 43 is '*essential*' primary health care. If so, the CteeESCR would not consider the *content* of the obligations of comparable priority to amount to *essential* primary health care, thus placing this content outside the scope of core obligations.

As mentioned earlier, the core obligations outlined in General Comment 14 demarcate the *essential* health needs that must be protected, as a matter of human rights, against governmental claims of resource scarcity.[174] The Committee further categorises these core obligations as *non-derogable* – States parties cannot justify its non-compliance with these obligations under any circumstances.[175] As observed by Forman and others, there is actually a shift from *derogable minimum core obligations* in General Comment 3 to *non-derogable core obligations* in General Comment 14.[176]

More specifically, General Comment 3 requires States parties to provide the minimum core content of health (i.e. essential foodstuffs, essential primary health care, basic shelter and housing, or the most basic forms of education), while General Comment 14 requires States parties to assure not only the substantive components of primary health care (i.e. access to essential food, access to basic shelter, housing, sanitation and water, access to essential medicines), but also the structural and procedural aspects of health (i.e. non-discrimination, equitable distribution of health

173 WHO, Declaration of Alma-Ata (n 167) arts VII2, VII3.
174 Forman and others (n 128) 28.
175 CteeESCR, General Comment 14 (n 1) para 47.
176 Forman and others (n 125) 537-538; Forman and others (n 128) 28.

facilities, goods and services, and a national public health strategy and plan of action).[177]

According to Forman and others, the shift from 'weaker duties of result' in General Comment 3 to 'stronger duties of conduct' in General Comment 14 may be an attempt to respond to the long-standing criticisms that 'the core is financially unfeasible for low and middle income countries.'[178] Forman and others' argument is implied by the discussion of the proposed General Comment 14 in 2000.[179] As mentioned earlier, the CteeESCR is cognisant that many of the poorest countries have severe resource constraints and even core obligations may be financially unfeasible for these countries to fulfil in reality. In such cases, countries with limited resources can begin to meet the core obligations in relation to the structural and procedural aspects of the right to health. In fact, core obligations such as non-discrimination, equitable distributions and plans of action are relatively cost-free and can generally be achieved with minimum resource implications.[180] For example, countries with limited resources can develop a comprehensive national health strategy or plan of action for the accomplishment of health goals as the first step to meet their core obligations.[181] Thus viewed, it is not surprising to see that these structural and procedural obligations are identified as core obligations in General Comment 14.

In addition, although to a very limited degree still subject to available resources, the substantive components of core obligations (i.e. essential drugs, essential food, as well as basic shelter, housing, sanitation, and water) by and large reflect the basic needs for survival and for living a life of dignity.[182] States parties are expected to have access to the resources needed for ensuring these basic rights to subsistence. In consideration of the reality that some of the poorest countries may still not have sufficient resources, the Committee imposes the obligation of international assistance and cooperation on richer countries to make resources available to these countries.[183]

177 CteeESCR, General Comment 14 (n 1) para 47.
178 Forman and others (n 128) 537.
179 CteeESCR, 'Twenty-Second Session, Summary Record of the 10th Meeting Held at the Palais Wilson, Geneva' (n 160) paras 24-32.
180 Forman and others (n 128) 28.
181 Chapman and Russell (n 123) 11.
182 Katharine Young, 'The Minimum Core of Economic and Social Rights: A Concept in Search of Content' (2008) Yale Journal of International Law 113, 156; Eibe Riedel, 'The Human Right to Health: Conceptual Foundations' in Andrew Clapham and others (eds), *Realizing the Right to Health* (Rüffer&Rub 2009) 32.
183 Chapman and Russell (n 123) 11.

By contrast, obligations of comparable priority, such as the prevention, treatment and control of epidemic and endemic diseases as well as the provision of appropriate training for health personnel and health education, may not reflect subsistence needs. Rather, they may reflect 'next in line' health needs,[184] which are still subject to progressive realisation and resource constraints. Viewed in this light, it is acceptable that these obligations are not considered to fall within the core of the right to health. Nevertheless, as Forman and others rightly note,

> [i]t must be questioned whether a theory of the right to health that prioritizes essential medicines but not reproductive health care and infectious disease control is not flawed in terms of both human rights theory and public health practice.[185]

It is difficult to justify a concept of essential primary health care that includes the provision of essential drugs as the one and only health intervention, but not the provision of reproductive health care and immunisation against infectious diseases.[186]

Secondly, although the CteeESCR explicitly outlines six core obligations in General Comment 14, it fails to clarify what constitutes *essential* primary health care. Instead of providing a comprehensive list of core obligations that are absolute essential, General Comment 14 enumerates the core obligations in a non-exhaustive fashion. However, beyond essential drugs and two underlying determinants of health, the types of health facilities, goods and services that fall within the scope of the core obligations remain underspecified.[187]

On the one hand, if the Committee identifies a wide variety of health needs as core obligations, it may be too demanding for poorer countries faced with severe resource constraints. As Chapman points out, while it is possible to define core obligations that can be applied to all countries regardless of their levels of development and available resources, 'defining such standard requires "think small"', i.e. narrowing the core to relatively few elements.[188] In addition, as the epidemiological profiles vary from one country to another, health challenges in each country also vary widely. For instance, in some rich countries obesity is a major health challenge, while in some of

184 Forman and others (n 143) 6.
185 ibid.
186 Forman and others (n 128) 30.
187 Forman and others (n 143) 6.
188 Chapman (n 148) 196.

the poorest countries it is still undernutrition. Therefore, in practice the requirement of essential primary health care also varies from country to country.[189] Furthermore, as some commentators argue, a well-defined list of essential primary health care may end up providing selective rather than comprehensive primary health care.[190] To this degree, it is pragmatic to prescribe the absolute essential elements of the right to health as core obligations and leave it to each State to identify its own package of essential primary health care.

On the other hand, as mentioned, the conceptual deficit leads to an unclear relationship between core obligations and obligations of comparable priority under the right to health. If reproductive health care and infectious disease control are recognised as *non-essential* primary health care, what constitutes *essential* primary health care? The lack of definitional clarity as to which health facilities, goods or services fall within the core content runs the risk that only essential drugs will be demarcated as required by the core obligation and thus prioritised in the allocation of resources. States are likely to claim lack of resources as a reason for not providing other types of primary health care. Consequently, the limited enumeration of core obligations may erode, rather than develop the scope of core obligations. To a lesser extent, it may even undermine the broader legitimacy of the CteeESCR's interpretation of core obligations.[191]

2.3.2.3 Scholarly debate over the core concept

The limited specificity of the Committee's interpretation of the core obligations has generated vigorous scholarly debate regarding the concept. Some attempts have been made to fill the conceptual gap by extending core obligations to general primary health care. For example, Hunt asserts that,

> a State has a core obligation to ensure a minimum "basket" of health-related services and facilities, including essential food to ensure freedom from hunger, basic sanitation and adequate water, essential medicines, immunization against the community's major infectious diseases, and sexual

189 UNGA, 'Report of the Special Rapporteur on the Right of Everyone to the Enjoyment of the Highest Attainable Standard of Physical and Mental Health, Paul Hunt' (n 27) para 52.

190 People's Health Movement, WHA66: Statement on Universal Health Coverage (24 May 2013). <www.phmovement.org/en/node/7600> accessed 20 October 2017. Cited in Forman and others (n 143) 7.

191 Forman and others (n 128) 30.

> and reproductive health services including information, family planning, prenatal and post-natal services, and emergency obstetric care.[192]

In addition, the Committee on the Rights of the Child (CteeRC) holds in its General Comment 15 that States parties have core obligations under children's right to health to ensure 'universal coverage of quality primary health services, including prevention, health promotion, care and treatment services, and essential drugs'.[193] Here, we see that both the CteeRC and Hunt have extended the core obligations regarding health to more general primary health services. A possible critique of this approach is that this interpretation of core obligations overlaps with the content of obligations with comparable priority outlined in paragraph 44 of General Comment 14. Also, extending the scope of non-derogable core obligations may place unrealistic financial burdens on poorer countries in order to meet these obligations.

Some other scholars are critical of the Committee's interpretation of non-derogable core obligations more generally. For example, Tobin argues against the Committee's list of core obligations in General Comment 14, which in his view is 'neither principled nor practical'.[194] Considering resource scarcity and the need for a nationally variable list of core obligations, Tobin argues for a more 'modest and practical vision' of the core of the right to health with a narrower set of obligations of conduct and result.[195]

Although the Committee distinguishes *obligations of conduct* from *obligations of result* in its General Comment 3,[196] it does not specify into which of these categories core obligations fall.[197] This prompted a discussion of whether the right to health should be conceptualised as implying an obligation of result or conduct, which took place at a conference held in Maastricht, the Netherlands in 1997.[198] According to the Maastricht Guidelines on Violations of Economic, Social and Cultural Rights, an 'obligation of result requires States to achieve specific targets to satisfy a substantive

192 UNGA, 'Report of the Special Rapporteur on the Right of Everyone to the Enjoyment of the Highest Attainable Standard of Physical and Mental Health, Paul Hunt' (n 27) para 52.
193 United Nations Committee on the Rights of the Child, 'General Comment No. 15: The Right of the Child to the Enjoyment of the Highest Attainable Standard of Health (Art. 24)' (17 April 2013) UN Doc CRC/C/GC/15, para 73 (b).
194 Tobin (n 35) 243-252.
195 ibid.
196 CteeESCR, General Comment 3 (n 4) para 1.
197 Forman and others (n 125) 537-538.
198 Chapman (n 148) 196.

standard' (eg the provision of essential drugs in accordance with the WHO Action Programme on Essential Drugs); while an 'obligation of conduct requires action reasonably calculated' to realise the enjoyment of the right to health (eg the adoption and implementation of a plan of action to provide essential drugs).[199]

As mentioned, Tobin argues for core obligations incorporating both conduct- and result-based duties. In terms of obligations of conduct, he divides them into two types: (1) an obligation to ensure that States acknowledge the interdependence of the right to health with other human rights; and (2) an obligation to take reasonable efforts to develop an appropriate health strategy or plan through a collaborative and participatory process.[200] In terms of obligations of result, Tobin acknowledges that it is not appropriate to construct a definitive or exhaustive list of obligations of result. He explains that the health matters to be prioritised in a particular country are influenced by local conditions, namely the health needs of the population and the capacity of the State to address these needs. As such, he argues for 'the development of a presumptive list of result obligations', including 'the provision of selective and integrated primary health care and the provision of food and water necessary to survive.'[201] In particular, he foresees that the provision of essential elements of primary health care, when integrated with participatory process, can develop a widely accepted model that 'all states should be capable of adopting with appropriate assistance'.[202]

By contrast, as mentioned in subsection 2.3.2.1, Chapman proposes an approach with a focus on obligations of conduct.[203] She argues against an approach based on obligations of result, given the absence of reliable data for assessing the progress in meeting health goals. According to Chapman, countries in some cases lack a proper system for collecting accurate data, while in some other cases, countries intentionally misreport health data so as to hide domestic health problems, in particular incidents such as HIV/AIDS and abortion. Consequently, she argues that government should be evaluated in terms of obligations of conduct rather than result.[204]

199 International Commission of Jurists, Maastricht Guidelines on Violations of Economic, Social and Cultural Rights (26 January 1997), para 7.
200 Tobin (n 35) 245.
201 ibid 246-248.
202 ibid 251.
203 Chapman (n 148) 202-203.
204 ibid.

A related debate over the core concept extends to whether core obligations are intended to be universally applicable or be tailored to national settings.[205] The drafting history of General Comment 14 reflects that core obligations are supposed to provide a universal set of essential health care standards that can be applied to all countries, irrespective of resource constraints and levels of development.[206] Nevertheless, many scholars doubt that a one-size-fits-all approach to the core obligations of the right to health is appropriate.[207] As explained earlier, the health conditions vary in different countries. Each country has its own burdens of disease, different populations within the country may have specific health needs, and the capacity of the health system to address these needs also varies.[208] Therefore, some scholars propose to identify essential health needs within a legally binding framework by integrating treaty text, international guidelines, State practice, judicial decisions, and academic scholarship.[209] They believe that such an integrated approach is likely to establish a more practical and feasible conception of the core obligations concerning essential health needs, which can be applied within different contexts.[210]

For example, Forman and others argue for the identification of the content of essential health benefits packages provided by the public health sector of domestic governments at various income levels. They believe that such research will illustrate 'current policy approaches to "core" health needs' and 'what low and middle income countries consider to be economically feasible'.[211] In fact, many countries have already defined their own national essential health care packages. Some countries have drawn on international guidelines provided by the World Bank or the primary health care approach outlined in the Alma-Ata Declaration.[212] Some other countries have developed their own national packages on other bases, such as responding to national health needs through participatory process or an assessment of available resources.[213] Nevertheless, researchers have observed an imbalanced translation of

205 Forman and others (n 128) 29.
206 CteeESCR, 'Twenty-Second Session, Summary Record of the 10th Meeting Held at the Palais Wilson, Geneva' (n 160) paras 24, 27.
207 Forman and others (n 128) 29.
208 ibid; Forman and others (n 143) 8.
209 Forman and others (n 125) 542.
210 Forman and others (n 143) 7.
211 ibid.
212 ibid.
213 ibid 8.

these essential health care packages into health guarantees.[214] Therefore, it is still important to develop the substantive content of an essential health care package in line with the core obligations under the right to health.

2.3.2.4 Summary

General Comment 14 outlines core obligations with which States parties must comply under any circumstances. These core obligations are intended to address the challenges posed by progressive realisation and prevent against governmental claims of resource scarcity and inadequate international assistance. Core obligations have the potential to advance health equity and the priority of essential health needs in domestic laws, policies, and adjudication. However, General Comment 14 does not provide any guidance as to which primary health care, beyond essential drugs, should fall within the scope of the core (i.e. essential primary health care). It also fails to specify whether the core of the right to health (care) is intended to be universally applicable or to be tailored to national-settings. Human rights scholars have provided important insights into these issues; nevertheless, there is no consensus on how to determine core obligations of the right to health care. Certainly, much more work has to be done to address the conceptual deficits identified in this section.

While acknowledging that the Committee's interpretation of the core obligations as set out in General Comment 14 requires improvement, in light of the document's authoritativeness, this study follows the same interpretation. Consequently, the understanding of the core content of the right to health care adopted by this study is limited to essential primary health care. States parties are not permitted to limit the right to health care below the level of essential primary health care in all of its promotive, preventative, curative and rehabilitative dimensions. More specifically, States parties undertake at least four non-derogable core obligations under the right to health care, as shown in Table 2.3. These core obligations are universally applicable in all countries, irrespective of resource constraints and their levels of development. Nevertheless, these non-derogable core obligations are just a starting point; a State should move continuously and expeditiously to the realm of progressive realisation after meeting its core obligations.

214 ibid.

2.3.3 Essential elements of the right to health care: AAAQ-AP

General Comment 14 recognises a set of 'essential elements' of the right to health care by stating that that health-care facilities, goods and services should be available, accessible, acceptable, and of good quality.[215] This set of principles is generally referred to as the 'AAAQ'. The AAAQ standards provide a comprehensive framework for assessing a State's compliance with the right to health care at the domestic level.[216] In addition to the AAAQ, accountability and participation ('AP') are also considered as key elements of the right to health care.[217] In the sections below, the meaning and implications of the AAAQ-AP principles will be discussed, so as to set the stage for the discussion of the implementation of the right to health care in China in chapters 3 and 4.

2.3.3.1 Availability

Availability requires a sufficient quantity of functioning public health and health facilities, goods and services, as well as health care programmes within a State.[218] These include: hospitals, clinics and other buildings, trained medical and professional personnel and essential drugs.[219] Although no concrete criteria for evaluating the availability of health care are provided in General Comment 14,[220] some indicators can be derived from the observations of the CteeESCR in its conclusions, such as the number of hospital beds and health care providers per inhabitant, the length of waiting time for admission to health care services, and the amount of resources allocated to health care.[221]

The assessment of the availability of health care may vary from country to country, depending on the level of development of each country, the health challenges it is facing given its unique epidemiological profiles, and its available resources.[222]

215 CteeESCR, General Comment 14 (n 1) para 12; Forman and Bomze (n 40) 46-47.
216 Toebes and San Giorgi (n 75) 407.
217 CteeESCR, General Comment 14 (n 1) paras 11, 17 and 55; CteeESCR, General Comment 9 (n 158) para 2.
218 CteeESCR, General Comment 14 (n 1) para 12 (a).
219 ibid.
220 ibid.
221 San Giorgi (n 1) 52.
222 CteeESCR, General Comment 14 (n 1) para 12 (a); Toebes and San Giorgi (n 75) 408.

Generally, the principle of availability requires governments to assess domestic health needs and to address the resource constraints to 'scal[e] up the provision of priority services to meet those needs'.[223] Notably, States are obliged to ensure the availability of essential primary health care, irrespective of resource constraints and their level of development.

2.3.3.2 Accessibility

Accessibility is crucial due to its relationship with the principles of non-discrimination, equality and equity.[224] Health facilities, goods and services have to be accessible to everyone within the jurisdiction of the State party without discrimination.[225] Accessibility has four overlapping dimensions: non-discrimination, physical accessibility, economic accessibility (i.e. affordability), and information accessibility.[226]

- Non-discrimination

Health facilities, goods and services must be accessible to all segments of society, including in particular the most vulnerable or marginalised groups of society.[227] The right to health care is closely related to and dependent upon the realisation of other human rights, including non-discrimination and equality.[228] According to the ICESCR, States parties undertake an obligation to ensure the *equality* of access to health care,[229] and to prevent and eliminate *discrimination* 'on the grounds of race, colour, sex, […] health status (including HIV/AIDS), sexual orientation and civil, political, social or other status',[230] in exercising the right to health care.[231]

More specifically, the principle of equality refers to 'equal treatment by law, before the law and in fact.'[232] Equality implies that the same standards and obligations must

223 Lawrence Gostin and others, *Advancing the Right to Health: The Vital Role of Law* (WHO 2017) 15.
224 Backman and others (n 1) 2055.
225 CteeESCR, General Comment 14 (n 1) para 12 (b).
226 ibid.
227 ibid.
228 ibid, para 3.
229 UNGA, ICESCR (n 1) art 3.
230 CteeESCR, General Comment 14 (n 1) paras 18, 19.
231 UNGA, ICESCR (n 1) art 2(2).
232 San Giorgi (n 1) 65.

be applied to everyone.[233] This means that vulnerable or marginalised groups should not be treated less favourably than other individuals and groups.[234] Remarkably, as Hunt rightly notes, equality is not always restricted to equal treatment; sometimes, it is also important for States to take measures in favour of vulnerable or marginalised groups. This is closely related to the concept of equity.[235] Therefore, tailored national health programmes must be designed to reach vulnerable and marginalised groups and to tackle the political, economic, social and cultural factors that hinder their access to health care.[236] This means, for example, that States have to provide those who do not have sufficient means to access health care with necessary health insurance.[237]

Discrimination is 'a *species* of inequality'.[238] General Comment 14 imposes an immediate obligation on States parties to guarantee the exercise of the right to health care by preventing any discrimination in access to health care, as well as to means and entitlements for its procurement on any internationally prohibited grounds.[239] For example, governments must ensure that people living with HIV/AIDS will not be denied access to health care because of their health status.

To summarise, the principles of non-discrimination and equality imply access to health care on a non-discriminatory basis, equal access to health care and equitable access to health care.[240]

- Physical accessibility

Health facilities, goods and services must be within safe physical reach of everyone, especially vulnerable or marginalised groups, such as ethnic minorities and indigenous populations, the elderly, people with physical disabilities, and people living in remote or inaccessible regions.[241] Physical accessibility requires States to build physical facilities and infrastructure so as to enable its populations to reach and

233 ibid.
234 Gostin and others (n 223) 18.
235 UNGA, 'Report of the Special Rapporteur on the Right of Everyone to the Enjoyment of the Highest Attainable Standard of Physical and Mental Health, Paul Hunt' (13 September 2006) UN Doc A/61/338, para 53.
236 ibid, para 54.
237 CteeESCR, General Comment 14 (n 1) paras 18, 19.
238 San Giorgi (n 1) 66-67.
239 UNGA, ICESCR (n 1) art 2(2); CteeESCR, General Comment 14 (n 1) paras 12(b), 18, 19, 30.
240 CteeESCR, General Comment 14 (n 1) paras 12, 18, 19, 36 and 43.
241 ibid, para 12 (b).

use health facilities, goods and services.[242] For example, elderly persons or persons with physical disabilities may not be able to access health care because of their limited mobility.[243] Thus, ramps should be built for people with limited mobility to access buildings and other places where health care is provided. Furthermore, health facilities and services at the community level should be accessible within a given time and distance, especially for those who live in remote areas. This requires the building of infrastructure (eg roads and bridges) and the provision of public transportation (eg bus, train or ferry services).[244]

- Economic accessibility (affordability)

Health facilities, goods and services, whether privately or publicly provided, should be affordable for all, including socially and economically disadvantaged groups and those with no fixed income.[245] According to General Comment 14, payment for health care services should be based on the principle of *equity*.[246]

It is worth noting that the concept of equity is not the same as equality. Generally speaking, equity is an ethical concept that is closely related to social justice or fairness.[247] Accordingly, health equity is an ethical value that can be defined as 'the absence of socially unjust or unfair health disparities'.[248] Like most value-based concepts, health equity cannot be measured according to concrete standards.[249] For operational reasons and for the purposes of measurement, Braveman and Gruskin define health equity on the basis of measurable criteria as 'the absence of disparities in health that are systematically associated with social advantage/disadvantage'.[250] Thus, equity in health care can be understood as 'fair arrangements that allow equal

242 Gostin and others (n 223) 18.
243 UNGA, 'Report of the Special Rapporteur on the Right of Everyone to the Enjoyment of the Highest Attainable Standard of Physical and Mental Health, Anand Grover' (4 July 2011) UN Doc A/HRC/18/37, para 25.
244 Gostin and others (n 223) 18.
245 ibid 19; CteeESCR, General Comment 14 (n 1) para 12(b).
246 CteeESCR, General Comment 14 (n 1) para 12 (b).
247 Paula Braveman and Sofia Gruskin, 'Defining Equity in Health' (2003) 57 Journal of Epidemiology and Community Health 254, 254-255.
248 Paula Braveman, Eleuther Tarimo, 'Social Inequalities in Health Within Countries: Not Only an Issue for Affluent Nations' (2002) 54 Social Science and Medicine 1621, 1623. Cited in Braveman and Gruskin (n 247) 254.
249 Braveman and Gruskin (n 247) 256.
250 ibid.

geographic, economic, and cultural access to available services for all in equal need of care'.[251] This requires, for example, that socially and economically disadvantaged groups (eg poorer households) are not disproportionately burdened with health expenses as compared to advantaged groups (eg richer households).[252] Accordingly, States should take legislative or policy measures to reduce excessive financial burdens from being imposed on individuals.[253]

It also deserves to be pointed out that health inequality is not a synonym for health inequity.[254] Equity in health focuses on resource allocation or other processes that drive a health system. It requires equitable health financing grounded in the principle of 'distributive justice', thus reducing unequal opportunities in access to health care associated with underlying social disadvantage or marginalisation, such as the poor, rural residents or racial, ethnic or religious groups.[255] In comparison, as discussed above, equality in the context of the right to health care refers particularly to equal access to health care on a non-discriminatory basis.

- Information accessibility

Information accessibility includes the right to 'seek, receive and impart information and ideas' in relation to health issues.[256] It is a key element in the patient-doctor relationship and is closely related to other concepts in medical law, such as privacy, confidentiality and informed consent. Information accessibility should not impair the right to privacy and confidentiality.[257] This means that health care providers must ensure that personal health data, especially sensitive information (eg HIV status), is kept secure and that privacy and confidentiality are respected.[258]

251 Shenglan Tang and others, 'Tackling the Challenges to Health Equity in China' (2008) 372 The Lancet 1493, 1493.
252 CteeESCR, General Comment 14 (n 1) para 12(b).
253 San Giorgi (n 1) 57; Gostin and others (n 223) 19.
254 Braveman and Gruskin (n 247) 255.
255 ibid 254; Paula Braveman and Sofia Gruskin, 'Poverty, Equity, Human Rights and Health' in (2003) 81 (7) Bulletin of the World Health Organization 539, 540-542.
256 CteeESCR, General Comment 14 (n 1) para 12(b).
257 ibid.
258 Gostin and others (n 223) 19.

2.3.3.3 *Acceptability*

The principle of acceptability provides that health facilities, goods and services should be delivered in ways that are respectful of medical ethics and confidentiality, culturally appropriate, and sensitive to gender and life-cycle requirements.[259] For instance, local cultural conceptions of health (eg regarding sexual and reproductive health care) and sickness must be taken into consideration in the provision of health goods and services at the community level.[260]

2.3.3.4 *(Good) quality*

The principle of quality requires that health facilities, goods and services be scientifically and medically appropriate and of good quality.[261] This requires skilled health professionals, processes for assuring the supply of scientifically approved and unexpired drugs and hospital equipment and other underlying determinants of health, such as safe and portable water and adequate sanitation.[262] Although indicators such as life expectancy, infant mortality rate and the number of health professionals with high education to some extent reflect the quality of the health care provided, given the breadth of the concept of equality it is difficult to assess the quality of health care.

Overall, as a matter of resource scarcity, States may not in practice be able to ensure that all health facilities, services and goods are sufficiently available, accessible, acceptable and of good quality within a short period of time. Trade-offs may exist between the availability, accessibility, acceptability and quality of health care provided. For example, while China has built up many village clinics and primary health care centres within physical reach of rural residents, the quality of health care provided in these places is rather poor. Another example is the provision of medicines in China.[263] While in general there is a sufficient quantity of medicines in China, medicines are sometimes less accessible in remote rural areas than in urban areas. Also, medicines may be available at a high price that is not affordable to all, thus

259 CteeESCR, General Comment 14 (n 1) para 12(c).
260 Backman and others (n 1) 2050.
261 CteeESCR, General Comment 14 (n 1) para 12(d).
262 ibid.
263 Backman and others (n 1) 2049-2050.

undermining the dimension of economic accessibility of the right to health care.[264] To some extent, given the limits of available resources, States are allowed to make trade-offs between the AAAQ principles when providing health care, especially in the process of resource allocation and priority setting. However, States must take deliberate, concrete and targeted steps to address these trade-offs and must 'move as expeditiously and effectively as possible' towards the full realisation of the right to health care.[265]

2.3.3.5 Accountability

Accountability is a central feature of human rights. The CteeESCR refers to accountability both implicitly and explicitly in its General Comments.[266] The Special Rapporteurs on the Right to Health have also emphasised the importance of accountability on a number of occasions. For example, Hunt asserts in his report that 'unless supported by some form of accountability, human rights run the risk of becoming mere window dressing'.[267] Hunt also notes that the implementation of the right to health care requires a range of effective, transparent, accessible and independent accountability mechanisms to be established by the State.[268] Accountability involves State actors being answerable to rights-holders, and being rewarded for good, or punished for bad, decisions and actions. As will be discussed further in chapters 5 and 6, accountability in the context of the right to health care is about fostering an effective and accountable healthcare system that functions for the benefit of the entire population.[269] Therefore, accountability is an essential component of the right to health care.

---

264 ibid.

265 CteeESCR, General Comment 14 (n 1) para 30.

266 ibid, para 55; CteeESCR, General Comment 9 (n 158) para 2.

267 UNGA, 'Report of the Special Rapporteur on the Right of Everyone to the Enjoyment of the Highest Attainable Standard of Physical and Mental Health, Paul Hunt' (n 2); UNGA, 'Report of the Special Rapporteur on the Right of Everyone to the Enjoyment of the Highest Attainable Standard of Physical and Mental Health, Paul Hunt' (n 27).

268 UNGA, 'Report of the Special Rapporteur on the Right of Everyone to the Enjoyment of the Highest Attainable Standard of Physical and Mental Health, Paul Hunt' (11 August 2008) UN Doc A/63/263, paras 8-18.

269 Lynn Freeman, 'Human Rights, Constructive Accountability and Maternal Mortality in the Dominican Republic: A Commentary' (2003) 82 International Journal of Gynaecology and Obstetrics 111, 111.

2.3.3.6 Participation

Health care systems should facilitate active and meaningful participation of all relevant stakeholders in all health-related decision-making, implementation and accountability at the community, national and international levels.[270] In particular, governments should establish institutional mechanisms to empower vulnerable and marginalised groups to participate in health-related decision-making processes that directly affect them, such as the formulation of national health laws and policies and the implementation, monitoring and evaluation of health interventions.[271] As mentioned in General Comment 14, States parties undertake a core obligation to adopt a national public health strategy and plan of action addressing the health concerns of the entire population through a participatory process.[272]

Participation is also closely related to other human rights principles. Effective participation relies on the right to seek, receive and impart health-related information and ideas on a non-discriminatory basis, with special attention being placed on sharing information with and seeking the views of disadvantaged individuals and groups.[273] Therefore, participation is also a central component of the right to health care.

2.4 States' core obligations arising from the right to health care

2.4.1 Progressive realisation

In light of resource constraints, the CteeESCR acknowledges that the enjoyment of economic, cultural and social rights, including the right to health care, generally cannot 'be achieved in a short period of time'.[274] Consequently, States parties are allowed to take deliberate, concrete and targeted steps, 'individually and through international assistance and cooperation', 'to the maximum of its available resources', to achieve progressively the full realisation of the right to health care.[275]

---

270 CteeESCR, General Comment 14 (n 1) para 11; Backman and others (n 1) 2051.
271 Helen Potts, 'Participation and the Right to the Highest Attainable Standard of Health' (University of Essex 2008) 15-18 <http://repository.essex.ac.uk/9714/1/participation-right-highest-attainable-standard-health.pdf> accessed 28 November 2017.
272 CteeESCR, General Comment 14 (n 1) para 43.
273 Potts (n 271)15-18.
274 UNGA, ICESCR (n 1) art 2(1); CteeESCR, General Comment 3 (n 4) para 9.
275 ibid; CteeESCR, General Comment 14 (n 1) para 30.

Progressive realisation grants States parties a margin of appreciation in taking steps and adopting measures most suited to their specific circumstances for implementing the obligations arising from the right to health care.[276] The CteeESCR respects the role of the State in formulating, adopting or implementing health-related laws and policies, in determining the optimum use of available resources, and in prioritising certain health demands over others.[277] However, the article of progressive realisation should not be interpreted as an 'escape clause', 'depriving the obligation of all meaningful content'.[278] Rather, States parties undertakes a specific and continuing obligation to take *all necessary steps* to 'move as expeditiously and effectively as possible' towards the full realisation of the right to health care.[279] If a State is not able to fully comply with its obligations due to resource constraints, it has the burden of proof to justify that every effort has been made to 'use all available resources at its disposal in order to satisfy, as a matter of priority,' the obligations arising from the right to health care.[280] The CteeESCR further emphasises the importance of 'distinguish[ing] the inability from the unwillingness of a State party to comply with its right to health obligations.'[281] If a State is unwilling to optimally use its available resources for the realisation of the right to health care, in principle this is a violation of the ICESCR.[282]

Viewed in this light, an assessment of the extent to which a State has complied with the progressive nature of its obligations is closely related to the circumstances within the State.[283] General Comment 14 does not provide any guidance for judging the reasonableness and adequacy of the steps taken, or for determining whether a State party's 'maximum available resources' have been deployed in implementing

276 CteeESCR, General Comment 14 (n 1) para 53; United Nations Economic and Social Council, 'An Evaluation of the Obligation to Take Steps to the "Maximum of Available Resources" under an Optional Protocol to the Covenant' (10 May 2007) UN Doc E/C.12/2007/1, para 11; San Giorgi (n 1) 33.

277 United Nations Economic and Social Council, 'An Evaluation of the Obligation to Take Steps to the "Maximum of Available Resources" under an Optional Protocol to the Covenant' (n 276) paras 11-12.

278 CteeESCR, General Comment 3 (n 4) para 9; San Giorgi (n 1), 33.

279 CteeESCR, General Comment 14 (n 1) paras 30, 47.

280 ibid, para 47.

281 ibid.

282 ibid.

283 United Nations Economic and Social Council, 'An Evaluation of the Obligation to Take Steps to the "Maximum of Available Resources" under an Optional Protocol to the Covenant' (n 276) para 10. Cited in Tobin (n 35) 233.

the right to health (care). Nevertheless, in a Statement regarding the evaluation of States parties' progressive obligation the CteeESCR suggested that it will consider the following factors:

> (a) The extent to which the measures taken were deliberate, concrete, and targeted towards the fulfilment of economic, social, and cultural rights;
> (b) Whether the State party exercised its discretion in a non-discriminatory and non-arbitrary manner;
> (c) Whether the State party's decision (not) to allocate available resources was in accordance with international human rights standards;
> (d) Where several policy options are available, whether the State party adopted the option that least restricts Covenant rights;
> (e) The time frame in which the steps were taken;
> (f) Whether the steps had taken into account the precarious situation of disadvantaged and marginalised individuals or groups, and whether they were non-discriminatory, and whether they prioritised grave situations or situations of risk.[284]

Notably, the Committee will only examine these factors when it considers a communication concerning an alleged failure of a State party to take steps to the maximum of its available resources.[285] Further, as will be discussed in chapter 6, only when States parties to the Optional Protocol of the ICESCR accept its competence can the CteeESCR receive and consider communications.[286] Nevertheless, the CteeESCR's approach suggests a domestic assessment as to whether a government has complied with the obligation of progressive realisation.

2.4.2 Obligations of immediate effect

Although the full realisation of the right to health care is to be attained progressively, States parties undertake a range of obligations of *immediate effect* that is not subject to progressive realisation. These obligations include: (1) guaranteeing the right to be exercised in a non-discriminatory manner; (2) taking steps towards the full realisation of the right to health care;[287] and (3) establishing a range of effective, transparent,

284 ibid, para 8. Quoted in Tobin (n 35) 234.
285 ibid.
286 UNGA, Optional Protocol to the International Covenant on Economic, Social and Cultural Rights (adopted on 10 December 2008, entered into force on 5 May 2013) UN Doc A/RES/63/117, art 10.
287 CteeESCR, General Comment 14 (n 1) para 30.

accessible and independent accountability mechanisms so as to ensure governmental accountability.[288]

More specifically, States parties must take deliberate, concrete and targeted steps towards the full realisation of the right to health care *within a reasonably short time* after the entry into force of the ICESCR.[289]

In addition, as defined by the ICESCR, States parties undertake an obligation of immediate effect to ensure that the exercise of the right to health care is not undermined by discrimination on the grounds prohibited by the Covenant.[290] Furthermore, the CteeESCR suggests in General Comment 14 that many measures for eliminating health-related discrimination can be pursued 'with minimum resource implications through the adoption, modification or abrogation of legislation or the dissemination of information.'[291] States are thus expected to adopt, modify or abrogate their domestic legislation so as to promote the equal enjoyment or exercise of the right to health care and to eliminate discrimination on the grounds recognised in the Covenant, including ethnic minorities, women, children, disabled persons, the elderly, or other status.[292] The Committee further stresses that States should adopt targeted and relatively low-cost programmes to protect vulnerable and marginalised groups even in times of severe resource constraints.[293]

Moreover, although not specially provided as obligations of immediate effect in General Comment 14, it is implied in the report of the Special Rapporteur on the Right to Health that States parties undertake an immediate obligation to establish a range of 'effective, transparent, accessible and independent mechanisms of accountability' in relation to obligations arising from the right to health care.[294] Similar to the measures for eliminating discrimination, many mechanisms for ensuring accountability are to a very limited degree subject to available resources and can thus be pursued immediately 'with minimum resource implications'.[295]

---

288 CteeESCR, General Comment 9 (n 158) para 2; UNGA, 'Report of the Special Rapporteur on the Right of Everyone to the Enjoyment of the Highest Attainable Standard of Physical and Mental Health, Paul Hunt' (n 27) para 51 (d).
289 CteeESCR, General Comment 3 (n 4) para 2; San Giorgi (n 1) 35.
290 UNGA, ICESCR (n 1) art 2 (2).
291 CteeESCR, General Comment 14 (n 1) para 18.
292 ibid.
293 ibid.
294 UNGA, 'Report of the Special Rapporteur on the Right of Everyone to the Enjoyment of the Highest Attainable Standard of Physical and Mental Health, Paul Hunt' (n 27) para 51 (d).
295 CteeESCR, General Comment 14 (n 1) para 18.

2.4.3 Core obligations to respect, protect and fulfil and violations of such obligations

In assessing whether a State has discharged its obligations arising from the right to health care, resource constraints are a decisive factor.[296] Given that fulfilling obligations to some extent depends on the resources available within a State, the State should prioritise core obligations in the allocation of resources when it takes steps to realise the right to health care.[297]

Read in conjunction with the obligations of immediate effect and in light of the Committee's compelling guidance on State obligations to respect, protect and fulfil rights,[298] I composed the following framework for assessing China's domestic implementation of the right to health care.

First, as summarised in Table 2.4, I selected two types of obligations as the criteria for the assessment, which are: (1) non-derogable core obligations; and (2) obligations of immediate effect.

(1) Non-derogable core obligations: as explained elaborately in subsection 2.3.2, paragraph 43 of General Comment 14 outlines six core obligations in relation to the right to health. The two core obligations regarding the underlying determinants of health are excluded from the discussion. As such, non-derogable core obligations include: the provision of essential drugs, non-discrimination, equitable distribution and the preparation of a comprehensive national health strategy. States parties cannot justify non-compliance with these four core obligations under any circumstances.[299] A State's failure to comply with these core obligations, including failing to adopt appropriate legislative or other measures, or the adoption of inadequate or insufficient legislative or other measures for discharging those obligations, would constitute a violation of the ICESCR.[300]

(2) Obligations of immediate effect: as discussed in section 2.4.2, States parties undertake a range of obligations of *immediate effect* that can be pursued 'with minimum resource implications'. However, the State can still attribute its failure to

296 CteeESCR, General Comment 3 (n 4) para 10.
297 OHCHR and WHO (n 56) 25.
298 CteeESCR, General Comment 14 (n 1) paras 33, 43.
299 ibid, para 47.
300 Toebes (n 6) 336-337.

discharge its obligations of immediate effect to a lack of available resources under certain circumstances. Nevertheless, I categorise obligations of immediate effect as core obligations because it is not possible for China to use resource constraints to justify its non-compliance with these obligations.

In brief, these two types of obligations were selected because they have the potential to guide policy-makers in formulating and implementing more equitable health policies through participatory process and to empower individuals to claim their right to health care before domestic courts. They can generate domestic action to guarantee essential health needs within a legally binding framework which has a certain degree of enforceability.[301] As just mentioned, a State cannot justify its non-compliance with non-derogable core obligations under any circumstances. As such, when courts are called upon to adjudicate claims regarding the denial of essential primary health care, the Chinese government cannot justify its failure to meet these core obligations on the basis of resource scarcity. In addition, given that obligations of immediate effect can be pursued with minimum resource implications, it is not possible for China to use resource constraints as a justification for its failure to discharge the obligations of immediate effect. Therefore, both non-derogable core obligations and obligations of immediate effect are considered as core obligations in this study and they can add much weight to claims against governments concerning the right to health care.

Second, I combined these two types of core obligations with the tripartite typology of obligations to respect, protect and fulfil the right to health care in various contexts. I also identified the violations of the core obligations to respect, protect and fulfil this right, irrespective of the national availability of resources and levels of development.

2.4.3.1 Core obligation to respect the right to health care

The core obligation to respect the right to health care requires States to respect equal access to health care and to refrain from interfering directly or indirectly with the provision of essential drugs and equitable distribution of all health facilities, goods and services.[302]

301 Forman and others (n 143) 7.
302 CteeESCR, General Comment 14 (n 1) paras 34, 48-52; OHCHR and WHO (n 56) 25..

The core obligation to respect would be manifestly violated if a State were to deny or limit access to health care to certain individuals or groups 'as a result of de jure or de facto discrimination'.[303] Taking China as an example, people with poor health status (eg people living with HIV/AIDS or Hepatitis B) may run the risk of being denied or having limited access to health care by public health care providers. Another example of the violation of the core obligation to respect is the suspension of legislation, failure to enforce relevant laws, or the adoption of any retrogressive measures that are incompatible with the core obligations under the right to health care.[304] Retrogressive measures include the adoption of laws or policies that interfere with the enjoyment of any component of the right to health care.[305]

2.4.3.2 Core obligation to protect the right to health care

The core obligation to protect the right to health care includes a State's obligation to adopt legislative or any other necessary measures to ensure that people have equal access to health facilities, services and goods provided by a third party.[306] It also includes an obligation to ensure that third parties (including private health care providers) do not threaten the availability, accessibility, acceptability and quality of health facilities, goods and services, nor limit access to certain health facilities, goods and services on the (international prohibited) grounds of discrimination mentioned in subsection 2.3.3.2.[307] States parties are also obliged to prevent third parties from coercing women to undergo harmful social or traditional practices and to ensure that these practices do not inhibit access to pre- and post-natal care and family planning.[308]

Violations of the core obligation to protect would occur if a State failed to take all necessary measures to prevent infringements of the right to health care by third parties. These include measures to ensure equal accessibility of health facilities, services and goods;[309] to discourage harmful social and traditional medical practices; or to regulate the activities of third parties so as to protect individuals from infringing the right to health care. Third parties include not only private hospitals or private

303 CteeESCR, General Comment 14 (n 1) para 18.
304 ibid, paras 48-50.
305 ibid, para 50.
306 ibid, paras 35, 48-52.
307 ibid, para 35.
308 ibid.
309 Toebes (n 6) 337-338.

insurers, but also industries like the fast food or tobacco industry. For example, it would constitute a violation of the core obligation to protect if a private insurance company refused to insure people living with HIV/AIDS and the State failed to take any action against the company.

2.4.3.3 Core obligation to fulfil the right to health care

The core obligation to fulfil the right to health care requires States to give sufficient recognition to non-discrimination and equality in the national legal and political systems, including through legislative implementation or the adoption of health policy.[310] States must also create conditions under which individuals would have non-discriminatory and equal access to health facilities, goods and services, especially for vulnerable or marginalised groups; ensure the provision of essential drugs in accordance with the WHO's requirements; ensure the equitable distribution of all health facilities, goods and services; and adopt and implement a national public health strategy and plan of action on the basis of a participatory and transparent process. It also requires States to put in place a range of effective, transparent, accessible and independent accountability mechanisms.[311]

Violations of the core obligations to fulfil include: (1) failure to recognise and/or implement the right to health care in the domestic legal and policy systems; (2) failure to provide essential drugs; (3) failure to adopt a national health strategy or plan of action for realising the right to health care; (4) failure to take legislative or other necessary measures to eliminate the inequitable distribution of health care; and (5) insufficient expenditure on and disproportionate resource allocation of essential health care, resulting in inequalities in access to health care, especially within vulnerable or marginalised groups.[312]

2.4.4 General obligations under the right to health care

In addition to the core obligations, States parties have a range of broader obligations to respect, protect, and fulfil the right to health care.[313] Yet, the lack of resources may

310 CteeESCR, General Comment 14 (n 1) para 36.
311 ibid, paras 36-37, 43; CteeESCR, General Comment 9 (n 158) para 2.
312 CteeESCR, General Comment 14 (n 1) para 52; Forman and Bomze (n 40) 50; Chapman (n 148) 210-214.
313 CteeESCR, General Comment 14 (n 1) paras 31-42.

arguably hinder a State's full compliance with these broader obligations.[314] When faced with resource constraints, the State still bears the burden of proof to justify that it has taken every effort to use all its available resources to discharge these obligations.[315]

Given the scope of this study, it is not possible to exhaustively analyse all of the legal obligations under the right to health care. Therefore, the following chapters will only assess the core obligations arising from the right to health care in the Chinese context.

2.5 CONCLUDING SUMMARY

This chapter has provided an overview of the right to health care as an essential component of the broader right to health framework. The right to health care is firmly embedded in international and regional human rights law. Many national constitutions also embrace this right. The right to health care can be understood as the right to access timely and appropriate health facilities, goods and services that are necessary for the realisation of the highest attainable standard of physical and mental health.

The scope of the right to health care covers access to medical care, preventative health care, curative health care, rehabilitative health care, mental health care, child health care, primary health care, palliative health care, the provision of essential drugs, and sexual and reproductive services, including family planning services and pre-and post-natal health care. It also includes the prevention, treatment and control of epidemic, endemic, occupational and other diseases. States may realise the right to health care progressively, depending on their available resources.

However, a State also undertakes a range of core obligations to respect, protect and fulfil the right to health care. Non-compliance with these core obligations would constitute a violation of the right to health. These core obligations are further divided into obligations of immediate effect and non-derogable core obligations in Table 2.4.

314 ibid.
315 ibid, para 47.

Table 2.4 Core obligations under the right to health care

Obligations of immediate effect	General Comment 14 para 30 UN Doc A/HRC/7/11, paras 51 (d)	• Guarantee the exercise of the right to health care without discrimination of any kind; • Take deliberate, concrete and targeted steps towards the full realisation of the right to health care;
		• Establish a range of effective, transparent, accessible and independent accountability mechanisms;
Non-derogable core obligations	General Comment 14 para 43	• The provision of essential drugs as defined by the WHO Action Programme on Essential Drugs; • Non-discriminatory and equal access to health facilities, goods and services, especially for vulnerable or marginalised groups; • Equitable distribution of all health facilities, goods and services; • The adoption and implementation of a national public health strategy and plan of action on the basis of a participatory and transparent process, with particular attention to vulnerable or marginalised groups.

Chapters 3 and 4 will assess China's legislative and policy commitments towards the realisation of the right to health care on the basis of the abovementioned core obligations. The assessment will also consider the AAAQ standards as set out in General Comment 14. The AAAQ standards provide an analytical framework for assessing China's compliance with the right to health care. However, to limit the scope of this study, I will mainly focus on availability and accessibility. In addition, I will also use accountability and participation as standards. In short, the AA-AP standards (i.e. availability, accessibility, accountability and participation) are selected as the criteria for assessing China's practice in chapters 3 and 4.

Chapter 3
China's Legislative Commitments towards the Right to Health Care

3.1 Introduction

The means by which the right to health care is given effect in the domestic legal order vary from one State to another, yet in many instances, legislation is 'highly desirable' and sometime 'indispensable' to ensuring the effective protection of the right to health care.[1] To fully comply with its obligations under this right, China has enacted a series of laws and regulations for providing solid legal ground for the promotion and protection of the right to health care.[2]

This chapter examines the legislative measures China has adopted to implement its (core) obligations under the right to health care. Section 3.2 first provides an overview of China's domestic legal and political system. Given that a culturally-rooted understanding of human rights has a clear impact on the research of the right to health care in China, this section also demonstrates the evolution of the Chinese conception of human rights and the general protection of human rights in China. Subsequently, section 3.3 first discusses the general practice of domestic application of international (human rights) treaties. This section begins with an introduction of the means by which international (human rights) treaties are given effect in domestic legal systems and some general observations regarding monism and dualism. It is followed by analyses of the direct effect and the precedence of these treaties.

1 United Nations Committee on Economic, Social and Culture Rights (CteeESCR), 'General Comment No. 14: The Right to the Highest Attainable Standard of Health (Art. 12 of the Covenant)' (General Comment 14) (11 August 2000) UN Doc E/C12/2000/4, paras 36, 53; CteeESCR, 'General Comment No. 3: The Nature of State Parties' obligations (Art.2 Para. 1 of the Covenant)' (General Comment 3) (14 December 1990) UN Doc E/1991/23, para 3.

2 United Nations Economic and Social Council, 'Implementation of the International Covenant on Economic, Social and Cultural Rights: Intial Reports submitted by States Parties under Articles 16 and 17 of the Covenant, Addendum, People's Republic of China' (4 March 2004) UN Doc E/1990/5/Add.59, paras 14, 145-209; United Nations Economic and Social Council, 'Implementation of the International Covenant on Economic, Social and Cultural Rights: Second Periodic Reports submitted by States Parties under Articles 16 and 17 of the Covenant, China' (6 July 2012) UN Doc E/C.12/CHN/2, ch 10 paras 1-9.

This section then moves to the discussion of China's specific practice. Section 3.4 forms the core part of this chapter, by critically examining the legislative measures China has taken to implement the right to health care in its domestic legal system. It conducts a secondary data analysis of China's existing health legislation and adopts the core obligations detailed in chapter 2 as the assessment criteria. Given the considerable number of Chinese laws at various levels, this section only provides a non-exhaustive analysis of the Chinese Constitution and the laws at the national level. Notably, legislation is not the only measure by which to implement the right to health care. There are other appropriate measures such as the adoption of national health policies and plans of action, or the establishment of judicial and other types of accountability mechanisms, which will be discussed further in chapters 4 and 7, respectively. Section 3.5 concludes with a discussion on the gaps between *de jure* and *de facto* implementation of the right to health care in China's legal system.

3.2 The background of China's human rights protection and health care system

3.2.1 China's political and legal system

3.2.1.1 China's political power structure

According to its Constitution, China is 'a socialist State under the people's democratic dictatorship led by the working class and based on the alliance of workers and peasants.'[3] China's current Constitution was promulgated in 1982 and amended in 2004. Chapter III of this Constitution, entitled 'Structure of the State', articulates that,

> [t]he National People's Congress of the People's Republic of China is the highest organ of state power. Its permanent body is the Standing Committee of the National People's Congress. The National People's Congress and its Standing Committee exercise the legislative power of the State.[4]

3 Constitution of the People's Republic of China (adopted and entered into force on 4 December 1982, amended on 14 March 2004) art 1 ('Chinese Constitution') <www.npc.gov.cn/englishnpc/Constitution/2007-11/15/content_1372965.htm> accessed 28 November 2017. The English version was obtained from the official website of the National People's Congress of the People's Republic of China (NPC).

4 ibid, arts 57-58.

Apart from being the 'the highest organ of state power' and the legislature, the National People's Congress (NPC) also supervises the work of four other State organs: the State Council, which is 'the highest organ of State administration';[5] the Central Military Commission, which 'directs the armed forces of the country';[6] the Supreme People's Court (SPC), which is 'the highest judicial organ';[7] and the Supreme People's Procuratorate (SPP), which is 'the highest procuratorial organ' and the State organ for legal supervision.[8] In contrast to many democratic States whose State power is divided into three separate organs (i.e. the executive, the legislature and the judiciary), it is generally believed that there is hardly any clear separation of powers in China because the NPC functions both as the legislature and the highest organ of State power that simultaneously supervises the executive and the judiciary.[9]

Furthermore, China's socialist political system has a unique feature - the Party leadership.[10] China's political power structure is thus characterised as the so-called 'Party-State', which generally means that the Communist Party of China (CPC) exercises its leadership role over the entire political system and functions as the uppermost decision-maker.[11] The Party leadership, although not mentioned in Chapter III of the 1982 Chinese Constitution, is recognised in its Preamble as being 'under the leadership of the Communist Party of China'.[12] The CPC's own constitution also explicitly recognises that the leadership by the CPC as one of the foundations for building the State.[13]

5 ibid, art 85.
6 ibid, art 93.
7 ibid, art 127.
8 ibid, arts 129, 132.
9 Zhining Ma, 'The Structure and Roles of China's Party-State System in Industrial Relations: An Updated Review' (2009) 7 China: An International Journal 370, 370-371.
10 The term 'Party leadership' has been mentioned in a considerable amount of Chinese legal and political documents, including the 1982 Constitution, statutory laws and government reports. Domestically, the Party leadership is deemed as the fundamental element of the socialist system with Chinese characteristics.
11 The concept 'Party-State' refers to 'party above the state' or 'party rule of the State'. See generally Larry Catá Backert, 'Party, People, Government and State: On Constitutional Values and the Legitimacy of the Chinese State-Party Rule of Law System' (2012) 30 Boston University International Law Journal 101, 101; Sarah Biddulph, *The Stability Imperative: Human Rights and Law in China* (UBC Press 2015) 1.
12 Chinese Constitution, preamble. The statement 'under the leadership of the Communist Party of China' is clearly mentioned five times in the preamble of the 1982 Chinese Constitution.
13 Constitution of the Communist Party of China (amended and adopted at the 17th National Congress of the Communist Party of China on 21 October 2007). The English version was obtained from the Central Compilation & Translation Bureau of China <www.cctb.net/bygz/wxfy/200912/P020130619516888170011.pdf> accessed 28 November 2017.

To sum up, China's political power structure can be understood as shown in Figure 3.1.[14] The State Council, namely the central government, is the highest executive organ of State power. The State Council follows the system of premier responsibility, while various ministries and commissions under the leadership of the State Council follow the system of ministerial responsibility. The main ministries and commissions that are responsible for health-related issues include the National Health and Family Planning Commission (NHFPC), the Chinese Food and Drug Administration (CFDA), the Ministry of Human Resources and Social Security (MOHRSS), the Ministry of Civil Affairs (MOCA), the Ministry of Finance (MOF) and the National Development and Reform Commission (NDRC).[15]

14 The CPC's leadership over the legislature, the judiciary, the executive and the procuratorate is not explicitly recognised in the CPC's constitution. Although according to the Organic Law of the National People's Congress [*Quanguo Renmin Daibiao Dahui Zuzhi Fa*], the presidium of the NPC nominates the leaders of the SPC and the SPP, in practice it is the CPC that nominates the members of the presidium of the NPC. In addition, in his speech on the 30th Anniversary of the Promulgation of the Constitution of the People's Republic of China in 2012, President Xi, Jinping affirmed that the CPC leads the people in promulgating the Constitution and laws. As such, it is generally believed that political power in China is divided into two parts – the CPC and the State organs. Western constitutional scholars normally look suspiciously at the CPC, given that it is the single ruling party in China and it has extra-constitutional power. In addition, when it comes to China's legal and judicial system, Western scholars tend to challenge whether there is judicial independence in China and question whether the Party leadership would be an obstacle to the rule of law. In the meantime, Chinese scholars and politicians also attack Western-style judicial independence. From my perspective, although the Party leadership may to some degree undermine the independence of the judiciary, the major obstacles are the systemic and institutional problems of China's entire judicial system. Nevertheless, although there has been an ongoing debate regarding the legitimacy of this Party-State system, it is not the aim of this chapter to challenge or justify China's current political structure. Rather, all analyses in this study are based on China's current political setting. See generally Larry Catá Backert, 'The Rule of Law, the Chinses Communist Party, and Ideological Campaigns: Sange Daibiao (the "Three Represents"), Socialist Rule of Law, and Modern Chinese Constitutionalism' (2006) 16 Journal of Transnational Law and Contemporary Problems 101; Randall Peerenboom, *China's Long March toward Rule of Law* (Cambridge University Press 2002); Susan Trevaskes, 'Political Ideology, the Party, and Politicking: Justice System Reform in China' (2011) 37 Modern China 315; Sarah Biddulph and others, 'Rule of Law with Chinese Characteristics: The Role of Campaigns in Lawmaking' (2012) 34 Law & Policy 373; Suli Zhu, 'Political Parties in China's Judiciary' (2006) 17 Duke Journal of Comparative & International Law 553.

15 State Council Organisation Chart, derived from the Official Website of the State Council of the People's Republic of China <http://english.gov.cn/state_council/2014/09/03/content_281474985533579.htm> accessed 28 November 2017.

Figure 3.1 China's political power[16]

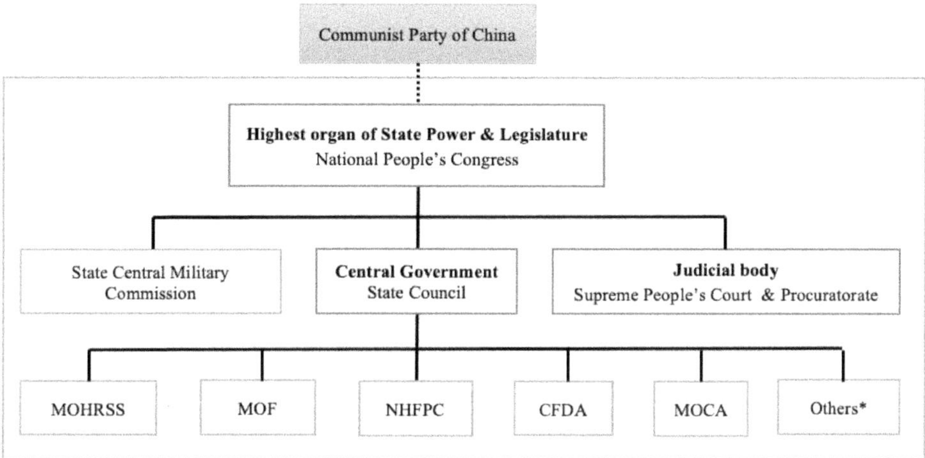

3.2.1.2 *China's health administration and health service delivery system*

China's health administration is composed of four levels. At the top level is the NHFPC, which serves as the major health authority at the national level, followed by provincial, municipal and county health bureaux as the main health authorities.[17] Provincial, municipal and county governments can lead the work of the health bureaux at the respective level. In the meantime, health bureaux are under the leadership and supervision of their respective superior health bureaux.[18] In addition to the NHFPC, other ministries and commissions under the State Council, such as the MOHRSS, MOCA, MOF and the NDRC, also take certain responsibilities for

16 Source: the author. China's constitutional structure as stipulated in the 1982 Constitution does not include the CPC. However, in order to reflect reality, the CPC is placed above the entire national organisation chart as a demonstration of the Party-State feature of China's political system. Furthermore, the NPC is placed in some scholarship on the same level as the State Council, the SPC and the SPP, so as to show that there is no clear balance between those state apparatuses. Again, given the aim of this section is to provide an overview of China's legal and political system, this constitutional structure is drawn upon the official legal and political documents.

17 China has reformed the ministries and commissions under the State Council. The NHFPC was established through merging the former Ministry of Health and the National Population and Family Planning Commission in accordance with the *State Council Institutional Reform and Transformation of Functions Plan.* State Council Institutional Reform and Transformation of Functions Plan [Guowuyuan Jigou Gaige he Zhineng Zhuanbian Fangan] (2013) <www.npc.gov.cn/wxzl/gongbao/2013-07/18/content_1810943.htm> accessed 28 November 2017. Author's translation. See also Qingyue Meng and others, 'People's Republic of China: Health System Review' (2015) 5 Health Systems in Transistion 16.

18 Meng and others (n 17) 1.

the planning, funding and insurance management of China's health system (see more detail in chapter 7).

China's health service delivery system encompasses both the public health system and the medical service delivery system.[19] There are both public and non-public health institutions in China according to their registration type and management type. Generally speaking, these health institutions are divided into three categories: (1) specialised public health institutions, (2) hospitals, and (3) primary health care institutions.[20] Firstly, the public health system consists of centres for disease control and prevention (CDC), institutions for specified diseases, maternal and child health institutions, health supervision and management institutions, to name just a few.[21] Secondly, China has a three-tiered medical service delivery system.[22] Since 1989, hospitals in China have been graded into three levels (Grade I, II and III) according to their size and function, the highest standard being Grade III.[23] Tertiary comprehensive hospitals are those national, provincial, municipal and medical school-affiliated hospitals that provide a high level of specialised outpatient and inpatient services (Grade III); secondary comprehensive hospitals are those located at county and district levels that provide general outpatient and inpatient services to local residents (Grade II); and primary hospitals (Grade I) are those located in a community that provide preventive, clinical treatment, inpatient and outpatient medical services for common diseases, and health administration. Primary hospitals are often regarded as primary health care facilities. Thirdly, in addition to hospitals, there are also primary health care institutions that provide basic medical services and public health services to residents within their regions.[24] These include community health centres (or stations thereafter) for urban residents and township health centres and village clinics for rural residents. Most village clinics are not owned by the government

19 ibid 20.
20 ibid 108.
21 ibid 20, 108, 130.
22 ibid 141.
23 See generally, Administrative Measures for the Classification of Hospitals (Interim Draft) [Yiyuan Fenji Guanli Banfa (Shixing Caoan)] (issued on 29 November 1989, revoked on 13 April 1998), art 4; Measures for the Assessment of Medical Institutions [Yiliao Jigou Pingsheng Banfa] (issued on 21 July 1995, revoked on 21 September 2011); Interim Measures for the Assessment of Hospitals [Yiyuan Pingsheng Zanxing Banfa] (issued on 21 September 2011) <www.nhfpc.gov.cn/yzygj/s3585u/201109/d2f032e736754c3ab74793779acb424c.shtml> accessed 28 Nov 2017. Author's translation.
24 Meng and others (n 17) 108.

but are affiliated with township health centres.[25] However, because a referral system is lacking in China, both urban and rural patients can freely choose any medical institution for receiving primary health care services, regardless of the Grade of the institution concerned.[26] As a result, problems that could have been solved at the primary level flood into secondary and tertiary hospitals through self-referral.[27]

Notably, given that China undertakes a non-derogable core obligation to provide essential primary health care, it is necessary to clarify the content of primary health care in the Chinese context before explaining the choice of terminology used to examine whether pre-existing legislation has prescribed the provision of essential primary health care. The term 'primary health care' has long been interpreted as 'entry-level health care' (*'chuji weisheng baojian'*) in China.[28] However, pursuant to the Alma-Ata Declaration, it is evident that entry-level or first-level health care services cannot cover the entire scope of primary health care, which pays particular attention to essential and fundamental health care. Since the new round of China's health care reform in 2006, the typology adopted in most Chinese legal and policy documents has changed from 'entry-level health care' to 'basic medical and health care (*'jiben yiliao weisheng'*)', which reflects a better understanding of the essence of primary health care.[29] As such, the analysis of primary health care will adopt the terms 'primary health care' and 'basic medical and health care' (as well as basic health care and basic medical care as key words thereafter) in English as well as *'chuji weisheng baojian'* and *'jiben yiliao weisheng'* in Chinese.

25 ibid 106-108, 139 -141.

26 ibid 137.

27 Margaret Chan, Keynote address at the International Seminar on Primary Health Care in Rural China (1 Novermber 2007) <www.who.int/dg/speeches/2007/20071101_beijing/en/> accessed 28 November 2017.

28 Guoping Xu and Jiaji Wang, 'Jichu Yiliao Weisheng Fuwu Yinggai zai Zhongguo Xinyigai zhong Dedao Zhengque Lijie he Quanmian Shishi [Primary Health Care: A Concept to be Fully Understood and Implemented in Current China's Health Care Reform]' (2015) 18 (32) Zhongguo Quanke Yixue [Chinese General Practice] 3893, 3893.

29 See for example Central Committee of the Communist Party of China, State Council, 'Opinions of the CPC Central Committee and the State Council on Deepening the Health Care System Reform' (2009) <www.china.org.cn/government/scio-press-conferences/2009-04/09/content_17575378.htm> accessed 28 November 2017. The English version was obtained from the official website of the State Council. State Council, 'The Twelfth Five-Year Plan for Health Sector Development' (2012) <www.wpro.who.int/health_services/china_nationalhealthplan.pdf> accessed 28 November 2017. The English version was obtained from the official website of the WHO Western Pacific Region.

3.2.1.3 China's legal system

China's domestic legal system is defined as a constitutionally-centred *'socialist system of laws with Chinese Characteristics'*.[30] In spite of this official definition, Chinese legal scholars generally remark that China's legal system is based on the Roman civil law system.[31] The Constitution is the highest law within China's jurisdiction. According to the 1982 Constitution and the Legislation Law, the official sources of laws and their hierarchies can be understood as follows:[32]

1. Constitution: enacted and promulgated by the NPC;
2. Laws (*'falv'*): enacted and promulgated by the NPC and the Standing Committee of the NPC (NPCSC);
3. Administrative regulations (*'xingzheng fagui'*): formulated and promulgated by the State Council;
4. Local regulations (*'difangxing fagui'*): enacted and promulgated by the local people's congresses (and their standing committees) in provinces and municipalities directly under the central government;
5. Self-governing regulations and seperate regulations (*'zizhi tiaoli' and 'dangxing tiaoli'*): enacted and promulgated by the local people's congresses in autonomous regions and counties;
6. Administrative rules (*'xingzheng guizhang'*), including:

- Local rules (*'difang zhengfu guizhang'*): formulated and promulgated by local governments;
- Department rules (*'bumen guizhang'*): formulated and promulgated by the ministries and commissions directly under the State Council, eg the NHFPC and the People's Bank of China;

30 Information Office of the State Council, 'White Paper on the Socialist Legal System with Chinese Characteristics' (2011). The English version was obtained from the official website of the State Council Information Office <www.scio.gov.cn/zfbps/ndhf/2011/Document/1036756/1036756.htm> accessed 28 November 2017.

31 Yanlong Han, 'Legal Protection of Human Rights in China' in Peter R Baehr and others (eds), *Human Rights: Chinese and Dutch Perspectives* (Martinus Nijhoff Publishers 1996) 91, 97; Mo Zhang, 'The Socialist Legal System with Chinese Characteristics: China's Discourse for the Rule of Law and a Bitter Experience' (2010) 24 Temple University & Comparative Law Journal 1, 1, 39.

32 Chinese Constitution, art 5; Legislation Law of the People's Republic of China [Lifa Fa] (adopted on 15 March 2000, entered into force on 1 July 2000, amended on 15 March 2015) (Legislation Law), arts 7, 65, 72, 80, 82, 92 <http://en.pkulaw.cn/display.aspx?cgid=245693&lib=law> accessed 28 November 2017. The English version was obtained from the academic database of authority – the pkulaw.

7. Military regulations and rules (*'junshi fagui guizhang'*): formulated and promulgated by the Central Military Commission.

In addition to statutory laws, the judicial interpretations (*'sifa jieshi'*) issued by the SPC to elucidate statutory provisions are of great importance to guide judgments and are directly applicable before China's domestic courts.[33]

With regard to health legislation more specifically, it is generally perceived that China has a four-tier legal framework for health protection. Along with the Constitution, health laws enacted and promulgated by the NPC and the NPCSC are on top of this framework (eg the drafting Basic Health Law as mentioned in chapter 1). As of 2017, there are 12 main health laws, which will be discussed further in section 3.4.3. The second layer of this framework contains health regulations formulated and promulgated by the State Council (i.e. administrative regulations). Currently, there are 40 health regulations at this level, including Nurse Regulation, Ordinance on Handling of Medical Malpractice, Ordinance on Traditional Chinese Medicines and so on so forth. The third layer is comprised of health regulations formulated and promulgated by the people's congresses (and their standing committees) at the provincial level (i.e. local regulations, self-governing regulations and seperate regulations). At the bottom of this hierarchy are health rules formulated and promulgated by local governments (i.e. local rules) or by the ministries and commissions under the State Council, in particular the NHFPC (i.e. department rules).[34]

3.2.1.4 China's judicial system

China's judicial system consists of four levels of courts, including the SPC at the national level, the High People's Courts at the provincial level, and the Intermediate and Basic People's Courts at the local level. In addition to the general courts, there

33 Vai Lo, 'Towards the Rule of Law: Judicial Lawmaking in China' (2016) 28 Bond Law Review 149, 150.

34 As of 2017, there are 12 health laws promulgated by the NPCSC. See generally, the official website of the NHFPC <http://en.nhfpc.gov.cn/regulations.html> accessed 28 November 2017; Meng and others (n 17) 17-19; Xin Liu and Hui Qin, 'Weishengfa Lilun Tixi Goujian de Qianti [Preconditions for the Construction of the Theoretical System of Health Law]' (2015) 4 Xingzhengfa Yanjiu [Research of Administrative Law] 55, 57.

are specialised courts, such as maritime, railway transportation and military courts.[35] Currently, there is no constitutional court under China's judicial system. Domestic courts do not have the power to review or interpret the Constitution.[36] Furthermore, as will be discussed further in section 3.4.2, constitutional provisions cannot be directly applied by China's domestic courts.

As mentioned earlier, there is no separation of powers between the executive, the legislature, and the judiciary in China, but only the separation of functions. Yet, Chinese scholars tend to perceive that the people's congress, government and court at respective levels function with mutual coordination and mutual restriction.[37] It is arguable that this regime would place the judiciary under the supervision of the legislature and potentially undermine judicial independence in China.[38] China's judicial system and judicial remedies for the right to health care will be further analysed in chapter 7.

3.2.2 China's ideology of human rights

3.2.2.1 The conception of human rights

Although China had ratified various international human rights treaties since 1980, it was not until 2004 that human rights were officially stipulated in written law.[39] One possible reason is that the Chinese society has been deeply influenced by the Confucian philosophy.[40] According to Confucius, the responsibilities and duties an individual undertakes to others, to society and to the State are more important than claiming one's own rights in social life.[41] This ideology is deeply rooted in Chinese

35 Yuwen Li, *The Judicial System and Reform in Post-Mao China: Stumbling Towards Justice* (Routledge 2014) 7.

36 ibid 8.

37 ibid 39.

38 ibid.

39 China ratified the Convention on the Elimination of All Forms of Discrimination Against Women in 1980, which was the first international human rights treaty China ever ratified. Nevertheless, no agreement has been reached as to whether human rights, as a concept of Western origin and a product of Western thinking, can and should be introduced into China. The inclusion of '*the State respects and preserves human rights*' in the 2004 amendment of the Constitution officially marked the start of legal protection of human rights in China.

40 Pinghua Sun, *Human Rights Protection System in China* (Springer 2014) 4-7.

41 ibid.

culture and may be responsible for the rare use of judicial mechanisms for seeking the enforcement of individual rights in China.

The Chinese conception of human rights has been constantly evolving since the adoption of China's reform and opening-up policy in 1979. In his 1985 speech entitled *Bourgeois Liberalization Means Taking the Capitalist Road*, the former leader Deng, Xiaoping pointed out that the perception of human rights in the West is inherently different from the Chinese understanding of human rights.[42] According to Deng, the Chinese conception of human rights is to ensure that human rights belong to *'all Chinese people'*. Deng contended that human rights can be divided into two categories: *'individual rights'* and *'collective rights'*. He further asserted that State sovereignty, or the *'State rights'* under the domain of collective rights are more important than individual rights or the 'Western human rights'.[43] Consequently, *individual (human) rights* are still not well recognised by China's top decision-makers.

In 1991, the Information Office of the State Council issued a White Paper entitled *Human Rights in China* and affirmed that the Chinese government highly values the UDHR.[44] This paper reiterates that the understanding of human rights varies among States, given their different political, social and cultural backgrounds. China derives its own conception of human rights in consideration of its historical and national conditions as well as its long practical experience. According to this white paper,

> [t]he human rights enjoyed by the Chinese citizenry encompass an extensive scope, including not only survival, personal and political rights, but also economic, cultural and social rights. The State pays full attention to safeguarding both individual and collective rights […]. The State provides guarantees in terms of system, laws and material means for the realization of human rights.[45]

42 Xiaoping Deng, 'Gao Zichanjieji Ziyouhua jiushi zou Zibenzhuyi Daolu [Bourgeois Liberalization Means Taking the Capitalist Road]' in *Deng Xiaoping Wenxuan 3 [Selected Works from Deng, Xiaoping]* (Renmin Publisher 1993) 125.

43 ibid 125; Sun (n 40) 91; Xiaoming Xia, 'Jianlun Deng Xiaoping de Renquan Sixiang [Brief Review on Deng Xiaoping's Conception of Human Rights]' 1995 (3) Xinjiang Shehui Kexue [Xinjiang Social Science] 76, 76-79.

44 The Information Office of the State Council, 'Human Rights in China' (1991) preface para 3. This document can be found on the official website of the Central People's Government of the People's Republic of China <www.gov.cn/zwgk/2005-05/24/content_488.htm> accessed 28 November 2017; The English version of this white paper was obtained from the State Council Information Office <http://china.org.cn/e-white/7/index.htm> accessed 28 November 2017.

45 ibid, preface para 4.

Remarkably, this white paper sets the highest priority for the right to subsistence and underlines that, 'the right to subsistence is the most important of all human rights, without which the other rights are out of the question'.[46] The right to subsistence entails the basic conditions for people to live with dignity and beyond.[47] As Sun asserts, the right to subsistence should not be regarded as a human right at the lower level, but a right with richer meanings, which guarantees personal dignity, the right to basic living standards, the right to health, and even the right to food and the right to housing.[48]

Since the publication of this white paper in 1991, China has become a State party to a wide range of international human rights treaties and the protection of human rights has gradually become an important issue for the Chinese government.[49] Table 3.1 summarises the major international human rights treaties China has ratified so far that recognise the right to health care. However, given that sovereignty is of the highest priority in China, it is unlikely for China to accept the competence of international treaty bodies to verify its compliance with these treaties.[50] In addition, China is reluctant to accept the supervision or monitoring of its implementation of human rights obligations under these treaties by various international supervisory mechanisms. Up to now, China has refused to accept most forms of supervision or monitoring at the international level, except through reporting procedures to treaty bodies.[51]

In addition, China has also issued a series of white papers with respect to the protection of human rights and the right to health in particular, which will be discussed in more detail in chapter 4.

46 ibid, chapter I para 1.
47 Sun (n 40) 88.
48 ibid 89.
49 Sun (n 40) 47; Biddulph (n 11) 1.
50 Mullen Wim, 'Chinese Practice in UN Treaty Monitoring Bodies: Principled Sovereignty and Slow Appreciation' in Hitoshi Nasu and Ben Saul (eds), *Human Rights in the Asia-Pacific Region: Towards Institution Building* (Routledge 2011) 88-89.
51 ibid.

Table 3.1 Ratification status of major international human rights treaties in China[52]

Human Rights Instrument (Date into force)	Signature	Ratification (R)/Accession (A)
CERD (1969)		1981(A)
ICCPR (1976)	1998	
ICESCR (1976)	1997	2001(R)
CEDAW (1981)	1980	1980(R)
CAT (1987)	1986	1988(R)
CRC (1990)	1990	1992(R)
CRMW (2003)		
CRPD (2008)	2007	2008(R)

3.2.2.2 Legal protection of human rights

The inclusion of the provision '*the State respects and preserves human rights*' in the 2004 amendment of the Constitution was unprecedented in China's history and a big step forward for the legal protection of human rights.[53] This amendment turns the Chinese conception of human rights from a purely political concept into a legal concept. The entry of human rights into the Constitution requires the State to enact or amend its domestic laws in order to reflect the State's respect for and guarantee of human rights, including the right to health (care).[54] In addition, to comply with its obligation under human rights law, China has enacted a wide range of laws and regulations aimed at the promotion and protection of the right to health (care).[55] Section 3.4.3 will further discuss elements of the right to health (care), including core obligations arising from this right, that have been stipulated in China's health-related laws.

52 Source: summarised by the author.
53 Chinese Constitution, art 33.
54 Sun (n 40) 27.
55 United Nations Economic and Social Council, 'Implementation of the International Covenant on Economic, Social and Cultural Rights: Intial Reports submitted by States Parties under Articles 16 and 17 of the Covenant, Addendum, People's Republic of China' (n 2) paras 14, 145-209.

3.3 The domestic application of international (human rights) treaties

Ratifying an international (human rights) treaty (or acceding to the treaty thereafter) means that a State is bound by the treaty to which it is a party. However, the ratification of a legally binding treaty does not necessarily entail that it becomes domestic law. Domestic application of international (human rights) treaties is a complex matter. International treaties do not provide for any specific means by which they should be given effect in the domestic legal system. In practice, States have adopted a variety of arrangements, varying substantially from one State to another.[56] Notably, it cannot be presumed that treaty provisions are directly applicable before domestic courts even when they have domestic effect.[57] To complicate this matter further, when a treaty provision is directly applicable as international law but is incompatible with provisions of domestic law, the question of precedence arises.

This section discusses the general domestic application of international (human rights) treaties and China's specific practice by addressing three questions: (1) the means by which international (human rights) treaties are given effect in domestic legal system(s); (2) whether or not provisions of international (human rights) treaties are directly applicable before domestic courts; and (3) what is the legal status of treaty vis-à-vis domestic law, when the provisions of international (human rights) treaties and domestic laws are incompatible with each other? I adopted Van Dijk's terminology – which distinguishes between the internal effect, direct effect and precedence of treaties – for analysing these questions. Each of these matters will be dealt with in more detail below. In addition, given that the question of whether international customary law has legally binding force remains largely controversial in China, the discussion below is confined to international (human rights) treaties.[58]

56 Matthew Craven, 'The Domestic Application of the International Covenant on Economic, Social and Cultural Rights' (1993) 40 Netherlands International Law Review 367, 371; Paul Hunt and others, 'Implementation of Economic, Social and Cultural Rights' in Scott Sheeran and Nigel Rodley (eds), *Routledge Handbook of International Human Rights Law* (Routledge 2013) 550

57 Craven (n 56) 377-404.

58 Jerry Li and Sanzhuan Guo, 'China' in Dinah Shelton (ed), *International Law and Domestic Legal Systems: Incorporation, Transformation, and Persuasion* (Oxford University Press 2011) 194.

3.3.1 General legal doctrines of domestic application of international (human rights) treaties

3.3.1.1 Internal effect

Adhering to the principle of *pacta sunt servanda*, a State party to a ratified treaty is subject to a legally binding obligation to perform the treaty obligations in good faith.[59] Therefore, the first step after the ratification of international (human rights) treaties is to give effect to treaty obligations in the domestic legal system. Notably, the means by which treaty obligations are to be given *internal effect* is left to a State's discretion.[60]

Scholarly discussions of such methods generally distinguish between the two different theories of 'monism' and 'dualism', of which there are no generally agreed definitions. Given that the monist and dualist theories are not the focus of this chapter, this section sheds light on some general observations concerning the theories.

- Monism

States with a civil law background, such as Austria, France, Germany, the Netherlands, Japan and South Africa, generally have a monist system. The USA is also believed to adopt a monist system.[61]

In monist States, international law and domestic law form a unitary legal system.[62] Ratification of an international (human rights) treaty automatically leads to the incorporation of the treaty into a State's domestic legal system,[63] without the need for any implementing legislation (i.e. a statute, a decree, or delegated or secondary legislation).[64] Put simply, treaty provisions have legal effect (i.e. internal effect) as

59 Vienna Convention on the Law of Treaties (adopted on 23 May 1969, entered into force on 27 January 1980) 1155 UNTS 331, art 26.

60 Pieter Van Dirk, 'Domestic Status of Human-Rights Treaties and the Attitude of the Judiciary - The Dutch Case' in Manfred Nowak and others (eds), *Progress in the Spirit of Human Rights* (1988) 634.

61 David Sloss, 'Domestic Application of Treaties' in Hollis Duncan (ed), *The Oxford Guide to Treaties* (Oxford University Press 2011) 373.

62 Philip Alston and Ryan Goodman, *International Human Rights: The Successor to International Human Rights in Context* (Oxford University Press 2012) 1058.

63 Andrew Byrnes and Catherine Renshaw, 'Within the State' in Daniel Moeckli and others (eds), *International Human Rights Law* (Oxford University Press 2013) 461.

64 Sloss (n 61) 373.

such in the domestic order. This approach is labelled the adoption or 'automatic incorporation' of treaties.[65]

However, it should be noted that there are some exceptions. Some monist States (eg Germany and China[66]) operate a similar system of adoption, but require the legislative body's additional approval or an 'order of execution' prior to ratification, which is often known as 'quasi-automatic incorporation'.[67] For instance, Article 59 (2) of the German Constitution (i.e. the Basic Law for the Federal Republic of Germany) states that, 'treaties that regulate the political relations of the Federation or relate to subjects of federal legislation shall require the consent or participation, in the form of a federal law, of the bodies responsible in such a case for the enactment of federal law.'[68]

- Dualism

Most States with a common-law background have a dualist system, including the United Kingdom, Australia, New Zealand and Canada, as well as jurisdictions such as the Hong Kong Special Administrative Region of China. There are also a number of Scandinavian States with a civil law background that adopt this system, including Sweden, Norway and Denmark.[69]

In dualist States, international law and domestic law are considered to be two co-existing and parallel systems, with no subordinating relationship with one another.[70] International (human rights) treaties do not have internal effect; treaty provisions must be either incorporated or transformed into the domestic legal system.[71] According to Craven, in the case of incorporation, treaty provisions are incorporated into the domestic legal order and applied as national law, 'as they stand by being

65 Craven (n 56) 371-372; Van Dijk (n 60) 634.

66 Law of the People's Republic of China on the Procedures of the Conclusion of Treaties [Dijie Tiaoyue Chengxu Fa] (adopted and entered into force on 28 December 1999), art 7. The English version was obtained from the official website of the Bureau of Legislative Affairs of the State Council <www.mfa.gov.cn/chn//pds/ziliao/tytj/tyfg/t70826.htm> accessed 28 November 2017.

67 Craven (n 56) 372.

68 Basic Law for the Federal Republic of Germany (23 May 1949) (the German Constitution), art 59 (2) <www.btg-bestellservice.de/pdf/80201000.pdf> accessed 28 November 2017.

69 Sloss (n 61) 370.

70 Emilian Ciongaru, The Monistic and Dualistic Theory in European Law <www.ugb.ro/Juridica/Issue1EN/10_Teoria_monista_si_dualista_in_dreptul_europeanCiongaruEN.pdf> accessed 28 November 2017.

71 Craven (n 56) 371-373; Van Dijk (n 60) 634-636.

appended in the text of the act or in its accompany Schedule'.[72] An example is the UK Merchant Shipping Act.[73] By contrast, in the case of transformation, treaty provisions are transformed into domestic law by a separate legislative act amending or supplementing existing domestic legislation, without any specific reference to the relevant treaty provisions.[74]

3.3.1.2 Direct effect

It is important to note that internal effect should be separated from direct effect. Even if a treaty is given the status of domestic law, domestic courts may still decline to apply treaty provisions. As Sloss points out, only if 'domestic law authorizes a domestic court to apply that treaty provision as a rule of decision' will a treaty provision have 'direct effect' or be 'directly applicable' in domestic courts.[75] As Van Dijk correctly notes, in assessing the effective implementation of a (human rights) treaty, the means by which a treaty is given effect in domestic law is not of decisive importance; what really matters is the attitude of the court towards such treaty provisions.[76]

Many scholars have discussed the direct effect of treaties; nevertheless, there is little consensus on the use of terms, such as 'direct effect', 'directly applicable', 'invocability' or 'self-executing'.[77] Conceptually speaking, these terms all denote different notions, but 'direct effect' and 'invocability' are very often closely linked in the judicial practice of courts in States that adopt a monist approach. Put simply, if a private party is empowered to invoke a treaty provision before a domestic court, this provision is 'invocable'; or in other words the provision has 'direct effect', or is 'directly applicable' in domestic courts.[78] Some States, for example the USA, also distinguish between treaty provisions that are self-executing and non-self-executing. However, 'self-executing' as such is a very complex concept. There is no generally

72 ibid.
73 ibid. The International Labour Conventions is incorporated into the UK legal system as the Merchant Shipping Act.
74 ibid.
75 David Sloss, 'Treaty Enforcement in Domestic Courts: A Comparative Analysis' in David Sloss (ed), *The Role of Domestic Courts in Treaty Enforcement: A Comparative Study* (Cambridge University Press 2009) 11.
76 Craven (n 56) 377; Van Dijk (n 60) 632.
77 Craven (n 56) 376.
78 Sloss (n 75) 11.

agreed definition of this term.[79] To avoid the confusion inherent in the term 'self-executing', I use the terms 'direct effect' and 'directly applicable', which mean that 'a treaty as a whole or its relevant provisions may be applied by judicial or administrative authorities without requiring further legislative intervention.'[80]

The analysis of direct effect is mainly aimed at monist States that operate a system of adoption, but sometimes it is also of consequence for dualist States in the event that treaties are incorporated into the domestic legal system.[81] Almost all monist States recognise, at least theoretically, that (at least some) treaty provisions can be directly applied by domestic courts.[82] Nevertheless, as Sloss observes, most courts in monist States prefer to apply treaty provisions indirectly rather than directly, which 'erodes the practical significance of the traditional distinction between monist and dualist States'.[83]

3.3.1.3 Precedence

The direct applicability of a treaty provision may give rise to the question of the legal status of international (human rights) treaties vis-à-vis domestic law, especially in the event that the treaty provision is incompatible with domestic legislation. Normally, when a treaty is given effect in domestic law by means of incorporation or transformation, provisions of such a treaty receive the same legal status as other provisions of domestic law of the same kind; while the legal status of a treaty recognised in domestic law by way of adoption should be determined on the basis of international or domestic law and/or practice.[84]

In some instances, treaty provisions have a status equivalent to that of constitutional provisions. An example is the European Convention on Human Rights

79 Scholars have extensively explained the self-execution doctrine, with different definitions and different reasons to distinguish from self-executing and non-self-executing treaty provision. See for example Sloss (n 61) 386-388; Robert Dalton, 'National Treaty Law and Practice: United States' in *Duncan and others* (eds), *National Treaty Law and Practice* (Martinus Nijhoff Publishers 2005) 788.

80 Craven (n 56) 379; Van Dijk (n 60) 636-637.

81 ibid, 378-379.

82 Sloss (n 61) 375.

83 ibid.

84 Van Dirk (n 60) 638.

in Austria, which has the same status as the Austrian Federal Constitutional Law.[85] In some other cases, treaty provisions have a status superior to that of provisions of domestic laws. For instance, the 1958 French Constitution provides that ratified or approved treaties shall prevail over Acts of Parliament upon publication.[86] The same applies in Germany.[87] In the USA, self-executing treaties are treated as ordinary federal law, so they will prevail over both State legislation and federal subordinate legislation.[88]

3.3.1.4 General observations

As just discussed, it is a matter of State discretion to adopt either a monist or dualist approach to give effect to international (human rights) treaties.[89] Nevertheless, the distinction between monism and dualism is far from clear-cut: the approach employed by the State may reflect both monist and dualist characteristics, depending on the nature and content of the international (human rights) treaty concerned.[90]

In fact, what really matters is not the monist or dualist approach a State adopts to give effect to international (human rights) treaties in its domestic legal system, but how the State discharges its obligations arising from these treaties. In terms of the legal status of international (human rights) treaties, provisions of these international (human rights) treaties may have status equivalent to that of constitutional provisions or that of domestic legal provisions, depending on international or domestic law

85 Ohlinger Theo, 'Austria and Article 6 of the European Convention on Human Rights' (1990) 1 European Journal of International Law 286, 286.

86 Constitution of October 4, 1958 (the French Constitution), art 55 <www.conseil-constitutionnel.fr/conseil-constitutionnel/english/constitution/constitution-of-4-october-1958.25742.html> accessed 28 November 2017.

87 Byrnes and Renshaw (n 63) 462.

88 David Moore, 'The Supremacy Clause and International Law: A Response to Jordan Paust' JURIST - Forum (1 July 2012) <www.jurist.org/forum/2012/07/david-moore-international-law.php> accessed 28 November 2017. Article VI Paragraph II of the US Constitution is commonly regarded as the 'Supremacy Clause', which provides that the federal constitution, federal law, and ratified treaties normally prevail over state laws and even state constitutions. Under this clause, state courts are bound by the supreme law and in case of conflict between federal and state law, the federal law must be applied even though state constitutions are subordinate to federal law. However, as explained in the preceding part, even if the Supremacy Clause declares a ratified treaty to be the supreme law of the land and thereby qualified as enforceable federal law, the treaty itself must be considered as self-executing before it can be directly applied before the courts.

89 Craven (n 56) 371.

90 Anthony Aust, *Modern Treaty Law and Practice* (Cambridge University Press 2007) 187.

and/or practice. Given these reasons, the traditional monistic-dualistic dichotomy is gradually losing ground. Indeed, the key issue to be addressed is whether the adoption, incorporation or transformation of international (human rights) treaties in domestic legal systems can ensure the effective protection of human rights.

3.3.2 Application of international (human rights) treaties in China

China has ratified a wide variety of international (human rights) treaties and has gradually implemented its treaty obligations. As explained earlier, international treaties do not provide for any specific means by which they should be given the force of law domestically; it is left to China's discretion. Nevertheless, neither China's Constitution nor basic laws set forth any general provisions on the legal status of international (human rights) treaties in China's domestic legal system.[91] As such, it remains controversial: (1) whether an international (human rights) treaty is automatically incorporated into China's legal system (a monist approach) or transformed by any legislative act (a dualist approach); (2) whether treaty provisions are directly applicable in China's domestic courts in the case of adoption; and (3) whether provisions of international (human rights) treaties take precedence over provisions of domestic law. In academia, while some scholars agree that China adopts a monist approach,[92] many others reject the use of both the monistic and the dualistic views to explain China's domestic application of international (human rights) treaties.[93] Considering that monism and dualism are blurred in State practice and that this dichotomy is by and large a theoretical distinction, it is not the aim of this study to argue whether China adopts a monist or dualist approach. The following subsections purport to provide an overview of China's general practice of implementing its international treaty obligations.

91 Hanqin Xue and others, 'National Treaty Law and Practice: China' in Duncan and others (eds), *National Treaty Law and Practice* (Martinus Nijhoff Publishers 2005) 163.

92 Most Chinese textbooks on international law contend that China has a monist system. See generally Haopei Li, *Tiaoyuefa Gailun [Introduction to Law of Treaties]* (Law Press 2003) 316-326; Sloss (n 61) 373.

93 See for example Hanqin Xue and Qian Jin, 'International Treaties in the Chinese Domestic Legal System' (2009) 8 (2) Chinese Journal of International Law 299, 305; Bjorn Ahl, 'Chinese Law and International Treaties' (2009) 39 HKLJ 737, 739; Li and Guo (n 58) 167-170.

3.3.2.1 Application of international treaties: general practice

The Chinese Constitution does not stipulate the means by which international treaties are to be given effect in the domestic legal system. International treaties in principle have legally binding force, except for those provisions to which China has made reservations. Nevertheless, not all treaties automatically become part of China's domestic law. Given the different nature of ratified treaties, how these treaties are given effect in China's domestic legal order also varies.[94] Generally speaking, both adoption and transformation can be observed within China's practice.

- Adoption

Many international treaties are automatically incorporated (i.e. adoption) into China's domestic system and have legal effect as such.[95] This practice is deduced from dozens of China's existing laws. For example, Article 17 of 1982 Trademark Law provides that,

> [a]ny foreign person or foreign enterprise intending to apply for the registration of a trademark in China shall file an application in accordance with any agreement concluded between the People's Republic of China and the country to which the applicant belongs, or according to the international treaty to which both countries are parties, or on the basis of the principles of reciprocity.[96]

A similar provision is found Article 20 of the 1984 Patent Law, among others.[97] When treaties are given effect in the domestic legal order by way of adoption, the question arises as to whether the provisions of these treaties are directly applicable in domestic courts. In fact, China's domestic courts have already applied a number of international treaties when adjudicating civil cases with foreign elements,[98] including

94 Xue and Jin (n 93) 300.

95 Zhaojie Li, 'The Role of Domestic Courts in the Adjudication of International Human Rights: A Survey of the Practice and Problems in China' In Benedetto Conforti and other (eds), *Enforcing International Human Rights Treaties in Domestic Courts* (Martinus Hijhoff Publishers 1997) 339.

96 Trademark Law of the People's Republic of China (adopted on 23 August 1982, entered into force on 1 March 1983, amended on 30 August 2013), art 17. The English version was obtained from the official website of the Ministry of Commerce. <http://english.mofcom.gov.cn/article/policyrelease/Businessregulations/201303/20130300045770.shtml> accessed 28 November 2017.

97 Patent Law of the People's Republic of China (adopted on 12 March 1984, entered into force 1 April 1985, amended on 27 December 2008), art 20. The English version was obtained from the official website of the State Council. <http://english.gov.cn/archive/laws_regulations/2014/08/23/content_281474983043612.htm> accessed 28 November 2017.

98 Xue and Jin (n 93) 310.

the 1980 United Nations Convention on Contracts for the International Sale of Goods, the 1929 Warsaw Convention on the Unification of Certain Rules Relating to International Carriage by Air, and many other treaties that contain commercial elements.[99] Furthermore, some domestic laws explicitly authorise courts to give precedence to provisions of international treaties. For example, Article 142 of the General Principles of the Civil Law states that,

> [i]f any international treaty concluded or acceded to by the People's Republic of China contains provisions differing from those in the civil laws of the People's Republic of China, the provisions of the international treaty shall apply, unless the provisions are ones on which the People's Republic of China has announced reservations.[100]

The same principle is restated in Article 260 of the Civil Procedural Law, among others.[101] The precedence of international treaties clearly indicates the direct effect of these treaties.[102] It should be noted, however, that giving precedence to the treaty provision over a conflicting provision of domestic law does not amend or repeal the latter – the domestic law provision remains in force.[103] An amendment or repeal of existing domestic law is required if domestic law is incompatible with international treaties.

- Transformation

In many other cases, international treaties are transformed into China's domestic legal system by enacting new legislation or amending existing legislation. If the subject matter of a treaty is not covered by pre-existing domestic laws, national legislation will be enacted so as to transform treaty obligations. For example, China is party to the 1975 Vienna Convention on Diplomatic Relations and the 1979 Vienna

---

99 ibid.

100 General Principles of the Civil Law of the People's Republic of China (adopted on 12 April 1986, entered into force 1 January 1987, amended on 27 August 2009) ('General Principles of the Civil Law'), art 142. The English version was obtained from the official website of the NPC. <www.npc.gov.cn/englishnpc/Law/2007-12/12/content_1383941.htm> accessed 28 November 2017.

101 Civil Procedure Law of the People's Republic of China (adopted and entered into force on 9 April 1991, amended on 27 June 2017), art 260. The English version was obtained from the official website of the NPC. <www.npc.gov.cn/englishnpc/Law/2007-12/12/content_1383880.htm> accessed 28 November 2017.

102 Li (n 95) 340; Sicong Zuo, 'Zhijie Shiyong Tiaoyue Wenti Yanjie [Research on the Direct Application of Treaties]' (2008) 3 Legal Research 88, 94.

103 Van Dijk (n 60) 639.

Convention on Consular Relations. Nevertheless, these two treaties as such do not have internal effect in China's domestic legal system. China enacted the Regulations Concerning Diplomatic Privileges and Immunities in 1986 and the Regulations Concerning Consular Privileges and Immunities in 1990, respectively, to transform the provisions of these two treaties into its domestic legal system.[104] This is a feature of a dualist approach. In dealing with matters concerning diplomatic or consular privileges and immunities, China's domestic courts and administrative departments are to apply the two Regulations rather than the treaty provisions.[105] Another example is China's ratification of the 1982 UN Convention on the Law of the Sea. In 1992, the Law of the People's Republic of China on the Territorial Sea and the Contiguous Zone was enacted so as to transform relevant provisions of the 1982 Convention into China's domestic legal system.[106]

If the subject-matter of a treaty can be addressed through pre-existing domestic laws, then treaty provisions are generally transformed into China's domestic legal system by amending or revising pre-existing laws, either prior to or after China's ratification of the treaty concerned. This method is the most common way by which China implements its international treaty obligations.[107] One representative example is in the area of trade law. As Xue and Jin observe, after joining the World Trade Organization (WTO), 'China has repealed, abrogated, revised, enacted and promulgated more than 3000 domestic laws, administrative regulations and administrative orders to ensure compliance with WTO rules.'[108] In settling trade disputes, domestic courts and administrative departments should provide remedies in accordance with China's domestic laws. Only when domestic remedies have been proved to be insufficient can WTO rules and standards be applied.[109]

104 Regulations of the People's Republic of China Concerning Diplomatic Privileges and Immunities (adopted on 5 September 1986, entered into force 5 September 1986) <www.npc.gov.cn/englishnpc/Law/2007-12/12/content_1383938.htm> accessed 28 November 2017; Regulations of the People's Republic of China Concerning Consular Privileges and Immunities (adopted and entered into force on 30 October 1990). The English version was obtained from the official website of the NPC. <www.npc.gov.cn/englishnpc/Law/2007-12/12/content_1383903.htm> accessed 28 November 2017.

105 Xue and Jin (n 93) 306.

106 Law of the People's Republic of China on the Territorial Sea and the Contiguous Zone (adopted and entered into force on 25 February 1992). The English version was obtained from the official website of the NPC. <www.npc.gov.cn/englishnpc/Law/2007-12/12/content_1383846.htm> accessed 28 November 2017.

107 Xue and Jin (n 93) 306; Li and Guo (n 58) 170.

108 Xue and Jin (n 93) 306.

109 ibid 308-309.

To sum up, instead of adopting a pure monist or dualist approach, China has adopted the methods of both adoption and transformation to give effect to international treaties, depending on the subject matter and nature of the treaty concerned. The legal status of international treaties should be considered in the specific context provided by each law.

3.3.2.2 Application of international human rights treaties

When it comes to international human rights treaties more specifically, the lack of constitutional clarification makes China's domestic application of human rights treaties a complex issue. Some Chinese scholars believe that international human rights treaties are automatically incorporated in China's domestic legal system.[110] Their argument is evidenced by many State reports that China has submitted to the human rights treaty bodies. For example, in the common core document that China submitted to the Office of the United Nations High Commissioner for Human Rights (OHCHR), it stated that,

> [t]o render international human rights agreements consistent with domestic law and make them a part of the domestic legal system, [...]. Once approved, the instrument is binding under Chinese law and China must honour the corresponding obligations: no further special legal transformation is required to turn it into domestic law.[111]

Some other Chinese scholars believe that international human rights treaties are given internal effect in China's domestic legal system by way of transformation.[112] Their argument is based on the fact that many domestic laws contain provisions regarding obligations under international human rights treaties, even though these laws do not explicitly refer to the relevant treaty. Examples include the 1990 Law on the Protection of Disabled Persons and the 1992 Law on the Protection of Women's Rights and Interests, to name just a few. These scholars thus conclude that China has adopted legislative acts amending or supplementing pre-existing laws to make sure that its domestic laws conform with human rights treaty provisions.[113]

110 Li and Guo (n 58) 169.
111 United Nations International Human Rights Instruments, 'Core Document Forming Part of the Reports of States Parties' (11 June 2001) UN Doc HRI/CORE/1/Add.21/Rev.2, para 51.
112 Xue and Jin (n 93) 309.
113 Xue and Jin (n 93) 309-310.

Although no consensus has been reached concerning the means by which international human rights treaties are given effect in China's domestic legal order, Chinese scholars generally agree that provisions of human rights treaties cannot be directly applied by domestic courts.[114] This claim is supported by the 1990 Human Rights White Paper, which provides that 'a human rights system must be ratified and protected by each sovereign State through its domestic legislation.'[115] This white paper to some degree represents the official stance of China's domestic application of international human rights treaties.[116] Such an official statement is also observed in the periodic reports submitted by China to human rights treaty bodies.[117] Viewed in this light, the protection of human rights depends largely on domestic laws.

Given the lack of direct applicability of human rights treaties, it is of pivotal importance to examine how treaty obligations have been transformed into China's domestic legal system through legislative measures. As will be discussed in section 3.4, there is a wide variety of health-related laws containing provisions implementing obligations under the right to health care, although none of these domestic laws explicitly refer to the relevant human rights treaties.

3.4 The legislative implementation of the right to health care in China

3.4.1 General introduction and methodology

Aside from the monist or dualist dichotomy, China clearly has a legal obligation to give sufficient recognition to the right to health care in its domestic legal order, preferably by way of legislative implementation.[118] In addition, as noted by the CteeESCR, the incorporation of the norms concerning the right to health care in the domestic legal order can considerably 'enhance the scope and effectiveness of remedial measures' and 'enable[s] courts to adjudicate violations of the right to health,

114 ibid; Li and Guo (n 58) 169.

115 Information Office of the State Council, Human Rights in China (1991) ch x. The English version was obtained from the official website led by the State Council Information Office. <www.china.org.cn/e-white/7/7-L.htm> accessed 28 November 2017.

116 Qiwu Zhu, Zhongguo Guojifa de Lilun yu Shijian [The Theory and Practice of International Law in China] (Law Press 1998); Ahl (n 91) 366; Li (n 95) 344.

117 Xue and Jin (n 93) 309-310.

118 CteeESCR, General Comment 14 (n 1) para 36.

or at least its core obligations, by direct reference to the Covenant.'[119] In line with the earlier analysis of the direct effect of international human rights treaties in China, it is desirable to give effect to the right to health care by means of legislative acts amending or supplementing pre-existing laws. Furthermore, China is also obliged to amend or repeal pre-existing domestic laws that are clearly incompatible with the core obligations under the right to health care.[120] Violations of the right to health care may occur if China fails to do so.

It is worth pointing out that, in addition to legislative measures, judicial measures are also key to the domestic implementation of this right. If there has been a failure on the part of the State to comply with the obligations, or at least with the core obligations under the right to health care, the aggrieved person(s) should have access to effective judicial or other appropriate remedies to redress this failure.[121] As illustrated in the previous chapter, China indeed undertakes an obligation of immediate effect to establish a wide range of effective, transparent, accessible and independent accountability mechanisms, including judicial mechanisms. The legislative and judicial measures enable the courts to adjudicate at least violations of the core obligations of the right to health care by reference to the right as given effect in domestic legislation. It should be noted, however, that not all provisions of China's health-related legislation are directly applicable in its dometic courts. Therefore, the following subsections will (1) examine whether, and if so, the degree to which China has enacted, amended or repealed its domestic legislation for the implementation of the right to health care; and (2) discuss whether the provisions of such legislation are applicable in domestic courts. The judicial measures China has taken to implement the right to health care will be discussed in chapter 7.

The method for this assessment was introduced in chapter 1. I derived key words from the core obligations outlined in chapter 2 for the assessment. The AA-AP standards – availability, accessibility, accountability and participation have also been taken into consideration. I searched not only keywords in the English-language versions of the legislation, but also the official Chinese-language versions so as to ensure the accuracy of this assessment. Furthermore, to prevent errors in English translation, I chose the official version published on the database on the

119 ibid, para 60.
120 ibid, para 48.
121 ibid, para 59.

official website;[122] if the official version was not available, I turned to the academic database of authority – the pkulaw ('*beida Fabao*'),[123] and verified the accuracy of its translation by reference to the original Chinese-language version. If there was no English translation available, I provided the translation myself.

3.4.2 The Chinese Constitution and the right to health care

Forming the core of the entire legal system, the Chinese Constitution is the basis for enacting domestic laws. The Constitution sets out general rules as to how the State is structured and society governed. In addition, it sets fundamental principles to which the State should adhere. Therefore, the inclusion of health or health care as a right in the Constitution is of great importance. It reflects China's constitutional commitment towards the assurance of health and health care for its people.[124]

The following subsections will provide a detailed analysis of the constitutional provisions concerning human rights protection in general and the core obligations under the right to health care in particular. The detailed content of the relevant constitutional provisions is summarised in Table 3.2.

3.4.2.1 'The State respects and preserves human rights'

As mentioned above, China has enshrined the respect for and protection of human rights in Article 33 of its Constitution, which was unprecedented in China's history and represented a big step forward for the legal protection of human rights. Many Chinese scholars even assert that the inclusion of 'the State respects and preserves human rights' into the Constitution marks a new era of human rights protection in China.[125] Structurally, this article forms part of chapter II of the Constitution which details the fundamental rights and duties of its citizens,[126] and includes most of the human rights recognised in international human rights treaties to which China is a

122 See generally 'The Database of Laws and Regulations' <www.npc.gov.cn/englishnpc/Law/Integrated_index.html> accessed 28 November 2017.
123 All translations of the legal documents on this online database are provided by the Legal Translation Research Centre of Peking University for reference <http://en.pkulaw.cn> accessed 28 November 2017.
124 Sun (n 40) 49.
125 ibid.
126 Chinese Constitution, ch II.

party.[127] However, the term 'human rights' was not explicitly adopted until the 2004 amendment of the Constitution.

More specifically, human rights are considered an important constitutional principle under Article 33. This article imposes a constitutional duty on the State to respect and preserve human rights.[128] It also stipulates that, '[e]very citizen is entitled to the rights and at the same time must perform the duties prescribed by the Constitution and other laws.'[129] Therefore, Article 33 also implies that human rights are the fundamental rights to which Chinese citizens are entitled.

Notably, instead of adhering to the typical typology of obligations to 'respect, protect and fulfil' human rights, the terms used in the official English version of the Constitution are that the State '*respects*' and '*preserves*' human rights.[130] There is no preparatory document explaining the choices of English translations between 'preserve' and 'protect'. However, when defining the State's obligation to 'preserve' human rights, most Chinese scholars tend to interpret it as 'protect'.[131] In my opinion, both 'preserve' and 'protect' refer to the obligation to protect as is generally recognised in most human rights documents; the choice of 'preserve' rather than 'protect' is just a matter of English translation. These two terms both have a meaning of the Chinese term '*baozhang*' that is originally used in the Constitution.

By contrast, I contend that the State's obligation to fulfil human rights is *intentionally* excluded from the Constitution. As is known to all, human rights cover not only economic, social and cultural rights, but also civil and political rights. However, at the time of writing, China has not yet ratified the ICCPR. Additionally, there is still some controversy concerning civil and political rights, such as the right to freedom of expression, the right to strike, and prohibition of death penalty. Since the obligation to fulfil human rights requires China to adopt appropriate legislative, judicial, administrative and other measures towards the realisation of all human rights, I assert that the obligation to fulfil human rights (including the obligation to fulfil the right to health care) is not guaranteed under Article 33 of the Constitution. In brief, it can first be deduced that there is a constitutional provision incorporating

127 See eg Chinese Constitution, arts 34-38.
128 ibid, art 33.
129 ibid.
130 ibid.
131 Sun (n 40) 54.

the obligations to respect and protect the right to health care, but the provision addressing the obligation to fulfil is still absent. Nevertheless, Article 33 remains of vital importance as it provides the ultimate legal basis for the legal protection of human rights, including the right to health care.

3.4.2.2 Constitutional provisions concerning non-discrimination and equality

In addition to the general article concerning the respect for and protection of human rights in China, the Constitution also contains articles that ensure equality and non-discrimination. Article 4 of the Chinese Constitution stipulates that,

> [a]ll nationalities in the People's Republic of China are equal. The State protects the lawful rights and interests of the minority nationalities and upholds and develops the relationship of equality, unity and mutual assistance among all of China's nationalities. Discrimination against and oppression of any nationality are prohibited.[132]

Article 33 also states that, '[a]ll citizens of the People's Republic of China are equal before the law. Every citizen enjoys the rights and at the same time must perform the duties prescribed by the Constitution and the law.'[133] Article 36 further prohibits discrimination on the ground of religion; it provides that '[n]o State organ, public organization or individual may discriminate against citizens who believe in, or do not believe in, any religion.'[134] Moreover, Article 48 guarantees women equal rights as men. It states that, '[w]omen in the People's Republic of China enjoy equal rights with men in all spheres of life, political, economic, cultural and social, and family life.'[135] Lastly, Article 89 ensures the equal rights of minorities in China. It requires the State Council to 'safeguard the equal rights of minority nationalities and the right of autonomy of the national autonomous areas.'[136] To sum up, discrimination on the grounds of gender, religion and ethnic origins is explicitly proscribed by the Constitution. It can thus be concluded that provisions concerning the right to equality and freedom from discrimination are well incorporated in the Chinese Constitution.

132 Chinese Constitution, art 4.
133 ibid, art 33.
134 ibid, art 36.
135 ibid, art 48.
136 ibid, art 89 (11).

3.4.2.3 Constitutional provisions concerning health and health care[137]

The Chinese Constitution refers to health and health care in many ways. As a general principle concerning health and health care, Article 21 requires the State to protect the people's health by developing medical and health services and establishing various medical and health facilities. In addition, Article 14 imposes a duty on the State to establish 'a sound social security system compatible with the level of economic development.'[138] As such, the government is obliged to provide health insurance that covers all of the people, which to some extent addresses the economic accessibility of health care. These two provisions imply a State obligation to ensure access to health care. Nevertheless, they do not explicitly specify that health care should be provided by the State free of charge, or oblige the State to provide universal health coverage.[139]

There are also several articles concerning health and health care in chapter II – the *Fundamental Rights and Duties of Its Citizens* of the Constitution. For example, Article 36 prohibits any individuals from making use of religion to impair the health of citizens.[140] Article 42 requires the State to promote occupational health.[141]

Most importantly, Article 45 guarantees citizens 'the right to material assistance from the State and society when they are old, ill or disabled' and prescribes the government to 'develop social insurance, social relief and medical and health services that are required for citizens to enjoy this right.'[142] Many Chinese legal scholars perceive 'material assistance' ('*wuzhi bangzhu*') as a specific formulation of the right to health (care) in China.[143] For example, Jiao, Hongchang, a leading scholar

137 See Table 3.2 for detailed constitutional provisions.
138 Chinese Constitution, art 14.
139 Jiangqing Yang, *Informal Payments and Regulations in China's Healthcare System: Red Packets and Institutional Reform* (Palgrave Macmillan 2017) 13.
140 Chinese Constitution, art 36.
141 ibid, art 42.
142 ibid, art 45.
143 See generally, Chengguang Wang, 'Lun Yi Baozhang Gongmin Jiankangquan wei Zongzhi Dazao Yiyao Weisheng Fazhi de Jianshi Jichu [Building Solid Foundation of Medicine and Health Care Law-ruling to Guarantee Citizens' Health Right]' (2016) 1 Yixue Yu Faxue [Medical Science and Jurisprudence] 1, 3; Christina Ho, 'Health Rights at the Juncture between State and Market: The People's Republic of China in Colleen Flood and Aeyal Gross (eds), *The Right to Health at the Public/Private Divide: A Global Comparative Study* (Cambridge University Press 2014) 271; Hongchang Jiao, 'Lun Zuowei Jiben Quanli de Jiankangquan [The Right to Health as a Fundamental Right]' (2010) 1 Zhongguo Zhengfa Daxue Xuebao [Journal of China University of Political Science and Law] 12, 19.

of constitutional law considers the right to material assistance as a positive right to health, which extends not only to health care services but also to other goods and services that constitute preconditions for health. Citizens can attain these goods and services through social insurance and social assistance.[144] Nevertheless, he argues that it should be the State rather than society that is ultimately responsible for providing material assistance; the obligations that Article 45(1) imposes on society should not exempt the State's obligation.[145]

I agree with Jiao that material assistance to some extent covers the provision of health care and that the Constitution should impose a clear obligation on the State. However, I doubt whether Article 45 is a specific formulation of the international right to health (care), given that this article has several elements that are not fully compliant with right to health standards. First, as a matter of human rights law, the State should guarantee *everyone* the right to health (care), rather than only citizens.

Second, Article 45 only obliges the State, as well as society, to provide *material assistance* to citizens if they are *old, sick, or disabled*. In other words, citizens can only claim their right to material assistance when they are old, ill or disabled. Although Article 12.2(d) of the ICESCR requires the State to create 'conditions which would assure to all medical service and medical attention in the event of sickness',[146] the right to health has a much broader scope. The content of the right to health (care) also includes the rights to maternal, child and reproductive health, as well as prevention, treatment and control of disease, to name just a few.[147] Furthermore, claiming the right to health (care) is not limited to specific health status (i.e. being old, ill, or disabled). Therefore, the right to material assistance cannot reflect the entire scope of the right to health (care).

Finally, as explained in chapter 2, a State undertakes a wide variety of obligations under the right to health (care). For example, the State undertakes the obligation to ensure equal access to health care and to guarantee the right to be exercised in a non-

144 Jiao (n 143) 19.

145 ibid.

146 United Nations General Assembly (UNGA), International Covenant on Economic, Social and Cultural Rights (ICESCR) (adopted 16 December 1966, entered into force 3 January 1976) (ICSECR) 993 UNTS 3, art 12.2(d).

147 ibid, art 12.2 (a)(b)(c).

discriminatory matter.[148] By contrast, Article 45 of the Constitution only imposes on the State the obligations to provide material assistance and to create conditions (eg social insurance, social assistance) for the enjoyment of the right to material assistance.[149]

To sum up, although Chinese citizens are entitled to material assistance when they are old, ill or disabled under Article 45 of the Constitution, this provision does not reflect the comprehensive nature of the international right to health (care). Therefore, while the right to material assistance and the right to health (care) share some similarities, Article 45 of the Constitution is not equivalent to the right to health (care) *per se*.

3.4.2.4 Non-direct applicability of constitutional provisions

A general perception is that constitutional provisions cannot be directly applied by China's domestic courts. Even though both Articles 21 and 45 impose duties on the Chinese government, while Article 45 also entitles the Chinese citizens to material assistance, in practice it is very difficult to seek a remedy for a violation of the right to health care by invoking constitutional provisions before domestic courts. The underlying reasons will be explained in detail in chapter 7.

Briefly speaking, the Chinese Constitution does not contain any provision regarding the direct applicability of constitutional provisions or constitutional review. As it currently stands, domestic courts, including the SPC, have not been granted the power to exercise constitutional review but can only request the NPCSC to review the constitutionality and legality of health-related laws and regulations.[150] However, the NPCSC has never initiated the review process in practice. Domestic courts have also not been given the power to exercise constitutional jurisdiction over legislative acts and governmental actions.[151] Furthermore, it remains largely controversial as to whether the infringement of constitutional rights is subject to judicial adjudication. In

148 CteeESCR, General Comment 14 (n 1) paras 30, 35.
149 Chinese Constitution, art 45.
150 Legislation Law, art 99.
151 Guobin Zhu, 'Constitutional Review in China: An Unaccomplished Project or a Mirage?' (2010) 43 Suffolk University Law Review 625, 644.

practice, right-holders have never claimed their constitutional right to health before any domestic court.[152]

Consequently, if the constitutional right to material assistance or the State's obligation to provide medical and health services under the Constitution have not yet been specified in separate laws and regulations, or if a legislative act itself violates the Constitution, then it would be extremely difficult, if not totally impossible, to seek judicial remedies.[153] Even though there are several provisions in the Constitution that cover essential elements of the right to health care, at present it is only possible to apply specific, rights-related legislation rather than constitutional provisions in domestic courts to redress violations of the right to health care.

In brief, constitutional provisions regarding health and health care play an important symbolic role in demonstrating China's commitment to the right to health care. However, taken alone, these provisions are not sufficient to implement China's core obligations under the right to health care. This symbolism should be accompanied by other legislative measures to practically implement such constitutional commitment, including the enactment of health laws.[154] Thus, section 3.4.3 moves on to assess the legislative measures China has taken to give effect to the core obligations under the right to health care.

Table 3.2 The Chinese Constitution (1982)[155]

Article 4	All nationalities in the People's Republic of China are equal. The State protects the lawful rights and interests of the minority nationalities and upholds and develops a relationship of equality, unity and mutual assistance among all of China's nationalities. Discrimination against and oppression of any nationality are prohibited; any act which undermines the unity of the nationalities or instigates division is prohibited.
Article 14	The State establishes a sound social security system compatible with the level of economic development.

152 Shengnan Qiu and Gillian MacNaughton, 'Mechanisms of Accountability for the Realization of the Right to Health in China' (2017) 19 Health and Human Rights Journal 279, 282.
153 ibid.
154 John Tobin, *The Right to Health in International Law* (Oxford University Press 2012) 184.
155 Chinese Constitution, arts 4, 14, 21, 33, 36, 42, 45, 48, 49.

Article 21	The State develops medical and health services, promotes modern medicine and traditional Chinese medicine, encourages and supports the setting up of various medical and health facilities by the rural economic collectives, State enterprises and institutions and neighbourhood organisations, and promotes health and sanitation activities of a mass character, all for the protection of the people's health.
Article 33	All persons holding the nationality of the People's Republic of China are citizens of the People's Republic of China. All citizens of the People's Republic of China are equal before the law. The State respects and preserves human rights. Every citizen is entitled to the rights and at the same time must perform the duties prescribed by the Constitution and other laws.
Article 36	Citizens of the People's Republic of China enjoy freedom of religious belief. No State organ, public organisation or individual may compel citizens to believe in, or not to believe in, any religion; nor may they discriminate against citizens who believe in, or do not believe in, any religion. The State protects normal religious activities. No one may make use of religion to engage in activities that disrupt public order, impair the health of citizens or interfere with the educational system of the State.
Article 42	Through various channels, the State creates conditions for employment, enhances occupational safety and health, improves working conditions and, on the basis of expanded production, increases remuneration for work and welfare benefits.
Article 45	Citizens of the People's Republic of China have the right to material assistance from the State and society when they are old, ill or disabled. The State develops social insurance, social relief and medical and health services that are required for citizens to enjoy this right.
Article 48	Women in the People's Republic of China enjoy equal rights with men in all spheres of life, in political, economic, cultural, social and family life.
Article 89	The State Council exercises the following functions and powers: (11) to direct and administer affairs concerning the nationalities and to safeguard the equal rights of minority nationalities and the right to autonomy of the national autonomous areas.

3.4.3 The Chinese health legislation

3.4.3.1 An overview of China's health law system

Generally speaking, China's health law system is fragmented in nature. There is no umbrella health law at the national level that sets out general rules as to how the health system should be structured and governed, and how health rights and interests be protected.[156] In addition, there is no academic consensus as to how the Chinese

156 At the time of writing, China is drafting its Basic Health Law, which will serve as an umbrella law.

health law system should be constructed.[157] Chinese scholars hold opposing views over the connotations and extension of health law. Some scholars assert that the health law system should be developed on the basis of the rights of life and health under the General Principles of Civil Law; in this case, the Environmental Protection Law and Law on the Prevention and Control of Atmospheric Protection would constitute part of the entire health law system.[158] Other scholars contend that the construction of China's health law system should be led by a basic, fundamental health law, followed by, *inter alia*, public health law, law on medical services and medical insurance, law on health promotion and international public health law.[159]

According to the classification of the NHFPC, health-related legislation in China can be divided into four categories: (1) public health; (2) health-related goods, such as food, drugs, medical equipments and cosmetics; (3) medical care and services; and (4) family planning. So far, health-related legislation at the national level consists of 12 laws ('*falv*') as detailed in Table 3.3, 40 administrative regulations ('*xingzheng fagui*') and a wide variety of administrative rules ('*xingzheng guizhang*').[160]

In addition to the specific health-related legislation, there are also a few general legal provisions regarding health-related rights. These provisions are, *inter alia*, Article 98 of the General Principles of Civil Law,[161] Articles 23-32 of the Social Insurance Law[162], and Article 61 of the Tort Law.[163]

Given this wide range, it is not possible to take a comprehensive approach and analyse all of the relevant provisions. Consequently, this subsection only focuses on

157 Liu and Qin (n 34) 55.

158 Chongqi Wu, *Zhongguo Weisheng Faxue [Chinese Health Law]* (Peking Union Medical College Press 2006) 25-28. Cited in Liu and Qin (n 34) 55.

159 Dongfeng Shi and others, 'Goujian Woguo Gonggong Weisheng Falv Tixi de Taolun [Discussion on the Construction of China's Public Health Law System)' (2004) 1 Zhongguo Gonggong Weisheng [Chinese Public Health] 80, 80-81.

160 Meng and others (n 17) 17-19; Liu and Qin (n 34) 57; See also the official website of the NHFPC <http://en.nhfpc.gov.cn/regulations.html> accessed 28 November 2017.

161 General Principles of the Civil Law, art 142.

162 Social Insurance Law of the People's Republic of China (adopted on 28 October 2010, entered into force on 1 July 2011) [Shehui Baoxian Fa] ('Social Insurance Law'), arts 23-32 <www.mohrss.gov.cn/gjhzs/GJHZzhengcewenjian/201506/t20150625_212401.htm> accessed 28 November 2017. The English version was obtained from the official website of the MOHRSS.

163 Tort Law of the People's Republic of China (adopted on 26 December 2009, entered into force on 1 July 2010) [Qingquan Zeren Fa] ('Tort Law'), art 61 <www.lawinfochina.com/Display.aspx?lib=law&Cgid=125300> accessed 28 November 2017. The English version was obtained from the academic database of authority – the pkulaw.

laws at the national level (i.e. *'falv'*) that include provisions addressing the right to health care. The analysis is based on the core obligations set out in chapter 2. The health-related laws are divided into three groups as shown in Table 3.3:

(1) 12 main health laws;[164]

(2) specific laws concerning vulnerable and marginalised groups;[165]

---

164 Drug Administration Law of the People's Republic of China (Revised) (adopted on 28 February 2001, entered into force on 1 December 2001, amended on 24 April 2015) ('Drug Administration Law') <http://eng.sfda.gov.cn/WS03/CL0766/61638.html>; Frontier Health and Quarantine Law of the People's Republic of China (adopted on 2 December 1986, entered into force on 1 May 1987, amended on 27 August 2009) ('Frontier Health and Quarantine Law') <www.npc.gov.cn/englishnpc/Law/2007-12/12/content_1383943.htm>; Law of the People's Republic of China on Prevention and Treatment of Communicable Diseases (Revised) (adopted on 28 August 2004, entered into force on 1 December 2004, amended on 29 June 2013) ('Law on the Prevention and Treatment of Communicable Diseases') <www.npc.gov.cn/englishnpc/Law/2007-12/12/content_1383919.htm>; Law of the People's Republic of China on the Red Cross Society (Revised) (adopted and entered into force on 24 February 2017) ('Law on the Red Cross Society') <http://www.npc.gov.cn/englishnpc/Law/2007-12/12/content_1383814.htm>; Law of the People's Republic of China on Maternal and Infant Health Care (adopted on 27 October 1994, entered into force on 1 June 1995, amended on 27 August 2009) ('Law on Maternal and Infant Health Care') <www.npc.gov.cn/englishnpc/Law/2007-12/12/content_1383796.htm>; Law of the People's Republic of China on Blood Donation ((adopted on 29 December 1997, entered into force on 1 October 1998) ('Law on Blood Donation') <www.npc.gov.cn/englishnpc/Law/2007-12/11/content_1383576.htm>; Law of the People's Republic of China on Licensed Doctors (adopted on 26 June 1998, entered into force on 1 May 1999, amended on 27 August 2009) ('Law on Licensed Doctors') <www.npc.gov.cn/englishnpc/Law/2007-12/11/content_1383574.htm>; Law of the People's Republic of China on Population and Family Planning (adopted on 29 December 2001, entered into force on 1 September 2002, amended on 27 December 2015) (' Law on Population and Family Planning') <www.gov.cn/english/laws/2005-10/11/content_75954.htm>; Law of the People's Republic of China on Prevention of Occupational Diseases (adopted on 27 October 2001, entered into force on 1 May 2002, amended on 5 Nov 2017) ('Law on the Prevention of Occupational Diseases') <www.npc.gov.cn/englishnpc/Law/2007-12/10/content_1383440.htm>; Food Safety Law of the People's Republic of China (Revised) (adopted on 24 April 2015, entered into force 1 October 2015) ('Food Safety Law') <http://en.pkulaw.cn/display.aspx?cgid=247403&lib=law>; Mental Health Law of the People's Republic of China (adopted on 26 October 2012, entered into force on 1 May 2013) ('Mental Health Law') <http://en.pkulaw.cn/display.aspx?cgid=187194&lib=law>; Law of the People's Republic of China on Traditional Chinese Medicine ('Law on Traditional Chinese Medicine') (adopted on 25 December 2016, entered into force on 1 July 2017) <http://en.pkulaw.cn/display.aspx?cgid=287286&lib=law>; The English versions were obtained from the official website of the Chinese government as well as the academic database of authority – the pkulaw.

165 Law of the People's Republic of China on Regional National Autonomy (adopted on 31 May 1984, entered into force on 1 October 1984, amended on 28 February 2001) ('Law on Regional National Autonomy') <www.npc.gov.cn/englishnpc/Law/2007-12/13/content_1383908.htm>; Law of the People's Republic of China on the Protection of Disabled Persons (Revised) (adopted on 24 April 2008, entered into force 1 July 2008) ('Law on the Protection of Disabled Persons') <www.npc.gov.cn/englishnpc/Law/2011-02/14/content_1620414.htm>; Law of the People's Republic of China on the Protection of Minors (Revised) (adopted on 29 December 2006, entered into force on 1 July 2007, amended on 26 October 2012) ('Law on the Protection of Minors') <www.npc.gov.cn/englishnpc/Law/2007-12/12/content_1383869.htm>; Law of the People's Republic of China on the

(3) general laws containing right to health elements.The detailed content of these health-related provisions is summarised in Table 3.4 (at the end of this chapter).[166]

Table 3.3 Health-related laws

Main health laws in China	
1986	Frontier Health and Quarantine Law (as amended in 2009)
1994	Law on Maternal and Infant Health Care (as amended in 2009)
1997	Law on Blood Donation
1998	Law on Licensed Doctors (as amended in 2009)
2001	Drug Administration Law (Revised) (as amended in 2015)
2001	Law on Population and Family Planning (as amended in 2015)
2001	Law on Prevention of Occupational Diseases (as amended in 2017)
2004	Law on Prevention and Treatment of Communicable Diseases (Revised) (as amended in 2013)
2012	Mental Health Law
2015	Food Safety Law (Revised)
2016	Law on Traditional Chinese Medicine
2017	Law on the Red Cross Society (Revised)
Specific laws concerning vulnerable and marginalised groups	
1984	Law on Regional National Autonomy (as amended in 2001)
1992	Law on the Protection of Women's Rights and Interests (as amended in 2005)
2006	Law on the Protection of Minors (Revised) (as amended in 2012)
2008	Law on the Protection of Disabled Persons
2012	Law on Protection of the Rights and Interests of the Elderly (Revised) (as amended in 2015)
General laws containing right to health elements	
1986	General Principles of Civil Law (as amended in 2009)
2009	Tort Law
2010	Social Insurance Law

Protection of Women's Rights and Interests (adopted on 3 April 1992, entered into force 1 October 1992, amended on 3 April 2005) ('Law on the Protection of Women's Rights and Interests') <www.npc.gov.cn/englishnpc/Law/2007-12/12/content_1383859.htm>; Law of the People's Republic of China on Protection of the Rights and Interests of the Elderly (Revised) (adopted on 28 December 2012, entered into force on 1 July 2013, amended on 24 April 2015) ('Law on the Protection of the Rights and Interests of the Elderly') <www.npc.gov.cn/englishnpc/Law/2007-12/11/content_1383583.htm> accessed 28 November 2017; The English versions were obtained from the official website of the Chinese government and the academic database of authority – the pkulaw.

166 General Principles of the Civil Law, art 142; Social Insurance Law, arts 23-32; Tort Law, art 61. The English versions were obtained from the official website of the Chinese government as well as the academic database of authority – the pkulaw.

Given that the obligations of immediate effect include an abstract obligation to 'take steps' and an obligation to establish accountability mechanisms that will be discussed in chapter 7, I only focus on guaranteeing the non-discriminatory exercise of the right to health care under the obligations of immediate effect and combine its assessment with non-discrimination under non-derogable core obligations. Thus, the results of the assessment are concluded in two parts: provisions concerning equality and non-discrimination, and provisions concerning elements of other non-derogable core obligations (i.e. the provision of essential drugs, the equitable distribution of health resources and the adoption of a national public health strategy and plan of action).

3.4.3.2 Provisions concerning non-discrimination and equality

This subsection focuses on the principles of non-discrimination and equality. China is obliged to enact, amend or repeal legislation to promote equality (especially for those who do not have sufficient means with the necessary health insurance and health-care facilities) and to prevent discrimination on any internationally prohibited ground.[167] In fact, China has enacted and promulgated several laws for protecting vulnerable and marginalised groups, including ethnic groups, women, disabled persons, children and the elderly. Other health laws or general laws also contain provisions that address non-discrimination and equality (as detailed in Table 3.4). I selected a number of keywords (both in English and Chinese) for searching these legal provisions, including 'discrimination (*qishi*)', 'equal/equality (*pingdeng*)', 'equity/equitable (*pingjun/gongzheng/jundeng/henping*)', 'medical (*yiliao*)', 'health/health care (*jiankang/weisheng*)', 'disabled (*canji*)', 'women (*funv/nvxing*)', 'ethnic minority (*shaoshu minzu*)', 'minor (*ertong*)' and 'the elderly (*lao*)'. In addition, as explained in chapter 2, it is important for a State to take measures in favour of vulnerable or marginalised groups, and to tackle economic, social and cultural factors that hinder their access to health care. For example, the Chinese government should provide those who cannot afford health care with necessary health insurance. As such, the key words 'insurance (*baoxian*)', 'affordability (*fudan*)' and 'out-of-pocket cost/expenditure (*geren huafei/zhifu*)' were also selected for this assessment.

167 CteeESCR, General Comment 14 (n 1) para 36.

First, as detailed in Table 3.4, this subsection concludes that currently, the five specific laws concerning vulnerable and marginalised groups all have provisions addressing discrimination on the basis of age (i.e. the elderly and minors), gender (i.e. women), ethnic groups and health status (i.e. the disabled). No other specific laws have been enacted for the elimination of other types of discrimination.

Second, there are a variety of health laws addressing equal access to health care in a non-discriminatory manner, especially for people with a specific health status (eg a positive HIV status), people living in rural areas and people who cannot afford the costs of medical and health care. For example, Article 5(2) of the Mental Health Law prohibits discrimination against patients with mental disorders. Article 28(3) of the Mental Health Law further provides that medical institutions should not refuse to make a diagnosis for any patient with suspected mental disorders.[168] Similar prohibitions on the refusal of medical institutions to diagnose occupational diseases and infectious diseases can also be found in other legislation. For instance, the Law on the Prevention and Treatment of Communicable Diseases explicitly states that, 'no units or individuals shall discriminate against infectious disease patients, pathogen carriers and suspected infectious disease patients' and that 'medical agencies shall give medical treatment and on-the-spot rescue to the patients or suspected patients of infectious diseases or provide outpatient service to them'.[169] Therefore, medical institutions and health professionals should not discriminate against people living with HIV/AIDS and refuse to provide them with medical treatment. Article 24 of the Law on Licensed Doctors stipulates that medical or health institutions or health professionals should not refuse to give emergency treatment, irrespective of an individual's financial status.[170] Article 22 of the Law on Population and Family Planning also proscribes discrimination against women who bear female babies.[171]

Third, the five specific laws concerning vulnerable and marginalised groups all contain provisions addressing equal access to health care, with particular attention to *affordability*, which is an essential dimension of the *accessibility* of health care. For example, as shown in Table 3.4, there are a variety of provisions obliging the State to develop social insurance system and to provide social assistance to vulnerable or

168 Mental Health Law, arts 5(2), 28.
169 Law on the Prevention and Treatment of Communicable Diseases, arts 16(2), 52.
170 Law on Licensed Doctors, art 24.
171 Law on Population and Family Planning, art 22.

marginalised groups that face financial hardship. These provisions are, *inter alia*: Article 48 (2) of the Law on the Protection of Disabled Persons, Article 28 (1) of the Law on the Protection of Women's Rights and Interests, and many articles in the Law on the Protection of the Rights and Interests of the Elderly.

Fourth, there are also a handful of provisions in health-related laws and general laws that address the *affordability* of health care. For example, Article 24 of the Law on Population and Family Planning imposes an obligation on the State to establish a basic medical insurance system so as to promote family planning.[172] China's Social Insurance Law contains 10 articles regarding China's basic medical insurance system.[173] This Law requires that the State should establish and improve a basic medical insurance system to provide basic universal insurance coverage over all Chinese citizens.[174] It also imposes an obligation on the State to subsidise people who cannot afford their personal contributions so as to address the affordability of the right to health care.[175] More specifically, it states that,

> for the persons enjoying the minimum living safeguard, the disabled persons who have lost the ability to work and the seniors aged 60 years or more and minors of low-income families, their personal contributions shall be subsidized by the government.[176]

As a result, vulnerable and marginalised groups such as the elderly, minors and disabled people would have equal and affordable access to health care.

3.4.3.3 Provisions concerning elements of other non-derogable core obligations

This subsection adopts the same method as subsection 3.4.3.3 in order to assess the extent to which elements of other non-derogable core obligations under the right to health care (i.e. the provision of essential drugs, the equitable distribution of health resources and the adoption of a national public health strategy and plan of action) have been incorporated in China's health-related laws (see Table 3.4 for detailed provisions). The key words (both in English and Chinese) selected for searching these legal provisions are, *inter alia*, primary health care, essential drugs, resource

172 ibid, art 24.
173 Social Insurance Law, arts 23-32.
174 ibid, arts 24-25.
175 ibid, arts 25.
176 ibid.

allocation, and national health policy and plan of action, terms regarding availability, accessibility and participation are also included. In brief, these key words include: 'primary (*jichu/chuji*)', 'basic/essential (*jiben*)', 'health/healthcare (*jiankang/weisheng*)', 'medical (*yiliao*), 'medicines/drugs (*yaowu/yaopin*)', 'availability/available (*kede/huode*)', 'accessibility/accessible (*keji*)', 'resource (*ziyuan*)', distribution/allocation (*fenpei*)', 'equity/equitable (*pingjun/gongzheng/jundeng/henping*)', 'policy/plan/strategy (*zhengce/jihua/celue*)', and 'participation (*canyu*)'.

The result of this survey shows that the five specific laws concerning the protection of vulnerable and marginalised groups and the twelve main health laws contain many elements of other non-derogable core obligations arising from the right to health care.

Seven out of the twelve health laws include provisions concerning elements of other non-derogable core obligations. With regard to the provision of essential primary health care and essential drugs, these provisions do not specifically stipulate primary health care as such, but articulate medical treatment in general. For example, Article 68 of the Mental Health Law states that 'health administrative departments of the people's governments at or above the county level shall organize medical institutions to provide free basic public health services for the patients with severe mental disorders.'[177] Article 44 of the Law on the Prevention of Occupational Diseases articulates that medical or health institutions providing occupational disease diagnosis cannot refuse to give occupational disease diagnoses upon request.[178] Other examples include Article 52 of the Law on the Prevention and Treatment of Communicable Diseases and Article 2 of the Law on Maternal and Infant Health Care. Nonetheless, none of these health laws prescribe the provision of essential drugs. The Law on the Prevention of Occupational Diseases, the Law of Maternal and Infant Health Care and the Law on Traditional Chinese Medicine also contain provisions regarding the adoption of a national public health strategy or plan of action and the reasonable distribution of resources, although the term 'equitable' is not adopted.

In addition, the five specific laws concerning the protection of vulnerable and marginalised groups also contain provisions regarding other non-derogable core obligations. In terms of the provision of essential primary health care and essential drugs, Article 48 of the Law on the Protection of Disabled Persons and Article 29 of

177 Mental Health Law, art 68.
178 Law on the Prevention of Occupational Diseases, art 45.

the Law on the Protection of the Rights and Interests of the Elderly stipulate that the State must guarantee basic medical needs and provide a subsidy for basic medical care to those experiencing financial hardship. Article 40 of the Law on Regional National Autonomy, Article 6 of the Law on the Protection of Disabled Persons and Article 67 of the Law on the Protection of the Rights and Interests of the Elderly also make it possible for vulnerable and marginalised groups to participate in the enactment of health laws, the formulation health policies and design of health programmes.

Furthermore, the General Principles of Civil Law, which is the fundamental component of China's current civil law system, articulates that 'citizens shall enjoy the rights of life and health.'[179] It also stipulates that the State bears civil liability if its organs or personnel violate the rights and interests of citizens (including health rights) and cause damages.[180] It should be noted that health is regarded as a personality right rather than a human right or fundamental right in this Law.[181]

The Tort Law contains similar articles. Chapter VII of this Law addresses the liability for medical malpractice in China. There are several provisions regarding *information accessibility*. For example, the Law imposes an obligation on health providers to supply a patient's medical history data upon their request.[182] It prescribes that 'a medical institution shall be at fault constructively for any harm caused to a patient if it conceals or refuses to provide the medical history data related to a dispute'.[183] In addition, medical institutions and health professionals shall treat personal health data with confidentiality. If any private data is revealed or any of the medical history data is available to the public without the consent of the patient, and causes harm to the patient, the medical institution shall assume tort liability.[184]

In terms of violations of the right to health care, the Administrative Procedure Law provides aggrieved individuals or groups with an opportunity to hold the administrative organs accountable and to seek judicial remedies. Article 12 of this Law states that the people's courts shall accept the complaints filed by citizens, legal persons or other organizations, including: (1) infringement of personal rights (including

179 General Principles of Civil Law, art 98.
180 ibid, art 121.
181 Lixin Yang, *Rengequanfa [Law of Personality]* (China Legal Publishing House 2006) 145–161.
182 Tort Law, art 61.
183 ibid, art 58.
184 ibid, art 62.

health rights) and other legal rights and interests; (2) refusal by an administrative organ to perform its statutory duties and responsibilities in respect of the protection of personal rights, property rights and other legal rights and interests, or its failure to respond to a request for its performance; or (3) cases where an administrative organ fails to compensation, a minimum subsistence fee or social insurance benefits according to the law.[185] Moreover, aggrieved individuals and groups are entitled to receive compensation under Article 27 of the State Compensation Law.[186]

Nevertheless, no provisions of these health-related laws have stipulated the provision of essential drugs as a core obligation under the right to health care. Moreover, these laws fail to clarify what kind of essential health care China is obliged to provide in order to ensure equal access for its people, nor have they scoped out a national package of such essential health care. These issues are expected to be solved by the drafting of the *Jiben Yiliao Weisheng Fa [Basic Health Law]*, an umbrella law that links the Constitution to specific health laws and regulations that China has been in the process of drafting since 2014.[187] This Law will serve as China's most fundamental legislation for the health care system. It is also expected to lay down some general principles for promoting people's right to health care, articulating the State's obligations arising from international human rights treaties and the Constitution, institutionalising policies and practice that have been proven to be effective, and defining the essential health care that China is obliged to provide.[188]

---

185 Administrative Procedure Law of the People's Republic of China (adopted on 4 April 1989, entered into effect on 1 October 1990, amended on 27 June 2017), arts 12(6), (10), (12) <www.lawinfochina.com/display.aspx?lib=law&id=23600> accessed 28 November 2017. The English version was obtained from the academic database of authority – the pkulaw.

186 Law of the People's Republic of China on State Compensation Law (adopted on 12 May 1994, entered into force 1 January 1995), art 27 <www.npc.gov.cn/englishnpc/Law/2007-12/12/content_1383753.htm> accessed 28 November 2017. The English version was obtained from the official website of the NPC.

187 Meng and others (n 17) 18.

188 Wang (n 143) 2, 4-6; Yunliang Chen, 'Jiben Yiliao Fuwu Fazhihua Yanjiu [Research on the Legalization of Basic Medical Services]' (2014) 2 Falv Kexue – Xibei Zhengfa Daxue Xuebao [Science of Law - Journal of Northwest University of Political Science and Law] 73, 76-84; Xin Liu and Xianjie Lian, 'Lun Jiben Yiliaoweishengfa de Lifa Dingwei jiqi Zhuyaoneirong [Legislative Orientation of Basic Health Law and the Main Content]' (2014) 22 Zhongguo Weisheng Fazhi [China Health Law] 23, 24-27.

3.5 Concluding summary

This chapter systematically examined the legislative measures China has taken to give effect to the right to health care in its domestic legal system. Overall, it can be observed that China has enacted and amended its domestic laws where necessary to comply with its right to health obligations arising from international treaties. The principles of non-discrimination and equality have been confirmed in the 1982 Constitution as over-arching principles. Most of the laws also include an explicit reference to non-discrimination and equality. In addition, a number of health-related laws have relevant provisions containing elements of other non-derogable core obligations. Moreover, there are also provisions concerning judicial remedies to redress violations of health-related rights, albeit not entirely equivalent to the right to health care *per se*. However, regardless of these legal provisions, the following gaps between *de jure* and *de facto* implementation of the right to health care have been identified.

First of all, the provision of essential primary health care and of essential drugs, which fall within the scope of core obligations under the right to health care, are not clearly stipulated in China's domestic health legislation. Although China has taken the step to draft its Basic Health Law so as to guarantee basic medical and health care services to its people, it is still not certain whether this fundamental health law will have an explicit articulation of the right to health care. It should be pointed out, however, that the provision of (essential) primary health care and essential drugs has been repetitively mentioned in China's policy documents, which will be discussed in chapter 4.

Secondly, although China has enacted legislation to ensure the right to receive medical treatment and reduce patients' financial burden, some of the provisions remain ambiguous, which may lead to implementation challenges.[189] For example, as mentioned, the Social Insurance Law outlines China's overall medical insurance system. However, it fails to detail what these medical insurance programs should provide.[190] Article 26 of this Law only stipulates that the three health insurance schemes shall be governed by the *relevant provisions* of the State.[191] However, it

189 Ho (n 143) 273-275.
190 ibid 271-272.
191 Social Insurance Law, art 26.

remains uncertain what these relevant provisions are. Furthermore, many of the provisions regarding legal liabilities are vague, promising only 'disciplinary actions in accordance with law' to those who may try to embezzle or refuse to pay benefits in a timely manner.[192] As Ho points out, the lack of details regarding how aggrieved individuals and groups can file their complaints makes it difficult, if not impossible, to invoke the legal rights enshrined in the Social Insurance Law before the courts.[193]

Thirdly, it is not sufficient to merely give effect to the core obligations under the right to health care in China's domestic legal order. Arguably, China has largely enacted or amended domestic legislation to respect, protect and fulfil the core obligations; yet, these obligations only represent the minimum essential levels that China is required to meet in order to comply with the (minimum requirements under) right to health care. As explained in chapter 2, the reason for conducting a 'bottom line' assessment is that China cannot attribute its failure to meet these obligations to a lack of available resources or any other circumstances. It is easier to hold the Chinese government to account when identifying its violations of such obligations. Nevertheless, it is apparent that China also undertakes a broader range of obligations to respect, protect and fulfil the right to health care, and to progressively establish an acceptable, accessible, acceptable health care system of good quality.

Lastly, it deserves to be noted that the adoption of legislative measures 'is by no means exhaustive of the obligations of States parties.'[194] Therefore, this study will continue to explore other appropriate measures for the implementation of the right to health care. Among other measures, the CteeECSR suggests that the enjoyment of the right to health care will often be enhanced 'in part, through the provision of judicial or other effective remedies'.[195] These remedial measures are in line with the understanding of 'accountability' adopted and discussed in more detail, together with the analysis of China's administrative law, including the aforementioned Administrative Procedure Law, in chapter 7. In addition, administrative, budgetary and other measures, which often comprise policies, are also essential. As such, chapter 4 will examine what national health policies China has adopted for its domestic implementation of the right to health care.

192 ibid, art 89; Ho (n 143) 273.
193 Ho (n 143) 273.
194 CteeESCR, General Comment 3 (n 1) para 4.
195 ibid, para 5.

Table 3.4 Provisions of specific laws and health-related laws[1]

Specific laws concerning vulnerable and marginalised groups	
Legislation	**Provisions concerning non-discrimination and equality**
Law on Regional National Autonomy	Article 9(1) State organs at higher levels and autonomous agencies in ethnic autonomous areas uphold and develop the socialist relationship of equality, unity and mutual assistance among all of China's nationalities; (2) Discrimination against and the oppression of any nationality is prohibited. Article 11(2) No State organ, public organisation or individual may compel citizens to believe in, or not to believe in, any religion, nor may they discriminate against citizens who believe in, or do not believe in, any religion. Article 48 Autonomous agencies of an ethnic autonomous area guarantee equal rights for the various nationalities in the area. Article 52 The organ of self-government of a national autonomous area shall guarantee that citizens of the various nationalities in the area enjoy the rights of citizens prescribed in the Constitution and shall educate them in the need to perform their duties as citizens.
Law on the Protection of Disabled Persons	Article 3(1) Disabled persons shall enjoy equal rights with other citizens in political, economic. cultural and social fields, in family life and other aspects. The citizen's rights and personal dignity of disabled persons shall be protected by law; (2) Discrimination against, the insulting of and infringement upon the rights of disabled persons shall be prohibited. Article 4 The State shall provide disabled persons with special assistance by adopting supplementary methods and supportive measures with a view to alleviating or eliminating the effects of their disabilities and external barriers and ensuring the realisation of their rights. Article 48 (2) The people's government at various levels shall, according to relevant regulations, provide relief and subsidies for basic medical care and rehabilitation services and for the instalment and replacement of the necessary assist devices; (3) The local people's government at various levels shall provide, in light of the specific conditions, nursing subsidies for disabled persons who cannot take care of themselves in their daily lives.

1 The table was drawn upon my survey of the five specific laws concerning the protection of vulnerable and marginalised groups and 12 main health laws. The source of the laws and the English translation was given in chapter 3.

Specific laws concerning vulnerable and marginalised groups	
Legislation	**Provisions concerning non-discrimination and equality**
Law on the Protection of Minors	Article 10(2) No female or handicapped minors may be discriminated against.
Law on the Protection of the Rights and Interests of the Eldly	Article 3(3) Discriminating against, insulting, maltreating or abandoning the elderly shall be forbidden. Article 5 (1) The state shall establish a multi-level social security system to gradually increase the security level for the elderly; (2) The state shall establish and improve the social elderly care service system, which is based on families and supported by communities and institutions. Article 29(1) The State shall guarantee the basic medical needs of the elderly through the basic medical insurance system. The individual premiums that should be paid by the elderly enjoying the minimum subsistence guarantee and the elderly in the qualified low-income families for participating in the new rural cooperative medical service and urban residents' basic medical insurance shall be subsidized by the governments; (2) When formulating medical insurance measures, the relevant departments shall give favourable consideration to the elderly. Article 30(2) For the elderly who cannot take care of themselves in the long-term and are experiencing financial hardship, the local people's government at all levels shall provide them with nursing subsidies according to their degree of disability. Article 31(1) The State shall provide relief for the elderly in financial hardship with respect to basic living, medical treatment, residence and so on; (2) The local people's government at all levels shall, in accordance with the relevant provisions, provide support or relief to the elderly who are unable to work, have no source of income or supporters or whose supporters are truly unable to provide for or support them; (3) The local people's government at all levels shall, in accordance with the relevant provisions, provide relief to the elderly without sources of income such as those who are vagrants or beggars or are abandoned. Article 37(2) The local people's government at all levels shall gradually provide elderly care service subsidies for the elderly in financial hardship.

Specific laws concerning vulnerable and marginalised groups	
Legislation	**Provisions concerning non-discrimination and equality**
Law on the Protection of the Rights and Interests of the Eldly	Article 52 (1) The people's government at the county level or above and relevant departments shall, in accordance with the economic and social development and special needs of the elderly, formulate measures for preferential treatment for the elderly and gradually increase the level of preferential treatment; (2) The people's government shall give same preferential treatment to the elderly of other cities who permanently reside in their administrative regions.
Law on the Protection of Women's Rights and Interests	Article 2(1) Women shall enjoy equal rights with men in all aspects of political, economic, cultural, social and family life; (2) Equality between men and women is a basic State policy. The State takes the necessary measures to gradually improve the systems for protecting the rights and interests of women, in order to eliminate all forms of discrimination against women; (3) The State protects the special rights and interests enjoyed by women according to law; (4) Discriminating against, maltreating, abandoning, and physically abusing women are prohibited. Article 28 (1) The State develops social insurance, social relief, social welfare and medical and health services to guarantee that women enjoy social insurance, social relief, social welfare and health care services, and other rights and interests. Article 29 (1) The State promotes a childbearing insurance system, and establishes other sound security systems relating to childbearing; (2) Local people's governments at various levels and the departments concerned shall, in accordance with relevant regulations, provide the necessary childbearing relief to needy women. Article 36 The State guarantees that women enjoy equal rights with men relating to their persons. Article 38 (1) Women's right of life and health is inviolable.

Specific laws concerning vulnerable and marginalised groups (continued)	
Legislation	**Provisions concerning elements of other non-derogable core obligations**
Law on Regional National Autonomy	Article 11(3) No one may make use of religion to engage in activities that disrupt public order, impair the health of citizens or interfere with the educational system of the State. Article 40 Autonomous agencies in ethnic autonomous areas shall make independent decisions on plans for developing local medical and health services and for advancing both modern medicine and the traditional medicine of the nationalities. Autonomous agencies in ethnic autonomous areas shall see to a more effective prevention of endemic and local diseases, provide better protection for the health of women and children, and improve medical and sanitary conditions.
Law on the Protection of Disabled Persons	Article 5(4) People's governments at various levels and the departments concerned shall keep in close contact with disabled persons, solicit their opinions and fulfill their own respective duties in the work for disabled persons. Article 6 (1) The State shall adopt measures to ensure that disabled persons, in accordance with law and through various channels and in various forms, participate in the management of State affairs, economic and cultural undertakings and social affairs; (2) Opinions of disabled persons and their organisations shall be solicited for the formulation of laws, regulations and rules and public policies involving major issues concerning their rights and interests and the undertakings for disabled persons; (3) Disabled persons and their organisations have the right to put forward opinions and suggestions to government departments at various levels concerning the protection of disabled persons' rights and interests and the development of the undertakings for disabled persons, etc. Article 15 The State ensures that disabled persons enjoy the right to rehabilitation services. Article 46(1) The State shall ensure that disabled persons enjoy all social security rights; (2) The government and society shall take measures to improve social security for disabled persons so as to guarantee and improve the life of disabled persons. Article 52 The State and society shall take measures to gradually improve accessible facilities [...].
Law on the Protection of Minors	Not relevant

Specific laws concerning vulnerable and marginalised groups (continued)	
Legislation	**Provisions concerning elements of other non-derogable core obligations**
Law on the Protection of the Rights and Interests of the Elderly	Article 3 (1) The State shall protect the lawful rights and interests of the elderly; (2) The elderly shall have the right to obtain material assistance from the State and society, the right to enjoy social services and social preferential treatment and the right to participate in social development and share achievements in development. Article 4(1) Actively responding to the ageing of a population is a long-term strategic task of the State; (2) The State and society shall take measures to improve various rules for the protection of the rights and interests of the elderly, and gradually better the conditions that guarantee the living, health and safety of the elderly and their participation in social development, so that they are provided for, have access to necessary medical care, […] enjoy themselves. Article 37(1) The local people's government at all levels and relevant departments shall take measures to develop urban and rural community-based elderly care services, […] various forms of services such as living care, emergency rescue, medical care, mental comfort, and psychological counselling. Article 49(1) The people's government at all levels and relevant departments shall bring the medical and health services for the elderly into the urban and rural medical and health service plans, and include the health management, common disease prevention and so on concerning the elderly into the basic public health service projects of the State. It shall be encouraged to provide health care, nursing, hospice care and other services for the elderly. Article 67 (1) Where major issues concerning the rights and interests of the elderly are involved in the formulation of laws, regulations, rules and public policies, the opinions of the elderly and the organisations of the elderly shall be heard; (2) The elderly and the organisations of the elderly shall be entitled to put forward opinions and suggestions with respect to the Protection of the Rights and Interests of the Elderly, undertakings regarding the development of the aging and so on to the state authorities.
Law on the Protection of Women's Rights and Interests	Article 51 (1) Women have the right to bear children, in accordance with relevant regulations of the State, as well as the freedom not to bear any child; (3) The State institutes a system of premarital health care and health care for the pregnant […]. The people's government at various levels shall take measures to ensure women's access to technical services for family planning in order to improve their reproductive health.

Main health laws in China	
Legislation	**Provisions concerning non-discrimination and equality**
Drug Administration Law	Not Relevant
Frontier Health and Quarantine Law	Not Relevant
Law on the Prevention and Treatment of Communicable Diseases	Article 16(2) No units or individuals shall discriminate against infectious disease patients, pathogen carriers and suspected infectious disease patients. Article 52 Medical agencies shall give medical treatment and on-the-spot rescue to the patients or suspected patients of infectious diseases or provide outpatient service to them.
Law on the Red Cross Society	Not Relevant
Law on Maternal and Infant Health Care	Not Relevant
Low on Blood Donation	No Relevant
Law on Licensed Doctors	Article 24 Doctors shall take immediate measures to treat emergency patients; no doctor may refuse to give emergency treatment to such patients.
Law on Population and Family Planning	Article 22 It is prohibited to discriminate or maltreat the women who bear female babies or the women who are incapable of bearing children. And it is prohibited to discriminate, maltreat or abandon female babies. Article 24 The State shall establish and perfect the basic pension insurance, basic medical insurance, maternity insurance, public welfare and other social security systems to promote family planning.

Main health laws in China	
Legislation	**Provisions concerning non-discrimination and equality**
Law on the Prevention of Occupational Diseases	Not Relevant
Food Safety Law	Not Relevant
Mental Health Law	Article 5(2) No news reports or literary and artistic works may contain content that discriminates against or insults patients with mental disorders. Article 28 (3) A medical institution which has received a patient with suspected mental disorders who is sent for diagnosis shall not refuse to make the diagnosis.
Law on Traditional Chinese Medicine	Not Relevant

Main health laws in China	
Legislation	**Provisions regarding elements of other non-derogable core obligations**
Drug Administration Law	Not Relevant
Frontier Health and Quarantine Law	Not Relevant
Law on the Prevention and Treatment of Communicable Diseases	Article 17(2) The health administration department under the State Council shall draw up plans and schemes for the State for the monitoring of infectious diseases. The health administration […] shall draw up plans and work schemes for monitoring infectious diseases in their own administrative areas. Article 52(1) Medical agencies shall give medical treatment and on-the-spot rescue to the patients or suspected patients of infectious diseases or provide outpatient service to them, keep written records of the cases and other relevant materials and preserve them properly. (2) [...] A medical agency that does not have the capability needed for treatment shall transfer the patients and the copies of their medical records to a medical agency that has such capability [...].
Law on the Red Cross Society	Not Relevant
Law on Maternal and Infant Health Care	Article 2(1) The State shall develop the maternal and infant health care undertakings and provide necessary conditions and material aids so as to ensure that mothers and infants receive medical and health care services. (2) The State shall support and assist the maternal and infant health care undertakings in outlying and poverty-stricken areas. Article 3(2) The undertakings of maternal and infant health care shall be included in the plans for national economic and social development.

Main health laws in China	
Legislation	**Provisions regarding elements of other non-derogable core obligations**
Low on Blood Donation	Not Relevant
Law on Licensed Doctors	Article 24 Doctors shall take immediate measures to treat emergency patients; no doctor may refuse to give emergency treatment to such patients.
Law on Population and Family Planning	Article 30 The State establishes premarital health care and maternal health care systems to prevent or reduce the incidence of birth defects and improve the health of newborns.
Law on the Prevention of Occupational Diseases	Article 44(3) No medical and health institutions providing occupational disease diagnosis shall refuse an employee's request for occupational disease diagnosis.
Food Safety Law	Not Relevant
Mental Health Law	Article 4(2) The lawful rights and interests of the patients with mental disorders in terms of education, employment, medical treatment, obtainment of material assistance from the State and society and other lawful rights and interests shall be protected by law. Article 28(4) A medical institution which has received a patient with suspected mental disorders who is sent for diagnosis shall not refuse to make the diagnosis. Article 30(1) The hospitalisation of patients suspected of mental disorders shall adhere to the principle of free will.

Main health laws in China	
Legislation	**Provisions regarding elements of other non-derogable core obligations**
Mental Health Law	Article 68(1) The health administrative departments of the people's government at or above the county level shall organize medical institutions to provide free basic public health services for the patients with severe mental disorders; (2) [...] The people's government at the county level shall, in accordance with the relevant provisions of the State, provide financial assistance for patients with severe mental disorders living in hardship to participate in the basic medical insurance [...] (3) If patients with mental disorders still have difficulties after the payment of medical expenses from the basic medical insurance or the medical expenses cannot be paid by the basic medical insurance, the departments of civil affairs shall give priority to providing them with medical assistance. Article 74 Where a medical institution and its staff have committed any of the following acts, the health administrative department of the people's government at or above the county level shall order them to make rectifications and give them a warning; and if the circumstances are serious, impose or order the imposition of disciplinary actions of demotion, removal from office or dismissal on the directly responsible person in charge and other directly liable persons according to law, and may order the relevant medical staff to suspend the practicing activities for a period of not less than one month but not more than six months: (1) refusing to make a diagnosis of the patients with suspected mental disorders who are sent for diagnosis [...].
Law on Traditional Chinese Medicine	Article 6 The State shall strengthen the building of a TCM service system, make rational planning on and allocate TCM service resources, and provide guarantee for citizens' obtainment of TCM services. Article 49 The responsible department of government at the county level and above shall include health institutions that provide traditional Chinese medicine into the basic medical insurance schemes and place the diagnosis of traditional Chinese medicine, drugs, herbal preparations on the reimbursement list.

Chapter 4
China's Policy Commitments towards the Right to Health Care

4.1 Introduction

As elaborated in chapter 3, although a handful of Chinese health laws reflect elements of the right to health care, such as non-discrimination and equality, most laws remain ambiguous as to what kind of essential health care the Chinese government must deliver in order to ensure equal access for all right-holders. The existing legal framework is ill-equipped to regulate China's health care system, which is experiencing a fast pace of reform.

In contrast, more precise health policies play a prominent role in the implementation of the right to health care in China, because they generally represent the political health manifesto of the Communist Party of China (CPC) and the central government.[1] This is in line with the United Nations Committee on Economic, Social and Cultural Rights' (CteeESCR) approach that recommends the adoption of not only legislative measures but also, *inter alia*, administrative, financial, educational, and social measures.[2] With this in mind, it is important to assess what policies China has formulated to progressively achieve the full realisation of the right to health care.

Since the launch of its new round of health care reform (NHR) in 2006, China has issued a considerable number of national health policies. These health policies explicitly state the government's political commitments, priorities, budgetary decisions and course of action, reflecting the overall goal to establish a basic health care system in which both urban and rural residents would have access to safe,

1 Editorial, 'What to Expect for China's Health in the Future' (2017) 389 (10066) The Lancet 226, 226.

2 United Nations Committee on Economic, Social and Cultural Rights (CteeESCR), 'General Comment No. 3: The Nature of State Parties' obligations (Art.2 Para. 1 of the Covenant)' (14 December 1990) UN Doc E/1991/23, para 7 (General Comment 3).

efficient, convenient and affordable health services by 2020.[3] As noted by many Chinese scholars, China's commitment to ensuring access to basic health care highly corresponds with the concept of Universal Health Coverage (UHC) as defined by the WHO. After having been included as one of the health targets specified in the United Nations Sustainable Developments Goals (SDGs),[4] UHC now certainly constitutes one of China's political commitments to be achieved by 2030. Some scholars even conclude that the overall goal of the current health care reform, if accomplished, will enable China to achieve UHC by 2020.[5]

The World Health Organisation (WHO) has labelled UHC as 'a practical expression of the concern for health equity and the right to health'.[6] It is evident that UHC to some extent overlaps with the obligations arising from the right to health (care).[7] For example, while the right to health (care) requires the provision of equal and timely access to essential primary health care, including in particular essential medicines,[8] UHC also includes access to quality essential health services and safe, effective, quality and affordable essential medicines.[9] Thus, an underlying assumption of this chapter is that efforts towards achieving UHC would contribute to the progressive realisation of the right to health care in China.

However, as noted by Dainius Puras, the present UN Special Rapporteur on the Right to Health, not all paths towards UHC conform with the requirements of the

3 Central Committee of the Communist Party of China, State Council, 'Opinions of the CPC Central Committee and the State Council on Deepening the Health Care System Reform' (2009) <www.china.org.cn/government/scio-press-conferences/2009-04/09/content_17575378.htm> accessed 28 November 2017. The English version was obtained from the official website of the State Council.

4 United Nations General Assembly (UNGA), 'Transforming Our World: the 2030 Agenda for Sustainable Development' (adopted on 25 September 2015) UN Doc A/RES/70/1, Goal 3.8.

5 See for example Qingyue Meng and Ling Xu, 'Monitoring and Evaluating Progress towards Universal Health Coverage in China' (2014) 11 PLOS Medicine 1, 1; Qingyue Meng and others, 'People's Republic of China: Health System Review' (2015) 5 Health Systems in Transistion 25, 159, 168, 184; William Hsiao and others, Universal Health Coverage: The Case of China (UNRISD Working Paper No. 2014-15) 15; Lilin Liang and John Langenbrunner, The Long March to Universal Coverage: Lessons from China (The World Bank 2013) V,

6 World Health Organisation (WHO), Anchoring Universal Health Coverage in the Right to Health: What Difference Would It Make? (WHO 2015) 1 <http://apps.who.int/iris/bitstream/10665/199548/1/9789241509770_eng.pdf> accessed 28 November 2017.

7 Audrey Chapman, 'Assessing the Universal Health Coverage Target in the Sustainable Development Goals from a Human Rights Perspective' (2016) 16 BMC International Health and Human Rights 1, 2.

8 CteeESCR, 'General Comment No. 14: The Right to the Highest Attainable Standard of Health (Art. 12 of the Covenant)' (General Comment 14) (11 August 2000) UN Doc E/C12/2000/4, para 17.

9 UNGA, 'Transforming Our World: the 2030 Agenda for Sustainable Development' (n 4) goal 3.8.

right to health (care).[10] Therefore, it is vital to evaluate the extent to which UHC is consistent with the right to health standards and to identify human rights omissions in the formulation and implementation of UHC. As such, this chapter seeks to first identify the gaps between efforts towards achieving UHC and efforts that are essential to the realisation of the right to health (care). Second, this chapter purports to further specify the current approach towards UHC from the perspective of the right to health framework and propose a human rights-based UHC. The aim of proposing a rights-based approach is to help States identify a national package of essential health care that is in line with the right to health standards.

Subsequently, the proposed rights-based UHC is applied to the Chinese context in this chapter. It mainly considers the following questions: to what extent has the right to health care been explicitly implemented in China's health policies? Which policy instruments have been taken by the Chinese government to expand UHC? Are the efforts that China has taken to scale up UHC in line with the right to health framework? What are the impacts of policy changes on equal and timely access to health care? After evaluating China's efforts to provide UHC and the right to health care, this chapter offers recommendations for scaling up a rights-based UHC as a way to promote the right to health care in the Chinese context. To summarise, this chapter moves from a purely legal approach to evaluate the extent to which China has committed itself to the right to health care through policy measures.

Section 4.2 first summarises major health policies issued since the NHR in 2006. This section also compares UHC with the right to health care and examines whether achieving UHC would nevertheless leave some requirements of the right to health care unfulfilled. To refine UHC and bring it in line with right to health standards, a rights-based approach to UHC is suggested and applied to the Chinese context. Specific attention will be paid to the core obligations arising from the right to health (care) (section 4.3). Section 4.4 identifies some remaining challenges and some next steps to be taken for promoting equal access to (basic) health care in China.

10 WHO, 'Positioning Health in the Post-2015 Development Agenda' (October 2012) WHO Discussion Paper 1-4. Cited in Dainius Puras, 'Foreword: Universal Health Coverage – A Return to Alma-Ata and Ottawa' (2016) 18 Health and Human Rights Journal 7, 8.

4.2 An appraisal of China's policy commitments to the right to health care

Implementing the right to health (care) through the adoption of policies is a firmly established approach in the right to health framework. As a party to the ICESCR, China has a legally binding obligation to pursue the full realisation of the right to health care through appropriate measures, including administrative, financial, educational, and social measures,[11] which often have the nature of a policy. Furthermore, the CteeESCR notes that States undertake a non-derogable core obligation to 'adopt and implement a national public health strategy and plan of action' to address the health concerns of the entire population, which is not subject to resource constraints.[12]

However, as the WHO observes, health values are very often not equally translated into tangible reforms.[13] Thus, taking a rights-based approach to health policy is of vital importance. First of all, the right to health (care) imposes a wide range of legally binding obligations on States. As suggested by Forman and others, a rights-based approach serves to guide the formulation of national health policies by informing policy-makers what the legally prioritised health needs are.[14] Of equal importance is that this approach can assist the advancement of equal access to health care, given that it focuses on non-discrimination and pushes for the participation of the vulnerable segments of society in all health-related decision-making processes at both the national and local levels.[15] In comparison with UHC, the right to health (care) has the potential to help States identify a package of essential health care by providing a relatively clear elaboration of core obligations.

Therefore, by incorporating the right to health care into national health policies, strategies and plans, the Chinese government could respond to the legally prioritised health needs of the entire population and ensure equal access to health care for all. The following subsections thus offer an appraisal of the extent to which China has committed itself to the right to health care in its health policies. This subsection

11 CteeESCR, General Comment 3 (n 2) para 7.

12 CteeESCR, General Comment 14 (n 8) paras 43(f), 47.

13 WHO, 'The World Health Report: Primary Health Care: Now More than Ever' (WHO 2008) 25 (WHR 2008).

14 Lisa Forman and others, 'What Could a Strengthened Right to Health Bring to the Post-2015 Health Development Agenda? Interrogating the Role of Minimum Core Concept in Advancing Essential Global Health Needs' (2013) 13 BMC International Health and Human Rights 1, 1-11.

15 CteeESCR, General Comment 14 (n 8) para 43(f).

begins with the definition of policy in the Chinese context and scopes out what types of policy fall under the realm of health policy.

4.2.1 The scope of health policy in the Chinese context

Policy is generally perceived as the 'authoritative decisions made in the legislative, executive, or judicial branches of government that are intended to direct or influence the actions, behaviours, and decisions of others.'[16] It is also regarded as the 'authoritative decisions and guidelines that direct human behaviours toward specific goals either in the private or the public sector.'[17] More specifically, the WHO defines health policy as 'the decisions, plans and actions undertaken to achieve specific health care goals within a society'.[18] Although the definition of policy varies among different scholars, there is one element in common: policy is an authoritative decision that goes beyond the individual sphere and affects society in its entirety. This decision can be made by an individual or a group (eg the president, parliament, legislature, or public health commissions) that has the power to implement the decision.[19]

In the Chinese context, the term *policy* is generally perceived in two ways – in a broad sense and more narrowly. If interpreted broadly, policy is a collection of normative documents and policy documents (as shown in the Figure 4.1). According to this approach, normative documents can be further divided into legislative documents and general normative documents. As discussed in chapter 3, legislative documents are hard laws, which include the Constitution, statutory laws *(falv)*, administrative regulations (*xingzheng fagui*), local regulations (*difangxing fagui*), self-governing regulations (*zizhi tiaoli*) and seperate regulations (*danxing tiaoli*), administrative rules (*xingzheng guizhang*) and military regulations and rules (*junshi fagui guizhang*). It goes without saying that legislative documents are legally binding.

In comparison, if the term policy is interpreted more narrowly, it refers to general normative documents and policy documents (as shown in the grey part of Figure 4.1),

16 Beaufort Longest, *Health Policymaking in the United States* (2nd Edn Health Administration Press 1998) 243, cited in Joel Bern Teitelbaum and Sara Wilensky, *Essentials of Health Policy and Law* (Jones and Bartlett 2007) 11.
17 B Hanley, 'Policy Development and Analysis' in Diana J Mason and Judith K Leavitt and others (eds), *Policy and Politics in Nursing and Health Care* (3rd Edn WB Saunders 1998) 125-138. Cited in Teitelbaum and Wilensky (n 16) 11.
18 WHO, 'Health policy' <www.who.int/topics/health_policy/en/> accessed 25 January 2017.
19 Teitelbaum and Wilensky (n 16) 12.

which do not have legally binding force. The formats of policy under this approach include administrative decisions (*jueding*), opinions (*yijian*), guidance (*zhidao*), notifications (*tongzhi*), or plans (*guihua*). Notably, there may be some confusion between department rules (*bumen guizhang*) and policy (in the narrow sense). Both of them can be issued by the ministries and commissions under the State Council, including the National Health and Family Planning Commission (NHFPC), in the format of guidance. However, according to the Legislation Law, department rules can *only* be promulgated by the order of the State Council;[20] while policy – in the narrow sense – can be published in different forms including notifications, opinions and guidelines, either by the State Council or by the ministries and commissions under the State Council.

This chapter discusses policy in its narrow sense, i.e. the policy documents and general normative documents regarding the right to health (care). Given that neither type of document is legally binding, it is not necessary to further identify whether a certain policy is a general normative document or a policy document. The following subsections only distinguish between different types of policy based on their content. Subsection 4.2.2 discusses human rights-related documents while subsection 4.2.3 discusses health-related documents.

Figure 4.1 The scope of policy in the Chinese context

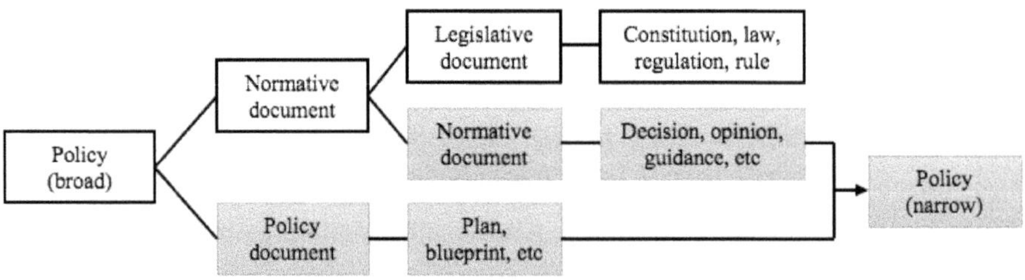

20 Legislation Law of the People's Republic of China [Lifa Fa] (adopted on 15 March 2000, entered into force on 1 July 2000, amended on 15 March 2015) (Legislation Law), art 76 <www.npc.gov.cn/englishnpc/Law/2007-12/11/content_1383554.htm> accessed 28 November 2017. The English version was obtained from the official website of the NPC.

4.2.2 Human rights-related documents

Human rights have been regarded as a Western ideology for a long time and the Chinese conception of human rights has evolved over time. It was not until 1991 that human rights were formally recognised in an official document entitled *Human Rights in China*. Since then, a significant number of human rights documents have been published, including human rights white papers and national human rights action plans (NHRAPs). These documents not only identify China's achievements in promoting and protecting human rights but also set out clear and concrete goals that inform the development of human rights implementation in China.

4.2.2.1 Human Rights White Papers

The first-ever human rights white paper – Human Rights in China – was published in 1991. Great importance was attributed in this paper to the right to subsistence, which includes, inter alia, the right to health.[21] The statement that 'public health services are a necessary guarantee for the human rights to life and health' was also included in the paper.[22] Since this white paper was issued, China has ratified most of the major human rights treaties and successively published a series of human rights white papers (see more detail in Table 4.1).[23] Apart from these documents, China has also periodically reported its progress concerning human rights protection in a series entitled P*rogress in China's Human Rights*.[24] These documents pay particular attention to vulnerable and marginalised groups. For example, the principles of non-discrimination and equality as well as the promotion of health have been reiterated in documents such as *The Situation of Chinese Women 1994*, *The Situation of Children in China 1996*, *National Minorities Policy and Its Practice in China 2000* and *Gender Equality and Women's Development in China 2015*. In addition, the document entitled *China's Social Security and Its Policy 2004* comprehensively and

21 Pinghua Sun, Human Rights Protection System in China (Springer 2014) 89.

22 Information Office of the State Council of the People's Republic of China, *Human Rights in China* (1991) chapter III para 14 < http://china.org.cn/e-white/7/7-III.htm > accessed 25 January 2016.

23 These papers were obtained from the official website of the State Council of the People's Republic of China <http://china.org.cn/e-white/≥ accessed 25 January 2017.

24 This series of white paper includes 'Progress in China's Human Rights' in 1995, 1996, 2000, 2003, 2004, 2009, 2012, 2013 and 2014 <www.china.org.cn/e-white/> accessed 25 January 2017.

systematically demonstrated China's social security system. The document clarifies three basic medical insurance (BMI) schemes and it explained how the State supports the poor, the disabled, the elderly, the unemployed and the people from rural areas to receive basic medical and health care.[25]

In terms of the right to health more specifically, China published a document called *Medical and Health Services in China 2012*. This white paper clearly pointed out that, 'China pays great attention to protecting and improving its people's health.'[26] It also introduced various measures that China had taken to establish its basic medical and health care system and to ensure the provision of safe, effective and affordable basic medical and health care to both urban and rural residents.[27] Moreover, while acknowledging the progress China had made in developing its health care system, this paper also recognised that such improvement still fell short of the public's demands for health care.[28]

In general, these human rights white papers present a systematic review of the efforts that China has taken in compliance with its human rights obligations.[29]

Table 4.1 Human rights white papers

Year	White paper
1991	Human Rights in China
1994	The Situation of Chinese Women
1996	The Situation of Children in China
2000	National Minorities Policy and Its Practice in China
2004	China's Social Security and Its Policy

25 China's Social Security and Its Policy (September 2004), section III <www.gov.cn/english/official/2005-07/28/content_18024.htm> accessed 19 November 2017. The English version was obtained from the official website of the State Council.

26 Information Office of the State Council, Medical and Health Services in China (December 2012), forward <http://english.gov.cn/archive/white_paper/2014/08/23/content_281474982986476.htm> accessed 19 November 2017. The English version was obtained from the official website of the State Council.

27 ibid.

28 ibid, section II.

29 Sun (n 21) 64.

Year	White paper
2006	The Development of China's Undertakings for the Aged
2011	New Progress in Development-oriented Poverty Reduction Program for Rural China
2011	The Socialist Legal System with Chinese Characteristics
2012	Medical and Health Services in China
2015	Gender Equality and Women's Development in China

4.2.2.2 National Human Rights Action Plans

In addition to the white papers, China also released three NHRAPs: the *National Human Rights Action Plans 2009 – 2010*, *National Human Rights Action Plans 2012 – 2015* and *National Human Rights Action Plans 2016 – 2020.*[30] The primary purpose of drawing up such plans was to identify the steps through which China could improve the promotion and protection of human rights, as recommended by the World Conference on Human Rights.[31] By placing human rights improvements in public policy, a government can set up concrete goals, devise practical programmes and engage all relevant sections of the government and society to ensure the promotion and protection of human rights.[32] As such, these three NHRAPs not only reaffirmed China's constitutional commitment to respect and guarantee human rights, but more importantly, they transformed the human rights cause in China from the realm of idealism into the realm of practice and routine.[33]

30 Information Office of the State Council of the People's Republic of China, National Human Rights Action Plans 2009 – 2010 (13 April 2009) <www.gov.cn/english/official/2009-04/13/content_1284128.htm>; National Human Rights Action Plans 2012 – 2015 (11 June 2012) <www.china.org.cn/government/whitepaper/node_7156850.htm> accessed 28 November 2017 (National Human Rights Action Plans 2012 – 2015); National Human Rights Action Plans 2016 – 2020 (August 2016) <http://english.gov.cn/archive/publications/2016/09/29/content_281475454482622.htm> accessed 28 November 2017 (National Human Rights Action Plans 2016 – 2020).

31 The World Conference on Human Rights, Vienna Declaration and Programme of Action, 1993, para 71 part II. <www.ohchr.org/EN/ProfessionalInterest/Pages/Vienna.aspx> accessed 25 January 2017.

32 Office of the United Nations High Commissioner for Human Rights (OHCHR), 'Handbook on National Human Rights Plans of Action' (UN 2002) 9 <www.ohchr.org/Documents/Publications/training10en.pdf> accessed 28 November 2017.

33 ibid 94; Sun (n 21) 81-82.

- NHRAP 2012-2015

In its NHRAP 2012-2015, the Chinese government set out five goals for the development of human rights. One of the goals was to provide comprehensive protection to economic, social and cultural rights of all members of society while another goal was to take proactive measures to alleviate the human rights situations of vulnerable segments of society.[34] Attention was also paid to civil and political rights, human rights education as well as the international exchange and cooperation on human rights. In particular, chapter I of this NHRAP concerned the promotion and protection of economic, social and cultural rights, including the right to health care. It stated that China would initially establish a basic medical and health care system covering both rural and urban residents by 2015. Efforts would also be made to promote equal access to basic public health care services and strengthen the construction of primary health care (PHC) institutions and training centres for general practitioners. In addition, it noted the enactment of Mental Health Law and the drafting of Basic Health Law.[35]

More importantly, this plan specified the targets to be achieved by 2015 and the benchmark for evaluating the progress made towards the realisation of the right to health care. For example, the targets set out that by 2015 China would manage to cover 60 million more people through the three BMI schemes than in 2010. According to the targets, the number of people enrolling the Urban Residents' Basic Medical Insurance (URBMI) and the New Rural Cooperative Medical Schemes (NRCMS) should have amounted to 1.32 billion by 2015. The reimbursement rate for inpatient care covered by the three BMI schemes was expected to reach 75% while the reimbursement rate for outpatient care covered by both the URBMI and the NRCMS was expected to increase to 50%. The premium paid by the government under the URBMI and NRCMS should have risen to 360 RMB or above by 2015. To strengthen the construction of PHC services, China also intended to train 150,000 general practitioners by 2015.[36]

34 National Human Rights Action Plans 2012 – 2015, introduction.
35 ibid, section I.
36 ibid.

• NHRAP 2016-2020

The NHRAP 2016 - 2020 was released in September 2016. In light of the fact that the Chinese government is determined to establish a basic medical and health care system covering all residents by 2020, this most recent plan is of great importance to the promotion and protection of the right to health care during this period.[37] This plan set out five goals that are consistent with the ones in the NHRAP 2012-2015. Furthermore, it acknowledged the stark disparities between rural and urban development, the weak legal protection of human rights and remaining challenges in such fields as health care, food and drug safety and care for the elderly. Although not specifically mentioning health care in its goals, it placed emphasis on the promotion of equal access to public services, which include health care services.[38]

In terms of the right to health care, this new plan reiterated the goal of establishing a basic medical and health care system that covers all residents by 2020 and set specific objectives to scale up UHC. For example, the coverage of the three BMI schemes should be maintained at 95% or above. Maternal insurance should also be integrated into these three schemes. Another example is that the Insurance Programme for Catastrophic Diseases (IPCD) covering both rural and urban residents should be fully implemented. In addition, the government should accelerate the steps to establish a national BMI network and a trans-regional mechanism for medical claim settlement. Patients who meet the referral requirement should be able to directly settle their medical claim for inpatient treatment, regardless of the region of enrolment.[39] Moreover, the government should endeavour to ensure equal access to basic public health services. Furthermore, efforts should be made to improve the capacity for providing PHC services and the geographic accessibility of PHC institutions. By 2020, the government aims to ensure two general practitioners for every 10,000 persons and 2.5 practitioners or assistants for every 1,000 persons. Additionally, all patients should be able to reach PHC institutions within 30 minutes. Moreover, special attention should be paid to drug safety. In addition to improving the national essential medicines system (NEMS), the government should also take measures to

37 Central Committee of the Communist Party of China, State Council (n 3).
38 National Human Rights Action Plan of China 2016-2020, introduction.
39 ibid, section I.

promote the drug supply and procurement mechanism as well as the inspection and testing system and particularly strengthen the monitoring of adverse drug reaction.[40]

- Evaluation of the NHRAPs

Numerous measures have been taken to implement the NHRAPs and remarkable progress has been made in the last five years. According to the evaluation report issued by the Information Office of the State Council, the goals set out in the NHRAP 2012-2015 were all achieved.[41] Nevertheless, in spite of this accomplishment, problems remain in the supervision and evaluation of the implementation of the NHRAPs.

As suggested by the Office of the United Nations High Commissioner for Human Rights (OHCHR), all relevant sections of the government should be involved in the monitoring process to ensure that appropriate responsibility is taken for the implementation of national human rights action plans. More importantly, the representatives of vulnerable and marginalised groups and CSOs should be encouraged to participate in the supervision and evaluation of the implementation of the plans.[42] This suggestion was reflected in the NHRAPs. In addition, a joint meeting mechanism was established to monitor and evaluate the implementation of the NHRAPs.[43] This mechanism, serving as the national coordinating committee, is led by the Information Office of the State Council and the Ministry of Foreign Affairs, and is comprised of the legislative and judicial branches and the responsible ministries and commissions under the State Council. The media and CSOs are also encouraged to participate in the work of this joint meeting mechanism.[44] However, there are some flaws in this joint meeting mechanism. Both the plan itself and the evaluation report fail to clarify whether the representatives of vulnerable groups or CSOs participated in the implementation, supervision and evaluation of the implementation of the NHRAP 2012-2015. Furthermore, the initial supervision and evaluation work was conducted by the departments that were responsible for the implementation of this plan. Even

40 ibid.
41 Information Office of the State Council, 'The Evaluation Report of the National Human Rights Action Plan 2012-2015)' (14 June 2016) <www.scio.gov.cn/zxbd/wz/Document/1480082/1480082.htm> accessed 19 November 2017. Author's translation.
42 OHCHR (n 32) 20-21.
43 National Human Rights Action Plans 2012 – 2015, section VI.
44 ibid.

though academics also made external evaluations, their work was mainly based on the self-evaluation reports submitted by these departments.[45] The accuracy of the data thus relied largely on the credibility of the responsible departments.

Therefore, a more rigorous, transparent and independent external evaluation is needed in the joint meeting mechanism.[46] Measures should also be taken to promote the participation of vulnerable and marginalised groups and CSOs in the supervision and evaluation of the implementation of the NHRAPs. Remarkably, although the CPC and the governments at all levels are determined to take effective measures to achieve the aims and complete the tasks set out in the NHRAPs, there are no mechanisms for holding them accountable for violations of the human rights obligations stated in the NHRAPs.[47] The establishment of appropriate non-judicial accountability mechanisms should thus be required by and detailed in the plan to make the government more accountable for their right to health obligations and other human-rights obligations.

4.2.3 Health-related documents

In addition to the human rights-related documents, the content of the right to health care has also been reflected in various health-related documents. Health has been placed at the core of China's policy agenda over the past decade. A significant volume of documents has been issued to direct the reform of the entire health care system and to regulate different sections of this system. These documents reflect China's political commitments, priorities, budgetary decisions and course of action for promoting and protecting the health of the entire population.[48] By setting concrete goals and proposing practical activities to achieve these targets, these health-related documents have the potential to transform the right to health (care) commitments into tangible actions and eventually advance equal and timely access to basic health care.

For example, the *'Healthy China 2030' Plan*, which was endorsed by the Central Committee of the CPC and the State Council in 2016, announced that health would be put at the centre of the country's entire policy-making machinery and become

45 ibid.
46 OHCHR (n 32) 98.
47 National Human Rights Action Plans 2012 – 2015, section VI.
48 Health policy, the official website of the WHO <www.who.int/topics/health_policy/en/> accessed 28 November 2017.

an explicit national political priority.[49] This plan is the first medium- to long-term national strategic plan in the health sector since the founding of China.[50] It represents the government's commitment to provide essential health care for all by 2020 and to achieve health equity by 2030.[51] This plan also implies that equal access to basic health care, which is an entitlement arising from the right to health care, has become a policy imperative for Chinese health policy-makers. In 2016 and beyond, this plan will be delineated in strategic programmes or action plans, which are expected to spell out more detailed goals and concrete implementation measures for lower-level apparatuses of government to take steps.[52] Another example is the *Opinions on Deepening the Health Care System Reform* which marked the start of China's NHR in 2006. This document was the first official document to call for the establishment of a basic medical and health care system covering both rural and urban residents by 2020.[53] As well as the documents concerning the reform of the entire health care system, there is also a wide range of documents focusing on specific areas of the health sector, including the reforms of the BMI schemes, PHC institutions and public hospitals as well as the establishment of a NEMS.

Table 4.3 (at the end of chapter 4) presents an overview of the major health-related documents issued by the State Council and the responsible ministries and commissions under the State Council, such as the NHFPC and the Ministry of Human Resources and Social Security (MOHRSS), as of January 2017. The aim of this chapter is to evaluate China's policy commitments towards the right to health care, with particular attention to core obligations. For this reason, the summary of the health polices is limited to general health policies that address primary health care, essential medicines, equality and non-discrimination (with particular attention paid to the reform of the three BMI schemes), equitable distribution of health care, and

49 Central Committee of the Communist Party of China, State Council, '"Healthy China 2030" Plan' (25 October 2016) <www.gov.cn/zhengce/2016-10/25/content_5124174.htm> accessed 28 November 2017. Author's translation.

50 National Health and Family Planning Commission, 'Interpretation of the 'Healthy China 2030' Plan' (26 October 2016) <www.nhfpc.gov.cn/guihuaxxs/s3586s/201610/a2325a1198694bd6ba42d6e47567daa8.shtml> accessed 19 November 2017. Author's translation.

51 Central Committee of the Communist Party of China, State Council (n 49), section I.

52 WHO, Healthy China 2030 (From Vision to Action) <www.who.int/healthpromotion/conferences/9gchp/healthy-china/en/> accessed 28 November 2017.

53 Central Committee of the Communist Party of China, State Council (n 3).

the adoption of a comprehensive and participatory national plan of action. It also explores whether the process for adopting these health policies was participatory and transparent.

As shown in Table 4.3, the provision of access to basic medical and health care services, repetitively mentioned in many health-related documents, forms the core of the current health care reform. Several elements of the right to health care, including core obligations, are reflected in China's national health policies, even though the term 'right to health' is not explicitly stated.

However, as explained in chapter 1, when screening health-related documents and relevant publications, we witness an inconsistent use of terminology. Taking the *Opinions on Deepening the Health Care System Reform* as an example (see Table 4.3 for more detail), if literally translated from the Chinese language, the overall goal stated in this document is to establish a basic medical and health care system covering both rural and urban residents by 2020.[54] The document further specifies that this basic system is comprised of four major areas: public health services, medical services, medical security, and drug production and supply. It also notes that the basic principle of this reform is to ensure universal access to basic medical and health care services.[55] The official English version of the Opinions states the following:

> [b]y 2020, the basic health care system covering urban and rural residents shall have been fundamentally established [...] everyone shall have access to [*sic*] basic health care services [...]. Four systems covering urban and rural residents shall be established, including the public health service system, [*sic*] health care service system, medical security system, and a secured pharmaceutical supply system, with an aim to forming a "four in one" basic health care system.[56]

The same problem occurred in a handful of other policy documents such as the *Planning and Implementation Plan of Deepening Health System Reform during the Twelfth Five-year Plan* and the *Thirteenth Five-Year Plan for Deepening the Health Care System Reform*. Some Chinese scholars interpret these policy commitments as

54 ibid, section II.
55 ibid.
56 ibid.

a requirement to achieve UHC by 2020.[57] Among them, some have further specified the commitment as the achievement of 'universal health coverage of primary care'[58] or 'universal health insurance coverage'.[59] Setting aside the translation deficit, I find it too early to draw the conclusion that the establishment of a basic medical and health care system covering both rural and urban residents is equivalent to UHC or the obligations under the right to health (care). It is yet not clear whether access to basic health care services is equivalent to what UHC entails. And more importantly, does universal access to basic health care or UHC suffice to realise the right to health care in China? Section 4.2.4 will explore the concept and content of UHC in detail and offer a comparative analysis of UHC and the right to health (care).

4.2.4 A comparative normative analysis of Universal Health Coverage and the right to health care

When evaluating China's progress towards the realisation of the right to health care, it is important to clarify what China has committed to in its national health policies. It is evident that priority has been given to the achievement of universal access to basic health care in China's policy-making. Nonetheless, a clearer conceptual framework is needed before it is possible to conclude that the efforts China has made towards universal access to basic health care or UHC are in line with the obligations under the right to health care. As such, this subsection begins by identifying the normative content of UHC in authoritative sources and how it is linked to the right to health care.

4.2.4.1 The changing definitions of Universal Health Coverage

The concept of UHC can be traced back to the 2005 World Health Assembly (WHA) resolution. In this resolution, the WHA noted the importance of further developing

57 See eg Meng and others (n 5) 25, 159, 168, 184; Hsiao and others (n 5) 15; Qingyue Meng and others, 'Consolidating the Social Health Insurance Schemes in China: Towards an Equitable and Efficient Health System' (2015) 386 The Lancet 1484, 1490; Liang and Langenbrunner (n 5) V; Winnie Yip and others, 'Early Appraisal of China's Huge and Complex Health-care Reforms' (2012) 379 The Lancet 833, 833; Hao Yu, 'Universal Health Insurance Coverage for 1.3 Billion People: What Accounts for China's Success?' (2015) 119 Health Policy 1145, 1145.

58 William Hsiao and others (n 5) 1.

59 Yu (n 57) 1145.

health financing systems in many countries so as to ensure all people 'access to necessary services while providing protection against financial risk.'[60] Access to necessary services and financial risk protection – were then defined as universal coverage, or UHC.[61] This definition was further detailed as 'access to key promotive, preventive, curative and rehabilitative health interventions for all at an affordable cost, thereby achieving **equity in access**'.[62] It can thus be deduced that universal coverage for all does not necessarily mean coverage for everything, but refers to access to necessary health services (promotion, prevention, treatment and rehabilitation).[63]

The twin goals of UHC (i.e. access to necessary services and financial risk protection) were reaffirmed in *The World Health Report 2008 – Primary Health Care*. This report acknowledged that a fundamental step for a State to take to promote health equity is 'universal coverage.'[64] More specifically, this report states that,

> universal access to the full range of personal and non-personal health services they need, with social health protection [...] ensure that services are available, accessible and produce quality care for those who need them, without exposing them to the risk of catastrophic expenditures.[65]

Although the goal of financial risk protection remained the same, the services to be covered by UHC were expanded in the 2008 report to include the full range of health services. This report also identified three critical areas to be considered when measuring progress towards UHC, i.e. the breadth, depth and height of coverage, which are generally presented as the 'UHC Cube' (this will be discussed further in section 4.2.4.2).[66] The breadth of coverage refers to the proportion of people who

60 World Health Assembly (WHA), 'Sustainable Health Financing, Universal Coverage and Social Health Insurance' (16-25 May 2005) Resolutions and Decisions WHA58.33 <http://apps.who.int/medicinedocs/documents/s21475en/s21475en.pdf> accessed 19 November 2017.

61 WHO, 'The World Health Report: Health Systems Financing – The Path to Universal Coverage' (WHR 2010) (WHO 2010) ix.

62 Emphasis in original. WHO, 'Social Health Insurance: Sustainable Health Financing, Universal Coverage and Social Health Insurance, Report by the Secretariat' (7 April 2005) WHA Doc A58/20, para 2. <http://apps.who.int/gb/archive/pdf_files/WHA58/A58_20-en.pdf> accessed 19 November 2017; Lisa Forman and others 'What Do Core Obligations under the Right to Health Bring to Universal Health Coverage' (2016) 18 Health and Human Rights Journal 23, 24.

63 WHO, WHR 2010 (n 61) 22.

64 WHO, 'The World Health Report 2008: Primary Health Care (Now More than Ever)' (WHR 2008) (WHO 2008) 25.

65 ibid.

66 ibid 25-27; Lawrence Gostin and others, *Advancing the Right to Health: The Vital Role of Law* (WHO 2017) 13-15.

enjoy social health protection; the depth of coverage is 'the range of essential services that are necessary to address people's health needs effectively'; and the height of coverage is 'the proportion of the costs covered by pooled funds'.[67] In this report, the WHO seemed, based on the definition provided in the 2005 WHA resolution, to limit the full range of health services to essential services. However, the WHO did not clarify the scope of essential services in the 2008 report, choosing only to note the importance of defining 'essential packages' of benefits when moving towards UHC. Given each country's specific national context, the WHO also left it to the discretion of each country to define its own package. Nonetheless, it suggested that each country set clear priorities and ration care and trade-offs between the breadth and depth of coverage when defining their essential benefits package.[68]

The World Health Report 2010 – Health System Financing reiterated the two key elements of UHC: (1) all people have 'access to needed health services (including the prevention, promotion, treatment and rehabilitation) of sufficient quality to be effective'; and (2) the use of health services does not expose the user to financial hardship.[69] According to this report, services covered under UHC include a set of *needed* preventive, promotive, curative and rehabilitative health services that everyone has the right to use.[70] More specifically, as its title suggests, this report focused on financial access to essential health services and the extent of financial risk protection provided under UHC. This report paid particular attention to the importance of developing national health financing systems towards UHC.[71] Considering national contexts, this report also acknowledged different approaches each country may take along the three dimensions of the UHC Cube and balance trade-offs between the range of services, the proportion of the population and the proportion of costs that can be covered when making policy choices.[72] As noted in the report, no countries can fully achieve UHC that covers 100% of the population for 100% of health costs and 100% of the needed services, with no waiting lists.[73] Thus, UHC, similar to the right to health care, allows for progressive realisation.[74] As

67 ibid.
68 ibid 26-27.
69 WHO, WHR 2010 (n 61) xvi, 6.
70 ibid xvi.
71 ibid 9
72 ibid 12.
73 ibid 2, 12.
74 WHO (n 6) 5.

just mentioned, all countries should make choices and balance trade-offs on the basis of their own level of development, availability of funds, epidemiological situation and people's expectations. As such, there is no one-size-fits-all approach.[75] The sets of health services included in the UHC package are determined upon each country's domestic context. What is critical is that these health services respond to the priority health needs of the population.[76] The question then arises as to how government budgets should be prioritised so as to offer more health services, extend coverage to more people or cover more health costs by pooled funds. The 2010 report suggested several methods for countries to improve both access to health services and financial risk protection in a more equitable manner. These include means for raising sufficient funds, removing financial barriers to access, and ensuring the effective use and equitable distribution of available resources.[77]

Furthermore, the concept of UHC was endorsed by the 2012 United Nations General Assembly (UNGA) resolution. It defined UHC as:

> [a]ll people have access, without discrimination, to nationally determined sets of the needed promotive, preventive, curative and rehabilitative basic health services and essential, safe, affordable, effective and quality medicines, while ensuring that the use of these services does not expose the users to financial hardship, with a special emphasis on the poor, vulnerable and marginalized segments of the population.[78]

This resolution reaffirmed that under UHC, all people would have access to *needed basic* health services. Moreover, it extended the content of UHC from health care services to health goods, namely essential, safe, affordable, effective and quality medicines. Remarkably, this resolution also recognised 'the responsibility of Governments to urgently and significantly scale up efforts to accelerate the transition towards universal access to affordable and quality health-care services'.[79] Furthermore, the General Assembly drew attention to health equity and non-discriminatory access in this resolution. For example, it specified that the implementation of UHC depends

75 ibid, 12.
76 ibid.
77 WHO, WHR 2010 (n 61) xi, 3, 12.
78 UNGA, 'Global Health and Foreign Policy' (adopted 6 December 2012) UN Doc A/67/L.36, para 10 <www.un.org/ga/search/view_doc.asp?symbol=A/67/L.36&referer=https://www.google.nl/&Lang=E> accessed 28 November 2017.
79 ibid, para 8.

on 'a resilient and responsive health system that provides comprehensive primary health care services, with extensive geographical coverage, including in remote and rural areas, and with a specific emphasis on access to populations most in need.'[80] Particular attention was also paid to the needs of vulnerable and marginalised groups, with the aim of enhancing their ability to realise their right to health care.[81] In addition, this resolution highlighted the importance of transparency, inclusiveness and equity in the decision-making process, which would 'allow for the input of all stakeholders and develop policies that perform effectively and reach clear and measurable outcomes for all, build accountability and, most crucially, are fair in both policy development processes and results'.[82]

Nevertheless, ambiguity remains in this resolution. Although it is clear from the definition above that essential medicines are part of UHC, the range of health services is yet not defined beyond needed basic health services (prevention, promotion, treatment and rehabilitation).[83] This is partially because the resolution acknowledged each country's 'particular epidemiological, economic, sociocultural, political and structural context.' Therefore, it allows each country to determine its own sets of basic health services and essential medicines, which to some extent leaves a precise understanding of what UHC entails unspecified.

The World Health Report 2013 – Research for Universal Health Coverage also embraced the two facets of UHC: (1) the provision of and access to high-quality health services; and (2) financial risk protection. According to this report, health services refer to 'methods for promotion, prevention, treatment, rehabilitation and palliative care' and 'ways of taking action on social and environmental determinants both within and beyond the health sector'.[84] Here, the WHO seems to expand services covered under UHC to the full spectrum of services that are 'sufficient to health needs, both in quantity and quality' and to encompass underlying determinants of health.[85] Remarkably, although essential medicines were not specifically mentioned in the report, the WHO noted that a health system moving towards UHC should

80 ibid, para 9.
81 ibid, para 14.
82 ibid, para 12.
83 Forman and others (n 14) 4.
84 WHO, 'The World Health Report: Research for Universal Health Coverage' (WHR 2013) (WHO 2013) xi.
85 ibid xi, 6.

assure access to essential medicines and health products.[86] The WHO also explicitly stated the goal of financial risk protection in this report, i.e. that 'no out-of-pocket payments that exceed a given threshold of affordability - usually set at zero for the poorest and most disadvantaged people.'[87]

However, similar to other world health reports, the 2013 report did not define the coverage of services in all settings; rather, it acknowledged that 'the health services that are necessary and the people who need them should be defined with respect to the causes of ill-health, the technologies and instruments for intervention, and the cost'.[88] Accordingly, governments should determine priorities in improving health, national sets of needed health services, appropriate mechanisms for financial risk protection and supporting policies on the basis of their own epidemiological contexts and their financial capacity to pay for these services.[89] As with the General Assembly resolution discussed above, the definition of UHC in the 2013 report was somewhat ambiguous.

UHC was also selected as one of the key targets of the overarching goal 'to ensure healthy lives and promote well-being for all at all ages' under the Sustainable Development Goals (SDGs). In particular, SDG 3.8 includes an explicit political commitment to 'achieve universal health coverage, including financial risk protection, access to quality essential health-care services and access to safe, effective, quality and affordable essential medicines and vaccines for all.'[90]

As a global target adopted by the UNGA, SDG 3.8 reflects the commitment of Member States of the UN to provide each other with political support in their efforts to ensure universal access to quality essential health care services and access to safe, effective, quality and affordable medicines and vaccines without the risk of financial hardship. In addition to SDG 3.8, SDG 3.7 also includes another explicit political commitment to 'ensure universal access to sexual and reproductive health-care services, including for family planning, information and education, the integration of reproductive health into national strategies and programmes'.[91] Because they are mentioned separately, the commitments made in SDG 3.7 regarding sexual

86 ibid 15.
87 ibid 6-7.
88 ibid 21-22.
89 ibid 4.
90 UNGA (n 4) goal 3.8.
91 ibid.

and reproductive health care services, may lead to a possible assumption that such services do not fall within the scope of *essential* health care services covered under UHC. In addition, since none of the targets under SDG 3 are prioritised, there is very little guidance for governments regarding how they should prioritise between the goal's various targets. For these reasons, a clear clarification of what UHC entails is still lacking in the definition of SDG 3.8, which again makes it difficult to identify the precise content of UHC.

A further criticism can be made regarding the two proposed indicators included in SDG 3 to measure progress towards UHC. Indicator 3.8.1 focuses on the coverage of essential health services, while indicator 3.8.2 is about financial protection when using health services.[92] However, as Chapman points out, the limit of focusing on coverage averages would possibly mask disparities in coverage across population groups, especially the exclusion of those most vulnerable and marginalised groups, which may be the problem of many low- and middle-income countries.[93] Moreover, using insurance coverage as an indicator for financial protection may not present the impoverishing impact of health expenditures.[94]

In brief, UHC generally stands for universal access to a set of health services for all without financial hardship. However, what we have witnessed through the shifting definitions of UHC is that the coverage of health services varies considerably. Regardless of the growing global consensus regarding its importance, no agreement has been reached as to the conceptual definition, meaning and scope of UHC.[95] Moreover, as explained above, the range of services, the proportion of the population and the proportion of cost can never be as universal as the concept's name suggests.

---

92 WHO, Monitoring Universal Health Coverage (2016) <https://unstats.un.org/sdgs/files/meetings/iaeg-sdgs-meeting-03/3rd-IAEG-SDGs-presentation-WHO--3.8.1-and-3.8.2.pdf> accessed 28 November 2017.

93 UNGA, 'Report of the Special Rapporteur on the Right of Everyone to the Enjoyment of the Highest Attainable Standard of Physical and Mental Health, Dainius Puras' (5 August 2016) UN Doc A/71/304, para 80; Marc Roberts and others, 'Disaggregating the Universal Health Coverage Cube: Putting Equity in the Picture' (2015) 1 Health Systems & Reform 22, 23; Audrey Chapman, 'The Problems with the Proposed Indicators for Monitoring Universal Health Coverage in the Sustainable Development Goals' Health and Human Rights Journal Blog (17 March 2016) <www.hhrjournal.org/2016/03/the-problems-with-the-proposed-indicators-for-monitoring-universal-health-coverage-in-the-sustainable-development-goals/> accessed 28 November 2017.

94 ibid.

95 Gilbert Abiiro and Manuela De Allegri, 'Universal Health Coverage from Multiple Perspectives: A Synthesis of Conceptual Literature and Global Debates' (2015) 15 BMC International Health and Human Rights 1, 2.

Yet, the WHO suggested three indicators in its world health reports for measuring progress towards UHC.[96] These indicators will be discussed further below.

4.2.4.2 Evaluating progress towards Universal Health Coverage

As shown in Figure 4.2, the WHO has identified three dimensions to consider when evaluating the progress made towards UHC (the so-called 'UHC Cube'), which raise three critical questions: *who* is covered, *which services* are covered, and *how much* cost is covered? Again, due to resource constraints, no country can assure all necessary health services to the entire population without any cost for individuals. What people can expect under UHC is access to essential health services and essential, safe, affordable, effective and quality medicines that they need, without being subjected to financial hardship.

Figure 4.2 The UHC Cube[97]

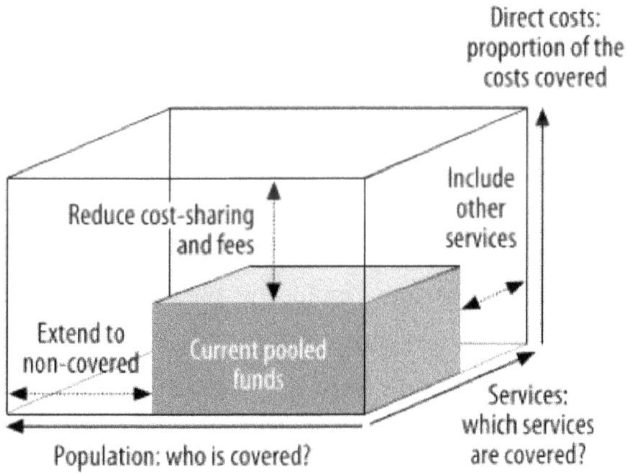

Given each country's different national contexts and burden of diseases, it is not possible to define a universally applicable essential benefits package.[98] The WHO has thereby acknowledged that each country may take different approaches towards these

96 WHO, WHR 2008 (n 64) 26; WHO, WHR 2010 (n 61) xv; WHO, WHR 2013 (n 84) 7.

97 Source: the World Health Reports. See generally WHO, WHR 2008 (n 64) 26; WHO, WHR 2010 (n 61) xv; WHO, WHR 2013 (n 84) 7.

98 Gorik Ooms and others, 'Is Universal Health Coverage the Practical Expression of the Right to Health Care' (2014) 14 (3) BMC International Health & Human Rights 1, 5.

three dimensions and balance trade-offs between the range of services, the proportion of population, and the proportion of costs that can be covered when making policy choices. Countries must make such choices based on their level of development, the availability of funds, their epidemiological situation and people's expectations.[99]

Nevertheless, it is worth noting that the WHO does not provide any 'bottom line' of essential health care under the concept of UHC; the lack of a mechanism to enforce UHC seems to implicitly permit a level of health care provision in a country which, due to the country's national context, fails to address standard health concerns.[100] This raises concerns as to whether countries will reduce health care downwards to merely provide essential health care, or provide selective rather other comprehensive health care.[101] It may also lead to greater disparities between rich and poor countries. Nevertheless, while UHC has some flaws, it does have the potential to improve human health and well-being. In addition, the flaws may be addressed if UHC is anchored in the right to health care.

4.2.4.3 Universal Health Coverage anchored in the right to health care

It is widely perceived that UHC is an aspiration anchored in the right to health.[102] As labelled by the WHO, UHC is 'by definition, a practical expression of the concern for **health equity and the right to health**'.[103] In its General Comment 15 the Committee on the Rights of the Child (CteeRC) also highlights the importance of 'ensuring universal coverage of quality primary health services, including prevention, health promotion, care and treatment services, and essential drugs'.[104] Therefore, an underlying assumption is that measures taken for promoting UHC would automatically advance the right to health. However, some scholars argue that UHC is not sufficient to ensure the right to health since UHC focuses *only* on health care while the right to

99 WHO, WHR 2008 (n 64) 26; WHO, WHR 2010 (n 61) xv; WHO, WHR 2013 (n 84) 7.
100 WHO (n 6) 11.
101 Forman and others (n 62) 31.
102 Ooms and others (n 98) 2; WHO, WHR 2013 (n 84) 6.
103 Emphasis in original. WHO, 'Positioning Health in the Post-2015 Development Agenda' (October 2012) WHO Discussion Paper 1, 3.
104 United Nations Committee on the Rights of the Child, 'General Comment No. 15: The Right of the Child to the Enjoyment of the Highest Attainable Standard of Health (Art. 24)' (17 April 2013) UN Doc CRC/C/GC/15, para 73 (b).

health also encompasses underlying determinants of health.[105] It is arguable that the absence of other determinants within UHC limits its capacity to promote the right to health at large. Nevertheless, given the focus of this chapter, it is certainly feasible to assess whether efforts towards scaling up UHC would improve the right to health care in China. While conducting this assessment, I intend to refine UHC by taking a right to health-based approach. Therefore, the following subsection offers a comparative analysis of the norms of UHC and the right to health care as shown in Table 4.2, mainly based on the 2012 UNGA Resolution and General Comment 14, given the authority of these two documents.[106] The analysis below is based on the components outlined in this table.

Table 4.2 Overlap of UHC with the right to health care (source: the author)

Key factors of UHC (2012 UNGA Resolution)	Right to Health Care (General Comment 14)
Trade-offs acknowledged	Progressive realisation and core obligations acknowledged
Nationally determined sets of services, no bottom line	Core obligations and obligations of compatible priority which are legally binding
Cost-effectiveness	Equitable distribution of health facilities, goods and services
Access to the needed promotive, preventive, curative and rehabilitative basic health services	Essential primary health care
Essential, safe, affordable, effective and quality medicines	Provision of essential drugs, as from time to time defined under the WHO Action Programme on Essential Drugs
Transparent, inclusive and equitable decision-making processes	Participatory and transparent processes, with particular attention paid to vulnerable and marginalised groups
Access for all, without discrimination	Access for all, without discrimination Equality
Emphasis on the poor, vulnerable and marginalised segments of the population	Emphasis on vulnerable and marginalised groups
Financial risk protection	Affordability (economic accessibility) Equity

105 Gorik Ooms and others, 'Universal Health Coverage Anchored in the Right to Health' (2013) 91 Bull World Health Organ 2, 2; Gorik Ooms and others (n 98) 2.

106 UNGA, 'Global Health and Foreign Policy' (adopted 6 December 2012) UN Doc A/67/L.36, para 10; CteeESCR, General Comment 14 (n 8) para 43; See also Chapman (n 93) 3-7; Ooms and others (n 105) 3-5; WHO (n 6) 10-11.

The first observation that can be made here is that in comparison with the two sets of norms listed in Table 4.2, both the WHO and the CteeESCR acknowledge the difficulties of each country to provide all forms of health care to all people. UHC is an ongoing 'work in process' rather than a final status to be achieved. It allows for trade-offs. Continuous efforts are required to expand UHC and to promote equal access to health care for all. Therefore, UHC is in line with the principle of progressive realisation under the right to health care.

Nevertheless, while the WHO acknowledges that each country needs to balance trade-offs between the range of services, the proportion of the population and the proportion of costs that can be covered under UHC when making policy, the CteeESCR's approach is more straightforward. As this study contends, States undertake two sets of core obligations arising from the right to health care: (1) obligations of immediate effect, which are relatively cost-free and can generally be achieved with minimum resource implications; and (2) non-derogable core obligations, which are not subject to resources constraints – States cannot under any circumstances justify their non-compliance with these obligations (outlined in chapter 2).

More specifically, although efforts made to move towards UHC would to some degree contribute to the progressive realisation of the right to health care, human rights omissions may occur in the formulation and implementation of UHC, as will be explained below. The following subsections summarise the gaps between efforts made to achieve UHC and what is required under the right to health care on the basis of two questions: (1) which health services are covered; and (2) who is covered?

- Which health services are covered?

As discussed earlier (section 4.2.4.1), the coverage of health services varies considerably, due to the diverse definitions of the UHC provided in different official documents:

- 2005 WHA Resolution: *necessary* services
- 2008 World Health Report: a *full* range of *needed* health services
- 2010 World Health Report: *needed* health services
- 2012 UNGA Resolution: nationally determined sets of the *needed basic* health services and *essential medicines*
- 2013 World Health Report: *high-quality* health services as well as *essential*

medicines and health products
- 2016 SDG 3.8: *quality essential* health-care services as well as *safe, effective, and affordable medicines and vaccines of sufficient quality*

As it currently stands, UHC only provides for universal access to a set of health services (and essential medicines). However, UHC does not explicitly identify which health services are covered, leaving States with the discretion to decide their own nationally determined sets of services.

In contrast, the right to health care provides relatively clear standards to which States must adhere – core obligations. More specifically, States have a non-derogable core obligation to 'ensure the satisfaction of the minimum essential levels of rights recognised in the Covenant, including essential primary health care'.[107] The CteeESCR further enumerates a relatively small but fundamental number of core obligations in relation to the right to health care, including one substantive component of primary health care – the provision of essential medicines. However, as argued in chapter 2, beyond the provision of essential medicines the CteeESCR is less explicit in detailing which elements of essential health care fall within the scope of core obligations.[108] This matter is further complicated by the fact that the CteeESCR identifies a number of obligations of comparable priority, which leaves the relationship between core obligations and obligations of comparable priorities unclear.

Nevertheless, despite these conceptual deficits, the interpretation of core obligations is still clearer than the definition of UHC:[109] States undertake a clear, non-derogable obligation under the right to health care to provide essential medicines. Arguably, the provision of essential medicines under UHC is also reflected in the definitions provided in the 2012 UNGA resolution and SDG 3.8. To this extent, UHC conforms with the right to health care. It deserves pointing out, however, that essential medicines are a *legally prioritised* health need under the right to health care. There are no circumstances in which any State is able to justify its failure to provide essential medicines. Therefore, when determining national essential health packages, it is of vital importance to include essential medicines, as this is certainly a legally binding obligation under the right to health care.

107 CteeESCR, General Comment 14 (n 8) para 43.
108 ibid.
109 ibid.

In determining which services should be covered by national essential health packages, another relevant issue concerns the prioritisation of the health needs of vulnerable and marginalised groups and their participation in the processes of health-related decision-making. Although the 2012 UNGA resolution acknowledges that 'governance to move towards universal health coverage involves transparent and inclusive and equitable decision-making processes',[110] this does not necessarily indicate that right-holders, especially vulnerable or marginalised groups, are provided with the conditions to participate in those processes. By contrast, the right to health care pays particular attention to participation, especially of vulnerable or marginalised groups.[111] States undertake a non-derogable core obligation to adopt a national public health strategy or plan of action through a participatory process. Dainius Puras, the present UN Special Rapporteur of the Right to Health, also advocates in his report that governments should make an explicit commitment to prioritising vulnerable segments of society in the process of expanding coverage or in determining which services to provide under UHC so as to prevent inequality.[112]

This brings to the next question as to which health services should be prioritised under UHC. A widely accepted principle under the UHC is cost-effectiveness.[113] The principle of cost-effectiveness is implied by General Comment 14, which states that, 'inappropriate health resource allocation can lead to discrimination that may not be overt'.[114] Accordingly, cost-effectiveness requires governments to fairly distribute its maximum available resources and to prioritise the needs of vulnerable or marginalised groups. This principle is applied when deciding the provision of expensive, curative health services accessible to a small group of people or primary and preventative health care benefitting a large group of people.[115] Clearly, the principle of cost-effectiveness is in line with the core obligation of equitable distribution.

However, as a WHO report suggests, the principle of cost-effectiveness may run the risk of pushing the rationing of care below the minimum essential level of the

110 UNGA, 'Global Health and Foreign Policy' (adopted 6 December 2012) UN Doc A/67/L.36, para 13.

111 CteeESCR, General Comment 14 (n 8) paras 11, 17, 54.

112 UNGA, 'Report of the Special Rapporteur on the Right of Everyone to the Enjoyment of the Highest Attainable Standard of Physical and Mental Health, Dainius Puras' (n 93) para 76.

113 WHO (n 6) 8.

114 ibid; CteeESCR, General Comment 14 (n 8) para 19.

115 ibid.

right to health (i.e. essential primary health care). Even if the level of health care provided in a country fails to address standard health concerns given the country's national context, UHC does not seem to prohibit this.[116] As a result, the national package of essential health care may not live up to the minimum level of health services to which all people should have access regardless of national context and cost-effectiveness.[117] As mentioned above, the right to health care can be considered to refine UHC by providing for a clear core obligation to prioritise the provision of essential medicines in resource allocation.

- Who is covered?

Both UHC and the right to health care provide for *universal* access to health care, which means that all people should be covered. However, as Hsiao and others observe, universal access does not necessarily guarantee everyone *equal* access to health care.[118] As will be discussed further in the Chinese context (section 4.3.2.4), people from urban and rural areas join different BMI schemes and therefore have different outpatient and inpatient service packages.

In comparison, the right to health care pays particular attention to vulnerable and marginalised groups within society. Equality, as an important principle under the right to health care, indicates that States take measures in favour of vulnerable or marginalised groups. For example, national health programmes must be designed so as to overcome the political, economic, social and cultural challenges that vulnerable and marginalised groups face in relation to access to health care.[119]

This brings us to the issue of non-discrimination. UHC aims to eliminate financial barriers to access to essential health care, which can at least bring an end to discrimination on the ground of financial status. To this extent, efforts made to achieve UHC through the removal of financial barriers contribute to the realisation of the right to health care. Nevertheless, UHC provides less clarity regarding other causes of discrimination.[120] In comparison, non-discrimination as a core obligation under the

116 WHO (n 6) 11.
117 ibid 5-13.
118 Hsiao and others (n 5) 1.
119 Gostin (n 66) 18.
120 WHO (n 6)11.

right to health care goes further by requiring governments to identify inequalities in access to health care that arise from discrimination on any internationally prohibited grounds, as detailed in chapter 2. UHC's focus on financial discrimination may result in a lack of attention being paid to other forms of discrimination, for example, *de facto* discrimination across regions.[121] Therefore, in addition to financial risk protection, it is desirable that UHC pays more attention to vulnerable and marginalised groups, with the aim of enhancing their ability to realise the right to health care. In addition, while expanding coverage percentages, decision-makers should also address other disparities in access to health care. Consequently, efforts towards UHC can provide protection against financial exclusion or any other discriminatory exclusions in the sets of health care provided nationally.

To summarise, to a certain degree UHC is consistent with standards under the right to health. However, right to health omissions have also been identified in the formulation and implementation of UHC. Therefore, we cannot conclude that China's efforts towards universal access to basic health care or UHC suffice to realise the right to health care. Nonetheless, this study contends that core obligations under the right to health care do have the potential to address the shortcomings of UHC. The following subsection continues to explore what core obligations can contribute to the refinement of UHC.

4.2.4.4 Reconciling core obligations under the right to health care with Universal Health Coverage

Decision-makers often face the question of how the State's internationally binding obligations fit with their obligations to fairly set health policy priorities along the three dimensions of UHC (the range of services, the proportion of the population covered, and the proportion of costs covered).[122] Arguably, decision-makers with different responsibilities may take different approaches to improving the health of the population. For example, health planners may take a utilitarian approach in order to maximise health benefits across the population, while legislators and judges make decisions based on the State's responsibility to protect the right to health care.

121 ibid.

122 Benedict Rumbold, 'Universal Health Coverage, Priority Setting, and the Human Right to Health' (26 April 2017) The Lancet Viewpoint 1, 1.

Nevertheless, these two approaches are not necessarily irreconcilable. Rather, as observed by Rumbold and others, the right to health care can aid priority-setting by informing decision-makers what the legally prioritised health needs are. Vice versa, by applying right to health standards that extend beyond utilitarian calculations, efforts towards UHC can indeed contribute to the realisation of the right to health care.[123]

As explained in the previous section, core obligations under the right to health care can refine the UHC in the following ways:

Firstly, core obligations answer the question of who the decision-makers are. In other words, when making health-related decisions, all stakeholders, including vulnerable and marginalised groups in particular, should be involved in the decision-making processes. National health strategies or plans of action should be designed through a transparent and participatory process, and the prioritised health needs of vulnerable and marginalised groups should be taken into consideration.

Secondly, the right to health framework provides for a minimum essential level of health care that each country should provide even when facing resource scarcity, i.e. essential primary health care. More specifically, States undertake a non-derogable core obligation to provide essential medicines. As such, decision-makers should set the provision of essential medicines as the top health policy priority. In addition to this non-derogable core obligation, States should discharge a handful of obligations with comparable priority. States should also reflect these obligations in domestic health policies and programmes. If they fail to do so, States have the burden of proof to demonstrate that the maximum available resources have been used.

Thirdly, non-discrimination as a core obligation under the right to health care provides a compelling framework for addressing issues of discrimination (extending beyond financial discrimination), exclusion and power asymmetries. This means, for example, that if decision-makers fail to provide all population with equal access to health care or to fairly distribute health resources, the right to health framework will provide legal recourses. As will be discussed in part 2 if the status quo in a given country fails to meet the core obligations under the right to health care, this right allows individuals as right-holders to hold responsible decision-makers to account.

123 ibid.

In this regard, litigation can be a mechanism for redress.[124]

4.3 The evaluation of progress towards the realisation of the right to health care in China

As shown in Table 4.3, China has issued a substantial number of national health policies to move towards UHC.[125] Clear progress towards basic UHC has been made since the launch of China's NHR in 2006, which has included the expansion of health insurance coverage to nearly 95% of the entire population,[126] and the establishment of a national essential medicines system (NEMS) that significantly improves the availability and (economic) accessibility of essential medicines.[127] This section seeks to reflect on the major health care reforms and evaluate whether the policy changes have had a positive impact on equal access to basic health care. Within this context, the following subsections focus on China's policy commitments concerning access to basic health care (i.e. access to essential medicines) and financial risk protection (health insurance coverage). The assessment is based on the core obligations under the right to health care.

4.3.1 Major health care reforms

As the world's most populous country, China has long struggled with the establishment of a health care system that functions for the entire population. Before China initiated the NHR, the health care system had long been criticised for being '*kanbingnan, kanbinggui*' (which literally means that access to health services was limited and unaffordable).[128] During that time, the widening health inequities and insufficient

124 ibid 2.

125 National Health Policies, the official website of the WHO <www.who.int/nationalpolicies/en/> accessed 20 November 2017.

126 Information Office of the State Council of the People's Republic of China, *Progress in China's Human Rights in 2014* (2015), ch I <http://english.gov.cn/archive/white_paper/2015/06/08/content_281475123202380.htm> accessed 28 November 2017.

127 Wenhui Mao and Wen Chen, 'The Zero Mark-up Policy for Essential Medicines at Primary Level Facilities' in Improving Health System Efficiency (WHO 2015) 4; WHO and OCED, Health at Glance Asia/Pacific 2014: Measuring Progress towards Universal Health Coverage (OECD 2014), 83; The State Council of the People's Republic of China, *Implementation Plan for the Recent Priorities of the Health Care System Reform (2009-2011)* (2009), para 2.

128 Alexander Korolev, 'Deliberative Democracy Nationwide? - Evaluating Deliberativeness of Healthcare Reform in China' (2014) 19 Journal of Chinese Political Science 151, 157.

government stewardship eroded public support for and trust in China's health care system and even challenged the government's legitimacy.[129] To deal with this difficult situation, the central government launched its NHR in 2006.[130] As will be explained further below, China's health care reforms can be divided into three phases.

4.3.1.1 Phase one: Before China's reform and opening-up in 1979

Following the Soviet Union's socialist model, China has adopted a highly centralised planned economic system since the foundation of the People's Republic of China in 1949. Private ownership, including private medical practice or private ownership of health facilities, were all replaced by public ownership.[131] The government, both at the central and local levels, played a central role in financing and managing the health care system. Hospitals were State-owned; health services were provided by health professionals who were employed by the State.[132]

During this phase, the medical security system comprised three major components: a cooperative medical scheme (CMS); a medical insurance scheme for government employees; and a medical insurance scheme for labourers. The CMS was a financial risk protection mechanism in rural areas. It was based on mutual assistance and jointly funded by communes, the government budget, and patients' out-of-pocket payments. Very basic health care was provided under the CMS, generally by township health centres or 'barefoot doctors' (who are equivalent to community health workers but receive less training).[133] In urban areas, the medical insurance scheme for government employees was established, covering civil servants, employees of public institutions, and university and college students. This scheme was mainly funded by the government and covered costs for both outpatient and inpatient services. Public, State-owned enterprises (SOE) organised and financed hospitals and clinics for workers in the form of the medical insurance for labourers. Funds for this scheme were raised from the revenue of SOEs. Workers' family members were also covered under this scheme,

129 Shenglan Tang and others, 'Tackling the Challenges to Health Equity in China' (2008) 372 The Lancet 1493, 1496.
130 Korolev (n 128) 157.
131 Meng and others (n 5) 160.
132 Winnie Yip and William Hsiao, 'What Drove the Circles of Chinese Health System Reforms' (2015) 1 Health Systems & Reform 52, 54.
133 ibid; Meng and others (n 5)162.

and could receive 50% reimbursement for their medical expenses. Community health clinics and hospitals, mainly financed by local governments, also provided basic health services to urban residents who were not affiliated with SOEs.[134]

During this period, the Chinese government gave priorities to health prevention and primary health care (PHC) to reconstruct its health care system. Remarkable progress was made despite severe resource constraints. For example, during that period, the mortality rate of children under the age of five dropped tremendously, from 200 to 57 per 1,000 live births. Life expectancy also rose from 45 to almost 68 years.[135]

4.3.1.2 Phase two: 1980s to 2006

From the 1980s until 2006, the central government did not follow the socialist model after embarking on its economic reform in 1978. This period has long been criticised for being '*kanbinnan, kanbingui*' (meaning that access to health services is limited and unaffordable).[136] One remarkable feature of this reform was the transition from a planned economy to a market economy, which not only influenced the economic sector but also had a significant impact on the health sector.[137] During this transition, there was a significant drop in government revenue. Given the fiscal constraints, by the early 1990s government subsidies for public health facilities had fallen from 60% to merely 10% of the facilities' total revenues.[138] To compensate for this financial gap, the Chinese government allowed public health care providers to charge patients directly for services as their main source of revenue. The government also allowed a 15% profit margin on drugs. What's more, health policy during this phase even encouraged public health care providers to deliver 'income-earning sideline services', such as 'special wards' or 'special attendance', which further widened inequalities concerning access to health care.[139] These health policies turned public health care providers into *de facto* for-profit entities. Misaligned incentives led to the over-prescription of drugs and tests, and out-of-pocket payment skyrocketed as a result.

134 Yip and Hsiao (n 132) 54.
135 ibid 55.
136 Korolev (n 128) 157.
137 Meng and others (n 5) 163.
138 ibid 164; Yip and Hsiao (n 132) 55.
139 Yip and Hsiao (n 132) 55.

Furthermore, health institutions paid little attention to maternal and children's health, epidemic control and health education.[140]

The outbreak of the Severe Acute Respiratory Syndrome (SARS) epidemic in 2003 placed this misguided health care system under the spot light and triggered public outcry.[141] Public dissatisfaction with the health care system even challenged the government's legitimacy.[142] In July 2005, the central government officially admitted that this reform was unsuccessful and that a new round of health care reform would be initiated the following year.[143]

4.3.1.3 Phase three: 2006 to the present

China's NHR was initiated in 2006. After three years of preparation and debate, the Chinese government issued the *Opinions of the Central Committee of the Central Party Committee and the State Council on Deepening the Reform of the Pharmaceutical and Healthcare Systems* in 2009, which marked the beginning of the NHR.[144] The primary goal of the NHR is to provide safe, efficient and affordable basic health care for all Chinese residents by 2020. Remarkably, the Opinions reaffirmed the government's role in financing health care. Five reform priorities were also targeted: (1) the expansion of health insurance coverage to insure at least 90% of the population; (2) the establishment of a national essential medicines system; (3) the improvement of the primary care delivery system for providing basic health care and managing referrals to specialist care and hospitals; (4) the provision of equal access to public health services; (5) the stimulation of the pilot reform of public hospitals.[145]

Since the Opinions was issued in 2009, steps have been taken to ensure universal access to basic health care for both rural and urban residents. For example, as Table 4.3 demonstrates, a wide variety of health policies were issued to move closer to UHC. More specifically, a total amount of 850 billion CNY (approximately 115 billion

140 Meng and others (n 5) 164-166.
141 ibid 24.
142 Tang and others (n 129) 1493-1499.
143 Korolev (n 128) 157.
144 Central Committee of the Communist Party of China, State Council (n 3).
145 The State Council, 'Implementation Plan for the Recent Priorities of the Health Care System Reform (2009-2011)' (2009).

euros) was invested in the NHR.[146] Three basic medical insurance (BMI) schemes were also established, expanding the coverage of health insurance from 29.7% in 2003 to nearly 95% by the end of 2014.[147] In addition, to ensure access to essential medicines, the NEMS was established in 2009, which significantly improves the availability and (economic) accessibility of essential medicines.[148]

On the basis of the core obligations identified in chapter 2 and the standards of availability and accessibility, the following subsections discuss the impacts of policies on China's progression towards right to health-based UHC and the remaining challenges, in two core areas: financial risk protection (i.e. equal access and affordability of health care) and access to essential medicines.

4.3.2 Basic medical insurance system

Over the past decade, China has gradually reformed its health care system and managed to provide basic UHC to over 1.3 billion individuals. This achievement has been marked as 'unparalleled' by the World Bank.[149] One of the most important components of China's UHC is the provision of basic medical insurance covering both urban and rural residents. To eliminate financial barriers in achieving universal access to basic health care and to promote health equity, China has invested a great amount of money in the health sector (CNY 850 billion) and established three BMI schemes through the NHR to reduce out-of-pocket payments.[150] By the end of 2014, these three major insurance schemes, which include the UEBMI, URBMI and NRCMS, covered over 95% of the entire population.[151] For the poor in both urban and rural areas who cannot afford their premium, the Medical Financial Assistant schemes help them to enrol in the BMIs and also provide additional reimbursements for their medical expenses.[152] The establishment of the basic medical security net

146 Yip and others (n 57) 833.

147 Information Office of the State Council, 'Progress in China's Human Rights in 2014' (2015), ch I <http://english.gov.cn/archive/white_paper/2015/06/08/content_281475123202380.htm> accessed 28 November 2017.

148 Mao and Chen (n 127) 4; WHO and OCED (n 127) 83; The State Council, 'Implementation Plan for the Recent Priorities of the Health Care System Reform (2009-2011)' (2009), para 2.

149 Liang and Langenbrunner (n 5) v.

150 Meng and others (n 5) 71.

151 Information Office of the State Council (n 147).

152 Meng and others (n 5) 78.

has also led to the significant decrease of 24.6% in out-of-pocket expenditure as a share of total expenditure on health. This was the largest reduction in out-of-pocket payments in all Asia-Pacific countries between the years 2000 and 2012.[153]

4.3.2.1 The Urban Employees' Basic Medical Insurance

The Urban Employees' Basic Medical Insurance (UEBMI) was launched in 1998 as the government's first step towards re-establishing its medical security system in urban areas. The UEBMI is a mandatory basic medical insurance for urban employees of State-owned or private enterprises.[154]

Most of the funding for this insurance scheme comes from employees and employers. Local governments, mainly at the municipal level, decide the specific contribution rate for employers and employees, as well as the level of deductibles and reimbursement caps, according to their own economic level. In general, contributions from employees should be no less than 2% of their average income and contributions from employers should be at least 6% of their monthly income. Retired persons are not required to make contributions. Self-employed individuals and workers that have been laid-off can voluntarily enrol in the UEBMI by paying the premium contributed by both the employers and employees, on the basis of the specific municipal city's average income in the previous year.[155] The raised funds are distributed into two separate accounts: the pooling fund (i.e. Social Pooling Account or 'SPA') and a personal account for each individual benefitting from the scheme (i.e. Medical Savings Account or 'MSA'). All employees' contributions and about 30% of employers' contributions go into the MSA; the remainder of the employers' contributions goes to the SPA. The two accounts are managed separately and pay for different services: the MSA covers outpatient and emergency services as well as drug expenses, while the SPA covers inpatient services. The reimbursement rate of these services is decided by local governments, mainly municipal human resources and social security bureaux.[156]

4.3.2.2 The Urban Residents' Basic Medical Insurance

153 WHO and OECD (n 127) 83.
154 State Council, 'Decision on Establishing Urban Employee Basic Medical Insurance Scheme' (1998).
155 Meng and others (n 5) 78-86
156 ibid.

In 2007, the State Council issued guiding opinions to establish its Urban Residents' Basic Medical Insurance (URBMI).[157] According to the guidelines, urban residents who are not covered by the UEBMI can enrol in the URBMI on a voluntary basis. The main purpose of the URBMI is to prevent all urban residents without formal employment from being impoverished by chronic or catastrophic diseases. The URBMI was first piloted in 79 cities before being expanded on a national basis in 2010, gradually extending to cover all unemployed urban residents.

The funding of this insurance scheme mainly comes from individuals. The government also provides some subsidies, as supplementary to the premium contributions. The premium is determined by local governments at the municipal level in accordance with the local economic level, medical care expense level, and the participants' household income level. There are extra governmental subsidies available to low-income families, the disabled, and teenagers.[158] Urban residents enrolled with URBMI are eligible for the reimbursement of outpatient visits, inpatient services and designated pharmacies that are under included in the national insurance list.[159]

4.3.2.3 The New Rural Cooperative Medical Scheme

In 2003, the State Council issued guidelines to further enhance the rural health care system, with the aim of re-establishing the rural cooperative medical system. The New Rural Cooperative Medical Scheme (NRCMS) was first piloted in selected counties and gradually expanded nationwide. By the end of 2012, it covered more than 98% of all rural residents.[160]

The NRCMS was organised and supported by the government, and voluntarily participated in by rural residents at the household level. Approximately 80% of the total NRCMS fund was provided by government subsidies, while the remainder was supplied through individuals' premiums. The central government has the ultimate

157 State Council, 'Guiding Opinions of the State Council about the Pilot Urban Residents' Basic Medical Insurance' (2007).

158 See generally Meng and other (n 5) 78-86; <www.albertoforchielli.com/2015/11/13/the-chinese-healthcare-system-how-it-works-and-future-trends/> accessed 28 November 2017.

159 Meng and others (n 5) 78.

160 (Former) Ministry of Health, Ministry of Finance, Ministry of Agriculture, 'Opinions on Establishing New Rural Cooperative Medical Scheme' Guoban fa [2003] No.3.

responsibility for subsiding the central and western regions of China.[161] The NRCMS provides partial coverage for inpatient and catastrophic outpatient services. The pooling administration authority at county level can decide the scope, level and amount of reimbursement according to local economic development levels.[162]

4.3.2.4 The issue of health equity

The three basic medical insurance schemes have contributed to an overall improvement in the accessibility, and especially the affordability, of health care. However, as Hsiao and others have correctly pointed out, broader health insurance coverage does not necessarily guarantee everyone equal access to affordable health care.[163] In fact, as shown in Annex 3, significant gaps exist between these three BMI schemes, including the coverage of benefits, reimbursement rates and ceilings, as well as the list of drugs that may be reimbursed. In general, the UEBMI has a broader coverage of benefits, which includes both inpatient and general outpatient services. In comparison, the URBMI and NRCMS cover impatient services and limited outpatient services. In addition, the UEBMI has a much higher reimbursement rate and ceiling than that of the URBMI and NRCMS.[164] In terms of the disparity between the drugs that could be reimbursed, the UEBMI and URBMI shared the same national reimbursement drug list established by the MOHRSS, according to which a total of 2,127 drugs can be reimbursed. Each province is also allowed to make its own supplementary reimbursement drug list.[165] In contrast, the NRCMS does not have a unified national reimbursement drug list; the NRCMS authority, which is usually the health and family planning bureaux at the municipal level, has the right to determine its own county, town and village drug lists. Generally, a county list is suggested to include 800-1,200 drugs.[166] Obviously, the UEBMI and URBMI have a much wider coverage

161 Meng and others (n 5) 65.
162 ibid 78-86.
163 William Hsiao and others (n 5) 1.
164 ibid 16-17.
165 Ministry of Human Resources and Social Security, 'Guojia Jiben Yiliaobaoxian, Gongshangbaoxian he Shengyubaoxian Yaopin Mulu [National Reimbursement Drug List for National Basic Medical Insurance, Work-related Injury Insurance and Maternity Insurance]' (2009) Author's tranlation.
166 (Former) Ministry of Health, 'Weishengbu Guanyu Tiaozheng he Zhiding Xinxing Nongcun Hezuo Yiliao Baoxiao Yaowu Mulu de Yijian [Opinions on the Adjustment and Formulation of Medical Reimbursement Drug List for New Rural Cooperative Medical Scheme 2009]' Author's translation.

than the NRCMS.

Moreover, since the insurance funds are pooled at the municipal level for the UEBMI and URBMI, and at the county level for the NRCMS, local governments have the authority to determine the coverage of benefits, the level of deductibles, co-payments, reimbursement rates and ceiling, as well as the supplementary reimbursement drug list, depending on the development levels of the local economy. Disparities across regions are thus observable, especially between rural and urban areas and across the eastern and western regions of the country.[167] The fragmentation of risk pools also has a negative impact on portability, given the restrictions on claiming benefits outside of the region of enrolment, resulting in the inefficiency of the whole insurance system.[168] Particularly, it may lead to unequal access to health care among specific members of the population, especially migrant workers.[169]

The disparities across populations with different social-economic status and between rural and urban areas constitute *de facto* discrimination in equal access to health care. As a party to the ICESCR, China undertakes an obligation of immediate effect to eliminate all forms of discrimination in the provision of health care.[170]

In early 2016, one step was taken to close the gaps between rural and urban residents. The Chinese government announced its decision to merge the URBMI and NRCMS in a bid to develop a unified basic medical insurance system.[171] According to the *Opinions on Integrating the Basic Medical Insurance Systems for Urban and Rural Residents* issued by the State Council, the integrated insurance would unify, *inter alia*, the coverage, the reimbursement rate and ceiling, the reimbursement drug list, and fund raising policies and management of both schemes, thus improving equal access to health care for both urban and rural residents. Under this new scheme, all insured residents would enjoy the same payment standards and scope of subsidies, although still subject to the local economic level and different from the UEBMI.

167 See Annex 3 for the detailed comparison.

168 If patients want to seek medical care outside of the city/county of enrolment, they first have to pay out-of-pocket, then claim a reimbursement afterwards in their own region. This often happens when patients want to receive special care in tertiary hospitals in big cities such as Beijing and Shanghai. See Liang and Langenbrunner (n 5) 27.

169 ibid.

170 CteeESCR, General Comment 14 (n 8) para 19.

171 State Council, 'Guanyu Zhenghe Chengxiang Jumin Jiben Yiliao Baoxian Zhidu d Yijian [Guideline on the Integration of Urban Residents' Basic Medical Insurance and New Rural Cooperative Medical Scheme]' (2016). Author's translation

Therefore, the implementation of the integrated scheme should pay attention to some key aspects, including in particular the increase of portability for migrant workers, the establishment of cross-region reimbursement mechanisms and raising the risk pooling from the city/county level to the provincial level.

4.3.3 The provision of essential medicines

Access to essential medicines is globally perceived as a fundamental component of the right to health care and of universal access to health care as recognised in the SDGs.[172] As discussed in chapter 2, the Committee on Economic, Social and Cultural Rights emphasises in its General Comment 14 that States undertake a core obligation to 'provide essential drugs, as from time to time defined under the WHO Action Programme.'[173] According to the latest WHO definition, essential medicines are 'those that satisfy the priority health care needs of the population. Essential medicines are selected with due regard to their public health relevance, evidence of efficacy and safety, and comparative cost-effective.'[174] Moreover, 'essential medicines are intended to be available within the context of functioning health systems at all times, in adequate amounts, in the appropriate dosage forms, with assured quality, and at a price the individual and the community can afford.'[175] While internatioanlly essential medicines are defined within the framework of the WHO Model Lists of Essental Medicines, it remains a national responsibility to decide which medicines are essential.[176] However, in fulfilling its core obligtion under the right to health care, a State should select essential medicines that reflect the prioritised health needs of its population. It is thereby necessary to evaluate how China translates this recognition into action, and how access to essential medicines as a core obligation arising from the right to health care inspires China's national health policy.

172 Hans Hogerzeil and others, 'Is Access to Essential Medicines as Part of the Fulfilment of the Right to Health Enforceable throught the courts?' (2006) 368 The Lancet 305; Hans Hogerzeil and Zafar Mirza, 'The World Medicines Situation 2011: Access to Essential Medicines as Part of the Right to Health' (WHO 2011) 4.

173 CteeESCR, General Comment 14 (n 8) para 43.

174 WHO, The Selection and Use of Essential Medicines: WHO Technical Report 985 (2013) 4.

175 WHO, The Selection and Use of Essential Medicines: WHO Technical Report 933 (2006) 54.

176 ibid; UNGA, 'Report of the Special Rapporteur on the Right of Everyone to the Enjoyment of the Highest Attainable Standard of Physical and Mental Health, Anand Grover' (1 May 2013) UN Doc A/HRC/23/42, paras 3-6..

4.3.3.1 Current reform of China's National Essential Medicines System

One of the core obligations that China undertakes under the right to health care is the provision of essential medicines.[177] To promote equal access to affordable essential medicines with assured quality, the current health care reform has given priority to the establishment of a national essential medicines system (NEMS). In 2009, China issued the *Implementation Opinions on Establishing the National Essential Medicines System* to direct the development of the NEMS.[178] The Opinions defined essential medicines in the same fashion as the WHO. It also required the government to set up a basic platform for the NEMS by 2011 and to reach its full implementation by 2020.[179] To achieve this goal, between 2009 and 2011 a comprehensive set of essential medicines policies (EMP), including the selection, production, procurement, distribution, pricing control, reimbursement, quality control and rational use of essential medicines were carried out (as shown in Table 4.3).[180]

As a core element of the NEMS, the National Essential Medicines List (NEML) (primary section) was published in 2009 (but was no longer in effect). The 2009 NEML included a total of 307 generic medicines, which was then updated to 520 generic medicines in 2012.[181] However, even though the *Administration of National Essential Medicines List* requires the NEML to in principle be adjusted every three years, the list has not been updated since 2012.[182] Many provinces have also formulated a supplementary essential medicines list according to the local economic level and local needs. Most importantly, all medicines listed on the NEML are included in the reimbursement drug list of the three BMIs, with a higher reimbursement ratio than that

177 CteeESCR, General Comment 14 (n 8) para 43(d).

178 The Ministry of Health, National Development and Reform Commission, Ministry of Industry and Information Technology, Ministry of Supervision, Ministry of Finance, Ministry of Human Resources and Social Security, Ministry of Commerce, China Food and Drug Administration and State Administration of Traditional Chinese Medicine of the People's Republic of China, 'Guanyu Jianli Guojia Jiben Yaowu Zhidu de Shishi Yijian [Implementation Opinions on Establishing the National Essential Medicines System] (2009), para 1. <www.nhfpc.gov.cn/zwgk/wtwj/201304/f2a0d9cbc33f45e091a9d4a936c6fe58.shtml> accessed 28 November 2017 Author's translation.

179 ibid, para 19.

180 Meng and others (n 5) 87.

181 Mao and Chen (n 127) 15.

182 National Health and Family Planning Commission, 'Guojia Jiben Yaowu Mulu Guanli Banfa[Administration of National Essential Medicines List]' (2015). Author's translation.

of unlisted medicines, leading to an observable drop in out-of-pocket expenditure.[183]

To further promote the affordability of essential medicines, a zero-mark-up policy was introduced in 2009 to eliminate drug mark-ups as a compensation mechanism.[184] This policy was first implemented in public PHC institutions between 2009 and 2011. Its implementation in secondary and tertiary hospitals is now gradually being expanded. Remarkably, local governments were required to grant a special subsidy to compensate PHC institutions for the reduced drug profit and to maintain the daily operation of these institutions.[185]

According to the EMP, all government-run PHC institutions were required, by the end of 2011, to be equipped with and use drugs listed on the NEML as well as the respective provincial supplementary list. Moreover, these institutions were only allowed to prescribe and sell essential medicines at procurement price without mark-up (i.e. the zero-mark-up policy).[186] The implementation of these EMP has had a positive impact on the reduction in out-of-pocket payment.[187] However, at the present stage of reform, EMP may have a perverse effect on access to affordable and quality essential medicines at PHC institutions for a number of reasons that will be discussed further below.[188]

4.3.3.2 The impact of China's Essential Medicines Policy

The elimination of drug mark-ups has removed economic incentives for the over-prescription of drugs and promoted the rational use of medicines. However, an alternative compensation mechanism for PHC institutions has not yet been properly formulated. Ultimately, this may negatively affect the availability of essential medicines. According to EMP, PHC institutions are not allowed to sell non-essential medicines or mark up drug prices, thus the major way for them to generate revenue is by charging for medical services, the importance of which is currently underestimated in China. Therefore, the operation of PHC institutions relies largely

183 Mao and Chen (n 127) 4; WHO and OCED (n 127) 83.
184 Meng and others (n 5) 176.
185 Mao and Chen (n 127) 13-14.
186 ibid 4 14--21.
187 WHO and OCED (n 127) 83.
188 Mao and Chen (2015) 23; Shanlian Hu, 'Essential Medicine Policy in China: Pros and Cons' (2013) 16 Journal of Medical Economics 289, 291-292.

on financial subsidies from local governments. For those PHC institutions in less developed regions, there is very often insufficient funding from the local government to support them. Furthermore, there is no specific law or regulation stipulating the government's responsibility in this regard. Consequently, it is difficult for those institutions to maintain their daily operation and development. This leads to health professionals, who can benefit from drug mark-ups, leaving the institutions. Thus, the lack of a proper compensation mechanism has a negative impact on the availability and accessibility of health services and goods, including essential medicines.[189]

Secondly, the zero-mark-up policy may also have a negative impact on the implementation of EMP due to the lack of a well-designed incentive programme. The health and family planning bureaux adopted EMP to restrict PHC institutions to sell only essential medicines. However, this was done through an administrative mandate rather than through an incentive programme, and the authority failed to state any concrete goals in the EMP. Therefore, PHC institutions as well as their physicians are generally not very motivated to fulfil EMP and to promote the use of essential medicines.[190]

Thirdly, although price control measures were taken to promote the affordability of essential medicines, they may lead to the lower availability and poor quality of essential medicines. To compete with others in the tendering procedures, pharmaceutical companies tend to decrease the price of their products. Indeed, some companies may even submit bids below cost.[191] However, since there are no strong financial incentives, a pharmaceutical company may not produce essential medicines to its full capacity, resulting in a shortage of certain medicines. What is even worse is that to ensure the affordability of essential medicines, local authorities very often pay most attention to the price of medicines – less emphasis is placed on the quality of the medicines.[192] The press has revealed several scandals regarding poor-quality medicines produced by selected pharmaceutical companies. Corruption was also reported in the tendering process. Therefore, a comprehensive monitoring mechanism is of great importance in the production and procurement processes of

189 Hu (n 188) 291-292. Gang Cheng and others, 'Woguo Jiben Yaowu Lingchalv Zhengce Cunzai de Wenti yu Tiaozheng Celue [Zero Mark-up Policy of Essential Medicines System in China: Problems and Recommendations]' (2011) 4 (10) China Health Policy Research 39, 40-41.

190 ibid 41.

191 Hu (n 188) 292; Sarah Barber and others, 'The Reform of the Essential Medicines System in China: A Comprehensive Approach to Universal Coverage' (2013) 3 (1) Journal of Global Health 1, 3-5.

192 Barber and others (n 191) 5.

essential medicines. [193]

4.4 Concluding summary

Chapter 4 has moved from the purely legal approach of the previous chapters to evaluate China's policy commitments towards the right to health care. As demonstrated in this chapter, China has issued a wide variety of national health policies over the past decades, and has achieved considerable progress towards UHC.[194] This progress is reflected in an effort to expand the proportion of the population covered by UHC from 29.7% in 2003 to nearly 95% by the end of 2014. It is also reflected in China's effort to gradually expand the range of health services provided under UHC, from covering only inpatient services to include outpatient services and catastrophic diseases. China has also established the NEMS to ensure access to essential medicines. In addition, the affordability of health care services and goods has been significantly improved through the establishment of three BMI schemes. Some of these efforts towards UHC have indeed promoted the progressive realisation of the right to health care in China.

Nevertheless, it is too soon to conclude that China's policy commitments towards UHC is equivalent to its fulfilment of the (core) obligations under the right to health care. As explained earlier, measures adopted to achieve UHC have nevertheless left some requirements of the right to health care unfulfilled. This includes, in particular, the protection of individuals from all types of discrimination in the nationally determined set of essential health care.

This chapter thus proposed a refinement of UHC by reconciling core obligations under the right to health care with UHC. As informed by core obligations, in determining national UHC, all stakeholders, including vulnerable and marginalised groups in particular, should be involved in decision-making through a transparent and participatory process. The prioritised health needs of vulnerable and marginalised groups should be taken into consideration. In addition, the provision of essential medicines should be set as the top priority for health policy-making. Moreover, non-discrimination as a core obligation under the right to health care provides a compelling framework for addressing issues of discrimination (extending beyond financial

193 Hu (n 188) 292.
194 National health policies, the official website of the WHO <www.who.int/nationalpolicies/en/≥ accessed 25 January 2017.

discrimination), exclusion and power asymmetries. This means, for example, that if decision-makers fail to provide the entire population with equal access to health care or to fairly distribute health resources, the right to health framework will provide legal recourse. If the status quo in a given country fails to meet the core obligations under the right to health care, this right allows individuals, as right-holders, to hold responsible decision-makers to account. In this regard, litigation can be a mechanism for redress.

In light of this, I identified the remaining challenges to achieving UHC from a human rights perspective, in spite of its impressive accomplishments. Although China's UHC has reached over 95% of the entire population, disparities between people with different socio-economic status and between rural and urban areas have resulted in *de facto* discrimination in equal access to health care. The fragmentation of risk pools also had a negative impact on portability, which may lead to the inefficiency of the whole insurance system as well as unequal access to health care for specific population such as migrant workers (i.e. geographic discrimination). In terms of access to essential medicines, the lack of an appropriate compensation mechanism for PHC institutions (i.e. a well-designed incentive programme for health professionals) and the lack of proper pricing control measures would continue to negatively affect the availability, accessibility and quality of essential medicines. Finally, as will be discussed in chapter 7, we witnessed the inclusion of society in health policy-making, although this approach was not entirely transparent and participatory. No particular attention has been paid to the vulnerable and marginalised groups and their prioritised health needs.

Making progress towards the right to health care requires the Chinese government to take further steps to address these challenges and to strengthen the building blocks of the health system. While there are numerous approaches, this study chose to consider these challenges through the lens of accountability and to assess the implementation of the right to health care in the context of China's unique legal, political and social background.

Table 4.3 Main health-related documents in China

Year	Title of Documents	Key Content Regarding the Right to Health (Care)
1998	**Decision on Establishing Urban Employee Basic Medical Insurance Scheme**	**Target population:** employees (including retirees) in urban areas (mandatory) **Premium levels:** cities at the prefecture level and municipal level for Beijing, Shanghai and Tianjin **Fundraising:** individual contributions and employer contributions **Fund pooling:** social pooling and personal savings accounts **Service package:** N/A **Fund management:** MOHRSS
2003	**Opinions on Establishing New Rural Cooperative Medical Scheme**	**Principle and goal:** each province (region or municipality) should launch the pilot in 2-3 counties and gradually expand the pilots and ultimately achieve nation-wide implementation of the NRCMS by 2010. **Target population**: residents in rural areas (voluntary) **Premium levels**: counties at the prefecture level **Fundraising**: individuals contribute no less than 10 RMB per year; local governments contribute no less than 10 RMB per person per year, central government subsidises 10 RMB per year in central and western regions (excluding cities) **Fund pooling:** social pooling **Service package**: inpatient services or catastrophic medical expenses **Fund management**: MOH (currently the NHFPC)
2007	**Guiding Opinions of the State Council about the Pilot Urban Resident Basic Medical Insurance**	**Principle and goal:** capable provinces can launch the pilot in 2-3 cities in 2007, increase the pilot cities to 80% and achieve nation-wide implementation of the URBMI by 2010. **Target population**: unemployed residents (including students) in urban areas (voluntary) **Premium levels**: cities at the prefecture level

Year	Title of Documents	Key Content Regarding the Right to Health (Care)
2007	**Guiding Opinions of the State Council about the Pilot Urban Resident Basic Medical Insurance**	**Fundraising**: individual contributions; local governments contribute no less than 40 RMB per person per year, central government subsidises 20 RMB per year to residents in central and western regions (excluding cities); central government provides additional allowance to special groups of people such as poor or disabled students and children, the elderly and the disabled **Fund pooling:** social pooling **Service package**: inpatient services or outpatient services for critical-illness **Fund management**: MOHRSS
2009	**Opinions on Deepening the Health Care System Reform**	**Tenet:** a basic medical and health care system is a public good which should be made accessible to all **The overall goal:** establish a basic medical and health care system covering both rural and urban residents by 2020, and ensure the provision of safe, efficient, convenient and affordable medical and health care services **Short-term target:** by 2011, effectively alleviate residents' economic burden in seeking medical care and the problem of being 'kanbinnan, kanbingui (meaning that access to health services is limited and unaffordable)'
2009	**Implementation Plan for the Recent Priorities of the Health Care System Reform (2009–2011)**	**Five reform priorities and their targets, tasks and policies:** Expand the **BMI coverage**: average enrolment rate of the three BMIs will be increased to 90% or above within three years, government subsidy for the URBMI and NRCMS to 120 RMB per person per year and the reimbursement cap for NRCMS will be increased to six times the income of local farmers; a trans-regional mechanism will be established to settle health care fees incurred outside of the area; Establish a preliminary **NEMS**: announce the NEML by 2009; all pharmacies and health care institutions are required to stock and sell EM; as of 2009 all government-run PHC institutions are required to ensure the availability and accessibility of EM and sell EM with zero mark-up, other health care institutions are to use EM in accordance with rules; all EM are to be included in the reimbursement drug list with a higher reimbursement ratio than that of non-EM;

Year	Title of Documents	Key Content Regarding the Right to Health (Care)
2009	**Implementation Plan for the Recent Priorities of the Health Care System Reform (2009–2011)**	Establish a basic **public health** system with equal access for all residents; increase major national public health programmes for major disease prevention and control such as Tuberculosis and HIV/AIDS; increase average per capita basic public health funding to 20 RMB or above in 2012; Improve the **PHC delivery system**: within three years, support constructing around 2,000 county-level hospitals, ensure that each county has at least one county hospital that meets the industry standard; complete the construction of 29,000 township health centres; support constructing village clinics in remote and border areas, ensure that each administrative village has one clinic; strengthen the building of a health professional system for PHC; reform the compensation mechanism for PHC institutions; Spur the pilot reform of **public hospitals**: reform the management, operation and supervision of public hospitals; push forward the reform of the compensation mechanism for public hospitals; accelerate the formulation of a health care delivery system within both public and private hospitals.
2009	**National Essential Medicines List (Primary Section) (2009 Version)**	The NEML is divided into two parts: the part to be used by the PHC and public health institutions and the other part to be used by all other health care institutions. In total, it includes 205 chemical drugs and biological products and 102 TCM, and Chinese herbal medicines.
2009	**Implementing Opinions on Establishing the National Essential Medicines System**	**The Opinions requires to:** define EM and NEMS; set up a National Essential Medicines Working Committee ('NEMWC') responsible for the policies that will direct NEMS, as well as the formulation, approval and adjustment of the NEML; announce the NEML by 2009 and in principle adjust the list every three years; the NDRC determines the pricing policy for the NEML, provincial governments perform centralised online public biding and procurement; all government-run PHC institutions are required to ensure the availability and accessibility of EM and sell them with zero mark-up, local governments are required to establish a subsidy mechanism; all EM are to be included in the reimbursement drug list with a higher reimbursement ratio than that of non-EM; the supply of EM that are with uncertain usage but clinically indispensable must be guaranteed.

Year	Title of Documents	Key Content Regarding the Right to Health (Care)
2009	**Implementing Opinions on Establishing the National Essential Medicines System**	**Key targets:** each province (region or municipality) implements NEMS in at least 30% of the government-run city and county health care institutions by 2009, including: achieve provincial-level centralised online public bidding and procurement, incorporate consolidated distribution, use and sell EM with zero mark-up; preliminarily establish the NEMS by 2011 and fully implement the NEMS nation-wide by 2020.
2009	**Administrative Measures for National Essential Medicines List (Interim)**	The **Document** notes that: all government-run PHC institutions are required to be equipped with and use EM, while other health care institutions are required to use EM in accordance with rules; the NEML includes chemical drugs, biological products and TCMs; the management of Chinese herbal medicine pieces refers to other policies formulated by the State Council; the NEMWC is responsible for the policies directing the NEMS, as well as the formulation, approval, and adjustment of the NEML; the MOH is responsible for establishing a pool of experts; the selection of EM is conducted by experts randomly chosen from the pool; in principle, the NEML shall be adjusted every three years.
2009	**National Reimbursement Drug List for National Basic Medical Insurance, Work-related Injury Insurance and Maternity Insurance (2009 version)**	The List is divided into two parts: chemical drugs and biological products, and TCM and Chinese herbal medicines. When paid by BMI, chemical drugs and biological products and TCM are further divided into Category A and Category B (Work-related Injury Insurance and Maternity Insurance do not make this distinction); Chinese herbal medicine pieces are all listed unless otherwise excluded by these three insurances. Drugs on the NEML are all included in Category A of the national reimbursement drug list. Drugs under Category A shall be fully paid by the BMI, out-of-pocket payments by patients is not allowed.

Year	Title of Documents	Key Content Regarding the Right to Health (Care)
2009	**Opinions on the Adjustment and Formulation of Medical Reimbursement Drug List for New Rural Cooperative Medical Scheme**	The document was drafted on the basis of the NEML and clinical treatments. Taking into consideration the unbalanced development in different regions, different pooling funds and the capacity of health services delivery, the reimbursement drug list for NRCMS is based on the country (or above), town and village levels. Drugs listed on the NEML are all incorporated on the county list while the other two lists are allowed to incorporate other drugs. A county list is suggested to include 800-1,200 drugs while town list in principle has 300-500 drugs; EM have a 5%-10% higher reimbursement ratio than that of non-EM.
2012	**National Essential Medicines List (2012 version)**	The latest NEML includes 317 chemical drugs and biological products and 203 Chinese traditional patent medicines, and Chinese herbal medicines.
2012	**The Twelfth Five-Year Plan for Health Sector Development (2010-2015)**	**The overall goal:** by 2015, improve the accessibility, quality and efficiency of health care services as well as the patients' satisfaction; largely reduce out-of-pocket payments; and narrow the cross-regional gap for health resource allocation and the gap in the health status of the population **The 12th FYP requires China to:** initially establish (1) a public health service system for promoting equal access to public health services for urban and rural residents; (2) a standard and well-structured medical service system for providing secure, efficient, convenient and affordable basic medical services to urban and rural residents; (3) a multi-tiered health insurance system covering urban and rural residents, with the BMI as the core, and various types of complementary medical insurance and commercial health insurance as supplementary.

Year	Title of Documents	Key Content Regarding the Right to Health (Care)
2012	**The Twelfth Five-Year Plan for Health Sector Development (2010-2015)**	Further regulate the drug supply and assurance system on the basis of the NEMS to ensure equal access to safe and effective EM and promote the rational use of EM. Improve various institutional mechanisms to support the comprehensive, coordinated and sustainable development of the health sector and to ensure the sound operation of the health care system.
2012	**Planning and Implementation Plan of Deepening Health System Reform during the Twelfth Five-year Plan (2010-2015)**	**The overall goal:** by 2020, ensure universal access to basic medical and health care services. **The Plan calls requires China to:** Spur the development of UHC by 2015: the coverage of the three BMIs will increase by 3%; government subsidy for the URBMI and NRCMS will be increased to 360 RMB per person per year; the average reimbursement rate of the three BMIs for inpatients will reach 75% or above; URBMI and NRCMS will cover all outpatient services with a reimbursement rate higher than 50%; by 2015, fully establish regional mechanism to settle health care fees incurred within the area and basically achieve trans-regional mechanism to settle health care fees incurred outside of the area. Consolidate and improve the EM system and the new operational mechanism of PHC institutions: expand the regions implementing EM policy; update the NEML in 2012; regulate the procurement mechanism of EM; establish a system of GPs, train more than 150,000 GPs for PHC institutions by 2015 and ensure two or more GPs for 10,000 urban residents and equip each township health centres with GPs. Actively prompt the reform of public hospitals.
2013	**Opinions on Consolidating and Improving Essential Medicine System and New Operating Mechanism**	**The Opinions requires China to:** refine the centralised procurement and distribution system for EM; set out a schedule for regular adjustment of the NEML – in principle every three years; strengthen the supervision and management of the use of EM; deepen the reforms of human resources management and an increase in income at PHC institutions; refine multi-channel compensation mechanisms for PHC institutions; improve the capacity for PHC delivery; improve the village doctors' capacity.

Year	Title of Documents	Key Content Regarding the Right to Health (Care)
2015	**Administrative Measures for National Essential Medicines List**	The **Measures** was mainly based on the 2009 Administrative Measures for National Essential Medicines List. The main revisions are: (1) the inclusion of Chinese herbal medicines; (2) the expansion of the expert pool to include experts on drug supervision and on the management of drug production and supply; (3) the creation of certain conditions for the deletion of certain medicine; (4) the Health Department of People's Liberation Army General Logistics Department replaces the Ministry of Supervision to become a member of the NEMWC.
2016	**Guideline on the Integration of Urban Residents' Basic Medical Insurance and New Rural Cooperative Medical Scheme**	**Tenets:** strengthen the coordination between BMI, IPCD, MFA, emergency rescue and commercial insurance; ensure health justice, gradually narrow the gap narrow the gap between rural and urban areas and among different regions; ensure that rural and urban residents have the same basic insurance coverage; governments at various levels undertake their responsibility. **Basic Policies for the integration are to unify the following aspects of the two basic insurance schemes:** **Coverage:** all urban and rural residents not enrolled in the UEBMI are covered by this integrated insurance; **Fundraising method:** individual contributions and government subsidy; **Benefit package and reimbursement rate:** inpatient and outpatient services; reimbursement rate will stay at around 75%; **Insurance catalogue:** unify the reimbursement drug list and health care services catalogue for rural and urban residents; **Fund management:** the management responsibility will be placed under MOHRSS; **Premium levels:** in principal at municipal level.
2016	**'Healthy China 2030' Plan**	**Fundamental goal:** healthy for all; **Tenets:** health as a national strategic priority, health in all policies; reform and innovation, adhere to the government's role of promoting people's health; scientific development; fair and just; the improvement of equity in basic public health services, maintain the public nature of basic health services; narrow the gap in basic health services and health status between rural and urban areas, different regions and population.

Year	Title of Documents	Key Content Regarding the Right to Health (Care)
2016	**'Healthy China 2030' Plan**	**Strategic Goals:** build a basic health care system covering both rural and urban residents, improve people's health status, promote the efficiency of health care system, optimise health industries, provide everyone with access to basic health care services and physical exercise services; main health indicators will be among the top of middle- and high-income countries by 2020; continue to improve health care system and basically achieve health justice; main health indicators will reach the standards of high-income countries by 2030. **Key tasks:** Strengthen the health care services for specific groups of people: promote healthy aging, improve the health conditions of women and children; protect the health of the disabled. Improve UHC: refine the multi-tiered health insurance system with the BMI as the core, various types of complementary medical insurance and commercial health insurance as supplement; further improve the insurance programme for catastrophic diseases; strengthen the coordination between the BMIs, IPCD, commercial health insurance and medical financial assistance scheme for the poor; spur the establishment of trans-regional mechanism for medical claim settlement, achieve direct settlement for inpatient fees for the retired who reside outside of the enrolment area or for the patients with proper referral. Improve the NEMS: consolidate the NEMS; improve the EM guarantee for specific groups of people; improve the drug policy for rare disease and free treatment, increase the free supply of drugs for specific diseases such as HIV/AIDS; deepen the reforms drug review and approval. Further develop the tiered diagnosis and treatment system to ensure everyone access to basic health care services in their community within 15 minutes by 2030.
2016	**The Thirteenth Five-Year Plan for Deepening the Health Care System Reform (2016-2020)**	**Tenets:** health as a national strategic priority; ensure basic services, strengthen primary health care and establish effective mechanisms; ensure government's leading role in combination with market-oriented mechanism; spur the supply-side reform; promote the parallel development and interaction of health care delivery, health insurance and pharmaceuticals.

Year	Title of Documents	Key Content Regarding the Right to Health (Care)
2016	**The Thirteenth Five-Year Plan for Deepening the Health Care System Reform (2016-2020)**	**Key tasks:** Establish the tiered diagnosis and treatment system: optimise health service delivery system; improve the service capacity of the PHC institutions; encourage public hospitals to participate in tiered diagnosis and treatment; promote the diagnosis-cure-long-term care model; establish contracted health services with family doctors. Establish a modern hospital management system: establish proper compensation mechanism to eliminate drug make-up; reform human resources management and income system; establish performance-based assessment system. Scale up UHC: reform the fundraising and reimbursement ratio adjustment mechanism; deepen the reform of insurance payment methods; spur the integration of the BMI; improve the IPCD; promote the development of commercial insurance. Deepen the reform of the drug production and supply system: ensure the provision of low-cost, life-saving, and orphan drugs and drugs for children; deepen the reform of drug distribution system; promote the centralised procurement system for drug and high-value medical consumables, particularly 'two-invoice system'; consolidate the NEMS; promote national medicines policies. Establish comprehensive supervisory system: deepen the reforms of decentralisation, supervision and service level; develop a dynamic supervisory system; strengthen industry supervision; advocate third-party evaluation and industry self-discipline.

Year	Title of Documents	Key Content Regarding the Right to Health (Care)
2016	**The Thirteenth Five-Year Plan for Deepening the Health Care System Reform (2016-2020)**	**Key targets by 2017:** Expand the coverage of contracted health services with family doctors to 30% of the entire population, 60% of the key targets; Expand the tiered diagnosis and treatment to more than 85% pilot cities; Preliminarily establish trans-regional mechanism to settle inpatient fees incurred outside of the residence but in conformity with the dual referral regulation. **Key targets by 2020:** Per capita health expenditure as a share of total expenditure on health will drop to 28%; Establish a preliminary tiered diagnosis and treatment system; Expand the coverage of contracted health services with family doctors to the entire population; Maintain the health insurance coverage at 95% or above of the entire population; Gradually raise the level of pooling to provincial level and keep the reimbursement rate at around 75%; Preliminarily establish a traceability system for drug's manufacturing price.

Part 2

An Analytical Framework for Right to Health-based Accountability

CHAPTER 5
AN OVERVIEW OF RIGHT TO HEALTH-BASED ACCOUNTABILITY

5.1 INTRODUCTION

Part 2 of this study (chapters 5 and 6) offers, through the lens of accountability, a possible solution to the remaining challenges confronting China in its implementation of the right to health care. Accountability gives 'teeth' to human rights; it can be a powerful tool for promoting the right to health (care). Nevertheless, and despite the growing body of literature recognising its importance for advancing the right to health (care), accountability remains under-specified throughout human rights scholarship.

The purpose of chapter 5 is twofold. First, it aims to refine the concept of accountability (which remains an elusive concept in several disciplines) from a human rights perspective. One of the unique contributions of the right to health framework is that it provides a rather objective and comprehensive framework for accountability.[1] The norms and standards under the right to health (care) provide a compelling normative framework for defining right to health-based accountability and for developing effective accountability mechanisms to advance the right to health (care).[2] Although still subject to progressive realisation, the right to health (care) gives rise to a range of obligations of immediate effect, including an obligation to establish effective, transparent, accessible and independent mechanisms for accountability.[3]

The second purpose of this chapter is to explore how accountability can advance the right to health (care) at the domestic level. Accountability is vital to human rights

---

1 Office of the United Nations High Commissioner for Human Rights (OHCHR), 'Claiming the Millennium Development Goals: A Human Rights Approach' (2008), vii, 7.

2 OHCHR and Center for Economic and Social Rights, 'Who Will Be Accountable? Human Rights and the Post-2015 Development Agenda' (2013) 10.

3 United Nations Committee on Economic, Social and Cultural Rights (CteeESCR), 'General Comment No. 9: The Domestic Application of the Covenant' (General Comment 9) (3 December 1998) UN Doc E/C12/1998/24, para 2; United Nations General Assembly (UNGA), 'Report of the Special Rapporteur on the Right of Everyone to the Enjoyment of the Highest Attainable Standard of Physical and Mental Health, Paul Hunt' (31 Janauary 2008) UN Doc A/HRC/7/11, para 51 (d).

implementation,[4] because it reinforces the realisation of the right to health (care) by providing right-holders with an opportunity to call into question how State (and other relevant) actors have discharged their obligations under the right to health (care). In addition, it enables right-holders to hold responsible actors to account when they have failed to comply with their obligations.[5] Likewise, it also provides duty-bearers with an opportunity to inform right-holders about what they have done to achieve the full realisation of the right to health (care), and explain and justify their reasons for it.[6] Where violations of the right to health (care) have occurred, accountability implies the possibility of imposing consequences on responsible duty-bearers, including eventual sanctions where relevant.[7] Additionally, accountability allows victims of violations of the right to health (care) to claim remedies.[8] Importantly, right to health-based accountability is more than finding fault, imposing punishment, and seeking remedies. Rather, it is a process that comprises a range of elements, including monitoring, rectification, access to a remedy and public participation, among others.[9] All in all, accountability in the context of the right to health (care) is about fostering an effective and accountable health care system that functions for the benefit of the entire population.[10]

Chapter 5 provides an overview of right to health-based accountability. Section 5.2 first looks closely at the concept of 'accountability', which is still insufficiently defined in human rights literature. It outlines the present debate surrounding the concept of 'accountability' in different disciplines, including in particular the political discourse. It also introduces the principal-agent theory, which is a widely-

4 UNGA, 'Report of the Special Rapporteur on the Right of Everyone to the Enjoyment of the Highest Attainable Standard of Physical and Mental Health, Paul Hunt' (n 3) para 51 (d).
5 ibid
6 ibid
7 ibid; OHCHR and Center for Economic and Social Rights (n 2) 10.
8 CteeESCR, 'General Comment No. 14: The Right to the Highest Attainable Standard of Health (Art. 12 of the Covenant)' (General Comment 14) (11 August 2000) UN Doc E/C12/2000/4, paras 59-60.
9 Lynn Freeman, 'Human Rights, Constructive Accountability and Maternal Mortality in the Dominican Republic: A Commentary' (2003) 82 International Journal of Gynaecology and Obstetrics 111, 111; Helen Potts, 'Accountability and the Right to the Highest Attainable Standard of Health' (University of Essex Human Rights Centre 2008) 13 <http://repository.essex.ac.uk/9717/1/accountability-right-highest-attainable-standard-health.pdf> accessed 28 November 2017.
10 Freeman (n 9) 111.

used paradigm for analysing accountability.[11] Answerability and enforcement as two dimensions of accountability are also discussed in this section. Subsequently, section 5.3 discusses the various forms of accountability on the basis of three questions: who is accountable, for what are these actors accountable and to whom are these actors accountable. Building on the current debate on the general concept and different types of accountability, section 5.4 develops a definition of accountability from a human rights perspective. It also identifies three constituent elements of accountability in the context of the right to health (care), namely responsibility, answerability and enforcement. Before concluding, section 5.5 proposes a dynamic accountability process with four building blocks: monitoring, judgement, consequences and remedies.

5.2 Conceptualising accountability

Accountability has become a hotly debated topic within political science, governance, law, and human rights discourse over the past decades. A growing body of literature has drawn attention to the concept of accountability.[12] Nevertheless, as mentioned above, accountability remains an elusive concept in different disciplines. Scholars adopt varying definitions of accountability and consensus has yet to be reached as to the concept's components and overall meaning.

Before developing my main arguments, it is necessary to explain more thoroughly what accountability is. As such, this section offers a few general conceptual observations from various disciplines, including in particular the political discourse on the concept. It first explores the etymological and historical roots of accountability.

11 Sean Gailmard, 'Accountability and Principal–Agent Theory' in Mark Bovens, Robert Goodin and Thomas Schillemans (eds), *The Oxford Handbook of Public Accountability* (Oxford University Press 2014) 90.

12 See eg Andreas Schedler, 'Conceptualizing Accountability' in Andreas Schedler, Larry Diamond and Marc Plattner (eds), *The Self-restraining State: Power and Accountability in New Democracies* (Lynne Rienner Publishers 1999); Derick Brinkerhoff, 'Taking Account of Accountability: A Conceptual Overview and Strategic Options' (US Agency for International Development 2001) 1 <http://1qswp72wn11q9smtq15ccbuo.wpengine.netdna-cdn.com/wp-content/uploads/2011/07/IPC_Taking_Account_of_Accountability.pdf> accessed 28 November 2017; Mark Bovens, 'Analysing and Assessing Accountability: A Conceptual Framework' (2007) 13 European Law Journal 447; Melvin Dubnick, 'Seeking Salvation for Accountability' paper presented at th Annual Meeting of the American Political Science Association (2002) <http://mjdubnick.dubnick.net/papersrw/2002/salv2002.pdf> accessed 28 November 2017.

5.2.1 Accountability in different discourses

According to the Oxford English Dictionary, accountability is 'the fact or condition of being accountable', or 'responsibility'; while *being* accountable means that an actor is 'required or expected to justify actions or decisions' or 'able to be explained or understood'. In this sense, accountability stands for many other terms, including answerability, responsiveness and responsibility, to name just a few.[13] In his analysis of the term accountability, Dubnick distinguishes between accountability as a word and accountability as a concept. He notes that accountability as a word is extremely difficult to translate into other languages, and by extension, to other political and administrative settings. For example, the major roman languages, including French, Spanish, Italian and Portuguese, use various forms of *responsibility* in lieu of the English word *accountability*, which results in a less clear distinction between responsibility and accountability. In Japanese, there is only one equivalent word to accountability – ***'akauntabiritii'*** (the transliteration of accountability) – while at least seventeen Japanese words can be used to translate responsibility. Other languages, such as northern and eastern European languages, have shifted attention from accountability as a word to accountability as a concept. These languages translate accountability into terms closely related to account-keeping.[14] As a concept recently imported to China, there is no equivalent word in Chinese that could be used to translate 'accountability'. Nevertheless, the term ***'wen ze'***, with its connotations of 'questioning' and 'blaming', is used to reflect the idea of accountability in Chinese.[15]

Approached conceptually, accountability was originally rooted in accounting. According to Dubnick, the contemporary conception of accountability can be traced back to the reign of William I of England and his successors.[16] In 1085, all the property holders in the realm of King William I were required to 'render a count' of what they possessed in the terms set by the King's agent.[17] The King's agent then assessed and listed these possessions in the so-called Domesday Books. By doing

13 Dubnick (n 12) 2.
14 ibid 4.
15 Shengnan Qiu and Gillian MacNaughton, 'Mechanisms of Accountability for the Realization of the Right to Health in China' (2017) 19 Health and Human Rights Journal 279, 281.
16 Dubnick (n 12) 3,7.
17 ibid 7-8

so, everything in the King's realm was accounted for through census. In addition, King William I established a sworn obligation for property holders to 'give him an accounting of all that to which he could lay claim'.[18] This census was regarded as the first modern enactment of accountability as a foundation for governance. King William's approach was then gradually developed into a realm-wide administrative system that was ruled through centralised auditing and semi-annual account giving mechanisms.[19] The concept of accountability thus points to a unique relationship between sovereigns and subjects, the governor and the governed based on norms and values established by the governor, which is a defining element of accountability.[20]

Since the late 20th century, the concept of accountability has transformed from the traditional financial accounting into a much broader form of public accountability. The accounting relationship has also largely reversed: 'accountability' did not refer to the sovereigns holding their subjects to account; rather, it was the governor being held accountable by the governed.[21] In contemporary political discourse, scholars claim that the State-society relationship should be characterised in terms of the so-called 'social contract' where citizens yield their natural right of self-governance to the State as an exchange for the societal benefits deriving from State sovereignty. As such, the social contract 'shifted the balance of power away from the absolutist state, where the state, embodied in a monarch or authoritarian leader, ruled over citizens as subjects, toward government by consent of the governed'.[22]

Given that 'accountability' or 'being accountable' holds strong promises of fair and equitable governance, scholars tend to perceive accountability as a key attribute of both democracy and democracy quality, as well as one of the cornerstones of good governance.[23] Nonetheless, despite its importance to democratic governance, accountability has not yet been fully defined by several disciplines. It has become a conceptual umbrella that covers various distinct concepts, such as responsibility,

18 ibid 8.
19 ibid 8-9; Bovens (n 12) 448.
20 Dubnick (n 12) 9; Mark Bovens, 'Two Concepts of Accountability: Accountability as a Virtue and as a Mechanism' (2010) 33 West European Politics 946, 951.
21 Bovens (n 12) 449.
22 Brinkerhoff (n 12) 7.
23 Bovens (n 12) 449; Dubnick (n 12) 17; Larry Diamond, Marc Plattner and Andreas Schedler, 'Introduction' in Andreas Schedler, Larry Diamond and Marc Plattner (eds), *The Self-restraining State: Power and Accountability in New Democracies* (Lynne Rienner Publishers 1999) 2.

responsiveness, answerability, transparency, equity and governance.[24] For Koppell, for example, accountability encompasses no less than five dimensions, including transparency, controllability, responsibility and responsiveness.[25] Mulgan also notes that 'accountability has come to stand as a general term for any mechanism that makes powerful institutions responsive to their particular publics'.[26]

Broadly speaking, accountability exists when there is 'a relationship of power'.[27] As Brinkerhoff points out, a fundamental element of good governance is the question of how State power and authority are allocated and applied in public realms, including the provision of public goods and services (eg health facilities, goods and services), the selection of leaders and representatives, and the rule of law and order, to name just a few.[28] Public officials – both elected and appointed – exercise varying degrees of power when they carry out their functions on the basis of the positions they occupy.[29] But what assures citizens that these officials will exercise their power and authority in the best interests of society and not their own benefits? According to Brinkerhoff, systems, procedures and mechanisms that impose restraints on the power and authority of public officials and that create incentives for appropriate decisions and actions are the key.[30] Along similar lines, Schedler perceives accountability as a term to express the 'continuing concern for checks and oversight, for surveillance and institutional constraints on the exercise of power'.[31] He further offers a more abstract definition of accountability: 'A is accountable to B when A is obliged to inform B about A's (past or future) actions and decisions, to justify them and to suffer punishment in the case of eventual misconduct'.[32]

---

24 Bovens (n 12) 449; Schedler (n 12) 14-17; Dubnick (n 12) 17.
25 Jonathan Koppell, 'Pathologies of Accountability: ICANN and the Challenge of "Multiple Accountabilities Disorder"' (2005) 65 Public Administration Review 94, 94 <http://doi.wiley.com/10.1111/j.1540-6210.2005.00434.x> accessed 15 August 2017. Cited in Bovens (n 12) 450.
26 Richard Mulgan, *Holding Power to Account: Accountability in Modern Democracies* (Palgrave Macmillan UK 2003) 8.
27 Anne Goetz and others, 'Introduction' in Anne Marie Goetz and Rob Jenkins (eds), *Reinventing Accountability: Making Democracy Work for Human Development* (Palgrave Macmillan UK 2005) 8.
28 Brinkerhoff (n 12) 1.
29 ibid.
30 ibid.
31 Schedler (n 12) 13.
32 ibid 17.

Looking for definitions of accountability elsewhere, we see that accountability has been used to refer to 'the *obligation* of power-holders to take responsibility for their actions';[33] 'the *process* of holding actors (eg individuals, agencies and public, private and civil society organizations) responsible for executing their powers according to a certain standards';[34] or 'a *relationship* between an actor and a forum, in which the actor has an obligation to explain and to justify his or her conduct, the forum can pose questions and pass judgement, and the actor may face consequences'.[35] We therefore see that there are several possible conceptions of accountability: accountability as a relationship, a process or an obligation.

In brief, accountability exists when there is a relationship between actor A and actor B, where A, as well as the decisions and actions made by A, is subject to B's oversight. A is obliged to inform B about his (or her) (past or future) decisions and actions, to explain and justify the reason, and face (positive or negative) consequences. Understanding accountability means analysing the relationship between actor A and actor B. Scholars label these two actors differently: (1) actor A (i.e. those in authority): accountable actor, power-wielder, accountor or actor; and (2) actor B (i.e. those who are affected): overseeing actor, account-holder, accountee or forum. Whichever phrasing is used, these two actors can either be an individual (eg an official or civil servant) or an institution (eg a public agency or organisation). This relationship lies at the very heart of the research of accountability in the context of governance, which is known as the 'principal-agent theory'.[36]

For the remainder of this study, I will refer to the two actors involved in the accountability relationship as overseeing actor(s) and accountable actor(s).

---

33 United Nations Development Programme (UNDP), 'Fostering Social Accountability: From Principle to Practice' (2010) 8 <www.undp.org/content/dam/undp/library/Democratic Governance/OGC/dg-ogc-Fostering Social Accountability-Guidance Note.pdf> accessed 28 November 2017.

34 Martin Tisné, 'Transparency, Participation and Accountability: Definitions' Unpublished Background Note for Transparency and Accountability Initiative (2010) 2. Cited in Greg Barrett and others, 'Review of Impact and Effectiveness of Transparency and Accountability Initiatives: Synthesis Report' (2010) 4 <www.ids.ac.uk/files/dmfile/IETASynthesisReportMcGeeGaventaFinal28Oct2010.pdf> accessed 28 November 2017.

35 Bovens (n 12) 450.

36 ibid 451; Brinkerhoff (n 12) 9; Dubnick (n 12) 9; Gailmard (n 11) 91.

5.2.2 The principal-agent theory

This section addresses the relationship between the overseeing actor(s) and the accountable actor(s), which very often has the nature of a principal-agent relationship. In the principal-agent model, one actor (either an individual or institution thereof) – i.e. the agent – undertakes an action on behalf of another actor – i.e. the principal. The principal delegates its agent to exercise power on his (or her) behalf, while the agent represents the interest of his (or her) principal. This relation is shown in Figure 5.1.

Figure 5.1 The principal-agent model[37]

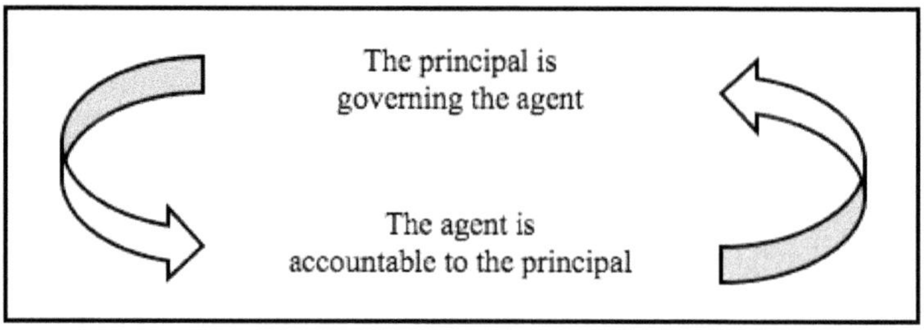

In the context of political discourse, a typical principal-agent relation is between voters, as principals, and their representatives to whom they delegate authority – i.e. agents – who give account to voters during elections. In such cases, the voters are overseeing actors while the elected representatives are accountable actors. Another example of the principal-agent relation is a State's parliament and its ministers. In a parliamentary system, elected representatives delegate the majority of their authorities to a cabinet of ministers. The ministers, being agents, regularly render political account to the parliament in relation to their performance.[38] Here, the ministers are accountable actors, while the parliament is an overseeing actor. This is a very typical example of political forms of accountability. Notably, in an internal hierarchical relation, an actor can both be a principal and an agent. For example, ministers are agents of parliament, but they can also be principals when they delegate

37 Paul Milgrom and John Roberts, *Economics, Organization, and Management* (Prentice-Hall 1992). Cited in Department for International Development, 'Accountability Briefing Note' (2008) 5 <www.gsdrc.org/docs/open/innovations-in-accountability/ia4.pdf> accessed 28 November 2017.

38 Bovens (n 12) 451; Riccardo Pelizzo and Frederick Stapenhurst, *Government Accountability and Legislative Oversight* (Routledge 2014) 8-9.

authority to various administrative organs or civil servants. Nevertheless, in many other types of accountability, overseeing actors are not necessarily principals of accountable actors. For instance, in a social accountability relationship where the media function as the watchdog of public interests and counterbalance the power of the executive, the legislature and the judiciary,[39] the media are not the principal of any of these State organs.

Generally speaking, the principal-agent relationship exists when there is a direct obligation resting upon an accountable actor(s) and an overseeing actor(s), perhaps due to the hierarchical relationship between these two actors, as in the examples mentioned above.

What is central to accountability is the question of how to ensure that an agent acts in the interests of his principal rather than for his own benefit. As Gailmard notes, the principal and the agent may have different preferences regarding the possible decisions and actions an agent may take.[40] Admittedly, given the need to allow at least some degree of discretion and the personal responsibility of the agent, the principal can never specify in advance or totally control every decision and action made by an agent.[41] It largely depends on the agent's self-discipline and professional ethics to act in compliance with his mandated duties. Nevertheless, such trust is limited and may result in abuses of power.[42] For this reason, other forms of control to protect the interests of the principal are required.

One important means of such protection is the capacity of a principal to call his agent to 'account'. As discussed, the original type of account was financial account, which often manifested in the form of a report on possessions, revenues and so forth. Other forms of account include a general report on the performance of an agent or an agent's response to a specific inquiry or investigation which requires the agent to inform his principal about what has been done or what is to be done, and to explain and justify the reason.[43] This gives rise to the need to establish mechanisms for preventing possible abuses of power from going unnoticed and mechanisms for evaluating the

39 Katrin Voltmer, 'The Media, Government Accountability, and Citizen Engagement' in Pippa Norris (ed), *Public Sentinel: News Media and Governance Reform* (The World Bank 2010) 140.
40 Gailmard (n 11) 92.
41 Mulgan (n 26) 8-9.
42 ibid 9.
43 ibid.

consequences of the agent's decisions and actions.[44] The capacity of a principal to call his agent to account, i.e. receiving information affected by or correlated with the agent's decisions and actions, forms the essential basis of accountability – i.e. the dimension of answerability, which will be discussed in detail in section 5.2.3.[45]

In addition to being called to account, an agent must also bear the consequences of his decisions and actions.[46] As Schedler correctly notes, 'inconsequential accountability is no accountability at all.'[47] Where the agent is found to have been at fault on the basis of available information and specific standards, effective rectification is needed.[48] There should be mechanisms for remedies available, by punishing the agent for his wrongdoings and compensating those who have been affected by the agent.[49] Notably, accountability implies more than sanctioning the agent – what it actually concerns is how to 'get the incentives right'.[50] Therefore, as well as sanctions, there should also be mechanisms for rewarding the agent when he takes the principal's preferred decisions and actions.[51] The capacity of the principal to reward good and to punish bad decisions and actions lies at the very heart of an accountability relationship, which is regarded as the dimension of enforcement.[52]

Answerability and enforcement, which are generally perceived in political discourse as the two dimensions of accountability, will be discussed further below.[53]

5.2.3 Answerability and enforcement: two sides of the same coin

While the concept of accountability may differ across disciplines, previous studies on accountability have generally recognised that accountability has two connotations: answerability and enforcement.[54]

44 Schedler (n 12) 16.
45 Mulgan (n 26) 9.
46 ibid; Schedler (n 12) 15.
47 Schedler (n 12) 17.
48 Mulgan (n 26) 9.
49 ibid.
50 Schedler (n 12) 16.
51 Gailmard (n 11) 92.
52 Mulgan (n 26) 9.
53 Schedler (12) 14; Bovens (12) 451; Pelizzo and Stapenhurst (n 38) 2.
54 ibid.

5.2.3.1 Answerability

Many scholars tend to perceive 'answerability' as the closest synonym of accountability, given that accountability indicates the ability of an overseeing actor to ensure that an accountable actor is answerable for his decisions and actions. Being accountable thus implies an obligation of an accountable actor to provide the overseeing actor with information about his decisions and actions, and to explain and justify their decisions in cases of failures; vice versa, holding the accountable actor to account implies a right of the overseeing actor to ask for information, explanation or justification as appropriate.[55] As such, answerability has two facets: an informational dimension and an explanatory dimension.

First, the informational dimension of answerability, as just explained, indicates a right of an overseeing actor to receive information, and a corresponding obligation of an accountable actor to release all necessary details about his decisions and actions by providing various types of data about the plans, procedures, or outcomes of his tasks.[56] This implies a one-way transmission of information from the accountable actor to the overseeing actor.[57]

Second, answerability extends beyond the provision of information;[58] an accountable actor may merely provide vague and abstract information concerning the issuance of a certain policy, without explaining the reason or consulting the relevant stakeholders. The increasing demand for specialised knowledge in policy-making and service delivery may undermine the overseeing actor's capacity to make sense of the information provided by the accountable actor, particularly for vulnerable and marginalised groups within society.[59]

Therefore, answerability also implies a parallel obligation of the accountable actor to explain what has been done or to be done and justify the reason for it, which is the explanatory dimension of accountability.[60] There needs to be a possibility for the overseeing actor to monitor the accountable actor and to question the adequacy of

55 ibid.
56 Schedler (n 12) 15; Bovens (n 12) 451; Pelizzo and Stapenhurst (n 38) 2.
57 Schedler (n 12) 14-15; Pelizzo and Stapenhurst (n 38) 2.
58 Bovens (n 12) 451.
59 Brinkerhoff (n 12) 9-10.
60 Pelizzo and Stapenhurst (n 38) 2.

the information or legitimacy of the decisions or actions made by him, particularly in the event of failures.[61] An example is that the accountable actor reveals the evidence upon which decisions or actions were based, such as expert testimony or supporting documentation.[62] Subsequently, the overseeing actor can, on the basis of available information and prevailing standards, judge the persuasiveness of the explanation and justification provided by the accountable actor regarding his decisions and actions.[63] The overseeing actor may administer a reward when passing a positive judgement, or impose sanctions on the accountable actor when passing a negative judgement.[64]

Based on the above, it can be concluded that the answerability element of accountability has the potential to create transparency.[65] The demand for information as well as explanation and justification are closely related to notions such as oversight and supervision. Given that it is not possible to completely control the accountable actor's decisions and actions, the overseeing actor may only monitor and ask for *ex post* explanation and justification.[66] As Schedler explains, answerability presupposes imperfect information. If the exercise of power were already transparent, it would be pointless to ask for more information; the overseeing actor would already know. Nevertheless, in reality, most information is not readily accessible. Thus, by demanding information, explanation or justification, answerability can prevent the opacity of power and keep accountable actor(s) under public scrutiny.[67]

Notably, in many cases, the accountable actor has much greater access to information about the government's resources, actions and performance, resulting in information asymmetries between the two actors. As such, accountability requires mechanisms for gathering information and evaluating the persuasiveness of the explanation or justification provided by the accountable actor, along with mechanisms of control and sanction.[68]

61 Bovens (n 12) 451.
62 ibid.
63 ibid.
64 ibid.
65 Schedler (n 12) 20.
66 ibid.
67 ibid.
68 Brinkerhoff (n 12) 9.

5.2.3.2 Enforcement

In addition to answerability, accountability encompasses another element - enforcement, i.e. the capacity of an overseeing actor, as appropriate, to reward or punish decisions or actions of an accountable actor.[69] While some early analyses of accountability were restricted to the stage of passing judgement, or even the stages of informing, explaining, justifying and debating,[70] it is now generally accepted that 'the possibility of imposing sanctions – not the actual imposition of sanctions – makes the difference between the non-committal provision of information and being held to account'.[71] As indicated in section 5.2.2, accountability without consequences would be regarded as an act of window-dressing rather than real constraints on power.[72] Therefore, an accountable actor is not only obliged to supply information about what he has done or plans to do and explain and justify the reasons for it, but also to bear the consequences of his decisions and actions.

When an accountable actor is found to have been at fault, such as through abuses of power, he will face negative consequences, including eventual sanctions,[73] which are often imposed pursuant to requirements, standards and penalties embedded in law, such as fines and disciplinary measures. However, negative consequences also include soft enforcement mechanisms, such as negative publicity and calling for the accountable actor's resignation.[74] Effective rectification also requires appropriate compensation for those who have been affected by the accountable actor's wrongdoings.[75] As important as finding fault, though, is the improvement of the accountable actor's performance and keeping his incentives to act responsibly by means of imposing positive consequences. Indeed, in order to encourage the accountable actor to repeat good decisions and actions, the overseeing actor could reward the accountable actor for acting in the best interests of the overseeing actor.[76]

69 ibid 15.
70 See for example Bovens (n 12) 451; Joseph G Jabbra and OP Dwivedi (eds), *Public Service Accountability: A Comparative Perspective* (Kumarian Press 1989) 5. Cited in Mulgan (n 26) 9.
71 Bovens (n 12) 451; Mulgan (n 26) 9.
72 Schedler (n 12) 15.
73 ibid.
74 Bovens (n 12) 451-452; Pelizzo and Stapenhurst (n 38) 2.
75 Mulgan (n 26) 9.
76 Gailmard (n 11) 92.

5.2.3.3 *Ex ante and ex post accountability*

Strictly speaking, accountability can only be exercised after the occurrence of the fact, i.e. '*ex post facto* accountability'.[77] The answerability element of accountability involves the evaluation of the decisions and actions made by the accountable actor; apparently, it is pointless to speak of evaluating something that does not actually exist. Nevertheless, this does not mean that an accountable actor can only be held accountable for *results*.[78]

Accountability is not only about *ex post* scrutiny, but also *ex ante* prevention and anticipation.[79] For instance, an overseeing actor can intervene whenever he thinks the accountable actor may act wrongly, ask for information about what has been done or will be done, as well as the explanation and justification for it, and evaluate the reasons given *before* bad decisions and actions have occurred in reality.[80] Viewed in this light, accountability has a preventive function. Furthermore, as mentioned above, by imposing potential (positive or negative) consequences, the overseeing actor can encourage the accountable actor to act in his best interests and prevent abuses of power. The accountable actor may adjust his decisions and actions in advance when he (or she) anticipates a negative judgement and the corresponding sanction, or repeat the decisions and actions that were rewarded before or may be rewarded. *Ex post* scrutiny can thus be an important input for *ex ante* decision-making.[81] Put simply, the preventive function of accountability helps to 'identify what works, so it can be repeated, and what does not, so it can be revised'.[82]

Accountability also has a corrective function. Where an accountable actor is found to have been at fault after *ex post* scrutiny, remedies should be put in place. Imposing negative consequences on an accountable actor for his wrongdoings is just one side of a coin; the other side requires that those affected are compensated. The retrospective nature differentiates accountability from responsiveness, which

77 Bovens (n 12) 453; The World Bank, 'Social Accountability in the Public Sector: A Conceptual Discussion and Learning Module' (2005) 6.
78 World Bank (n 77) 6.
79 Bovens (n 12) 453.
80 World Bank (n 77) 6-7. It should be noted that, in theory, it is possible to ask accountable actors to provide information, and explain and justify their decisions and actions *ex ante*. Nonetheless, it is not clear whether overseeing actors can influence the decision-making process in reality.
81 ibid.
82 Potts (n 9) 13.

involves proactive input into decision-making processes but does not encompass the elements of explanation, justification and consequences.[83]

5.2.4 Summary

The concept of account*ability* implies the *possibility* of an overseeing actor to call and hold an accountable actor to account. The accountable actor can be account*able* without truly being called and held to account.[84] All that is necessary is that the overseeing actor has the right to ask for reliable information (the informational dimension of answerability) or a valid explanation and justification (the explanatory dimension of answerability), and impose consequences (the dimension of enforcement), so as to prevent the accountable actor from abusing his authority or power and to ensure that the accountable actor acts in the best interests of the overseeing actor.

The exercise of accountability is of course not always so easy in practice. For example, when the wrongdoings of politicians are identified, citizens often state that 'we will hold them accountable' as a way of expressing their anger or frustration. Indeed, citizens can hold their elected politicians to account, but the exercise of this type of accountability happens mostly during the electoral period. It is arguably easier for an overseeing actor to hold an accountable actor to account when the former has a higher status than the latter. For example, it is apparent that it would be more difficult for citizens to hold their elected politicians to account than for a minister to hold his personnel to account. As I will discuss further below, the exercise of accountability depends largely on the nature of the relationship between an accountable actor and an overseeing actor, which answers the question: for what are accountable actors obliged to give account?

5.3 Types of Accountability

Several questions arise when we wish to hold public institutions or officials to account. For instance, for what are these actors to be held accountable? What standards do we use for holding them to account? The answers to these questions vary – accountability

83 Bovens (n 12) 453.
84 Mulgan (n 26) 10.

can take different forms, depending on (among other things) who is accountable, for what are they accountable and to whom are they accountable.[85]

Scholars have developed various typologies to define the content of different forms of accountability. Scholarly works suggest that a classic typology is based on the identity of an overseeing actor, i.e. to whom accountable actors are accountable. Different types of overseeing actors demand different kinds of information and apply different criteria according to which they can evaluate accountable actors' decisions and actions and pass judgment. According to the types of overseeing actors, we can at least distinguish the following kinds of accountability: political accountability, legal accountability, judicial accountability, quasi-judicial accountability, administrative accountability and social accountability. This typology will be discussed further in the context of the right to health (care) and with various forms of accountability mechanisms in chapter 6.

The subsection below does not intend to delineate all types of accountability, but is confined to one classic typology based on the question: to whom are accountable actors held to account? A very general reason for holding an actor to account would be that one is mandated to or volunteers to do so. Based on the nature of an accountable actor's obligation, accountability can be further divided into vertical, horizontal and diagonal accountability, which each involve different overseeing actors.[86] There are two different schools of thought on this division.

5.3.1 The prevailing view of vertical, horizontal and diagonal accountability

The prevailing view of vertical and horizontal accountability is derived from the spatial metaphor of power: '"above" equals power, "below" equals powerless'.[87] As such, vertical accountability describes a classic, top-down relationship between unequal actors: the more powerful (superior) actor holds the less powerful (inferior) actor accountable. Vice versa, the inferior actor can also hold the superior actor accountable. This concept concerns the hierarchy between the two actors, which often has the nature of a principal-agent relation. However, it leaves open the question of

85 Pelizzo and Stapenhurst (n 38) 2-7; Bovens (n 12) 454-460; Schedler (n 12) 21-25.
86 Bovens (n 12) 460; Pelizzo and Stapenhurst (n 38) 2-6.
87 Schedler (n 12) 23.

whether vertical accountability is exercised in a top-down or bottom-up manner.[88] A very common example of the former is bureaucratic accountability, sometimes also called internal accountability, in which higher-ranking public officials (principals) delegate their power to their subordinates (agents) and control the exercise of power by their subordinates. An example of the latter is electoral accountability in which citizens pose questions and pass judgement on their elected politicians through the election processes.[89] During periods in which no elections are taking place, citizens, CSOs or the media can also enforce standards of good performance on public officials and hold them accountable for misconducts, very often by naming and shaming.[90]

In comparison, horizontal accountability describes a relationship between equals: one actor holds another actor, that has roughly equal power, to account.[91] Horizontal accountability is often exercised through the separation of powers by the legislature, the judiciary and the executive, which conduct mutual 'checks and balances'. Simply speaking, horizontal accountability refers to the capacity of State institutions (or officials) to check abuses of power by other institutions within the State by requiring them to report 'sideways'.[92] For example, courts can hold administrative agencies to account through judicial proceedings. A strong, independent judiciary that can provide checks on the exercise of power is thus crucial.[93] Other institutions such as audit offices, anti-corruption agencies and bureaucratic supervision boards often exercise external horizontal accountability.[94] It should be noted, however, that despite their horizontal relationship, in which the two actors stand on an equal footing, the overseeing actor should be more powerful, 'at least in its sphere of competence'.[95] Additionally, an overseeing actor must be 'legally enabled and empowered', within the boundaries of its jurisdiction, to impose consequences (and especially sanctions) on an accountable actor who is found to have been at fault.[96]

88 ibid; Pelizzo and Stapenhurst (n 38) 3.
89 Pelizzo and Stapenhurst (n 38) 3.
90 Guillermo O'Donnell, 'Horizontal Accountability in New Democracies' in Andreas Schedler, Larry Diamond and Marc Plattner (eds), *The Self-restraining State: Power and Accountability in New Democracies* (Lynne Rienner Publishers 1999) 29-30.
91 Schedler (n 12) 23; Pelizzo and Stapenhurst (n 38) 3.
92 Pelizzo and Stapenhurst (n 38) 3.
93 The Department for International Development (DFID), *Briefing: Justice and Accountability* (May 2008) 3.
94 ibid 12.
95 Schedler (n 12) 23.
96 ibid 23-24.

In addition to the traditional concepts of accountability, 'diagonal accountability' recently emerged as an intermediate form of accountability.[97] There is increasing recognition that weak competence and a lack of legitimacy may undermine horizontal accountability institutions (eg independent supervisory institutions).[98] This implies that institutions of horizontal accountability themselves need to be held to account, raising the question of who should do this. A solution may lie in diagonal accountability, which directly entails vertical accountability actors (eg citizens) 'in the workings of horizontal accountability institutions' that have traditionally been the arena of public officials and institutions alone.[99] Combining elements of both vertical and horizontal accountability, 'by breaking the state's monopoly over responsibility for official executive oversight', diagonal accountability has the potential, as Pelizzo and Stapenhurst assert, to enhance civil society's watchdog role.[100]

5.3.2 Another school of thought on vertical, horizontal and diagonal accountability

Some scholars hold differing opinions regarding the distinction between vertical and horizontal accountability. For Bovens, for example, the distinction between vertical and horizontal accountability depends on whether the relations between the two actors have a principal-agent character or not.[101] According to Bovens, vertical accountability refers to a classic principal-agent relationship in which 'the forum formally wielders power over the actor'.[102] In his definition, the forum refers to the overseeing actor (the principal) while the actor refers to the accountable actor (the agent). Political accountability arrangements are the most common form of vertical accountability based on the principal-agent relationship. In these arrangements, the principal delegates his power to the agent and holds the agent accountable internally, along the lines of the 'chain of command'.[103] An example that has been repeatedly

97 Pelizzo and Stapenhurst (n 38) 5.
98 DFID (n 93) 11.
99 Pelizzo and Stapenhurst (n 38) 5.
100 ibid 5-6.
101 Mark Bovens, 'New Forms of Accountability and EU-Governance' (2007) 5 Comparative European Politics 104, 109.
102 Boverns (n 12) 460
103 ibid.

mentioned above is that parliament can hold its ministers accountable. Legal accountability is another example of vertical accountability. Although not based on the principal-agent relationship, an overseeing actor has the formal authority to hold an accountable actor to account through the court on the basis of domestic legislation.[104]

In contrast, an accountability relationship becomes one of horizontal accountability due to the absence of a hierarchy between the two actors involved and the lack of any formal obligation of account-giving.[105] In addition, in horizontal accountability relationships there is no formal obligation for the actor (i.e. the accountable actor adopted in this chapter) to render account to the forum (i.e. the overseeing actor). The obligation of account-giving is normally moral in nature and generally occurs on a voluntary basis with no intervention on the part of the forum.[106] Horizontal accountability is thus demand-driven, and operates from the bottom, which in this sense can also be regarded as social accountability.

Bovens regards most administrative accountability relationships as a form of diagonal accountability. An example is public institutions such as national human rights institutions and ombudsmen. In general terms, there is no direct hierarchical relationship between these institutions and other public officials and institutions; therefore, they have little power to enforce their compliance and impose sanctions. Nevertheless, these institutions can report directly or indirectly to those in authority (eg the parliament or ministers), and ultimately derive informal power from reporting.[107]

The above discussion has shown that accountability exists when there is a relationship between an overseeing actor and an accountable actor, in which the accountable actor is obliged to provide information on, explain and justify his decisions and actions, while the overseeing actor can question the accountable actor, pass judgement and impose consequences on him. We have also discussed various types of accountability and how the exercise of accountability can keep power under control and hold those responsible to account. The question remains, however: why is it important to discuss accountability in the context of human rights?

---

104 ibid.
105 ibid.
106 ibid.
107 ibid.

As noted in Hunt's reports, 'unless supported by some form of accountability, human rights run the risk of becoming mere window dressing'.[108] Accountability gives 'teeth' to human rights. Therefore, accountability is often regarded as an integral feature of human rights and is considered central to the domestic implementation of the right to health.[109] A follow-up question then arises: what role does accountability play in the progressive realisation of the right to health (care)? This question will be addressed by the analysis below.

5.4 Rights to health-based accountability: a conceptual framework

5.4.1 Defining right to health-based accountability

There are no specific provisions in international human rights treaties that define accountability, which remains an underexplored concept in human rights research. Nonetheless, despite the fact that the word *'accountability'* is not explicitly mentioned on the majority of occasions, accountability is included in a wide variety of international mechanisms (eg State reporting and individual communications) that allow the State parties' conformity with human rights standards to be evaluated.[110] Additionally, in its General Comment 9, the CteeESCR requires States parties to the International Covenant on Economic, Social and Cultural Rights (ICESCR) to enhance 'governmental accountability'.[111]

---

108 UNGA, 'Report of the Special Rapporteur on the Right of Everyone to the Enjoyment of the Highest Attainable Standard of Physical and Mental Health, Paul Hunt' (17 Janauary 2007) UN Doc A/HRC/4/28, para 57; UNGA, 'Report of the Special Rapporteur on the Right of Everyone to the Enjoyment of the Highest Attainable Standard of Physical and Mental Health, Paul Hunt' (n 3) para 51 (d).

109 UNGA, 'Report of the Special Rapporteur on the Right of Everyone to the Enjoyment of the Highest Attainable Standard of Physical and Mental Health, Paul Hunt' (11 August 2008) UN Doc A/63/263, para 8.

110 OHCHR, 'The Major Universal Human Rights Instruments and the Mechanisms for Their Implementations' in *Human Rights in the Administration of Justice: A Manual on Human Rights for Judges, Prosecutors and Lawyers* (United Nations Publication 2003) 42, 47, 60.

111 CteeESCR, General Comment 9 (n 3) para 2; CteeESCR, General Comment 14 (n 8) para 55.

Furthermore, scholars now also perceive accountability as an essential component of human rights practice.[112] In the context of the right to health (care) specifically, the importance of ensuring accountability has been emphasised in reports submitted by Hunt, the first UN Special Rapporteur on the Right to Health.[113] According to Hunt:

> [a]ccountability provides individuals and communities with an opportunity to understand how those with human rights responsibilities have discharged their duties. Equally, it provides those with human rights responsibilities the opportunity to explain what they have done and why. Where mistakes have been made, accountability requires redress.[114]

In addition to Hunt, Freeman also identifies that accountability is '[...] about developing a dynamic of entitlement and obligation between people and their government and within the complex system of relationships that form the wider health system, public and private'.[115] Following this understanding, accountability refers to the relationship between those who bear right to health obligations and those who are entitled to the right to health (care) under international human rights law.[116] In the current research, those who undertake a human rights obligation to provide information and to explain and justify their decisions and actions (whether taken or planned) are referred to as *duty-bearers*, while those who have the right to health (care) are labelled *right-holders*.

It is obvious that human rights form the basis of account-giving in this relationship. First of all, when identifying duty-bearers, it is clear that, as a matter of international human rights law, the State is ultimately accountable for its obligations under the right to health (care).[117] In addition, from a human rights perspective, all actors that operate on behalf of the State have a responsibility to promote and protect human

112 See for example Alicia Yamin, 'Beyond Compassion: The Central Role of Accountability in Applying a Human Rights Framework to Health' (2008) 10 (2) Health and Human Rights 1, 1; Paul Hunt and others, 'Implementation of Economic, Social and Cultural Rights' in Scott Sheeran and Nigel Rodley (eds), *Routledge Handbook of International Human Rights Law* (Routledge 2013) 550–554.

113 UNGA, 'Report of the Special Rapporteur on the Right of Everyone to the Enjoyment of the Highest Attainable Standard of Physical and Mental Health, Paul Hunt' (n 109) paras 3, 8.

114 ibid, para 9.

115 Freeman (n 9) 111.

116 Potts (n 9) 4.

117 CteeESCR, General Comment 14 (n 8) para 42.

rights within their spheres of responsibility.[118] In this context, '*the State*' generally encompasses the State itself and all '*State actors*' that have a responsibility mandated by the State to advance the right to health (care), including formal public institutions (eg parliament, the Ministry of Health and its branches, and local governments) and public officials (eg policy-makers and civil servants at different levels).[119] In addition, public health care providers, social security institutions or public health insurers all have responsibilities from a right to health perspective and are thus also regarded as duty-bearers.[120]

Instead of 'the State', this study uses 'State actors' to distinguish from non-State actors. The question of whether non-State actors are subject to international human rights obligations is receiving increasing amounts of scholarly attention. Certainly, at the national level, depending on a State's domestic laws and policies, non-State actors may be considered as duty-bearers. Nevertheless, given the scope of this study, my analysis of duty-bearers is confined to 'State actors'. Generally speaking, all State actors defined in this study are accountable actors, and in certain circumstances, some State actors also function as overseeing actors.

Moving to the identification of right-holders, as a matter of international human rights law, everyone enjoys the right to health (care) and is thus a right-holder that can hold duty-bearers to account. All individuals are entitled to ask duty-bearers for reliable information or a valid explanation and justification, as well as to impose consequences on them.[121] When there is a violation of the right to health (care), right-holders should have access to judicial or other appropriate remedies.[122]

Right-holders fall under the umbrella of overseeing actors. In addition to right-holders, overseeing actors also encompass other overseeing institutions that provide checks and balances on duty-bearers. Such institutions include constitutional courts, ombudsman offices and supreme audit institutions. The media also have a crucial role

118 Andrew Byrnes and Catherine Renshaw, 'Within the State' in Daniel Moeckli and others (eds), *International Human Rights Law* (2nd Edn Oxford University Press 2014) 469; Potts (n 9) 4.

119 OHCHR and Center for Economic and Social Rights (n 2) 11.

120 CteeESCR, General Comment 14 (n 8) para 42. General Comment 14 also states that all members of society have responsibility for the realisation of the right to health, including the private business sector (i.e. non-state actor). However, in the space given, the discussion will be limited to public actors. See also Derick Brinkerhoff, 'Accountability and Health Systems: Overview, Framework, and Strategies' (Partners for Health Reformplus 2003) 11-18.

121 Potts (n 9) 22.

122 CteeESCR, General Comment 14 (n 8) para 59.

to play in holding State actors (i.e. accountable actors) to account.

Put simply, the actors involved in right to health-based accountability include:

- Accountable actors: duty-bearers (State actors, eg the State, the Ministry of Health, civil servants);
- Overseeing actors: right-holders (everyone) and overseeing institutions (eg courts, national human rights institutions, the media).

In the reminder of this study, especially in chapters 6 and 7, I will use the terms accountable actors and State actors, as well as right-holders, overseeing actors and overseeing institutions.

5.4.2 Constituent elements of right to health-based accountability

A further analysis of right to health-based accountability leads to its constituent elements. As mentioned above, accountability has two dimensions: answerability and enforcement. Following a similar line of analysis, this study contends that right to health-based accountability embraces one more element: responsibility.[123] Responsibility answers the question: for what can accountable actors be held to account? In the debate on accountability more generally, no consensus has been reached as to what constitutes accountable behaviour. There are no specific criteria for good or bad decisions and actions because those criteria differ from role to role, time to time, and place to place.[124] Human rights contribute to this discussion by providing clear standards; human rights frameworks help to define the substantive responsibilities of State actors on the basis of relevant human rights standards and principles.[125] State actors are clearly accountable for their obligations arising from the right to health (care).

In short, right to health-based accountability, or human rights-based accountability more generally, comprises three different elements: (1) responsibility; (2) answerability; and (3) enforcement. The right to health framework provides a strong rationale for these components,[126] which are all necessary, but on their own insufficient, elements to achieving right to health-based accountability.

123 OHCHR and Center for Economic and Social Rights (n 2) 10.
124 Bovens (n 12) 450.
125 OHCHR and Center for Economic and Social Rights (n 2) 10-13.
126 ibid 10-16.

5.4.2.1 *Responsibility*

First, with respect to responsibility, the right to health framework clearly delineates the responsibilities of duty-bearers. State actors (including every local, national and international institution or official that is mandated by the State with responsibility for the implementation of the right to health) are obliged to respect, protect and fulfil its right to health commitments recognised in the relevant international human rights treaties to which the State is party.[127]

More specifically, as explained in depth in chapter 2, State actors undertake certain core obligations to respect, protect and fulfil the right to health care. Some detailed right to health standards are also provided in General Comment 14. For instance, health facilities, goods and services should be available, accessible, acceptable, and of good quality.[128] This AAAQ framework allows overseeing actors to assess State actors' decisions and actions accordingly.[129]

5.4.2.2 *Answerability*

This subsection does not intend to repeat the discussion of answerability and enforcement in section 5.2.3, the findings of which are followed here. To reiterate, answerability requires accountable actors (i.e. State actors) to be answerable to overseeing actors (i.e. right-holders and overseeing institutions).[130]

The right to health framework sheds light on the question concerning to whom State actors are answerable.[131] This framework requires that State actors are answerable to the entire population in a non-discriminatory manner.[132] More specifically, it requires State actors to create an environment for mobilising and empowering relevant stakeholders, including, in particular, vulnerable and marginalised groups

127 CteeESCR, General Comment 14 (n 8) para 33; OHCHR and Center for Economic and Social Rights (n 2) 11.
128 CteeESCR, General Comment 14 (n 8) para 12.
129 Brigit Toebes and Maite San Giorgi, 'Dutch Realities: Evaluating Health Care Reform in the Netherlands from a Human Rights Perspective' in Brigit Toebes and other (eds), *The Right to Health: A Multi-Country Study of Law, Policy and Practice* (Springer 2014) 407.
130 OHCHR and Center for Economic and Social Rights (n 2) 11, 14; Potts (n 9) 15; Schedler (n 12) 14-15.
131 OHCHR and Center for Economic and Social Rights (n 2) 14.
132 ibid.

(who have traditionally been excluded), to participate in all health-related decision-making processes.[133] The vulnerable and marginalised groups should be able to have *ex ante* input and make their prioritised health needs clear to State actors. By doing so, their health needs and concerns would not be neglected in the first place. Appropriate mechanisms (eg public hearings, online platforms) should be put into place so as to make it possible for right-holders (and overseeing institutions) to ask State actors for information, as well as explanation and justification for their decisions and actions.[134] These mechanisms also help to identify – when and what – policy adjustments are necessary.[135] Viewed in this light, the answerability dimension of accountability can establish a prospective process for dynamic communication between accountable actors (i.e. State actors) and overseeing actors (right-holders and overseeing institutions).

5.4.2.3 Enforcement

Finally, to be accountable, State actors should bear both positive and negative consequences, including, in particular, the imposition of sanctions for wrongdoings.[136] As is understood in the right to health framework, the State has an obligation to adopt appropriate means for ensuring accountability and to provide effective remedies.[137] These include incorporating the right to health norms into the State's domestic legal system, establishing judicial procedures under which violations of the right to health (care) can be investigated, and providing appropriate and effective access to justice and remedies to redress grievances.[138]

In brief, the right to health framework calls for: the establishment of effective, transparent, accessible and independent accountability mechanisms for monitoring the degree to which State actors are in compliance with their obligations arising from

133 Yamin (n 112) 2.
134 OHCHR and Center for Economic and Social Rights (n 2) 14.
135 United Nations Economic and Social Council, 'Economic, Social and Cultural Rights: The Right of Everyone to the Enjoyment of the Highest Attainable Standard of Physical and Mental Health, Report of the Special Rapporteur, Paul Hunt' (16 February 2004) UN Doc E/CN.4/2004/49, para 9.
136 Schedler (n 12) 15; OHCHR and Center for Economic and Social Rights (n 2) 14-15.
137 CteeESCR, General Comment 9 (n 3) para 2; CteeESCR, General Comment 14 (n 8) paras 54, 59-60.
138 CteeESCR, General Comment 14 (n 8) para 59-60; OHCHR and Center for Economic and Social Rights (n 2) 14 -16; Yamin (n 112) 2-3.

the right to health (care;) the imposition of consequences on State actors, including in particular sanctions when State actors fail to carry out their mandated obligations; and the adoption of measures to ensure effective and accessible remedies for victims of a violation of the right to health (care).[139]

5.5 A CONSTRUCTIVE ACCOUNTABILITY PROCESS

This study contends that right to health-based accountability is a process of making certain that accountable actors (i.e. State actors) inform overseeing actors (i.e. right-holders and overseeing institutions) about what they have done or plan to do for the realisation of the right to health (care), and explain and justify their reasons for doing so. It also entails that accountable actors are subject to consequences for their decisions and actions and that there are mechanisms for remedying failures and violations of the right to health (care). Nevertheless, it should be noted that while this study views accountability mostly as a *process*, it also implies the existence of an accountability-*relationship*, and an *obligation* for State actors to be accountable for the right to health (care).

139 CteeESCR, General Comment 14 (n 8) para 56; Potts (n 9) 17, 28; OHCHR and Center for Economic and Social Rights (n 2) 14, 16, 32.

The right to health-based accountability process can be understood as below:[140]

Accountable actors (i.e. State actors/duty-bearers) give account to overseeing actors (i.e. right-holders and overseeing institutions) on the basis of the right to health (care); 1. Monitoring: • Overseeing actors ask State actors about the extent to which they have respected, protected and fulfilled their obligations under the right to health (care); • State actors should release all necessary information and data concerning their decisions and actions; 2. Judgement: • Overseeing actors pose questions to responsible State actors; • State actors explain and justify their decisions and the reasons for them; • Overseeing actors evaluate the persuasiveness of the explanation and justification; • Overseeing actors pass positive or negative judgement; 3. Consequences: • Positive: overseeing actors reward State actors when passing a positive judgement; • Negative: overseeing actors impose sanctions or other forms of negative consequences on State actors when passing a negative judgement; 4. Remedies • When State actors are found to have been at fault, remedies should be put in place for those who have been affected by violations of the right to health (care).

Based on the above, I contend that a constructive accountability process encompasses four fundamental building blocks: monitoring, judgement, consequences and remedies (see the coloured blocks in Figure 5.2).

140 Source: the author. Adapted from Bovens (n 12) 452.

Figure 5.2 A comprehensive accountability process[141]

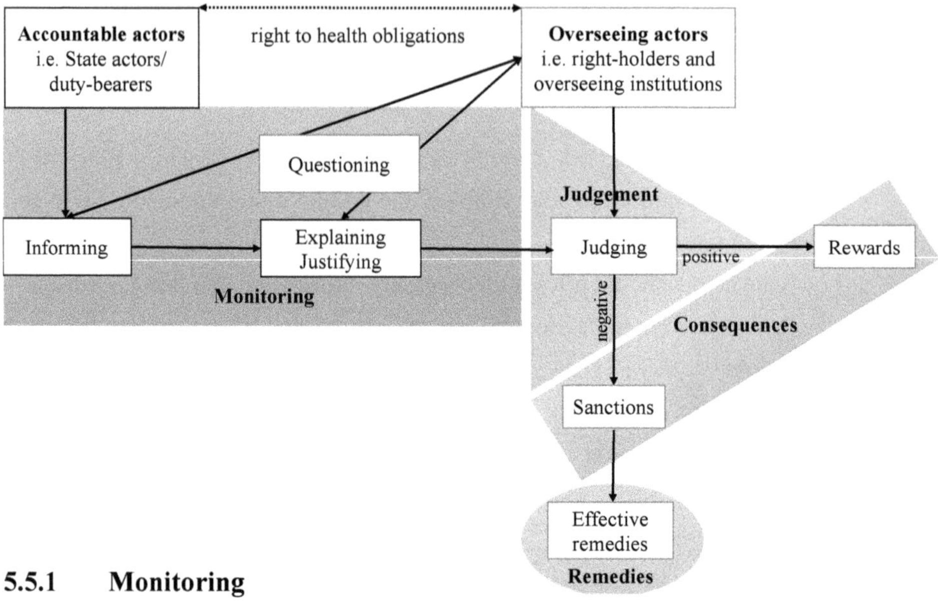

5.5.1 Monitoring

Right to health-based accountability involves the gathering of information and data so as to measure the degree to which State actors comply with their obligations under the right to health (care) and to identify what works, and what needs to be improved or revised.[142]

Monitoring involves a dynamic dialogue between accountable actors and overseeing actors, in which overseeing actors question accountable actors (i.e. State actors, in the context of the right to health) about their decisions and actions. Correlatively, accountable actors are required to inform overseeing actors about what they have done or plan to do, as well as explain and justify the reasons for their decisions and actions. In particular, overseeing institutions, such as human rights ombudsmen, can directly participate in and initiate the monitoring process on their own volition and question the responsible State actors directly. Alternatively, overseeing institutions can engage in the monitoring process upon a right-holder's request, which is very often the case for courts.

141 Source: the author.
142 Potts (n 9) 14.

Mechanisms should be established to monitor decision-making processes, the performance (and results thereof) of State actors, and to ensure the collection and analysis of appropriate and accurate information and data.[143]

5.5.2 Judgement

After obtaining the relevant information and data, overseeing actors will judge whether right to health commitments have been fulfilled and duties discharged.[144] Right-holders and overseeing institutions can adjudicate the persuasiveness of the explanation and justification provided by State actors on the basis of the available information and the right to health standards and principles.

Notably, the process of judgement by overseeing actors can keep health laws, regulations, policies, and programmes in conformity with right to health norms. As explained earlier, State actors may adjust their decisions and actions in advance when they anticipate a negative judgement and corresponding sanctions, or they may repeat the decisions and actions that have previously been rewarded or may be rewarded in the future. The judgement process thus has the potential to recognise good practices, identify obstacles that undermine the implementation of the right to health (care), and make practical recommendations so as to repeat what works and revise what does not work.[145]

Considering the complexity of a health care system, many countries have established an independent overseeing institution (eg national human rights institution) to provide professional judgement and assess the compliance of State actors with right to health standards, thus ensuring the objectivity and credibility of the accountability process. Mechanisms for the judging process will be discussed in detail in chapter 6.

143 Center for Reproductive Rights, 'The Role of Human Rights-based Accountability in Eliminating Maternal Mortality and Morbidity' (April 2011) 2, 5 <www2.ohchr.org/english/issues/women/docs/responses/CenterforReproductiveRights.pdf> accessed 28 November 2017.

144 Partnership for Maternal, Newborn and Child Health (PMNCH), 'National Accountability Mechanisms for Women's and Children's Health' (2012) 10 <www.who.int/pmnch/topics/part_publications/national_accountability_mechanisms.pdf> accessed 28 November 2017.

145 ibid.

5.5.3 Consequences

To hold State actors accountable, systematic mechanisms that enable right-holders or overseeing institutions to impose consequences on State actors are necessary at this stage. When right to health obligations (especially its core obligations) are not respected, protected or fulfilled, or violations of the right to health (care) occur, it is important to assure that State actors will be subject to various forms of enforceable negative consequences, including eventual sanctions. Very often, sanctions are imposed by overseeing institutions (eg courts) because right-holders in general cannot enforce sanctions themselves. Significantly, as explained above, right-holders and overseeing institutions may not only pass negative, but may also pass positive judgement on State actors. This allows positive aspects of a health care system to be repeated, thus making the accountability process both prospective and retrospective.

5.5.4 Remedies

Remedial action should be taken when violations of the right to health (care) occur. Victims of such violations should have access to judicial or other effective remedies. Overseeing institutions, including courts, national human rights institutions and patients' rights associations, should address violations of the right to health (care).[146] This includes but is not limited to reparation for the specific victims, the establishment of new legislation or the amendment of existing legislation, as well as revisions to health policies and programmes. Remedies can then be understood as measures that must be taken to rectify an undesired, unintended or harmful outcome.[147] Remedies will also be discussed further in chapter 6.

5.6 Concluding summary

A distinct feature of the right to health framework is that it reinforces (good) health practice through accountability. By the same token, without accountability, the

146 CteeESCR, General Comment 14 (n 8) para 59.
147 ibid.

right to health (care) is likely to become an empty promise. Right to health-based accountability thus has far-reaching benefits which strengthen health care systems and advance the right to health (care).

Right to health-based accountability, or human rights-based accountability more generally, is regarded as a dynamic and interactive process in which State actors are obliged to inform overseeing actors (i.e. right-holders and overseeing institutions) about their (past or future) decisions and actions, to justify them and to face positive or negative consequences for them. This process has the potential to ensure that all State actors discharge their obligations as planned, and that any unintended consequences are swiftly identified and addressed.

Enhancing right to health-based accountability involves not only integrating right to health norms and standards into the overall decision-making processes but also provides for the establishment of appropriate accountability mechanisms for facilitating the overall accountability process. International, regional and national accountability mechanisms can be created within and outside health care systems to monitor the conduct of State actors, to hold responsible actors to account, and to provide avenues for remedies and redress for violations of the right to health (care). The focus in chapter 6 thus shifts to an analysis of accountability mechanisms.

Chapter 6
Accountability Mechanisms for the Realisation of the Right to Health

6.1 Introduction

While calling for more accountability is certainly necessary for improving the realisation of the right to health,[1] it is even more important to ensure that accessible, transparent and effective accountability *mechanisms* have been established for exerting accountability. Accountability mechanisms enable overseeing actors to hold State actors to account and to provide redress for violations of the right to health (or indeed any human right). The purpose of this chapter is to explore the nature and scope of accountability mechanisms that can hold State actors accountable for their right to health obligations at various levels.

Section 6.2 first clarifies the distinction between 'accountability' and an 'accountability mechanism'. Subsequently, it proposes an analytical framework for analysing accountability mechanisms at different levels, within and outside health care systems. This framework is based on the three questions mentioned in chapter 5: who is accountable, for what are these actors accountable, and to whom are these actors accountable? Given that China is not a State party to any of the regional human rights treaties, the discussion in this chapter is confined to domestic and international accountability mechanisms. Paul Hunt, (one of the) former UN Special Rapporteurs on the Right to Health, has mentioned in several of his reports that the State undertakes a core obligation to establish a range of (domestic) accountability mechanisms so as to ensure the full enjoyment of the right to health.[2] Section 6.3 offers an overview of judicial, quasi-judicial, political, administrative and social accountability mechanisms at the domestic level and illustrates how overseeing actors (i.e. right-holders and

1 To allow the chapter to have a broader application, its focus is the right to health more generally (which also encompasses the right to health care), rather than the right to health care in particular.

2 See eg United Nations General Assembly (UNGA), 'Report of the Special Rapporteur on the Right of Everyone to the Enjoyment of the Highest Attainable Standard of Physical and Mental Health, Paul Hunt' (31 Janauary 2008) UN Doc A/HRC/7/11, para 51 (d); UNGA, 'Report of the Special Rapporteur on the Right of Everyone to the Enjoyment of the Highest Attainable Standard of Physical and Mental Health, Paul Hunt' (11 August 2008) UN Doc A/63/263, para 11.

overseeing institutions) can hold State actors (with right to health obligations) to account through these mechanisms. Section 6.4 pays particular attention to the media, which function in this study as both an accountability mechanism and as an external overseeing institution.[3] As will be discussed further in chapter 7, the media play a crucial role in exerting accountability in China. Nevertheless, the role of the media is perceived differently by scholars from different disciplines.[4] The aim of section 6.4 is thus to synthesise existing studies across disciplines and to provide a comprehensive analysis of the role of the media in generating accountability. Section 6.5 provides a general discussion of international mechanisms for monitoring States parties' compliance with their obligations under international human rights treaties. Section 6.6 summarises the key components of an analytical framework for right to health-based accountability, thus setting the stage for the discussion of accountability for advancing the right to health care in China in chapter 7.

6.2 An overview of accountability mechanisms

6.2.1 Accountability and accountability mechanisms: a conceptual clarification

As Hunt observes, accountability within health care systems is often very weak.[5] Research indicates that there are several causes for this, including relatively inadequate regulatory and institutional capacity to exercise oversight of health service providers' performance.[6] Additionally, in reality there is very often limited information and data

3 The definition of these terms will be provided in section 6.4.

4 See eg Derick Brinkerhoff, 'Taking Account of Accountability: A Conceptual Overview and Strategic Options' (US Agency for International Development 2001) 4-5 <http://1qswp72wn11q9smtq15ccbuo.wpengine.netdna-cdn.com/wp-content/uploads/2011/07/IPC_Taking_Account_of_Accountability.pdf> accessed 28 November 2017; Helen Potts, 'Accountability and the Right to the Highest Attainable Standard of Health' (University of Essex Human Rights Centre 2008) 23 <http://repository.essex.ac.uk/9717/1/accountability-right-highest-attainable-standard-health.pdf> accessed 28 November 2017; United Nations Development Programme (UNDP), 'Fostering Social Accountability: From Principle to Practice' (2010) 10; United Nations Children's Fund (UNICEF), 'Accountability for Children's Rights: With Special Attention to Social Accountability and Its Potential to Achieve Results and Equity for Children' (2015) 4.

5 UNGA, 'Report of the Special Rapporteur on the Right of Everyone to the Enjoyment of the Highest Attainable Standard of Physical and Mental Health, Paul Hunt' (11 August 2008) UN Doc A/63/263, para 12.

6 Derick Brinkerhoff, 'Accountability and Health Systems: Toward Conceptual Clarity and Policy Relevance' (2004) 19 Health Policy and Planning 371, 375-377.

available and accessible to right-holders to allow them to hold State actors to account. In light of these weaknesses, accessible, transparent and effective accountability mechanisms are important for establishing how State actors have discharged their obligations arising from the right to health. [7]

Nevertheless, there is considerable conceptual confusion when it comes to the term 'accountability mechanism'. Potts, an authoritative author in the field of right to health accountability, views an accountability mechanism (considered to be a *procedure*) as part of accountability itself, which she considers to be a *process*. In terms of accountability as a process, Potts asserts that accountability mechanisms, together with monitoring, participation and remedies, are essential elements of an effective accountability *process*.[8] When it comes to an accountability mechanism as a *procedure*, Potts holds that:

> an accountability mechanism is the procedure through which government is answerable for its acts or omissions in relation to right to health obligations. The procedure provides right-holders with an opportunity to obtain information on government action, and to ask for explanations. It also provides government with an opportunity to explain its actions.[9]

Potts then defines 'accountability' as 'the process which requires government to show, explain and justify how it has discharged its obligations regarding the right to the highest attainable standard of health'.[10] It deserves noting that Pott's definition of *accountability mechanism (a procedure)* and accountability (*process*) blur the distinction between accountability and accountability mechanisms.

In relation to this, a clear distinction between the concepts of *accountability* and *accountability mechanism* is lacking in most human rights research on accountability. I searched the term 'accountability mechanism' in the reports of the Special Rapporteurs on the Right to Health and in 15 papers addressing the issue of accountability from a human rights perspective. These studies have in common that they all emphasise the

7 UNGA, 'Report of the Special Rapporteur on the Right of Everyone to the Enjoyment of the Highest Attainable Standard of Physical and Mental Health, Paul Hunt' (n 5) para 11.
8 Potts (n 4) 13-14.
9 ibid 17.
10 ibid 13.

importance of establishing accountability mechanisms.[11] However, in the majority of these studies, the term 'accountability mechanism' remains undefined. Most scholars simply exemplify different types of accountability (eg judicial, political, administrative accountability) under the category of accountability mechanisms,[12] whereas some scholars consider accountability itself as a mechanism.[13]

Explanations provided in political discourse may help to clarify these two concepts. For instance, Bovens distinguishes between 'accountability as a virtue' and 'accountability as a mechanism'. Accountability, or being accountable, is seen as a virtue when it is used as 'a normative concept, as a set of standards for the behaviour of actors, or as a desirable state of affairs.'[14] This notion is closely linked to concepts such as 'responsiveness' and 'responsibility'. The locus of accountability studies in this regard is the behaviour of public agents, with a focus on the standards for assessing such behaviour.[15] However, as explained in chapter 5, given the absence of a general consensus regarding the standards for accountable behaviour in political discourse, it is not easy to substantively define accountability as a virtue. Nonetheless, the responsibility dimension of right to health-based (or human rights-based more generally) accountability has the potential to refine accountability as a virtue, as explained in chapter 5.

In comparison, accountability is seen as a mechanism when it is used in a narrower and more descriptive way, 'as an institutional relation or arrangement in which an agent can be held to account by another agent or institution'.[16] Bovens defines accountability as 'a *relationship* between an actor and a forum, in which the actor

11 See generally, UNGA, 'Report of the Special Rapporteur on the Right of Everyone to the Enjoyment of the Highest Attainable Standard of Physical and Mental Health, Paul Hunt' (n 5) para 11; Alicia Yamin, 'Beyond Compassion: The Central Role of Accountability in Applying a Human Rights Framework to Health' (2008) 10 Health and Human Rights 1, 5; Paul Hunt and Gunilla Backman, 'Health Systems and the Right to the Highest Attainable Standard of Health' (2008) 10 Health and Human Rights 81, 85; Office of the United Nations High Commissioner for Human Rights (OHCHR) and Center for Economic and Social Rights, 'Who Will Be Accountable? Human Rights and the Post-2015 Development Agenda' (2013) 32; Potts (n 4) 17; UNICEF (n 4) 8; Brinkerhoff (n 6) 373.

12 UNGA, 'Report of the Special Rapporteur on the Right of Everyone to the Enjoyment of the Highest Attainable Standard of Physical and Mental Health, Paul Hunt' (n 5) para 11; Yamin (n 11) 5; OHCHR and Center for Economic and Social Rights (n 11) 32.

13 See eg UNICEF (n 4) 8.

14 Mark Bovens, 'Two Concepts of Accountability: Accountability as a Virtue and as a Mechanism' (2010) 33 West European Politics 946, 947-949.

15 ibid.

16 ibid 948.

has an obligation to explain and to justify his or her conduct, the forum can pose questions and pass judgement, and the actor may face consequences'. This definition reflects a relatively narrow approach to accountability.[17] The locus of accountability studies such as Bovens' is the institutional relationship between the actor and the forum; and the focus is whether actors (i.e. accountable actors) 'are or can be held accountable *ex post facto*', rather than whether they have acted in an accountable way.[18] In this sense, accountability as a mechanism closely corresponds to the answerability and enforcement dimensions of right to health-based accountability, as mentioned in chapter 5. Seen as a mechanism, accountability encompasses a variety of accountability relationships. For example, it can be divided into legal, political, administrative and social accountability, the applicability of which is based on the type of the forum (i.e. overseeing actors) to which account is to be rendered.[19] Accountability as a mechanism in this sense is similar to the classification of accountability mechanisms under some human rights literature.[20]

To complicate matters further, accountability *as a mechanism* must be distinguished from an accountability *mechanism*. There is one striking difference between these concepts. Human rights scholars consider actors, such as courts, auditors and ombudsmen, as mechanisms for accountability.[21] In comparison, taking a broader approach, Bovens perceives accountability relationships, whether formal or informal in nature, as accountability mechanisms.[22] For example, being accountable to legal and administrative forums such as courts, auditors and ombudsmen, is an important mechanism for preventing and detecting the abuse of public powers; in Bovens' definition, courts, auditors and ombudsmen constitute the forum rather than the accountability mechanism *per se*.[23]

Based on Bovens' work, Kasuya and Takahashi claim that accountability as a mechanism encompasses both the components and the agents of accountability.[24] In their view, the agents can generate both vertical and horizontal mechanisms of

17 ibid 951.
18 ibid 948.
19 ibid 952-953.
20 See note 11.
21 See eg Yamin (n 11) 5.
22 Bovens (n 14) 955.
23 ibid.
24 Yuko Kasuya and Yuriko Takahashi, 'Streamlining Accountability : Concepts , Subtypes , and Empirical Analyses' (2012) 2, 14 <ssrn.com/abstract=2493654> accessed 28 November 2017.

accountability.[25] Elections are considered to be 'a primary mechanism of generating accountability', while 'voters are the agent of this accountability mechanism'.[26] However, Kasuya and Takahashi perceive oversight agencies (eg courts and ombudsmen), legislative oversight and judicial review as all being horizontal mechanism of accountability.[27] Following this understanding, *the court* that provides for judicial review is regarded as a mechanism of accountability, while *judicial review* itself is also regarded as a mechanism of accountability. Similar statements are also found in some human rights literature addressing accountability.[28]

I argue that if we do not distinguish more clearly between accountability mechanism and overseeing institutions (or Kasuya and Takahasi's agents of accountability), as shown in Table 6.1, the boundaries of each concept would become blurred. The agents of accountability (or the forum, overseeing actors, however termed) include, *inter alia*, voters, courts, ombudsmen and auditors. Still taking the court as an example, if an individual claims a State's violation of the right to health before a domestic court, this case will involve three parties: the victim (i.e. right-holder), the State (i.e. duty-bearer) and the court. The State is accountable to human right-holders as a matter of human rights law. Any victim of a violation of the right to health can hold the State to account by means of bringing a claim before the court, which is similar to voters holding their representatives to account through elections. Nevertheless, the natures of elections and courts are different. Rather than right-holders, it is the court, pursuant to the responsibility formally or legally conferred on it, that has the formal authority to directly compel the State to give account.[29] In this sense, the court functions as an agent of accountability. Human rights ombudsmen also directly hold the State to account, but their authority to do so derives from a State-mandated responsibility and is limited by the scope of their mandate. Therefore, I argue that it is necessary to distinguish agents of accountability from accountability mechanisms. However, I do not make a distinction between 'accountability as a virtue' and 'accountability as a

25 ibid 13-14. Kasuya and Takahashi use the term 'electoral' accountability rather than vertical accountability. Nevertheless, their essence is the same. I replace 'electoral' with 'vertical' accountability as used in chapter 5 to avoid terminology confusion.

26 ibid 15.

27 ibid 14.

28 See eg UNICEF (n 4); Potts (n 4).

29 Mark Bovens, 'Analysing and Assessing Accountability: A Conceptual Framework' (2007) 13 European Law Journal 447, 456.

mechanism'; instead, I see accountability as a constructive process that encompasses features of both definitions.

Lastly, to avoid conceptual confusion between the principal-agent relationship and the notion of accountable/overseeing actors adopted in chapter 5, I refer to *overseeing institutions* rather than *agents* of accountability. Overseeing actors include right-holders and overseeing institutions. Overseeing institutions can be further divided into horizontal institutions (eg courts, ombudsmen) and vertical institutions (eg CSOs and the media). In reality, in addition to intuitions that are established for the specific purpose of human rights protection (eg national human rights institutions), many other horizontal overseeing institutions already exist. This is also the reason for distinguishing between an *overseeing institution* and an accountability *mechanism*. The call for establishing accessible, transparent and effective accountability mechanisms does not necessarily mean that the State has to create new (horizontal or vertical) overseeing institutions for account-giving. What really matters is that institutional arrangements exist through which State institutions generate ongoing checks and balances for State actors' acts or omissions in relation to their right to health obligations. This means, for instance, that the State should establish an appropriate complaints procedure so that right-holders can bring a complaint of a violation of the right to health before a court, a tribunal or an ombudsman, or alternatively mandate overseeing institutions to actively engage in the protection of certain human rights (eg the right to health) through investigation or research.

To sum up, this study defines an *accountability mechanism* in a narrow sense, as an institutional arrangement that facilitates the process of account giving. Under right to health-based accountability, or human rights-based accountability more generally, right-holders and overseeing institutions can hold State actors to account, directly or indirectly, through an appropriate institutional arrangement – i.e. an accountability mechanism – such as judicial proceedings, constitutional review and public hearings, to name a few. State actors may face judicial, political, administrative or even social consequences such as naming and shaming.[30]

30 Yamin (n 11) 5.

6.2.2 Analytical framework for right to health-based accountability

6.2.2.1 Components of the analytical framework

Based on my arguments presented above, in order to structure the discussion in sections 6.3 and 6.4 of this chapter, I proposed an analytical framework for analysing accountability mechanisms at different levels, as shown in Figure 6.1. Components of this framework are actually components of right to health-based accountability (which can be applied to other human rights contexts) and are selected on the basis of the following questions: (1) who is accountable? (2) for what are these actors accountable? (3) to whom are these actors accountable? and (4) how can these actors be held to account? The answers to these questions are provided below.

Figure 6.1 Analytical framework for right to health-based accountability

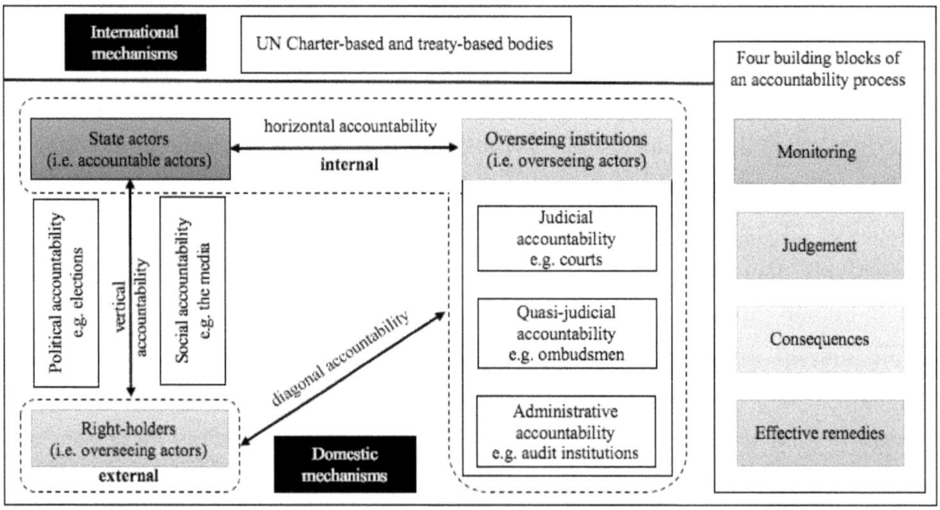

First, when it comes to the question of *who is accountable*, the answer is in principle clear: in this study, as discussed extensively in chapter 5, State actors are accountable for advancing the right to health. State actors include the State itself, as well as public institutions and public officials mandated by the State with responsibilities regarding the realisation of the right to health.

Second, the question arises: for *what* are State actors accountable? As repeatedly mentioned in previous chapters, *the State* (i.e. State actors) is ultimately accountable for guaranteeing the realisation of the right to health. In other words, State actors are accountable for their obligations under the right to health. International human rights law clearly sets out the standards and principles for respecting, protecting and fulfilling the right to health. As detailed in chapter 2, State actors are accountable for the core obligations of the right to health. One such obligation, which is the focus of the present chapter, is the obligation to establish appropriate accountability mechanisms. In addition to the core obligations, of which some (including the obligation to establish appropriate accountability mechanisms) have been held to be immediately enforceable,[31] State actors also undertake obligations of comparable priority, obligations of progressive realisation and some general obligations. Violations can occur if State actors fail to fully comply with these right to health obligations, and will result in State actors being held accountable, either *ex ante* or *ex post* (as explained in chapter 5). As part of the process of holding State actors accountable for such violations, they will be subject to negative consequences, including sanctions.

Monitoring States' progress in discharging right to health obligations requires the selection of appropriate indicators for evaluating both the circumstances under which State actors should be held accountable for particular conduct (process indicators), and long-term outcomes (outcome indicators).[32] As Yamin notes, these indicators can help to identify whether there are failures in the implementation of the right to health, for example in relation to the substantive AAAQ standards (i.e. whether there is a lack of availability, a lack of accessibility, a lack of acceptability, or a lack of quality), and whether there are failures in the State's legal and policy framework.[33] State actors are obliged to inform overseeing actors about what they have done or plan to do for the realisation of the right to health and to explain and justify the reasons for it. Notably, and as Brinkerhoff rightly notes, 'a country's socio-cultural, economic, and political relations shape how constitutions and laws interpreted and applied, and how public administration functions are exercised. These in turn, influence how accountability figures in governance'[34] Therefore, in determining whether actions or omissions amount to a violation of the right to health, the domestic context of each State matters.

31 Yamin (n 11) 7–8.
32 ibid, 9.
33 ibid.
34 Brinkerhoff (n 4) 8.

Once the matter of for what State actors are accountable has been determined, the next questions to address are to whom are they accountable, and how they can be held to account. These two questions will be discussed in detail in sections 6.3 and 6.4, but it should be immediately noted here that under right to health-based accountability (as well as other human rights-based accountability), State actors are first and foremost accountable to right-holders. Given that the relationship between individual right-holders and State actors is unequal, right to health-based accountability still falls within the realm of vertical accountability. Right-holders, as external overseeing actors, can enforce standards of good performance (i.e. right to health standards) on State actors. More specifically, right-holders can impose accountability on State actors directly and formally through electoral processes (a political accountability mechanism), or directly but informally through the media (a social accountability mechanism). Since elections are normally held every three to five years, there is an increasing demand for other internal State institutions to provide checks and balances on Sate actors on a day-to-day basis (i.e. horizontal accountability). These horizontal accountability institutions, or *overseeing institutions*, include constitutional or domestic courts (within judicial accountability), national human rights institutions (within quasi-judicial accountability) and audit institutions (within administrative accountability) that are parallel to the institutions mandated by the State for undertaking right to health obligations.[35] Furthermore, it is interesting to observe that there is a growing trend of engaging right-holders directly in the workings of horizontal accountability institutions via certain accountability mechanisms (i.e. diagonal accountability).[36]

Remarkably, the aforementioned horizontal overseeing institutions and their corresponding accountability mechanisms all have the purpose of advancing the right to health. The reasons that State actors give account to these institutions, however, vary. For example, the court, as a horizontal overseeing institution, can *directly* hold State actors to account on the basis of the responsibility formally or legally conferred on it.[37] Right-holders only be *indirectly* involved in the account-giving process, through

35 See generally Riccardo Pelizzo and Frederick Stapenhurst, *Government Accountability and Legislative Oversight* (Routledge 2014) 3-6; Andreas Schedler, 'Conceptualizing Accountability' in Andreas Schedler, Larry Diamond and Marc Plattner (eds), *The Self-restraining State: Power and Accountability in New Democracies* (Lynne Rienner Publishers 1999) 21-26.

36 For example, citizen advisory boards function as horizontal overseeing institutions for auditing government expenditures. Pelizzo and Stapenhurst (n 35) 5.

37 Bovens (n 29) 456.

certain accountability mechanisms for informing internal overseeing institutions about violations of the right to health. An accountability relationship then exists between overseeing institutions and State actors. Significantly, when they are informed of a situation by right-holders or through their own investigation (i.e. ombudsmen), overseeing institutions have the authority to determine whether State actors' decisions would amount to a violation of the right to health. They can then, contingent on their different mandates, impose judicial, quasi-judicial, or administrative consequences on State actors. By contrast, in a vertical accountability relationship, right-holders can allege, but do not have the authority to determine, violations of the right to health. However, in such settings, right-holders can nevertheless impose political (eg voting) or social (eg negative publicity, naming and shaming) consequences on State actors.

It is worth noting, however, that my argument here is based on my differentiation between an overseeing *institution* (i.e. 'the agent of accountability') and an accountability *mechanism*. If accountability mechanisms were considered to be congruent to overseeing institutions, then right-holders would be able to hold State actors directly to account through various types of accountability mechanisms. To this extent, courts or human rights ombudsmen, for example, would both be accountability mechanisms at the domestic level with the purpose of exerting accountability. Considering such horizontal overseeing institutions as accountability mechanisms, however, would over-simplify the whole accountability process. It would also mean that right-holders (as overseeing actors) could hold State actors (as accountable actors) to account by bringing a complaint before a court or human rights institution.

However, I argue that this over-simplified vision of accountability may undermine right to health-based accountability (or other human rights-based accountability) because it excludes checks and balances provided by overseeing institutions that are directly and actively involved in the process. Once again taking human rights ombudsmen as an example, they can indeed investigate right to health violations even in the absence of a victim, and hold State actors to account. This often happens in systematic and structural failures, for example when regulations and policies are incompatible with human rights standards and principles. In light of the analysis above, it is important to be more specific about accountability mechanisms and overseeing institutions in research on right to health-based accountability.

Lastly, the purpose of this chapter is to shed light on the general application of accountability mechanisms at domestic and international levels. Chapter 7 will further analyse accountability and accountability mechanisms under China's unique legal, political and social background.

6.2.2.2 An overview of findings

Based on the analytical framework, I conducted a literature review to map various types of accountability mechanisms for the implementation of the right to health at the international, regional and national levels. The literature was mainly obtained from the main electronic public health databases (eg Google Scholar, PubMed) and the United Nations documents databases (eg the WHO, OHCHR) by searching for key words such as accountability, accountability mechanisms, participation, health systems, and the right to health. The findings are summarised in Table 6.1. It is worth noting that the examples provided in relation to each overseeing actor and accountability mechanism are illustrative rather than exhaustive.

The findings are divided into three sections, each corresponding with one of the levels reviewed (the international, regional and domestic levels). In addition, examples of accountability mechanisms are discussed under three key headings, depending on the types of overseeing actors that drive the accountability processes, including judicial, quasi-judicial and non-judicial (i.e. political, administrative and social) accountability. This categorisation, informed by Potts' work, is favoured due to its previous application in the majority of human rights literature.[38] The following sections will illustrate how accountability mechanisms, both at the domestic and international levels, facilitate a constructive and dynamic right to health-based accountability process (which can be applied to more human rights contexts). Given that the exhaustion of domestic remedies is a prerequisite of some international mechanisms, section 6.3 will explore various types of domestic accountability mechanisms for facilitating a constructive accountability process, which under the proposed analytical framework consists of four key building blocks.

38 See generally Potts (n 4); UNICEF (n 4); OHCHR and Center for Economic and Social Rights (n 11).

Table 6.1 An overview of accountability mechanisms

	Types of accountability	Overseeing actor	Accountability mechanisms
International	Judicial	• N/A	• N/A
	Quasi-judicial	• UN treaty-based bodies (eg CteeESCR)	• Reporting mechanism • Complaints mechanism
	Non-judicial	• UN Charter-based bodies • Special Rapporteur • Inter-governmental organisations • CSOs (eg Global Health Watch)	• Universal periodic review • Special procedures
Regional	Judicial	• Regional courts (eg the European Court of Human Rights)	• Human rights litigation
	Quasi-judicial	• Regional treaty-based bodies (eg the European Committee of Social Rights)	• Complaints mechanisms
	Non-judicial	• Inter-governmental organisations • Parliamentary assemblies	• Investigation • Parliamentary reports
National	Judicial	• Constitutional courts • National courts • National tribunals	• Constitutional review • Human rights litigation • Statutory interpretation
	Quasi-judicial	• National human rights institutions (eg ombudsmen) • Health complaints tribunals • Patients' rights commissions or tribunals	• Public inquiries • Investigations and research • Complaints procedure
	Non-judicial • Political • Administrative • Social	• Voters • Parliamentary committees • Health councils • CSOs, the media	• Elections • Human rights impact assessments • Complaints procedure • The media

6.3 Domestic accountability mechanisms

6.3.1 Judicial accountability mechanisms

For a long time, human rights research on accountability has focused mostly on judicial accountability, or *justiciabililty*.[39] It should be noted here that justiciability is not the same as direct applicability, as discussed in chapter 3. While justiciability generally refers to whether matters can be appropriately resolved by courts, direct applicability concerns the question of whether treaty provisions can be directly applied before domestic courts without further elaboration.[40] In relation to economic, social and cultural rights (ESCR), the debate focuses on whether ESCR, including the right to health, are *justiciable*, or whether they can or should be subject to judicial or quasi-judicial adjudication.[41] The presumed non-justiciability of ESCR was based on an oversimplified and now outdated dichotomy of civil and political rights on the one hand and ESCR on the other. It has often been suggested that matters involving resource allocation in relation to ESCR should be left to an elected legislature rather than to unelected judges.[42] Such arguments have been rebutted by many scholars and human rights treaty bodies, including the Committee on Economic, Social and Cultural Rights (CteeESCR). In its General Comment 9, the CteeESCR states that 'it is appropriate to acknowledge that courts are generally already involved in a considerable range of matters which have important resource implications'.[43] It also observes that such a distinction between civil and political and ESCR would 'drastically curtail the capacity of the courts to protect the rights of the most vulnerable and disadvantaged groups in society.'[44]

---

39 Paul Hunt and others, 'Implementation of Economic, Social and Cultural Rights' in Scott Sheeran and Rodley Nigel (eds), *Routledge Handbook of International Human Rights Law* (Routledge 2013) 550.

40 United Nations Committee on Economic, Social and Cultural Rights (CteeESCR), 'General Comment No. 9: The Domestic Application of the Covenant' (General Comment 9) (3 December 1998) UN Doc E/C12/1998/24, para 5.

41 Hunt and others (n 39) 552.

42 CteeESCR, General Comment 9 (n 40) para 10; Abdullahi An-Na'im, 'To Affirm the Full Human Rights Standing of Economic, Social and Cultural Rights' in Yash Ghai and Jill Cottrell (eds), *Economic, Social and Cultural Rights in Practice: The Role of Judges in Implementing Economic, Social and Cultural Rights* (Interights 2004). Cited in Hunt and others (n 39) 552.

43 CteeESCR, General Comment 9 (n 40) para 10.

44 ibid.

Over the past two decades, we have witnessed a rapidly growing number of cases in relation to ESCR being adjudicated by domestic courts, in particular in Latin American countries and in South Africa.[45] The increasing body of national jurisprudence can be considered an affirmation of the justiciability of the right to health. Human rights scholars have discussed the decisions of domestic court extensively.[46] Box 6.1 provides a general overview of some representative examples of such decisions. While the approach and practice of courts around the world differ widely, empirical research suggests that such cases focus on the failure of States to immediately achieve a minimum standard of the realisation of the right to health or the failure to take adequate steps to realise this right more gradually.[47]

Box 6.1 National jurisprudence in relation to the right to health	
South Africa	*Minister of Health and others v Treatment Action Campaign and others* (2002)[48]
Fact	The case concerned the provision of Nevirapine, an anti-retroviral drug used to prevent mother-to-child-transmission (MTCT) of HIV in South Africa. The South African government announced that this drug would only be provided on certain research and training sites (2 pilot sites in each of the 9 provinces). The drug could also be obtained from private medical providers. As a result, mothers and their babies who did not have access to the pilot sites and could not afford access to private health care, were unable to gain access to Nevirapine. The Treatment Action Campaign launched a constitutional challenge against the South African Ministry of Health, alleging that the restriction on the procurement of Nevirapine was a violation of both the international and constitutional rights to health.
Decision	The Constitutional Court of South Africa found that the government's policy had not met its constitutional obligations to provide people with access to health care services in a manner that was reasonable and took account of pressing social needs. It also ordered the government 'to devise and implement a comprehensive and coordinated programme to progressively realize the right of pregnant women and their new-born children to have access to health services to combat mother-to-child transmission of HIV'.

45 Aart Hendriks, 'The Right to Health in National and International Jurisprudence' (1998) 5 European Journal of Health Law 389, 394–402; Hans Hogerzeil, Melanie Samson and Jaume Casanova, 'Ruling for Access: Leading Court Cases in Developing Countries on Access to Essential Medicines as Part of the Fulfilment of the Right to Health' (WHO 2004) 17-35; Daniel Wei Wang, 'Right to Health Litigation in Brazil: The Problem and the Institutional Responses' (2015) 15 Human Rights Law Review 617.

46 See eg Potts (n 4); OHCHR and Center for Economic and Social Rights (n 11); Yamin (n 11); Wang (n 45) 617.

47 OHCHR and Center for Economic and Social Rights (n 11) 39-41.

48 Minister of Health and Others v Treatment Action Campaign and Others (No 1) (CCT9/02) [2002] ZACC 16; 2002 (5) SA 703; 2002 (10) BCLR 1075 (5 July 2002).

Argentina	*Campodonico de Beviacqua, Ana Carina v Ministerio de Salud y Acción Social* (2000) [49]
Fact	The case was filed by parents on behalf of their son who suffered from Kostmann's disease (a severe bone disease with which children get frequent infections) and was entirely dependent on a specific drug named 'Neutromax 300'. From 1996 to 1998, this medicine had been given to the child free of charge by the National Bank of Antineoplastic Drugs (an agency dependent on the Ministry of Health). However, in 1998 the agency decided not to provide the medicine anymore. The agency argued that it was not obliged to provide the medicine and the previous provisions were made for humanitarian reasons.
Decision	The Supreme Court issued a declaratory order that required the Ministry of Health to oblige the National Bank of Antineoplastic Drugs to continue providing the drugs. It noted in its decision that the right to life was the 'first right of human beings' under the Constitution and that the right to health was part of the right to life. It also emphasised that the State had ratified a number of human rights treaties incorporating the rights to life and health to constitutional legal status. The State undertook a legal obligation to progressively realise the right to health under Article 12 of the International Covenant of Economic, Social and Cultural Rights to the maximum of its available resources.
India	*Laxmi Mandal v. Deen Dayal Haringagar Hospital and others* (2010)[50]
Fact	This case was brought by Laxmi Mandal on behalf of Shanti Devi, a woman who lived in poverty and died shortly after giving birth to a premature baby without any medical attention. She was denied medical treatment at several hospitals because she was unable to show a BPL (below poverty line) card for the free services under existing State-sponsored schemes, despite the fact that she qualified for one as she lived below the poverty line. The case was brought before the High Court of Delhi under Article 226 of the Indian Constitution. The issue to be decided by the court were the 'protection and enforcement of the basic, fundamental and human right to life under Article 21 of the Constitution.'
Decision	The High Court of Dehli found that there was a failure to properly implement the pre- and post-natal services which should have been available to the plaintiff. The court noted that it was inappropriate to place the burden on the poor to prove their eligibility for health services; rather, the State should ensure their access to these essential primary health care services. The Court noted in its decision that this case highlighted two critical 'survival rights' enforceable under Article 21 of the Indian Constitution that protects the right to life. One of the enforceable 'survival rights' is the right to health care, including the right to access public health facilities, to receive a minimum standard of treatment and care, the enforcement of the reproductive rights of the mother, and the right to nutrition and medical care of a new-born child until the age of six years.

In general, judicial accountability can be exercised when the right to health as a norm under international law has been adopted or transformed into a domestic legal system. Domestic courts generate judicial accountability by reviewing the

49 Campodonico de Beviacqua, Ana Carina v. Ministerio de Salud y Accién Social. Constitutional Court, File C.823.XXXV (Oct 24, 2000; Argentina)

50 Laxmi Mandal v. Deen Dayal Harinagar Hospital & Ors, W.P.(C) Nos. 8853 of 2008.

constitutionality, legality and soundness of health laws, regulations and policies as well as the decisions and actions made by State actors.[51] Viewed in this way, judicial accountability can be exercised both prospectively and retrospectively. First, the entrenchment of right to health norms in a domestic constitution and other laws makes it possible for right-holders to demand the enforcement of legislation through judicial accountability mechanisms. Second, if the State fails to enforce its law, right-holders have recourse to the courts and they can retroactively seek redress for the violations of the right to health through litigation.[52] For example, if a patient has been denied access to health care, he (or she) can file a claim against the State actors responsible for the violation of his right to health. The courts have the formal authority to determine whether certain conduct would amount to such violations. Domestic courts can hold State actors to account through statutory interpretation, through the identification of legislation or policies that are incompatible with human rights treaty obligations and through judicial review of executive decision-making.[53]

Furthermore, to address violations of the right to health domestic courts can provide judicial remedies, which include immediate redress for individual litigants as well as structural redress for systematic deficiencies that aims at a large number of people.[54] Potts distinguishes between four forms of redress that domestic courts can provide, including: (1) compensation for any economically assessable damage directly resulting from a violation of the right to health; (2) restitution, which involves the amendment of legislation or the reversal of a policy that is inconsistent with the right to health obligations; (3) rehabilitation, which includes the provision of needed health facilities, goods and services; and (4) satisfaction and guarantees of non-repetition, which concerns the formation of an effective accountability process in the long term, for example by establishing an overseeing institution.[55]

It is widely accepted that as a horizontal overseeing institution a court has a high capacity for enforcement. Courts are probably the most powerful overseeing actor in terms of holding State actors to account and providing victims with redress for violations of the right to health. Nevertheless, in the context of the right to

51 OHCHR and Center for Economic and Social Rights (n 11) 37.
52 ibid 39-40; Potts (n 4) 17-18; UNICEF (n 4) 8.
53 Potts (n 4) 18.
54 Hunt and others (n 39) 555.
55 Potts (n 4) 28-29.

health, critics allege that judicial intervention may distort health budgets in favour of privileged litigants who have the necessary resources to access the courts, as has occurred in Brazil.[56] Furthermore, considering that judicial proceedings are time-consuming, and given the uncertainty of their outcome, judicial accountability mechanisms have very often been regarded as a last resort in many countries.[57]

6.3.2 Quasi-judicial accountability mechanisms

Broadly speaking, quasi-judicial accountability is generated through independent (at least theoretically speaking) overseeing institutions established by the State, usually through a legislative act.[58] For the specific purposes of advancing and defending human rights, many countries have established national human rights institutions (NHRI) in the forms of human rights commissions, human rights ombudsmen and public defenders.[59] Other quasi-judicial institutions include health complaints tribunals and patients' rights commissions or tribunals. These independent institutions are (usually) established by the State on the basis of specific statutes, but their mandate and power vary.[60] Given their autonomous nature, quasi-judicial institutions normally function as a bridge between the State and society.[61]

These independent institutions exercise 'soft power' through a set of mechanisms for exerting quasi-judicial accountability and may have an impact on the realisation of the right to health and on the development of health laws and policies.[62] For example, in many countries NHRIs can 'act *sua sponte* to identify laws and policies that violate health-related rights.'[63] They can also conduct investigations into the implementation of the right to health and review health sector performance. In addition, through their complaints mechanisms quasi-judicial institutions can adjudicate complaints in relation to the national health service and independent health service providers, as well as health workers in general. Based on such investigations and reviews, these

56 Yamin (n 11) 5-7; Hunt and others (n 39) 554.
57 OHCHR and Center for Economic and Social Rights (n 11) 40.
58 See generally Yamin (n 11) 5; Potts (n 4) 18-19; UNICEF (n 4) 7.
59 Potts (n 4) 18-19.
60 ibid.
61 UNICEF (n 4) 7.
62 Potts (n 4) 18-19.
63 Yamin (n 11) 5.

institutions can make quasi-judicial decisions which may have an impact on existing laws and policies.[64]

However, the current impact of these bodies on the implementation of the right to health should not be over-estimated. As Yamin points out, of more than 100 NHRIs worldwide, only a small proportion have engaged in the work of monitoring and oversight of ESCR, and even fewer work in the particular field of the right to health.[65] Furthermore, country studies suggest that due to the limited capacity of quasi-judicial institutions, their decisions regarding complaints, their findings of reviews and investigations and their law and policy recommendations tend to be haphazard. The institutions' capacity may be undermined by budgetary or human resources, or by their mandate. The impact of their work also varies, depending on a State's domestic setting, including the degree of independence and public authority. For instance, based on their mandate, many NHRIs do not have the power to enforce their decisions.[66] For this reason, quasi-judicial institutions have a relatively low enforcement capacity compared to that of courts.

6.3.3 Political accountability mechanisms

Political accountability is aimed at ensuring that elected representatives fulfil their electoral promises, obtain and maintain public trust, aggregate and represent public interests, and respond to public demands and concerns.[67] Political accountability is normally exercised within a principal-agent relationship,[68] and can manifest itself in two main ways: electoral accountability and ministerial accountability.

First, in a narrow sense, political accountability exists between voters and elected representatives, where voters, being the primary principals, delegate their power to popular representatives through elections (i.e. vertical accountability). The elected representatives, in turn, transfer 'the drafting and enforcement of laws and policy to

64 See generally Yamin (n 11) 5; Potts (n 4) 19; UNICEF (n 4) 8; The UNICEF Office of Research, 'Championing Children's Rights: A Global Study of Independent Human Rights Institutions for Children: Summary Report' (2012) 5, 10 <www.unicef-irc.org/publications/pdf/championing2_eng.pdf> accessed 28 November 2017.

65 Yamin (n 11) 5.

66 See generally Yamin (n 11) 5; Potts (n 4) 18-19; UNICEF (n 4) 7.

67 Brinkerhoff (n 4) 8.

68 Mark Bovens (n 29) 455.

government'.[69] This narrow type of political accountability is also known as *electoral accountability*. Through electoral accountability, right-holders can participate in the formulation of health legislation, regulations and policies by voting for their representatives.[70] In this relationship, right-holders themselves are both overseeing actors and principals. During an electoral period, politicians seeking office are motivated to be more accountable to the electorate, so as to be elected by them. The electoral competition among political parties has the potential to overcome or even to prevent information asymmetries between politicians and voters because both the incumbent government and the opposition will disclose more information about their policies and performance. Based on the information obtained during the electoral period, voters can judge the incumbent government's performance *ex post facto* and reward good or punish bad performance by voting for representatives who can act in their best interests, and by voting against representatives who may have not kept their past electoral commitments or who may have violated human rights.[71] In this regard, political accountability is exercised retrospectively.[72]

Nonetheless, many scholars criticise elections for being 'blunt instruments', due to the following shortcomings.[73] The first weakness is that the length of time that passes between elections is quite long, often from three to five years. There is no tool for voters to directly check and control the incumbent government's behaviour during this period of time.[74] Secondly, voters have an uneven say in selecting their representatives.[75] Furthermore, the effectiveness of an election is very dependent on a fair and sound electoral system. Thus, a country's specific political context may hinder the operation of this mechanism.[76] In brief, voters have a relative low capacity to make their elected representatives answerable and to impose positive or negative consequences on them.

69 Mark Bovens (n 14) 955.
70 Mark Bovens (n 29) 455; UNICEF (n 4) 8; OHCHR and Center for Economic and Social Rights (n 11) 36-37.
71 UNICEF (n 4) 8.
72 Kasuya and Takahashi (n 24) 16.
73 See eg ibid; UNICEF (n 4) 8.
74 Catalina Smulovitz and Eurique Peruzzotti, 'Societal Accountability in Latin America' (11) 2000 Journal of Democracy 147, 147-158. Cited in Yuko Kasuya and Yuriko Takahashi (n 24) 16.
75 UNICEF (n 4) 8.
76 See eg Kasuya and Takahashi (n 24) 16; UNICEF (n 4) 8.

Second, in a broad sense, parliaments can generate political accountability during the period between elections.[77] In most parliamentary systems, elected representatives delegate the majority of their authorities to a cabinet of ministers, who then in turn entrust the execution of their tasks to a variety of public institutions and public officials or to various (more or less) independent administrative bodies and institutions.[78] Along each chain of delegation, the agents render political account to their principals – the principals can monitor the execution of their tasks by calling the agents to account.[79] More specifically, public institutions and public officials are accountable to their ministers, who give account to the parliament; this is also labelled *ministerial accountability*.[80] Parliament, in turn, then renders account to voters through (the) election.

Generally speaking, through political accountability parliaments (i.e. in a broad sense) evaluate the appropriateness of both substantive laws and policies and the processes of law- and policy-making. Parliaments also monitor and judge the performance of political actors.[81] More specifically, parliaments draft and implement laws and policies, scrutinise budget plans and place checks and balances on the government.[82] Parliaments are also in a position to ensure that legislative proposals respect and promote human rights, to amend legislation that is incompatible with human rights law, and to evaluate budgets and resource allocation on the basis of human rights standards and principles.[83]

Given the principal-agent relationship, parliaments can monitor the behaviour of the ministers and make them more accountable for implementing human rights, more specifically the right to health.[84] They normally exercise their oversight role through mechanisms such as hearings, inquires, investigations into and consultations regarding particular issues in relation to the right to health. As noted in a UN publication, the ability of parliaments to 'represent and bring complaints on behalf of their constituents' is an important 'parliamentary expression of vertical accountability,

77 Bovens (n 29) 455; Bovens (n 14) 955; OHCHR and Center for Economic and Social Rights (n 11) 36-37.
78 ibid.
79 ibid.
80 ibid.
81 Schedler (n 35) 22.
82 OHCHR and Center for Economic and Social Rights (n 11) 36-37.
83 ibid 36-37.
84 ibid.

which can bring marginal issues, including the concerns of minorities or vulnerable groups, to national attention.'[85]

6.3.4 Administrative accountability mechanisms

Administrative accountability concerns 'the expediency and procedural correctness of bureaucratic acts.'[86] It requires State actors to 'meet standards with regard to transparency, participation, reasoned decision and legality, and provide effective review of their actions.'[87] In the broadest sense, all States have their own internal mechanisms of accountability to ensure that those with delegated authority carry out their tasks pursuant to pre-determined purposes and performance standards.[88] In some studies on accountability, this broad form of administrative accountability is also regarded as horizontal accountability, for the reason that it provides checks and balances on a variety of public institutions and public officials across the State.[89] Some scholars assert that institutions exercising 'independent and external administrative and financial supervision and control', such as ombudsmen, audit offices, anti-fraud offices and other independent supervisory authorities (which in this study are categorised as quasi-judicial overseeing institutions), can generate this type of accountability.[90] Other scholars, however, divide this broad form of accountability into political, fiscal, administrative (in a narrow sense) and legal methods of achieving accountability.[91]

This study considers administrative accountability in a narrow sense, based on its internal hierarchical relationship. As already explained, public institutions and public officials give account to their ministers and the ministers are accountable to parliament. A broad type of political accountability exists between parliaments and their cabinets of ministers, in which parliaments still provide external checks and balances on the executive. The same applies to courts (which provide for judicial accountability) and to NHRIs (which provide for quasi-judicial accountability). While courts and NHRIs

85 ibid 37.
86 ibid.
87 ibid.
88 UNICEF (n 4) 9.
89 ibid.
90 Bovens (n 29) 456.
91 Adapted from UNICEF (n 4) 9.

are internal institutions of the State, they still provide external checks and balances on State actors that are subject to right to health obligations.

As noted in a UN report, 'no amount of external monitoring is likely to improve the performance of institutions or public officials if their internal systems of control are dysfunctional or corrupt'.[92] Administrative supervision *within* institutions is arguably a key determinant of the performance of State actors.[93] Inferior actors give administrative account to their superiors along on the basis of a 'chain of command'.[94] Public officials are accountable to more senior officers, to their supervisors, and ultimately to public audit offices.[95] It should be noted that while the present study perceives this internal form of accountability as *administrative* accountability, some scholars also consider it to be political accountability.[96]

Mechanisms of administrative accountability focus on the services, performances and outcomes of public institutions and public officials.[97] They include incentive-based management mechanisms as well as results-based management mechanisms, with an emphasis on providing rewards for good, and sanctions for bad, performance. By providing standards of conduct that public servants should uphold and standards of service delivery, the human rights framework can help public administrators in their development of administrative accountability mechanisms. In order to provide internal checks and balances, administrative institutions should also establish various channels for receiving complaints and grievances, including interactive websites, office boxes, and mail boxes.[98] Provided that administrative accountability is exercised through a chain of command, it is evident that it has a high enforcement capacity.

6.3.5 Social accountability mechanisms

Social accountability exists between society (individuals and CSOs) on the one hand and the State on the other. It generally refers to a form of accountability that emerges

92 OHCHR and Center for Economic and Social Rights (n 11) 37-38.
93 ibid.
94 Bovens (n 29) 458.
95 OHCHR and Center for Economic and Social Rights (n 11) 37-38.
96 Bovens (n 29) 458.
97 Martin Atela and Francis Wafula, 'Mapping Accountability Mechanisms: A Review of In-Country Accountability in Health Systems' (2015) 8.
98 OHCHR and Center for Economic and Social Rights (n 11)37-38.

through the actions of individuals and CSOs that aim to hold the State to account, as well as efforts by other actors (eg the media) to support these actions.[99] In this regard, social accountability can be perceived as a form of vertical accountability.

Nevertheless, a minority of scholars argue that social accountability is a form of horizontal accountability. For example, Bovens claims that in relation to social accountability, 'a hierarchical relationship is generally lacking between actor and forum, as are any formal obligations to render account'. He argues that account giving is normally based on a formal process, whereas in the case of social accountability, which is moral in nature, overseeing actors participate on a voluntary basis. As such, he perceives social accountability as a form of horizontal accountability.[100] However, it is not the aim of this section to argue whether social accountability is a form of vertical or horizontal accountability. Putting this debate aside, the definition of social accountability implies that social accountability exists between actors on an unequal footing and can be exercised in either a top-down or (in the absence of a principal-agent relation) bottom-up manner.

Social accountability can provide extra sets of checks and balances on a continuous basis through various mechanisms, such as social audits, citizen reports, public hearings and the media.[101] Social accountability can be initiated by individuals and CSOs, by the State, or by combinations of these actors. Most often, social accountability is demand-driven and triggered from the bottom up.[102] Individuals or CSOs can monitor the decisions and actions made by State actors in fulfilling their right to health obligations, expose violations of the right to health, and hold responsible State actors accountable through various social accountability mechanisms.[103] A particular feature of social accountability is that it has the ability to focus on the needs of vulnerable and marginalised groups; social accountability mechanisms provide avenues for those who have traditionally been excluded from or marginalised by society to participate in health-related decision-making processes in order to claim their rights more effectively.[104] For example, as will be discussed

99 UNDP (n 4) 10.
100 Bovens (n 29) 460.
101 UNDP (n 4) 10.
102 Carmen Malena and others, 'Social Accountability: An Introduction to the Concept and Emerging Practice' (Draft paper prepared for the World Bank 2004) 3.
103 OHCHR and Center for Economic and Social Rights (n 11) 44-45.
104 UNDP (n 4) 11.

further in chapter 7, patient groups can play an important role in exerting social accountability for the violations of the right to health care in China.

Therefore, social accountability is not only a retrospective process of urging State actors to adjust their malfeasance and to discipline themselves *ex post* through negative publicity (i.e. enforcement), but also a prospective process of establishing a dynamic dialogue between the State and society (i.e. answerability), which allows right-holders to participate and voice their concerns in the *ex ante* process of decision-making.[105]

A considerable number of case studies have proven that health governance and health service delivery can be improved by exerting social accountability, ultimately leading to the better implementation of the right to health (care).[106] Nevertheless, empirical research on the impact of social accountability has also shown that in some countries, pure bottom-up mechanisms may have a limited effect if they are detached from the 'incentive systems' established for keeping State actors' incentive right (explained in chapter 5) or when they are isolated and prevented from interacting with other social actors.[107] Therefore, these studies note the importance of taking a State-society synergistic approach to social accountability.

In their consideration of a wide range of social accountability mechanisms, Malena, Forster and Singh identify some key building blocks for successful social accountability. These include obtaining, analysing and disseminating information, mobilising public support, and advocating and negotiating change.[108] Furthermore, they assert that the capacities of both society and the State, and the synergy between these two actors are crucial factors of such success.[109] For example, if CSOs were only to have limited capacity to mobilise and effectively use the media, the effect of social accountability would be largely futile. In such cases, the State is required to create an enabling environment for CSOs to strengthen their capacity. The success of social accountability also depends on the capacity of the State itself – if the State machinery were to collapse, social accountability would lose all meaning. A well-functioning public administration that can respond to public demands in a timely and

105 ibid 18.
106 Potts (n 4) 22-23; UNICEF (n 4) 16-18; OHCHR and Center for Economic and Social Rights (n 11) 44.
107 OHCHR and Center for Economic and Social Rights (n 11) 45.
108 Malena and others (n 102) 3.
109 ibid 13.

effective manner is crucial in this regard.[110] Additionally, State-society synergy is also important for successful social accountability. Human rights scholars may argue that achieving State-society synergy is not possible in reality, given that human rights remain a challenge to some States, and that some States regard social accountability mechanisms, especially negative publicity, as a threat to their authority.[111] However, a 2005 World Bank report indicates that, without positive engagement of the State, 'unilateral social action often results in repression and violence by the state' and that 'the most productive results arise when both sides actively participate'.[112] Evidence also suggests that social accountability may be more fruitful when supported by the State.[113] As such, it is important to set up social accountability mechanisms for enhancing the synergy between the State and society.

Furthermore, Malena, Forster and Singh state that the media play a significant role in exerting social accountability.[114] Many human rights scholars share the same observation.[115] It is arguable that access to and the effective use of information is a key element for society to exert accountability. As society's main sources of information, the media are undoubtedly an indispensable component of social accountability.[116] While on the one hand the media can be used by the State to create a dialogue with society, they can also be used as a mechanism through which society holds State actors to account. Furthermore, as an independent institution the media can raise awareness of health issues, amplify public voices, and provide external checks and balances for State actors.

The question then arises: what is the precise role of (the) media in exerting social accountability? In general, the discussion of the role of the media remains evasive. Some scholars simply note that the media play a crucial role,[117] others describe the

110 ibid.
111 John Ackerman, 'Social Accountability in the Public Sector: A Conceptual Discussion' (2005) 12, 36-37.
112 ibid.
113 ibid.
114 Malena and others (n 102) 3.
115 See generally UNGA, 'Report of the Special Rapporteur on the Right of Everyone to the Enjoyment of the Highest Attainable Standard of Physical and Mental Health, Paul Hunt' (11 August 2008) UN Doc A/63/263, para 11; Potts (n 4) 23; UNICEF (n 4) 14-15.
116 Katrin Voltmer, 'The Media, Government Accountability, and Citizen Engagement' in Pippa Norris (ed) *Public Sentinel: News Media and Governance Reform* (The World Bank 2010) 140.
117 See generally UNGA, 'Report of the Special Rapporteur on the Right of Everyone to the Enjoyment of the Highest Attainable Standard of Physical and Mental Health, Paul Hunt' (11 August 2008) UN Doc A/63/263, para 11; Potts (n 4) 23; Malena and others (n 102) 13.

media as social accountability mechanisms, instruments or initiatives;[118] while still more scholars regard the media as an independent institution that exists parallel to CSOs and functions as a 'watchdog'.[119] Before addressing these questions, section 6.4 begins by stating how the term 'media' is understood in this study, based on a synthesis of scholarly work on the role of the media across different disciplines. Subsequently, section 6.4 provides an analysis of the media's role in exerting accountability from a human rights perspective.

6.4 The media's role in exerting accountability

'The *media*', according to the Oxford English Dictionary, refer to the main means of mass communication (broadcasting, publishing and the Internet) regarded collectively. In recent years, the communication revolution, especially the emergence of social media, has largely changed the way in which information is disseminated.[120] 'Social media' refers to the content and interactions that are created through social interactions between individuals and communities via mobile applications and highly accessible web-based technologies.[121] Social media, including social networking sites, online forums, blogs and micro-blogs, support and facilitate individuals and CSOs in the free dissemination of information and expose malfeasance of State actors in relation to the right to health.[122] By doing so, individuals and CSOs are likely to attract the attention of society on the one hand and the State on the other. State actors are expected to explain and justify what has been done and why, and may face consequences, including eventual sanctions imposed either by the superior institutions or by the

118 See generally UNDP (n 4) 10; UNICEF (n 4) 15.

119 Voltmer (n 116) 140; Brinkerhoff (n 6) 373; Sheila Coronel, 'Corruption and the Watchdog Role of the News Media' in Pippa Norris (ed), *Public Sentinel: News Media and Governance Reform* (The World Bank 2010) 111; Pippa Norris, 'Watchdog Journalism' in Mark Bovens, Robert Goodin and Thomas Schillemans (eds), *The Oxford Handbook of Public Accountability* (Oxford University Press 2014) 525.

120 International Council on Human Rights Policy (ICHRP), 'Journalism, Media and the Challenge of Human rights Reporting' (2002) 34 <https://ssrn.com/abstract=1551305> accessed 28 November 2017.

121 John Bertot, Paul Jaeger and Justin Grimes, 'Using ICTs to Create a Culture of Transparency: E-Government and Social Media as Openness and Anti-Corruption Tools for Societies' (2010) 27 Government Information Quarterly 264, 268.

122 UNDP, 'Reflecting on Social Accountability: Catalyzing Democratic Governance to Accelerate Progress towards the Millennium Development Goals' (2013) 16-21.

horizontal overseeing institutions.[123] Very often, social accountability in this regard is generated by pressuring State actors to respond to public demands in a timely and effective way and to adjust their decisions and actions in accordance with the right to health standards.[124] Notably, it is society *itself* that functions as the guardian of the right to health and spontaneously exposes positive or negative information in relation to health issues through the *media,* especially *social media*. The *media* (i.e. as a collection of technologies) plays a *passive* role as an important tool through which individuals and CSOs can disseminate information. The *media* is deemed to be one type of social accountability mechanism in this regard.

In addition to its passive role, the media can also function as an overseeing institution, similar to other formal institutions such as courts and human rights ombudsmen. In this sense, '*the media*' – i.e. the people running the media – take on an active role as the *watchdog* of State power. The watchdog role of the media has been increasingly recognised in Anglo-American systems.[125] Many liberal theorists perceive the media as an independent guardian grounded in civil society that actively and directly monitors or investigates government conduct, thus strengthening the accountability of powerful decision-makers.[126] The idea of a watchdog also reflects the liberal conception of *the media* as the 'Fourth Estate', an independent institution alongside other public institutions that provide external checks and balances to monitor public officials and institutions and to restrain abuses of power.[127] This is sometimes labelled 'media accountability'.[128] The core notion of *the media* as a watchdog is embedded in the very meaning of journalism, of which investigative reporting is a major form.[129] In this sense, watchdog journalists *actively* investigate the decisions and actions of State actors and expose their malfeasance.[130] They can also provide accurate, reliable and timely information and generate public awareness of issues regarding the right to health. Furthermore, watchdog journalism has a potential impact on agenda setting.[131] By bringing certain topics (eg violations of

123 ibid.
124 Adapted from OHCHR and Center for Economic and Social Rights (n 11) 44-45.
125 Coronel (n 119) 111; Norris (n 119) 525.
126 Norris (n 119) 525-528.
127 Norris (n 119) 525; Coronel (n 119) 111; Voltmer (n 116) 140.
128 Voltmer (n 116) 140.
129 Coronel (n 119) 111-113; Norris (n 119) 525.
130 Norris (n 119) 525-526.
131 Adapted from Norris (n 119) 531-532; Voltmer (n 116) 142-144.

the right to health) to the attention of the public, sometimes even causing public outrage, and by inviting State actors and independent experts to participate in the discussion, *the media* directly set the agenda for public debate, thus triggering effective responses from State actors and potentially transforming public concerns into the policy agenda.[132] By fulfilling this *active* role, *the media* have the capacity to strengthen social accountability and advance the right to health. However, it deserves pointing out that the media, as an overseeing institution, have certain limits. These include, for example, the accuracy of the news, which cannot always be assured. Other limits are the publication of fake news, the manipulation of negative publicity, and censorship.

To sum up, when fulfilling the role of watchdog, the media serve as an external overseeing institution that is parallel to CSOs, and which would otherwise serve as one type of social accountability mechanism. A subsequent question may be raised here: if *the media* is an external overseeing institution that is run by the people, then do *the social media* also function as an independent institution? From my perspective, even though the *social media* can be used to disseminate negative information regarding State actors' malfeasance, they are used by individuals and CSOs who function as watchdogs of the public interest and cannot be considered an overseeing *institution*. The *social media* only serve as a social accountability (rather than other types of accountability) mechanism. Additionally, the information disseminated through social media is generally on a random basis, and it is not always credible. The lack of investigative reporting limits the possibility of *social media* to be an overseeing institution.

It is worth noting that the media do not have any formal authority to compel State actors to be accountable to society, but can only achieve this through naming and shaming. Therefore, the media as an institution have a relatively low capacity for enforcement. Nevertheless, the media can generate social accountability through intermediary means by informing those with authority – either the superior of responsible State actors (i.e. vertical accountability) or other overseeing institutions (i.e. horizontal accountability) – to enforce compliance. The media in this sense derive an informal power of answerability and enforcement from other formal institutions. Not surprisingly, the success of this type of social accountability is also dependent

132 ibid.

on the engagement of the State.[133] In many cases, State institutions intervene and hold the relevant State actors accountable to prevent damage to the government's reputation caused by negative publicity and to win public trust and support.[134] In some other cases, due to information asymmetries, the superior institution or other horizontal institutions are not aware of malfeasance of State actors. These institutions will also intervene and hold the relevant actors to account when they are informed by the media, but mainly for internal administrative reasons.

Contrary to most democratic countries in which the media has long been advocated as the watchdog of power, many scholars cast doubt on the role of the media in countries (eg China) that suffer from political constraints and censorship.[135] Nevertheless, as will be further explored in chapter 7, this study contends that although subject to certain restrictions, (the) media can still play a role in advancing the right to health care in China.

6.5 International mechanisms for monitoring the implementation of the right to health

There is a wide variety of international mechanisms for overseeing whether States parties comply with or violate their international treaty obligations, including obligations under the right to health. This section provides a brief introduction to the UN Charter-based and treaty-based accountability mechanisms.

6.5.1 UN Charter-based accountability mechanisms

The current UN Charter-based bodies are the Human Rights Council ('HRC') and its subsidiaries. Charter-based international mechanisms include the procedures of the HRC, such as the universal periodic review ('UPR'), resolutions on certain human rights issues, and special procedures.[136] In particular, the UN Special Rapporteur on the Right to Health is mandated by the HRC through a special procedure to monitor

133 OHCHR and Center for Economic and Social Rights (n 11) 45.
134 Brinkerhoff (n 4) 3.
135 Norris (n 119) 530; Jingrong Tong and Colin Sparks, 'Investigative Journalism in China Today' (2009) 10 Journalism Studies 337, 344.
136 OHCHR and Center for Economic and Social Rights (n 11) 50.

the implementation of the right to health throughout the world.[137] Given the fact that UN Charter-based mechanisms only make recommendations for States parties, which they cannot enforce, the mechanisms only provide a limited degree of international political accountability.[138]

6.5.2 UN treaty-based accountability mechanisms

The UN human rights treaties all have corresponding monitoring bodies for overseeing the implementation of treaty obligations including those arising from the right to health. Each of the treaty bodies are invested with various competences to supervise States parties' compliance with their treaty obligations.[139] Simply speaking, the treaty-based mechanisms can be divided into two groups: the reporting mechanisms and the complaints mechanisms. There are three major procedures for bringing a complaint of a human rights violation before treaty bodies: (1) inter-State communications; (2) individual communications; and (3) inquires.[140] The UN treaty bodies consist of 10 to 23 independent experts who generally meet to consider States parties' reports under the State reporting procedure as well as complaints.[141]

Given the number of international human rights treaties, it would be unfeasible within the scope of this thesis to discuss various types of supervisory mechanisms under each treaty. For this reason, this section focuses on the human rights treaties to which China is party: the ICESCR, CERD, CRPD, CEDAW and CRC.[142] Table 6.2 provides an overview of the treaty provisions in relation to the reporting mechanisms and complaints mechanisms. The following subsections will discuss these treaty-based mechanisms in more detail, with particular attention to the mechanisms under the ICESCR and its Optional Protocol, which is the focus of this study.

---

137 See OHCHR, 'Special Rapporteur on the Right of Everyone to the Enjoyment of the Highest Attainable Standard of Physical and Mental Health' <www.ohchr.org/EN/Issues/Health/Pages/SRRightHealthIndex.aspx> accessed 28 November 2017.

138 OHCHR and Center for Economic and Social Rights (n 11) 50.

139 Jane Connors and Markus Schmidt, 'Protection' in Moeckli Daniel and others (eds), *International Human Rights Law* (Oxford University Press 2013) 376.

140 ibid; OHCHR and International Bar Association, 'Human Rights in the Administration of Justice: A Manual on Human Rights for Judges, Prosecutors and Lawyer (2003) 28-29 <www.ohchr.org/Documents/Publications/training9Titleen.pdf> accessed 28 November 2017.

141 ibid 28-29.

142 The CAT is excluded from the discussion as it does not specifically address the right to health care.

Table 6.2 An overview of treaty-based mechanisms

Instrument	State reporting	Individual communications	Inter-State communications	Inquiries
CERD	Art 9	Art 14	Arts 11-13	
ICESCR	Art 16	Optional Protocol	Optional Protocol	Optional Protocol
CEDAW	Art 18	Optional Protocol		Optional Protocol
CRC	Arts 44-45	Optional Protocol 3	Optional Protocol 3	Optional Protocol 3
CRPD	Art 35	Optional Protocol		Optional Protocol

6.5.2.1 State reporting

The reporting procedures are designed as mechanisms for monitoring the performance of States parties in relation to relevant international human rights treaties.[143] States parties are obliged to provide comprehensive information in an initial report and subsequent periodic reports that are submitted to the treaty body concerned. The reporting procedures can create a dialogue between the treaty body (which responds to the reports via 'concluding observations') and the State party in question, so as to facilitate regular and systematic evaluations of the measures taken, the progress made and the difficulties encountered in the implementation of treaty obligations. Viewed in this light, the reporting procedures have the capacity to generate *answerability*.

Generally speaking, a treaty-based monitoring body is established under the human rights treaty in question for the purpose of monitoring the progress made in the implementation of the treaty. There is one exception: Article 16 of the ICESCR requires States parties to report on progress to the United Nations Economic and Social Council (ECOSOC), which is the formal body entrusted with monitoring the Covenant.[144] The ECOSOC, in turn, established the United Nations Committee

143 Nihal Jayawickrama, *The Judicial Application of Human Rights Law: National, Regional and International Jurisprudence* (Cambridge University Press 2002) 133.

144 UNGA, International Covenant on Economic, Social and Cultural Rights (ICESCR) (adopted 16 December 1966, entered into force 3 January 1976) 993 UNTS, art 16-22. See also Brigit Toebes, *The Right to Health as a Human Right in International Law* (Intersentia/Hart 1999) 90; Lawrence Gostin, *Global Health Law* (Harvard University Press 2014) 252.

on Economic Social and Cultural Rights (CteeESCR) to review reports and make recommendations to States parties in the same manner as the other treaty bodies.[145]

While the reporting procedures can be effective mechanisms for supervising States parties' compliance with treaty obligations, they suffer from certain institutional weaknesses.[146] First of all, while States parties undertake a legally binding obligation to submit reports, the effectiveness of the mechanisms largely depends on the cooperation of States parties to submit a report before the date on which it is due, or even at all. Second, most States parties are reluctant to facilitate domestic debate and are likely to be self-laudatory regarding the content of the reports.[147] Third, the reporting procedures lack a degree of enforcement. Although a treaty-based monitoring body can request and remind a State party to submit a report, it does not have the authority to compel the performance of the reporting obligation.[148] Fourth, instead of issuing binding decisions, the monitoring bodies only provide recommendations and views.[149] Fifth, the levels of expertise and independence of the members of the treaty bodies have also been challenged, given that their concluding observations on States parties' reports are often very generally worded.[150] Therefore, the mechanisms found in international human rights treaties, which (with the exception of the CERD) consists exclusively of the reporting procedures, are relatively weak.

6.5.2.2 Inter-State communications

An inter-State communication allows one State party to initiate a complaint before the relevant treaty body against another State party which it believes is failing to fulfil its treaty obligations.[151] According to the Optional Protocol to the ICESCR (ICESCR-OP), a State party to the protocol may at any time declare that it recognises 'the competence of the Committee to receive and consider communications to the effect

145 OHCHR, Review of the Composition, Organization and Administrative Arrangements of the Sessional Working Group of Governmental Experts on the Implementation of the International Covenant on Economic, Social and Cultural Rights ECOSOC Resolution 1985/17; See also OHCHR and International Bar Association (n 138) 43.

146 Jayawickrama (n 143) 132-133.

147 ibid 133.

148 ibid.

149 Gostin (n 144) 71.

150 Philip Alston and Ryan Goodman, *International Human Rights, The Successor to International Human Rights in Context* (Oxford University Press 2012) 839.

151 Connors and Schmidt (n 139) 381.

that a State Party claims that another State Party is not fulfilling its obligations under the Covenant'.[152] The CERD and an Optional Protocol to the CRC (CRC-OP) also provide for such a mechanism.[153] This means that one State party may only initiate such a complaint mechanism if both States parties concerned have recognised the competence of the treaty body in question to receive inter-State communications. Nevertheless, given that this procedure has never been used in reality, it lacks practical import.[154] Moreover, except for the CERD, only few States have become party to the optional protocols mentioned above. As such, inter-State communications are very weak.

6.5.2.3 Individual communications

An individual communications procedure is an international complaints mechanism through which an individual or a group of individuals whose human rights (eg the right to health care) have been violated domestically can lodge a communication (or complaint) with the relevant treaty body for quasi-judicial adjudication.

Similar to inter-State communications, an individual communication will only be taken into consideration if the State party to the relevant treaty (and its optional protocol) recognises the competence of the treaty body to receive and consider such a communication. The utilisation of this mechanism also requires the exhaustion of all available domestic remedies.[155] The treaty body will then draw conclusions and recommendations, sometimes even induce the State party to modify its domestic legislation or take other appropriate measures so as to comply with its international

152 UNGA, Optional Protocol to the International Covenant on Economic, Social and Cultural Rights (adopted on 10 December 2008, entered into force on 5 May 2013) UN Doc A/RES/63/117, art 10.

153 UNGA, Optional Protocol to the Convention on the Rights of the Child on a Communication Procedure (adopted on 19 December 2011, entered into force on 14 April 2014) UN Doc A/RES/66/138, art 12; CERD, arts 11-13.

154 Connors and Schmidt (n 139) 381.

155 See generally UNGA, International Convention on the Elimination of All Forms of Racial Discrimination (CERD) (adopted on 21 December 1965, entered into force on 4 January 1969) 660 UNTS 195, art 14; UNGA, Optional Protocol to the International Covenant on Economic, Social and Cultural Rights (ICESCR-OP) (adopted on 5 March 2009, entered into force 5 May 2013) UN Doc A/RES/63/117, arts 1-9; UNGA, Optional Protocol to the Convention on the Rights of the Child on A Communication Procedure (CRC-OP) (adopted on 19 December 2011, entered into force 14 April 2014) UN Doc A/RES/66/138, arts 5-11; UNGA, Optional Protocol to the Convention on the Elimination of All Forms of Discrimination against Women (adopted on 15 October 1999, entered into force on 22 December 2000) UN Doc A/RES/54/4, arts 1-7.

treaty obligations.[156] It deserves pointing out that decisions regarding individual communications are not legally binding and thus cannot be enforced.[157] The compliance of a State with a decision made by a treaty body largely depends on the State's willingness as well as public support at the domestic level. Nevertheless, these decisions still have the potential to improve domestic implementation of human rights. A remarkable case in this regard is the decision of the Committee on the Elimination of Discrimination against Women (CteeEDAW) in *Alyne da Silva Pimentel Teixeria v Brazil*,[158] in which an international treaty body directly held its State party to account.

Similar to inter-State communications, except for the CERD, only optional protocols to the aforementioned human rights treaties provide for individual communications procedures. Only a relatively small number of States have become party to these optional protocols. Moreover, most States parties to the CERD and to optional protocols have not yet accepted the competence of treaty bodies to receive individual communications. Consequently, the individual communications mechanisms are also relatively weak for holding States to account.

6.5.2.4 Inquiries

The ICESCR-OP, the CEDAW-OP, and the CRC-OP allow their corresponding treaty bodies to conduct 'initiative confidential investigations' of grave or systematic violations of any of the human rights contained in the main treaty (eg the right to health care) through an inquiry procedure.[159] As with the complaints mechanisms explained above, treaty-based monitoring bodies can only conduct inquiries when States become party to the optional protocols and recognise the competence of the bodies to do so.[160]

All in all, international accountability mechanisms are relatively weak. They depend to a large extent on a State party's political will and capacity to fully comply with its treaty obligations at the domestic level.[161] While the reporting mechanisms

156 OHCHR and International Bar Association (n 138) 29.
157 Connors and Schmidt (n 139) 383.
158 United Nations Committee on the Elimination of Discrimination against Women (CteeEDAW), Communication No. 17/2008 (10 August 2011) UN Doc CEDAW/C/49/D/17/2008.
159 UNGA, ICESCR-OP (n 152) art 10; UNGA, CEDAW-OP (n 152) art 8; UNGA, CRC-OP (n 152) art 13.
160 Connors and Schmidt (n 139) 380.
161 ibid.

and complaints mechanisms can increase the answerability of a State, both types of mechanism lack a degree of enforcement. As it currently stands, State reporting is the only treaty-based mechanism available for monitoring China's compliance with its treaty obligations at the international level. China has not ratified any of the optional protocols that provide for complaints mechanisms and has not accepted the authority of any treaty body to determine human rights violations or publish its views and recommendations in this respect. Arguably, international accountability mechanisms are no more than empty rhetoric in relation to China. It is thus crucial that accessible, transparent and effective accountability mechanisms be established at the domestic level.

6.6 Concluding summary

Part 2 of this study has proposed an analytical framework for right to health-based accountability (which can also be applied to more human rights contexts), in order to set the foundations for the discussion of accountability in the Chinese context in chapter 7.

Firstly, part 2 distinguished and defined accountability from a human rights perspective. In this study, right to health-based (or more generally human rights-based) accountability is regarded as a dynamic and interactive process in which State actors are obliged to inform right-holders and overseeing institutions about their (past or future) decisions and actions, to explain and justify them and to face positive or negative consequences for them. In case of violations of the right to health, right-holders should have access to judicial or other effective remedies. Together, these aspects form the four building blocks that comprise the process of accountability: monitoring, judgment, consequences and remedies.

Secondly, this part identified three elements of (right to health-based) accountability: responsibility, answerability and enforcement. Responsibility is a particular contribution of the right to health framework to the current debate on accountability, and has the potential to refine the standards for accountable behaviour.

Thirdly, scholars have developed various typologies to define the content of different forms of accountability. This study is confined to two classic typologies. On the basis of the nature of the accountable actor's obligation, accountability can be further divided into vertical, horizontal and diagonal accountability, whilst based on the types of overseeing actors, it can be divided into judicial, quasi-judicial, political, administrative and social accountability. Judicial accountability mainly concerns courts' involvement in matters relating to ESCR. Quasi-judicial accountability is generated through independent overseeing institutions established by the State. Political accountability in a narrow sense exists between voters and elected representatives (electoral accountability), while in a broad sense, parliaments can also generate political accountability (ministerial accountability). Administrative accountability is based on internal hierarchical relationships and is exercised *within* institutions. Social accountability emerges through the actions of individuals and CSOs that aim to hold the State to account, as well as efforts by other actors (eg the media) to support these actions. Part 2 also extensively discussed the role of the media in exerting accountability, either as a social accountability mechanism or as an overseeing institution.

Fourthly, part 2 clarified the distinction between 'accountability' and an 'accountability mechanism'. Accountability mechanisms are the institutional arrangements that facilitate the process of accountability. Part 2 also discerned various types of mechanisms at the domestic level for generating judicial, quasi-judicial, political, administrative and social accountability for advancing the right to health.

Lastly, part 2 also discussed a handful of international supervisory mechanisms and State reporting, which despite being relatively weak, is the only treaty-based mechanism through which China's domestic implementation of the right to health can be monitored.

The analysis in part 2 was largely based on scholarly works that have a particular focus on democratic countries with competitive, free and fair elections. Little attention has been paid in the literature to accountability in other regimes. For many scholars, free election is a fundamental component, without which accountability is unlikely to exist in any meaningful way.[162] However, in my opinion, accountability could exist even with the absence of competitive elections. I will test this hypothesis in the following chapter by conducting an in-depth country study (i.e. China), so as to come to a greater understanding of right to health-based accountability. As such,

162 Bovens (n 29) 455, 465; Brinkerhoff (n 6) 374.

chapter 7 will explore how the implementation of the right to health care can be improved by exerting accountability within China's unique legal, political, and social background.

Part 3

Advancing the Right to Health Care in China - Towards Accountability

CHAPTER 7
ACCOUNTABILITY MECHANISMS FOR THE REALISATION OF THE RIGHT TO HEALTH CARE IN CHINA

7.1 INTRODUCTION

This chapter evaluates the extent to which right to health-based accountability can advance the right to health care within China's unique legal, political and social background. The purposes of such an assessment are threefold. First, as outlined in chapter 2, States undertake a core obligation to establish a range of effective, transparent, accessible and independent accountability mechanisms in relation to duties arising from the right to health (care).[1] In his mission to China in 2017, Philip Alston, the UN Special Rapporteur on Extreme Poverty and Human Rights, observed the existence of top-down mechanisms in China to control public officials; however, he also noted that 'it is extremely difficult to identify any effective mechanisms or avenues' that provide 'regularized avenues for citizens to complain and seek remedies for relevant abuses', 'despite the plethora of procedures that exist in theory'.[2] In light of this, by identifying existing mechanisms for exerting accountability in the context of the right to health care chapter 7 first examines whether China has discharged its core obligation to establish appropriate accountability mechanisms.

Second, previous (human rights or political science) scholarship addressing accountability has more or less focused on democratic countries with competitive, free and fair elections; relatively little attention has been paid to accountability in non-electoral regimes. This begs the question of whether the concept of accountability can be applied in the same fashion in non-electoral regimes. In fact, as explained in chapter 6, there is a considerable volume of literature and research criticising the effectiveness of elections for ensuring political accountability and aiming to identify

1 United Nations Committee on Economic, Social and Cultural Rights (CteeESCR), 'General Comment No. 9: The Domestic Application of the Covenant' (General Comment 9) (3 December 1998) UN Doc E/C12/1998/24, para 2; United Nations General Assembly (UNGA), 'Report of the Special Rapporteur on the Right of Everyone to the Enjoyment of the Highest Attainable Standard of Physical and Mental Health, Paul Hunt' (31 January 2008) UN Doc A/HRC/7/11, para 51 (d).

2 UNGA, 'Report of the Special Rapporteur on Extreme Poverty and Human Rights on His Mission to China, Philip Alston' (28 March 2017) UN Doc A/HRC/35/26/Add.2, paras 68-69.

other forms of accountability mechanisms to advance the right to health care. By taking China as a country study, this chapter can reach a greater understanding of accountability. States with similar legal and political settings can also draw lessons from China's experience.

Third, through extensive case analyses, this chapter explores the role that accountability can play in reducing abuses of power, assuring compliance with right to health standards and redressing violations of the right to health care within the context of China's current legal and political system. By identifying examples of good practice and obstacles to improved accountability, this chapter offers several recommendations for the enhancement of accountability. The recommendations, if fed directly into China's new round of health care reform (NHR), would eventually advance the right to health care in China.

To guide this country study, the chapter uses the analytical framework for right to health-based accountability developed in chapter 6 to identify connections between actors involved in China's health sector and to assess the capacity of overseeing actors to hold accountable actors (i.e. *State actors*) to account through various forms of domestic accountability mechanisms. Therefore, this chapter is structured as follows: section 7.2 identifies the key overseeing and accountable actors in China's health sector. Sections 7.3 to 7.7 then extensively discuss judicial, quasi-judicial, political, administrative and social accountability respectively, as well as the corresponding accountability mechanisms for exercising these types of accountability in light of China's reality. Section 7.8 concludes with some recommendations for establishing appropriate mechanisms for exerting right to health-based accountability in China.

7.2 Overseeing and accountable actors in China's health sector

As explained in chapter 5, right to health-based accountability in a narrow sense involves two actors: right-holders and duty-bearers. On the right-holders' side, everyone is entitled to the enjoyment of the highest attainable standard of health. On the duty-bearers' side, the State holds ultimately responsibility for the realisation of the right to health care.[3] All State organs (including both public institutions and public officials) to which the State has delegated the responsibility of performing

3 CteeESCR, 'General Comment No. 14: The Right to the Highest Attainable Standard of Health (Art. 12 of the Covenant)' (General Comment 14) (11 August 2000) UN Doc E/C12/2000/4, para 42.

obligations under the right to health care are also duty-bearers. In addition, public health care providers (i.e. public hospitals and health professionals) and social security institutions all have responsibilities from a human rights perspective and can thus be regarded as duty-bearers.

Nevertheless, as discussed in previous chapters, not only right-holders can hold duty-bearers to account. Therefore, this chapter uses the terms overseeing and accountable actors rather than right-holders and duty-bearers.

7.2.1 Overseeing actors

Overseeing actors include both right-holders and overseeing institutions. Clearly, patients are the major right-holders in the health care system who can (directly or indirectly) hold responsible State actors to account. But right-holders are not limited to patients. All individuals are right-holders as a matter of human rights law. Moreover, CSOs can also function as right-holders.

In addition to right-holders, other overseeing actors (i.e. overseeing institutions), including courts, complaints tribunals, people's congresses at various levels and the media, all have a role to play in exerting accountability for the realisation of the right to health care in China.

7.2.2 Accountable actors

In a broad sense, the discussion of duty-bearers in right to health-based accountability extends beyond State actors. A growing body of human rights scholarship also notes the responsibilities of non-State actors. Nevertheless, the analysis of accountable actors in this study is confined to duty-bearers as defined above (i.e. the State, State organs mandated by the State to discharge obligations arising from the right to health care, and other public institutions and public officials with responsibilities under the right to health care). In order to distinguish them from non-State actors, these accountable actors are all referred to as *State actors* in this study.

State actors normally include health ministries and specialised health institutions and commissions. As introduced in chapter 3, the National Health and Family Planning Commission (NHFPC) and the health (and family planning) bureaux at the provincial and local levels are the major authorities that undertake obligations arising from the right to health care in China. The NHFPC is responsible for making laws, regulations, policies and standards for health and family planning. It also develops national health plans and programmes and allocates health resources.[4] Arguably, the NHFPC is the key actor in the right to health-based accountability relationship. As a State organ under the leadership of the State Council, the NHFPC is directly accountable to the State Council and other overseeing institutions, and is indirectly accountable to society. Remarkably, the NHFPC also functions as an overseeing actor that provides internal checks and balances over health bureaux and other public institutions (and public officials) at the provincial and local levels.[5] The role of NHFPC will be discussed further in section 7.6.

Other ministries and commissions under the State Council are also engaged in health governance. Their responsibilities include the budgeting, planning, insurance management, and reforming of China's health care system.[6] For example, the Chinese Food and Drug Administration (CFDA) administers and supervises the manufacturing, procurement and utilisation of drugs, including essential medicines; the Ministry of Human Resources and Social Security (MOHRSS) is responsible for formulating health policies and standards concerning the basic medical insurance schemes; the Ministry of Civil Affairs (MOAC) is in charge of planning and making policies and standards related to the Medical Financial Assistance Programme for vulnerable groups within society; the Ministry of Finance (MOF) is the main source for public health funding and provides financial support for implementing health policies and programmes; and the National Development and Reform Committee (NDRC) is responsible for making all strategic decisions concerning national economic and social development and coordinates the development and reform of the health care system in China.[7]

Remarkably, to better understand the application of accountability mechanisms within China's unique legal, political and social framework, this chapter uses both descriptive and empirical approaches. I have not only identified the existing accountability mechanisms through literature review, but also investigated their

4 Qingyue Meng and others, 'People's Republic of China: Health System Review' (2015) 5 Health Systems in Transistion 30.
5 ibid, see also Derick Brinkerhoff, 'Accountability and Health Systems: Overview, Framework, and Strategies' (Partners for Health Reformplus 2003) 12.
6 Meng and others (n 4) 19-21.
7 ibid 30-31.

practical application through interviews with judges, officials from the health sector and people from civil society organisations (CSOs). Given time and financial constraints, I interviewed three judges, one person from the complaints tribunal, the founders of two CSOs, two officials from the health bureaux and one official from the food and drug administration to explore the operation of China's existing accountability mechanisms for claiming and redressing grievances of the right to health care. The case studies in this section are largely informed by the interviewees. However, among the nine interviewees, only the two founders of the CSOs allowed me to refer to their organisations in the written text. These two founders are Chuang Lei from Yiyou Charity, a non-governmental organisation for HBV carriers, and Hua Bai from BHL China League, a support network for people living with HIV/AIDS.

7.3 Judicial accountability

This section explores the possibilities of advancing the right to health care through judicial accountability. As explained in chapter 6, domestic courts can hold State actors to account on the basis of legally conferred responsibility. Normally, domestic courts generate judicial accountability by reviewing the constitutionality and legality of health laws and administrative regulations, rules and actions. When the right to health care is violated or State actors fail to discharge their (core) obligations under the right to health care, domestic courts can provide judicial remedies to those who are affected and sanction responsible State actors.[8] Domestic courts, as judicial overseeing institutions, provide horizontal accountability mechanisms that right-holders and other overseeing actors can use to claim violations of the right to health care. Domestic courts can hold State actors to account through the identification of laws that are not consistent with constitutional rights or international human rights obligations (if entrenched in the constitution or other statutes), judicial review of administrative decisions and actions, and statutory interpretation.[9] This section divides the judicial accountability mechanisms into two parts: constitutional accountability mechanisms and general judicial accountability mechanisms.

8 Office of the United Nations High Commissioner for Human Rights (OHCHR) and Center for Economic and Social Rights, 'Who Will Be Accountable? Human Rights and the Post-2015 Development Agenda' (2013) 39.

9 Helen Potts, 'Accountability and the Right to the Highest Attainable Standard of Health' (University of Essex Human Rights Centre 2008) 13 <http://repository.essex.ac.uk/9717/1/accountability-right-highest-attainable-standard-health.pdf> accessed 28 November 2017.

7.3.1 Constitutional accountability mechanisms

7.3.1.1 Constitutional review of legislation

According to Black's Law Dictionary, judicial review is 'a court's power to review the actions of other branches or levels of government; esp., the court's power to invalidate legislative and executive actions as being unconstitutional'.[10] Constitutional review, another label for judicial review, generally refers to the power of courts to examine whether legislation enacted by parliament or acts of the executive are consistent with the Constitution and to determine their validity.[11] The 1982 Chinese Constitution does not provide any provision regarding constitutional review. Domestic courts, including the Supreme People's Court (SPC), have not been granted, explicitly or implicitly, any power to exercise constitutional review.[12]

As explained in chapter 3, rather than a clear separation of powers as observed in most Western countries, in China there is only a separation of functions.[13] State power is centralised in the National People's Congress (NPC), as the highest State organ. The NPC and the Standing Committee of the NPC (NPCSC) also exercise the legislative power of the State. [14] The judiciary operates under the leadership and supervision of the NPC and NPCSC.[15] In addition to exercising legislative power, the NPC has the power to amend the Constitution and supervise its enforcement, while the NPCSC has the power to interpret the Constitution and supervise its enforcement.[16] The power of supervision implies that both the NPC and the NPCSC can provide (non-judicial) review of the constitutionality and legality of laws and administrative regulations and rules.

---

10 Black's Law Dictionary (9th Edn West 2009) 924.

11 Guobin Zhu, 'Constitutional Review in China: An Unaccomplished Project or a Mirage ?' (2010) 43 Suffolk University Law Review 625, 625.

12 ibid 625-626; Yuwen Li, *The Judicial System and Reform in Post-Mao China: Stumbling Towards Justice* (Routledge 2014) 8.

13 Zhining Ma, 'The Structure and Roles of China's Party-State System in Industrial Relations: An Updated Review' (2009) 7 China: An International Journal 370, 370-371.

14 Constitution of the People's Republic of China (adopted and entered into force on 4 December 1982, amended on 14 March 2004) arts 3, 57-58 <www.npc.gov.cn/englishnpc/Constitution/2007-11/15/content_1372965.htm> accessed 28 November 2017 (Chinese Constitution). The English version was obtained from the official website of the National People's Congress (NPC).

15 Chinese Constitution, art 67.

16 Chinese Constitution, arts 62, 67.

This implication is evident in the Legislation Law. According to Article 97 of this Law, the NPC has the authority to amend or repeal any improper national laws ('*falv*') enacted by the NPCSC, and to repeal any self-governing regulations ('*zizhi tiaoli*') that have been approved by the NPCSC but nevertheless contravene the Constitution. The NPCSC has the authority to repeal any administrative regulations ('*xingzheng fagui*') that contravene the Constitution or any (national) law, and to repeal any local regulations ('*difangxing fagui*') that contravene the Constitution or any (national) law and administrative regulation.[17] In addition, when they deem that 'any administrative regulation, local regulation, autonomous regulation, or separate regulation contravenes the Constitution or any law', a number of State organs, including the State Council, the SPC, and the Supreme People's Procuratorate (SPP), can submit a written *request* to the NPCSC for review.[18] The operating divisions of the NPCSC should refer such requests to the relevant specialised committees for their review and opinion.[19] Other State authorities, social organisations and citizens can also submit a written *recommendation* to the NPCSC for such a review.[20]

Nevertheless, as Zhang observes, since the enactment of the Legislation Law in 2000, the NPCSC has not activated the review process, notwithstanding the fact that it has already received a considerable amount of recommendations from citizens, legal professionals and other social organisations to do so.[21] The NPCSC is generally reluctant to activate the review process due to its concerns that doing so would open the floodgates and result in a significant volume of requests and recommendations that the body would not have the capacity to screen and study prior to initiating the process.[22]

As it currently stands, constitutional review of legislation is not possible within the Chinese people's congress system. The power to interpret the Constitution and supervise its enforcement resides with the NPC and NPCSC. Therefore, the only

17 Legislation Law of the People's Republic of China [Lifa Fa] (adopted on 15 March 2000, entered into force on 1 July 2000, amended on 15 March 2015), art 97 (Legislation Law) <www.npc.gov.cn/englishnpc/Law/2007-12/11/content_1383554.htm> accessed 28 November 2017. The English version was obtained from the official website of the NPC.

18 Legislation Law, art 99.

19 ibid.

20 ibid, art 100.

21 Xiang Zhang, 'The Selection Mechanisms of Constitutional Cases' [Xianfa Anjian de Shaixuan Jizhi] Chinese Yearbook of Constitutional Law 2012 [Zhongguo Xianfa Niankan] 98, 98.

22 ibid; Zhu (n 11) 639.

possibility for reviewing the constitutionality of laws and administrative regulations is to submit written requests or recommendations to the NPCSP to conduct *non-judicial review*. It is not yet certain whether, and if so when the NPCSP will initiate the procedure for constitutional review in practice.

7.3.1.2 Constitutional litigation – the 'judicialisation' of the Constitution

Another type of constitutional review concerns the jurisdiction of the SPC (as opposed to the NPC) to adjudicate violations of constitutional rights – the so-called 'constitutional judicialisation'.[23] The 1982 Constitution grants individuals the right to material assistance when they are old, ill or disabled; it also obliges the State to develop a comprehensive health system for the protection of the health of its people.[24] Nonetheless, the direct applicability of constitutional provisions remains underspecified in the Constitution. In practice, right-holders have never claimed their constitutional right to health before any domestic court.[25] This has given rise to a controversial debate concerning the question of whether constitutional rights are subject to judicial adjudication.

Under China's current legal and political system, the judiciary has not been granted any power to exercise constitutional jurisdiction over legislative acts.[26] However, given the complexity of this matter, it is too soon to conclude whether or not individuals can invoke constitutional provisions to seek a remedy for a violation of individual constitutional right before domestic courts.

Arguably, domestic courts have no power of constitutional adjudication. If the Constitution were to be interpreted, it must be by the NPCSC.[27] Nevertheless, as Morris points out, the definition of term 'interpretation' as used in the Constitution is contested.[28] To complicate this matter further, in the case *Qi Yuling v Chen Xiaoqi*

23 Robert Morris, 'China's Marbury: Qi Yuling v. Chen Xiaoqi - The Once and Future Trial of Both Education & Constitutionalization' (2012) 2 Tsinghua China Law Review 273, 287.
24 Chinese Constitution, arts 21, 45.
25 Shengnan Qiu and Gillian MacNaughton, 'Mechanisms of Accountability for the Realization of the Right to Health in China' (2017) 19 Health and Human Rights Journal 279, 282.
26 Zhu (n 11) 644.
27 Chinese Constitution, art 67.
28 Morris (n 23) 279.

and others (hereinafter Qi's case),[29] the SPC arguably acted beyond its authority and issued a judicial interpretation regarding the application of the Constitution.[30]

Box 7.1: *Qi Yuling v Chen Xiaoqi and others* - claiming constitutional right to education before the High People's Court of Shandong Province

Qi, Yulin and Chen, Xiaoqi were secondary school students in Shandong Province, China. In 1990, both students sat the entrance examinations for further education. Qi passed the exam while Chen failed. The same year, the Commercial School of Jining City in Shandong Province ('the School') sent Qi an admission letter. In order to continue Chen's study, Chen's father and the head of Chen's secondary school fraudulently intercepted Qi's admission letter without notifying her. By using Qi's name and the admission letter, Chen registered and studied at the School. The student profile kept by the School include a photo of Qi, whose facial features were obviously different from Chen's. Nevertheless, after pretending to be Qi for three years, Chen graduated and found a job at a local bank – an expected consequence of her education. In 1999, Qi finally discovered the incident and filed a lawsuit against Chen and others for infringing her rights, including the right to identity and the constitutional right to education.[31]

The High People's Court of Shandong Province was unsure whether to proceed with the complaint concerning a constitutional right. This is because no constitutional provisions had ever been applied in China's domestic courts before. According to Article 32 of the Organic Law of the People's Courts, the SPC 'gives interpretation on [*sic*] questions concerning [the] specific application of laws and decrees in judicial proceedings.'[32] Therefore, this matter was referred to the SPC, which issued its judicial interpretation, commonly referred to as the 'Response to Qi, Yuling's Case'.[33] In this Response, the SPC held that, 'by means of violating the right to identity, Chen Xiaoqi and others have infringed upon the fundamental right to education that Qi Yuling should enjoy in accordance with the constitutional provisions, and caused concrete damages to the appellant; they should assume civil liabilities accordingly.'[34]

On 23 August 2001, the High People's Court of Shandong Province gave its verdict in favour of Qi and confirmed that Chen had violated Article 46 of the Constitution.

29 *Qi Yuling v Chen Xiaoqi and others*, SUP. PEOPLE'S CT. GAZ. (Supreme People's Ct., June 28, 2001). The English translation of the trial is available at <www.lawinfochina.com/Case/List.asp> (search for Qi, Yuling) accessed 28 November 2017.

30 Morris (n 23) 283; Zhu (n 11) 645.

31 Chinese Constitution, art 46.

32 Organic Law of the People's Courts of the People's Republic of China (adopted on 1 July 1979, entered into force on 1 January 1980, amended on 31 October 2006), art 32 <www.npc.gov.cn/englishnpc/Law/2007-12/13/content_1384078.htm> accessed 28 November 2017. The English version was obtained from the official website of the NPC.

33 The Supreme People's Court of the People's Republic of China, '[Guanyu yi qinfan xingmingquan de shouduan qinfan xianfa baohu de gongmin shoujiaoyu de jiben quanli shifou ying chengdan minshi zeren de pifu [An official response of the SPC to whether those who violated the basic constitutional right to education by infringing the right to identity should assume civil liability]' Zuigao Fayuan Gongbao [Official Gazette of Supreme People's Court] Fashi (2001) No. 25. Author's translation. See also Zhu (n 11) 645; Morris (n 23) 289.

34 ibid.

Qi's case is known as the first, if not only, case that constitutes a judicial application of a constitutional provision. Qi's case has drawn considerable attention from scholars and commentators. For example, the former President of the Civil Chamber of the SPC, Huang, Songyou considers this case to be the beginning of an era of 'constitutional judicialisation'.[35] The concept of constitutional judicialisation is similar to the concept of direct applicability, which refers to introducing the Constitution into judicial proceedings as a legal basis for judicial adjudication.[36] Huang asserts that, '[a]mong all the kinds of laws applied in China, the Constitution used to be a source of embarrassment' and 'the majority of its content has been placed, neglected, "on the shelf" in China's judicial activities, having no practical legal effect.'[37] He further argues that, '[c]onstitutional judicialization is the requirement for enhancing the legal effect of the Constitution' and that constitutional judicialisation should be a prerequisite for ruling the country in accordance with the law and for building a socialist country that adheres to the rule of law.[38]

By contrast, some scholars argue that the SPC's interpretation is 'in effect an *ultra vires* action'.[39] Given that the Constitution explicitly affords the power to interpret the Constitution to the NPCSC,[40] the SPC cannot confer that power on lower courts by way of judicial interpretation. It is 'the meddling of the judiciary in the affairs committed by the Constitution to the NPC and the NPCSC'.[41] Moreover, some scholars argue that the Response 'is not an express or implied grant of the power of constitutional review'.[42] For example, as Morris observes, in its interpretation the SPC 'applied' the Constitution between private parties. However, the SPC did not 'construe any statute or rule by comparing it against the Constitution as a measure, least of all strike the latter down for being "unconstitutional"'.[43] Therefore, Morris

35 Songyu Huang, 'Xifa Sifahua Jiqi Yiyi – Cong Zuigao Renmin Fayuan Jintian de Yige Pifu Tanqi [Constitutional Judicialisation and its Significance – A Comment on Today's 'Response' by the SPC]' Renmin Fayuan Bao [People's Court Daily] (13 August 2001). Cited in Guobin Zhu (2010) 646.

36 ibid.

37 Huang (n 35). Quoted in Morris (n 23) 284. Morris' translation.

38 Huang (n 35). Cited in Zhu (n 11) 647. Zhu's translation.

39 Morris (n 23) 284.

40 Chinese Constitution, art 67.

41 Morris (n 23) 284.

42 Ulric Killion, 'China's Amended Constitution: Quest for Liberty and Independent Judicial Review' (2005) 4 Washington University Global Studies Law Review 43, 72.

43 Morris (n 23) 285-286.

asserts that Qi's case is above all 'a "safe" constitutional case for the SPC to flex its muscles and test the political water.' [44]

Notably, in 2008, the SPC officially announced that its judicial interpretation regarding Qi's case was 'no longer in use',[45] without explaining the reason for the withdrawal.[46] It is not certain whether the decision of the SPC will bring an end to constitutional litigation and even judicial reform on a larger scale.

All in all, as Kellogg comments, although the SPC's intervention in Qi's case has some flaws, 'what the Court was trying to accomplish was absolutely fundamental'.[47] Although no more courts have applied any constitutional provision after the withdrawal of the judicial interpretation on Qi's case, the possibility of claiming constitutional rights before China's domestic courts is still inspiring. Much more work has to be done with regard to judicial reform under the current people's congress system in China.

7.3.2 General judicial accountability mechanisms

As it currently stands, domestic courts cannot hold State actors to account through constitutional mechanisms. Neither can right-holders invoke constitutional provisions protecting the right to health care before domestic courts. Nevertheless, right-holders can claim remedies for a violation of the right to health care by invoking health-related legislation. Domestic courts can also hold responsible State actors to account through general judicial accountability mechanisms which will now be discussed.

7.3.2.1 Civil proceedings

Generally, right-holders can seek redress for a violation of the right to health care by bringing a lawsuit before China's domestic courts. Correspondingly, courts can

---

44 ibid.

45 SPC, Zuigao Renmin Fayuan Guanyu Feizhi 2007 Niandi Yiqian Fabu de Youguan Sifa Jieshi (Diqipi) de Jueding [The Supreme People's Court Decision on Abolishing Some Judicial Interpretations (the 7th Batch) issued before the End of 2007] Sup. People's Ct. (adopted on 18 December 2008, entered into force 24 December 2008). Author's translation.

46 Morris (n 23) 288-290.

47 Thomas Kellogg, 'The Death of Constitutional Litigation in China?' (2009) 9 China Brief: A Journal of Analysis and Information 1, 4-7 <https://jamestown.org/wp-content/uploads/2009/04/cb_009_7_02.pdf?x87069> accessed 28 November 2017.

sanction responsible State actors and provide judicial remedies to aggrieved right-holders by applying the relevant laws. It deserves pointing out, however, that in the majority of court jurisprudence no explicit reference has been made to the right to health care. Rather, this right is achieved through the application of other legal rights, such as 'the rights of life and health' prescribed under Article 98 of the General Principles of Civil Law (GPCL).[48] In other words, violations of the right to health care can be judicially redressed by invoking other health-related rights.

As discussed in chapter 3, although the right to health has not been transformed into specific human rights terms within China's domestic legislation, elements of the right to health care are reflected in a handful of health-related laws. In practice, there are a considerable number of health-related litigations. However, most concern medical malpractice and thus fall within the realm of civil proceedings on the basis of the GPCL or the Tort Law. The subject of these civil litigations is more the infringement of a civil right *of* health, or patient rights, than the violation of fundamental (human) right *to* health. For example, many health-related laws provide for duties incumbent on health care providers. If a health professional refuses (for example) to provide patients with immediate emergency measures where necessary, the patients can sue the health professional before the court on the basis of a violation of law.[49] However, in such civil proceedings, the two parties stand on an equal footing and the verdict concerning the denial of access to health care is not based on the right to timely and appropriate health care *per se*.

Briefly speaking, civil proceedings are often used to address disputes between patients and health care providers (including health professionals). Although the GPCL also stipulates that the State bears civil liability if State actors violate the rights and interests of citizens (including health rights) and cause damage thereto,[50] in the strictest sense of the word, right-holders cannot hold State actors accountable

48 General Principles of the Civil Law of the People's Republic of China (GPCL) (adopted on 12 April 1986, entered into force 1 January 1987, amended on 27 August 2009) <www.npc.gov.cn/englishnpc/Law/2007-12/12/content_1383941.htm> accessed 28 November 2017. The English version was obtained from the official website of the NPC. Article 98 of the GPCL articulates that 'citizens shall enjoy the rights of life and health.'

49 Law of the People's Republic of China on Licensed Doctors (adopted on 26 June 1998, entered into force on 1 May 1999, amended on 27 August 2009), art 24 <www.npc.gov.cn/englishnpc/Law/2007-12/11/content_1383574.htm> accessed 28 November 2017. The English version was obtained from the official website of the NPC.

50 GPCL, art 121.

for violations of the right to health care on a larger scale (eg for systematic failures in the health care system). However, right-holders can use civil proceedings to hold the relevant State actors (in most cases health care providers) accountable for violations of the right to health care. This can be done by a right-holder invoking elements of the right to health care that have been transformed into domestic laws (such as the State actors' duty to provide access to health care) rather than by directly invoking personal right to health care.

7.3.2.2 Administrative proceedings

State actors can be held accountable both *ex ante* and *ex post facto* through administrative proceedings. As mentioned in chapter 3, right-holders can seek judicial remedies before a court if an administrative organ: (1) infringes personal rights (including health rights) and other legal rights and interests; (2) refuses to perform its statutory duties and responsibilities in respect of the protection of personal rights and other legal rights and interests, or fails to respond to a request for its performance; or (3) fails to pay compensation, a minimum subsistence fee or social insurance benefits according to the law.[51] For example, if a social security institution (an administrative organ) refuses to reimburse health expenses to an individual without providing a valid reason for doing so, the aggrieved person can hold this institution to account through administrative proceedings.[52]

The aforementioned civil proceedings and administrative proceedings make it possible to exert *ex post facto* judicial accountability – i.e. after the occurrence of a fact or damage. However, the outcomes of these litigations only seem to benefit individual right-holders rather than right-holders generally. As Ho correctly points out, 'litigation may only stand in as an outlet for disgruntled individuals' if there is no genuine policy or structural change, albeit that the outcomes of such health-related claims may benefit other patients.[53]

---

51 Administrative Procedure Law of the People's Republic of China (APL) (adopted on 4 April 1989, entered into effect on 1 October 1990, amended on 27 June 2017), arts 12(6), (10), (12) <www.lawinfochina.com/display.aspx?lib=law&id=23600> accessed 28 November 2017. The English version was obtained from the academic database of authority – the pkulaw.

52 ibid, art 57.

53 Christina Ho, 'Health Rights at the Juncture between State and Market: The People's Republic of China in Colleen Flood and Aeyal Gross (eds), *The Right to Health at the Public/Private Divide: A Global Comparative Study* (Cambridge University Press 2014) 275.

Remarkably, as of 2015 in accordance with the amended Administrative Procedure Law (APL), domestic courts can also hold State actors to account *ex ante*. Before the amendment of the APL, the conventional understanding was that courts could not adjudicate claims against administrative organs with regard to the formulation of administrative regulations and rules, or decisions and orders with general binding force, even when these regulations and rules were incompatible with right to health standards.[54] The APL only aimed at regulating *concrete administrative acts ('juti xingzheng xingwei')* against specific individuals.[55] An example is the aforementioned social security institution that refuses to reimburse patients. According to the APL, the courts could not adjudicate cases against *abstract administrative acts* (*'chouxiang xingzheng xingwei'*), which have a general legally binding force upon a large but uncertain number of people.

Nonetheless, pursuant the amendment, the APL no longer distinguishes *concrete* or *abstract* administrative acts. Instead, Article 53 (1) of the amended APL states that,

> [w]here a citizen, a legal person, or any other organization deems that a regulatory document developed by a department of the State Council or by a local people's government or a department thereof, based on which the alleged administrative action was taken, is illegal, the citizen, legal person, or other organization may concurrently file a request for review of the regulatory document when filing a complaint against the administrative action.[56]

Accordingly, when they file a complaint against an administrative action it is possible for right-holders to file a request for judicial review in relation to the legality of the *regulatory document*. Nevertheless, Article 53 (2) clarifies that the regulatory documents do not include department rules (*'bumen guizhang'*).[57] This means that while domestic courts can review the legality of local regulations enacted by the local people's congresses and local rules formulated by local governments, courts still cannot review the legality of national laws (*'falv'*) enacted by the NPC and NPCSC, the *administrative regulations* formulated by the State Council, or the *department*

54 Administrative Procedure Law of the People's Republic of China (original) (adopted on 4 April 1989, entered into force 1 October 1990), art 13(2) <www.npc.gov.cn/englishnpc/Law/2007-12/12/content_1383912.htm> accessed 28 November 2017). The English version was obtained from the official website of the NPC.

55 APL, art 11.

56 ibid, art 53(1).

57 ibid, art 53(2).

rules formulated by the ministries and commissions under the State Council. This includes health-related laws, regulations and rules.

To conclude, litigation (i.e. a type of judicial accountability mechanism) makes it possible to hold responsible State actors judicially accountable. As of 2015, domestic courts can hold State actors to account both *ex ante* and *ex post*. Right-holders can not only seek redress for violations of the right to health care caused by concrete administrative acts, but also request the court to review whether the regulatory document on which the allegedly illegal administrative action was based, are compatible with the right to health norms included in relevant domestic legislation.

However, as Ho points out, '[l]itigation is a relatively weak tool in China.'[58] The cost, duration and the uncertainty of the outcome of a litigation often discourage right-holders from seeking redress through litigation.[59] Litigation is thus generally perceived as a last resort in China.

7.4 QUASI-JUDICIAL ACCOUNTABILITY

7.4.1 'Letters and visits'

China has not yet established any national human rights institutions (NHRI). However, China did establish 25 new State institutions in 2013 that perform comparable functions. These 25 institutions comprise the Ministries of Justice, Supervision, Human Resources and Social Security, as well as other government institutions mandated by the ministries and commissions under the State Council, including the State Bureau for Letters and Calls.[60]

Amongst the 25 State institutions that have functional responsibilities similar to those of a NHRI, the State Bureau for Letters and Calls is a specific overseeing institution established to deal with complaints. According to the Regulations on Complaint Letters and Visits ('*Xinfang Tiaoli*'), aggrieved individual(s) and group(s) can seek redress against public institutions and officials by lodging complaints at their local bureaux for letters and calls through personal visits, letters, phone calls

58 Ho (n 53) 273.
59 OHCHR and Center for Economic and Social Rights (n 8) 40.
60 United Nations Economic and Social Council, 'List of Issues in Relation to the Second Periodic Report of China (E/C.12/CHN/2), including Hong Kong), China (E/C.12/CHN-HKG/3) and Macao, China (E/C.12/CHN-MAC/2)' (11 February 2014) UN Doc E/C.12/CHN/Q/2/Add.1, para 1.

or online portals.[61] This mechanism is often referred to as the 'letters and visits' ('*xinfang*') or 'petitioning' procedure.[62] Notably, some scholars also regard 'letters and calls' as administrative mechanisms given that the bureaux for letters and calls are apparatuses of government and the determination of the complaints is a matter of official discretion.[63] Theoretically, after reviewing a complaint, a local bureau for letters and calls refers the complaint to a relevant specialised institution that has the authority to address the complaint.[64] Nevertheless, as Alston notes, this process is relatively opaque in practice, given that local bureaux lack sufficient staff and that no meaningful statistics are available as to the exact number and nature of petitions received and addressed.[65] Moreover, unlike NHRIs, these bureaux do not carry out investigations into the progress made towards the domestic implementation of human rights and do not identify human rights violations themselves.

In fact, the aforementioned 25 State institutions, including the State Bureau for Letters and Calls, are not established for the purpose of human rights promotion and protection and they have a range of other State-mandated responsibilities. It is relatively difficult, if not impossible, for these State institutions to maintain full independence and to effectively perform the same role as a NHRI. As noted by the United Nations Committee on Economic, Social and Cultural Rights, it is still necessary for China to 'establish an independent national human rights institution with a broad mandate to promote and protect human rights', including the right to health care.[66]

7.4.2 Mediation

In addition to independent oversight bodies, chapter 6 also introduced other overseeing institutions, such as patients' rights tribunals or health complaints

61 Regulation on Complaint Letters and Visits (adopted on 5 January 2005, entered into force on 1 May 2005), art 2 <www.lawinfochina.com/Display.aspx?lib=law&Cgid=56635> accessed 28 November 2017 (Regulation on Complaint Letters and Visits). The English version was obtained from pkulaw.

62 UNGA, 'Report of the Special Rapporteur on Extreme Poverty and Human Rights on His Mission to China, Philip Alston' (n 2) para 70.

63 Ho (n 53) 274.

64 Regulation on Complaint Letters and Visits, art 21.

65 UNGA, 'Report of the Special Rapporteur on Extreme Poverty and Human Rights on His Mission to China, Philip Alston' (n 2) para 70.

66 United Nations Economic and Social Council, 'Concluding Observations on the Second Periodic Report of China, including Hong Kong, China, and Macao, China' (13 June 2014) UN Doc E/C.12/CHN/CO/2, para 8.

tribunals, that can exert quasi-judicial accountability.[67] This type of quasi-judicial overseeing institutions is also present in China, very often in the form of medical mediation committees. In 2006, the first medical disputes mediation committee was established by the local government of the Pudong New District in Shanghai. According to the *Procedures of the Municipality of Shanghai on the Prevention and Mediation of Medical Malpractice Disputes*, the justice bureau is 'responsible for guiding people's mediation of medical malpractice disputes and promoting the standardization of such mediation.'[68] The people's mediation committee for medical malpractice disputes (MMMC) is a district- or county-based 'non-government[al] organization specializing in mediating medical malpractice disputes in the relevant jurisdiction, subject to the guidance of the district/county justice department.' The MMMC 'mediate[s] medical malpractice disputes according to law, free from any interference from any organization or individual' and provides the mediation free of charge.[69] Where necessary, having reached a mediation agreement, the parties to a dispute can apply for a judicial confirmation.[70] In light of the mediation, the MMMC may also submit written proposals for the prevention of medical malpractice disputes to the health and family planning bureau and the medical institutions.[71]

Gao and others conducted a survey of 37 medical institutions and 124 patients in 2011 and found that both medical institutions and patients were willing to work with MMMCs to solve medical disputes, although their reasons for choosing mediation varied.[72] For the medical institutions surveyed, the main reason was to maintain stability and keep their reputation unblemished. For the patients, motives included the practicality of the dispute mechanism, the simplicity of the procedure and the savings they would make in relation to both time and money.[73]

67 Potts (n 9) 19.
68 Shanghai Municipal People's Government, 'Procedures of Shanghai Municipality on Prevention and Mediation of Medical Malpractice Dispute' (adopted on 6 January 2014, entered into effect 1 March 2014), art 4 <www.shanghai.gov.cn/shanghai/node27118/node27386/node27408/n32231/n32235/u26ai39127.html> 28 November 2017. The English version was obtained from the official website of the Shanghai municipal people's government.
69 ibid, art 5.
70 ibid, art 39.
71 ibid, art 41.
72 Jianwei Gao and others, 'Shanghaishi 37 suo Yiliao Jigou he 124 wei Huanzhe Yihuanshuangfang Xieshang Jiejue Jiufen Xianzhuang Diaocha Fenxi [Survey and Analysis on Consultation Settlement of 124 Doctor-patient Disputes in 37 Medical Institutions in Shanghai]' in (2011) 15 Zhongguo Yiyuan [Chinese Hospitals] 47, 48. Author's translation.
73 ibid.

Arguably, mediation has now become a key mechanism for solving medical disputes.[74] However, unlike in many other countries where quasi-judicial overseeing institutions are autonomous bodies created pursuant to legislation, the Chinese MMMCs are mostly established in accordance with local rules ('*difang zhengfu guizhang*') and function under the leadership of the bureaux of justice at local levels. Therefore, strictly speaking, the Chinese MMMCs are not entirely independent. Their mandates are also different from those of general quasi-judicial overseeing institutions. The mandate of general quasi-judicial institutions includes not only determining complaints about public health services and health professionals, but also carrying out reviews of health sector performance and investigating and researching the health sector.[75] As Potts observes, the decisions of tribunals and the findings of the quasi-judicial institutions' investigations and research can assist health policy makers.[76]

In comparison, the mandate of the Chinese MMMCs is relatively limited. They do not have the authority to directly and actively investigate and review health sector performance, but only to submit written proposals to health bureaux and health care providers. In terms of complaints, they have a restricted mandate to mediate complaints concerning infringements of health rights caused by health care providers (including health professionals).

In light of the above, it can be concluded that the existing quasi-judicial overseeing institutions do not provide any independent oversight of violations of the right to health care. Quasi-judicial mechanisms, such as 'letters and visits' or mediation are relatively weak mechanisms for holding State actors to account. Therefore, it is important for China to establish independent quasi-judicial overseeing institutions with a broad mandate, as well as corresponding accountability mechanisms, to promote and protect the right to health care.

74 ibid.
75 Potts (n 9) 19.
76 ibid.

7.5 Political accountability

Political accountability generated through periodic elections is deemed to form the core of democracy.[77] Generally, voters participate in the formulation of health legislation, regulations and policies by delegating their authority to elected representatives.[78] They also hold the government to account by voting for representatives who can act in their best interests, and by voting against representatives who may have not kept their past electoral commitments or who may have violated human rights.[79] Given that China is a State with a single ruling party, this narrow sense of political accountability (electoral accountability) is not easily practicable in China.[80]

Nevertheless, as explained in chapter 5, there is a growing body of argument against elections as a blunt mechanism to hold State actors to account. This is because of the lengthy time that passes between elections, individuals' uneven influence in selecting representatives, and the lack of tools for directly checking and controlling the government's conduct.[81] In contrast, parliament can also generate political accountability and hold State actors to account more regularly (i.e. through ministerial accountability). This broad sense of political accountability is present in China and is exercised by the NPC. The Chinese NPC has a comparable function to parliament – according to Article 34 of the Chinese Constitution, citizens directly elect their representatives at the local level and indirectly elect them at the provincial and national level.[82] The indirectly elected representatives at the national level constitute the NPC and are accountable to their constituents. The following section examines how the NPC and its Standing Committee can exert ministerial accountability for the right to health care in three main ways.

---

77 Derick Brinkerhoff, 'Taking Account of Accountability: A Conceptual Overview and Strategic Options' (US Agency for International Development 2001) 5 <http://1qswp72wn11q9smtq15ccbuo.wpengine.netdna-cdn.com/wp-content/uploads/2011/07/IPC_Taking_Account_of_Accountability.pdf> accessed 28 November 2017.

78 Mark Bovens, 'Analysing and Assessing Accountability: A Conceptual Framework' (2007) 13 European Law Journal 447, 455.

79 United Nations Children's Fund (UNICEF), 'Accountability for Children's Rights: With Special Attention to Social Accountability and Its Potential to Achieve Results and Equity for Children' (2015) 8.

80 Qiu and MacNaughton (n 25) 283.

81 UNICEF (n 79) 8; Catalina Smulovitz and Eurique Peruzzotti, 'Societal Accountability in Latin America' (11) 2000 Journal of Democracy 147, 147-158. Cited in Yuko Kasuya and Yuriko Takahashi, 'Streamlining Accountability: Concepts, Subtypes, and Empirical Analyses' (2012) 16 <ssrn.com/abstract=2493654> accessed 28 November 2017.

82 Chinese Constitution, art 34.

First, the NPC, as the legislature of the State, has the responsibility to ensure that legislative proposals respect and promote the right to health care. Generally speaking, deputies of the NPC (elected representatives at the national level) can submit their legislative or other proposals at the annual meeting of the NPC. Individual citizens can theoretically participate in the health law-making process by making legal recommendations to these deputies. For example, Lei Chuang,[83] the director of the Yiyou Charity (the non-governmental organisation for HBV carriers) drafted a recommendation letter calling for the affordability of hepatitis B drugs and submitted them to Tang, Zuyi, who is the deputy to the NPC (the elected representative at the national level). Mr. Tang reviewed Lei's letter and found the suggestions crucial. He then included the suggestions in his legal proposal for the NPC.[84] Nevertheless, it remains uncertain whether Tang's proposal has been taken into consideration by the congress given the huge amount of proposals submitted for discussion. In addition, although Lei, Chuang's approach is inspiring, such occasional proposals do not create a regular avenue for right-holders to participate in the process of health law-making. It also deserves pointing out that the function of the NPC has long been criticised as 'rubber stamping', meaning that in practice they have little influence over the central government, and only pass proposals put forward by the government itself.[85]

Second, as mentioned in section 7.3, the NPC and its Standing Committee have the responsibility of ensuring that domestic legislation conforms with human rights law. The NPC has the authority to amend or repeal any improper national laws enacted by the NPCSC, while the NPCSC has the authority to repeal any administrative or local regulations that contravene the Constitution or any (national) laws. The NPCSC also has the power to review the constitutionality and legality of laws, administrative regulations and rules upon receiving a written request or recommendation.[86] Nevertheless, as section 7.3 explained it is a relatively 'untransparent and discretionary' process in reality.[87] As of yet, no concrete progress has been made to regularise this accountability mechanism.[88]

83 The interviewee as mentioned in section 7.2.
84 Based on my interview with Chuang Lei. See also report <www.yiyougongyi.org/h-nd-401.html> accessed 28 November.
85 Ma (n 13) 370–371.
86 Chinese Constitution, art 100.
87 UNGA, 'Report of the Special Rapporteur on Extreme Poverty and Human Rights on His Mission to China, Philip Alston' (n 2) para 71.
88 ibid.

Third, as the highest organ of State power, the NPC and NPCSC have the power to provide regular oversight of the work of the State Council and to hold the State Council to account.[89] More specifically, the NPC and NPCSC can review the State Council's proposals for health strategies. For example, as mentioned in section 7.2, the NDRC is a commission under the State Council that is responsible for drafting national health plans. These strategies will not enter into effect until they have been approved by the NPC.[90] This allows the NPC to make sure that proposals respect and promote the right to health care, such as the equitable distribution of health resources. Moreover, the NPC and NPCSC can hold the head of the NHFPC accountable for the ministry's performance,[91] including advising and supervising administrative decisions and actions in relation to the right to health care. For instance, Wenkang Zhang, the minister of the former Ministry of Health, was held accountable for the failure to protect public health and resigned after the outbreak of the SARS epidemic in China in 2003.[92] Political accountability can to some degree be achieved by the resignation of officials. However, as Qiu and MacNaughton note, the resignation constitutes a more 'political gesture' than a regularised political accountability mechanism.[93]

To summarise, although in theory the NPC and NPCSC can provide strong parliamentary oversight, mechanisms for political accountability remain relatively weak in practice – little progress appears to have been made regarding the practical functioning of the NPC and NPCSC.

7.6 Administrative accountability

This section discusses administrative accountability in a narrow sense, whereby inferior actors give administrative account to their superiors on the basis of a 'chain of command'.[94] This section focuses on administrative supervision within the State Council. The State Council operates under the leadership of the NPC, while the ministries and commissions operate under the leadership of the State Council. In

89 Chinese Constitution, art 67.
90 Qiu and MacNaughton (n 25) 284.
91 ibid.
92 ibid.
93 ibid.
94 Bovens (n 78) 458. Notably, this type of administrative accountability is also categorised as political accountability in other scholarship. However, this study only discusses political accountability that is either generated through elections or through parliamentary oversight.

other words, the State Council holds its ministries and commissions to account and gives account to the NPC and the NPCSC. Along similar lines, county, municipal and provincial governments are under the leadership of the State Council, which can hold its subordinate governments to account.[95] Actors in this relationship can become both the principal and the agent.

In the health sector more specifically, as observed by Alston, the institutional architecture of China's health sector is fragmented, with responsibility for designing, planning and financing policies being dispersed over various ministries and commissions.[96] In general, the State Council (a principal) delegates the majority of authority in relation to health to the NHFPC (an agent) for carrying out health-related responsibilities, while other ministries and commissions under the State Council, such as the CFDA, MOHRSS, MOF, MOAC and NDRC (agents) are also engaged in health governance (as shown in Figure 3.1).[97]

Obviously, the NHFPC is the core actor in administrative accountability concerning the right to health care. As discussed earlier, the NHFPC is an accountable actor that is directly accountable to other overseeing institutions (eg courts) and indirectly accountable to right-holders. Internally, the NHFPC can be both an accountable actor and an overseeing actor. The NHFPC is vertically accountable to its superior (the State Council) and is able to further delegate its authority as a principal to lower-level health (and family planning) bureaux (and other public institutions and public officials) that function as agents. Health bureaux are accountable to their respective superior health bureaux and ultimately to the NHFPC.[98] By the same token, governments at county, municipal and provincial levels (principals) can hold health bureaux (agents) to account at their respective levels. In brief, a local health bureau is accountable to both its superior health bureau and to the local government. The dual relationships can be understood as demonstrated in Figure 7.1 (taking only a local health bureau as an example).

95 Meng and others (n 4) 4, 16-19.
96 UNGA, 'Report of the Special Rapporteur on Extreme Poverty and Human Rights on His Mission to China, Philip Alston' (n 2) para 59.
97 Meng and others (n 4) 16-19.
98 ibid 1.

Figure 7.1 Relationship between governments and health bureaux (source: the author)

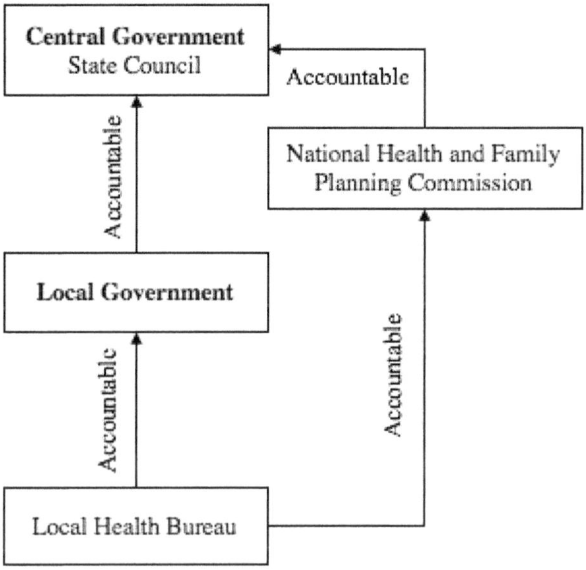

7.6.1 The cadre responsibility system

Administrative accountability pays attention to one particular question: how can we ensure that the agent(s) uses the power and authority delegated to him/her in the best interests of the principal(s) and not for his/her own benefit. In other words, how can the incentives of the principal(s) and the agent(s) be formally aligned?[99] As Brinkerhoff suggests, the systems, procedures and mechanisms that impose restraints on the power and authority of public institutions (and public officials) and that create incentives for appropriate decision-making and actions, matter.[100] In China, the central government relies considerably on top-down administrative mechanisms such as the cadre responsibility system that will be further discussed below. Scholars assert that administrative accountability mechanisms have been 'at least as salient as any mechanisms for judicial accountability'.[101]

99 Andreas Schedler, 'Conceptualizing Accountability' in Andreas Schedler, Larry Diamond and Marc Plattner (eds), *The Self-restraining State: Power and Accountability in New Democracies* (Lynne Rienner Publishers 1999) 16.
100 Brinkerhoff (n 77) 1.
101 Ho (n 53) 274.

In general, the cadre responsibility system is a specific performance management mechanism established for ensuring the accomplishment of higher-level policies in lower-level institutions.[102] In this system, lower-level authorities (inferiors) are monitored and disciplined by higher-level authorities (superiors), and give account to their superiors on the basis of a principal-agent relationship. Rewards and sanctions are given in accordance with the achievement of the performance targets allocated by the higher-level authorities.[103] Generally speaking, the performance assessment of a Chinese public official is based on an annual performance appraisal of the degree to which he/she has fulfilled a list of specified performance targets. In Gao's case study on the situation in Shaanxi Province it was found that there were two types of performance targets: (1) functional targets ('*zhineng zhibiao*'), which included targets specific to each institution and core targets that focused on economic objectives, such as economic growth (eg the growth of China's Gross Domestic Product); and (2) common targets ('*gongxing zhibiao*'), which included different kinds of political work, such as ensuring stability within society as well as family planning (eg the one-child-per-couple rate, which was used to assess the achievement of the one-child policy, until it was replaced by the two-child policy).[104] Gao summarises the performance targets set by a township government in Shaanxi Province in 2005 (as shown in Table 7.1, Gao's translation).[105]

102 Jie Gao, 'Performance Management in the People's Republic of China During the Market Reform Era: A Case Study of Two Counties in Shaanxi Province' (unpublished PhD dissertation, City University of Hong Kong) ii.

103 John Burns and Zhiren Zhou, 'Performance Management in the Government of the People's Republic of China: Accountability and Control in the Implementation of Public Policy' (2012) 2 OECD Journal on Budgeting 1, 14.

104 Gao (n 102) 7.

105 Adapted from Gao (n 102) 104. Gao's translation.

Table 7.1 Performance targets of a county in Xi'an City, Shaanxi Province, 2005

Functional targets	1. Conducting special educations on district. 2. Conducting ideology education of all Party members on the theme of 'keeping advancement of Party members'. 3. Organzing all Party members to learn the Party's Sixteenth Conference documents. 4. Ensuring more than 95% of the Party branches establish regular Party systems, such as weekly Party meetings. 5. Evaluating and rewarding excellent Party members and advanced Party organizations. 6. Training cadres in-charge-of Party affairs, and construction of Party branches. 7. Actively conducting activities of 'Learning Party Organizations'. 8. Developing, investigating and educating new Party members. 9. Coordinating all Party branches to celebrate the 84 birthday of the Chinese Communist Party. 10. Strengthening the collection and management of Party fees.
Common targets	1. Actively carry out activities on the theme of being a model civil servant. 2. Party building. 3. Ideology education, theory learning, and propaganda work. 4. Construction of a transparent and electronic-government. 5. Comprehensive social security (with veto power). 6. Family planning **(with veto power)**. 7. Safety production **(with veto power)**. 8. Handling of mass complaints and the cult religion of Falungong **(with veto power)**. 9. Personnel system reform in social service institutes. 10. Labor employment. 11. Other targets assigned by the County Party Committee and County Government. 12. Ensuring the implementation of the objective responsibility system. 13. Management work of civil servants, eg by categorizing personnel dossiers.

Gao found that targets with veto power (eg social security, family planning, safety production and the handling of mass complaints) were given top implementation priority by officials. According to Gao's field research,

> [a]ll interviewees agreed that targets with 'veto power' (those with clear personnel management consequences) were the most important task for leadership cadres and that the accomplishment

> of targets with veto power brought great pressure for local officials, especially for cadres in the leadership corps who were directly accountable for the failure of veto targets on behalf of their organizations.[106]

If a local official failed to meet the targets with veto power, he/she would not have the opportunity to attend the annual assessment, regardless of the achievement of other targets. The failure to meet targets with veto power would even result in severe sanctions, including demotion and dismissal.[107] The power of higher-level authorities to impose sanctions on local authorities for their failures is the key feature of this mechanism. In practice, the competence of local authorities to handle mass complaints and to maintain social security are the most important targets. Very often, when a local complaint draws public attention on a larger scale or even results in public outcry (via the media), the superior will soon intervene and hold the inferior to account for the sake of stability within society (labelled by Gao as 'social security'). Therefore, society can play a role in exerting administrative accountability. As will be discussed further in section 7.7.1, this administrative accountability mechanism, when associated with other social accountability mechanisms, especially the media, can be a powerful mechanism for controlling the performance of local officials and holding them to account.

7.6.2 General oversight mechanisms

In addition to the cadre responsibility system for monitoring internal performance, there are also a handful of general oversight mechanisms in China. For example, health bureaux oversee a variety of public institutions (and public officials, including public health care providers). The broad oversight mandate of health bureaux to oversee public institutions at their respective levels is often accompanied by disciplinary measures, such as warnings, demotion, dismissal from position and expulsion. The case in Box 7.2 demonstrates how a health bureau at the provincial level becomes an overseeing actor itself, addresses local failures and holds responsible actors to account within its mandate.

106 ibid (n 102) 132.
107 ibid; Burns and Zhou (n 103).

Box 7.2: Five instances of HIV transmission in Zhejiang Province caused by malpractice[108]
On 9 February 2017, the Health and Family Planning Commission of Zhejiang Province (ZPHFPC) reported HIV transmission incidents caused by staff negligence at the Zhejiang Traditional Chinese Medicine Hospital. At least five people were infected with HIV after a technician of the hospital reused pipettes on separate patients. This incident was reported to the ZPHFPC on 26 January 2017 and an emergency investigation was initiated immediately. The ZPHFPC also sent medical experts treat the infected patients and instructed relevant government agencies to provide compensation. Later, the NHFPC and the CFDA dispatched a team to Zhejiang Province to oversee the investigation into the incident. The technician directly responsible was taken into police custody for criminal investigation. Six officials of the hospital, including the director, two deputy directors and three department heads were also held accountable and dismissed from their positions.

In addition to the general oversight, right-holders can also bring a complaint to a local health bureau for violations of health-related rights, if not the right to health care *per se*, in the region concerned. The health bureau has to review the complaint and provide a written response as to whether it will take (disciplinary) measures to address the problem.

Box 7.3: Proscribed admission test of HBV[109]
In August 2017, a mother who was an HBV carrier (anonymous) became aware that her baby had been subjected to HBV tests for admission into kindergarten. She was very concerned whether her baby, also a HBV carrier, would be discriminated after the test. According to a regulatory document published by the MOHRSS, the Ministry of Education and the former Ministry of Health, physical examinations for school admission may no longer include an HBV test. With the help of the Yiyou Charity, this mother lodged a complaint to the relevant county health bureau against the maternal and infant hospital in Hejing County, Xinjiang Province. A couple weeks after receiving the complaint, the county health bureau announced that conducting a HBV test for school admission without parental permission was not allowed. The bureau required the county maternal and infant hospital to return the test fee to all children who had been tested without permission. The director of the hospital lost the opportunity to attend the annual assessment of the cadre's performance.

108 'China orders medical security campaign following malpractice-caused HIV infections' (UNAIDs 14 February 2017) <www.unaids.org.cn/en/index/topic.asp?id=1133&classname=Media%20 Reporting&class=2> accessed 28 November 2017.

109 This case was obtained from the interview with Yiyou Charity. The report of the case <www. yiyougongyi.org/h-nd-497.html> accessed 19 November 2017.

Furthermore, when receiving a complaint, the health bureau may not respond after the expiry of the prescribed time limit. If this is the case, or if the bureau replies that the complaint is not accepted, right-holders then have the right to apply to a higher-level health bureau to reconsider the complaint through the 'administrative reconsideration procedure' ('*xingzheng fuyi*').[110]

In brief, administrative supervision *within* institutions is a key determinant of the performance of State actors. Given the high capacity of enforcement, administrative accountability mechanisms are arguably a strong tool for holding responsible State actors to account. However, it deserves pointing out that, as Ma observes, although administrative accountability mechanisms are useful, they 'have been carried out without direct citizen involvement and, therefore, fall short of ensuring government accountable to society'.[111] Additionally, as mentioned in the introduction to this chapter, Alston has also noted that while there are top-down mechanisms to control public officials, in practice it is difficult for Chinese citizens to use these mechanisms to complain and seek remedies for human rights violations.[112] Therefore, the following section continues to explore whether society itself can be a powerful actor for generating accountability and what mechanisms are available for right-holders to hold responsible State actors to account.

7.7 Social accountability[113]

Society itself can become an overseeing actor and provide external checks and balances to ensure that State actors act in the public interest. Very often, social accountability is generated through direct or indirect actions of individuals and CSOs as well as through efforts by other actors (eg the media) to support these actions, with

110 Law of the People's Republic of China on Administrative Reconsideration (adopted on 29 April 1999, entered into effect 1 October 1999, amended on 1 September 2017), art 2 <www.npc.gov.cn/englishnpc/Law/2007-12/11/content_1383562.htm> accessed 28 November 2017. The English version was obtained from the official website of the NPC.

111 Jun Ma, 'The Rise of Social Accountability in China' (2012) 71 The Australian Journal of Public Administration 111, 112.

112 UNGA, 'Report of the Special Rapporteur on Extreme Poverty and Human Rights on His Mission to China, Philip Alston' (n 2) paras 68-69.

113 This section is largely based on my book chapter, Yi Zhang, 'The Media's Role in Ensuring Social Accountability for the Right to Health in China' in Marlies Hesselman and others (eds), *Socio-Economic Human Rights in Essential Public Services Provision* (Routledge 2016) 275-296.

an aim of mobilising demand for accountability.[114] However, there is now a trend that social accountability is facilitated by State actors in the name of achieving good governance.[115] In other words, social accountability can be initiated by individuals and CSOs, by the State, or by combinations of these actors.

Social accountability can be exercised on a continuous basis through various mechanisms, such as social audits, public hearings, NGO shadow reports and the media, to name just a few. In addition, aided by new information and communication technologies, new forms of social accountability mechanisms have been created over the past decade which empower vulnerable and marginalised groups to claim their rights more effectively.[116]

However, as explained in chapter 6, pure bottom-up social accountability mechanisms may be of limited effect if they are isolated and prevented from interacting with other (including State) actors. Empirical research has noted the importance of taking a State-society synergistic approach to social accountability.[117] Put simply, it is important that both society and the State are engaged in exerting social accountability. The State-society synergy is observed in the Chinese context and can be broken down into 'society-led social accountability' and 'State-led social accountability'. Society-led social accountability is driven by society to amplify its voice and advocate for individuals' right to health care. State-led social accountability, on the other hand, is mainly initiated by the State to re-establish the government's legitimacy and win back public trust in and support for the health care system. This section will discuss 'society-led social accountability' (section 7.7.1) and 'State-led social accountability' (section 7.7.2) respectively. This section will also discuss some limitations of existing mechanisms for exerting 'society-led social accountability' and 'State-led social accountability' in China (section 7.7.3).

7.7.1 Society-led social accountability

As mentioned in chapter 6, access to and the effective use of information, the mobilisation of public support, and the advocation and negotiation of change are the

114 United Nations Development Programme (UNDP), 'Fostering Social Accountability: From Principle to Practice' (2010) 10.
115 OHCHR and Center for Economic and Social Rights (n 8) 44.
116 ibid.
117 ibid 45.

key building blocks of successful social accountability. As the example in box 7.4 (below) illustrates, direct monitoring and pressure from society, when accompanied by publicity by the media, can indeed generate accountability. Society can impose pressure on State actors to explain and justify their decisions and actions (i.e. answerability) through various social accountability mechanisms. Although these mechanisms have a relatively low enforcement capacity (sanction very often comes in the form of public exposure or naming and shaming), they can be reinforced by other accountability mechanisms. For example, by drawing the attention of actors that have the formal authority to directly compel State actors to give account (eg courts or administrative institutions), individuals and CSOs can indirectly impose sanctions on responsible State actors. Viewed in this light, both the media and CSOs play a critical role in exerting society-led social accountability. In fact, the media have gradually become a powerful weapon for society to advocate the right to health care in contemporary China. The remainder of section 7.7.1 will first examine the role of the media in exerting society-led social accountability and will subsequently address the role of CSOs.

7.7.1.1 The role of the media

As discussed in chapter 6, the media can function both as an overseeing institution and a social accountability mechanism. Admittedly, the media's role as the watchdog of public interest (i.e. an overseeing institution) is less developed in China due to the State's influence over the media.[118] In fact, society has often questioned the credibility of news reports. This is because before the 2000s the media in China was mainly dominated by State-affiliated institutions, making it easier for the government to monopolise the dissemination of negative information.[119] As some commentators have noted, local authorities prevented many right-holders from complaining to

118 Jingrong Tong and Colin Sparks, 'Investigative Journalism in China Today' (2009) 10 Journalism Studies 337, 342; Pippa Norris, 'Watchdog Journalism' in Mark Bovens, Robert Goodin and Thomas Schillemans (eds), *The Oxford Handbook of Public Accountability* (Oxford University Press 2014) 531.

119 Gregory Distelhorst, 'Publicity-Driven Accountability in China: Qualitative and Experimental Evidence' (2012) MIT Political Science Department Research Paper Working Paper 2012-24, 8.

higher-level authorities about malfeasance at the local level.[120] However, new information and communication technologies (eg various types of social media) have eroded the government's capacity to control negative publicity and have facilitated various new media platforms, or 'social media'.

Most media, and social media in particular,[121] are now run by non-State enterprises (a significant difference from traditional media in China), allowing society another avenue for amplifying public demand, safeguarding public interests, and even holding responsible State actors to account. Through the use of the (social) media as a social accountability mechanism, grass-roots individuals[122] and CSOs no longer need to rely on traditional journalism to disseminate information, but can now initiate 'bottom-up' social accountability by monitoring and reviewing the decisions and actions of State actors, exposing their unlawful actions or misconduct, and restraining abuses of power.

Box 7.4: Forced late-term abortion in Shaanxi Province

In June 2012, three county-level family planning officials in the Shaanxi province forced Feng, Jianmei, a woman whose pregnancy was not in accordance with China's one-child policy,[123] to undergo an abortion during her seventh month of pregnancy.

An Internet user posted the information to an online forum and received widespread attention, with thousands of Internet users reposting it to other online platforms.[124] This post then became the most popular topic on Sina Weibo (China's version of Twitter) and was even reported by State-owned news websites.

120 Philip Chen and Di Wu, 'China's Evolution in Progressively Realizing the Right to Health' in in José Zuniga, Stephen P Marks and Lawrence O Gostin (eds), *Advancing the Human Right to Health* (Oxford University Press 2013) 165.

121 The media refers to the main means of mass communication (broadcasting, publishing and the Internet) regarded collectively. Social media refers to the content and interactions that are created through social interactions between individuals and communities via mobile applications and highly accessible web-based technologies, including social networking sites, online forums, blogs and micro-blogs. See section 6.4 for a thorough discussion.

122 The term 'grass-roots' here is different from the ordinary meaning of the term, which often refers to NGOs. Here, it is a translation of the Chinese word 'CaoGen', which represents individuals at the lowest/lower levels of society.

123 As of 1 January 2016, all Chinese couples are allowed to have two kids.

124 This news was first posted on Huashang BBS online forum and was accessed nearly 55,000 times as of September 2014 <http://bbs.hsw.cn/read-htm-tid-3697258.html> accessed 28 November 2017. After the original post, many major online forums and non-State-owned news websites reposted this news and it received tremendous social attention (for example, Netease News' post on the situation attracted nearly 389,000 Internet users' comments <http://comment.news.163.com/news_shehui7_bbs/83QP5TAI00011229.html> accessed 28 November 2017.

In response to this negative publicity, the higher-level government intervened and suspended the local officials responsible for the forced abortion. Later on, seven officials were either fired or admonished, and the local government was ordered to provide the woman with 70,600 RMB (roughly 9,100 EUR) as compensation.[125]

To diminish the nationwide outrage over such coercive measures in family planning, the NHFPC held a national press conference and reiterated that forced late-term abortions were strictly prohibited even under the one-child policy, that the legal rights of pregnant women should be maintained, and that forced abortion should not occur at any stage of pregnancy.[126] The statement brought an end to forced abortion in China and fundamentally changed the family planning regulations and policies at local levels.[127]

Feng's case is very much related to the three common targets for the annual performance appraisal of the cadres that have veto power mentioned in section 7.6.1 (Table 7.1): family planning, handling mass complaints and social stability (what Gao describes as 'social security'). The targets with veto power were the most important task for cadres' performance assessments and the implementation of these tasks were of the highest priority. In terms of family planning more specifically, local officials were responsible for ensuring that the one-child policy was respected, and would be held accountable by their superiors if they failed to do so.[128] It was not surprising to see that local family planning officials wish to prevent extra births. Another assessment criterion under the family planning was that there were no mass complaints regarding birth control.[129] Thus, the negative publicity and public outcry triggered after Feng's case played a considerable role in the higher-level authorities' prompt response to this case.

In addition to Feng's case, there appear to be at least a handful of cases in which citizens' legitimate or legal rights were ignored by State actors that have

125 The term they used to describe the money the government provided was assistance rather than compensation, as China's family planning law does not contain any provision for damages compensated to victims of abuse by government officials. The statement is available on Ankang government's website <www.ak.gov.cn/Content-47361.html> accessed 28 November 2017.

126 'China vows to prohibit late-term abortions' <http://china.org.cn/china/2014-01/08/content_31124328.htm> accessed 28 November 2017.

127 Firstly, this reiteration from the NHFPC contributed to the revision of laws at the municipal level. The family planning laws and regulations in some provinces included provisions relating to forced abortion and were abolished or revised after this reiteration. Secondly, under the previous one-child policy, parents would be charged social assistance fees if they gave birth to a second child. Local government officials thus have a financial stake in implementing this policy. The reiteration helps to warn local officials and prevents them from abuses of power.

128 Gao (n 102) 135-137.

129 ibid.

been successfully settled by drawing the attention of public institutions (eg the courts and administrative institutions) or exerting pressure on them to address State actors' failures and redress related grievances .[130] For example, the media played an important role in the 'Sun Zhigang incident', which led to the abolition of the Chinese custody and repatriation system.[131] As Cai has identified, very often the greater the disruptive and forceful resistance of individuals, the better the concessions or policy adjustments they can receive from the State as part of public remediation.[132] In fact, these society-led cases reveal a typical cycle for individuals or CSOs to hold State actors to account in China (see Figure 7.2).

Figure 7.2 A general cycle of how society-led social accountability can be generated[133]

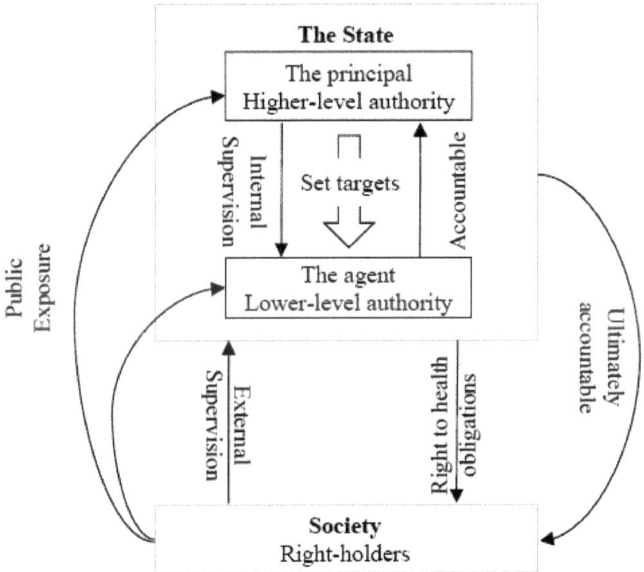

Generally speaking, the starting point of society-led social accountability is public exposure, very often through the media, of malfeasance by lower-level authorities (agents). As explained above, lower-level authorities in China are accountable to

130 Benjamin Liebman, 'Watchdog or Demagogue? The Media in the Chinese Legal System' (2005) 105 (1) Columbia Law Review 1, 65-90.

131 ibid 82-90.

132 Yongsun Cai, Collective Resistance in China: Why Popular Protests Succeed or Fail? (Stanford University Press 2010) 22-34.

133 Source: the author.

their superiors (principals) and are sensitive to the possible negative consequences of public exposure. Therefore, by exerting public attention or even public outrage, society-led social accountability can potentially lead to two positive results.

Taking Feng's case as an example, the local authorities had to maintain compliance with the one-child-per-couple rate set down by their superiors. If they could not achieve this, they would be held accountable by their superior for the failure of this target (which has veto power) and face severe sanctions, including demotion and dismissal. This was the major reason Feng was forced to go into labour. In addition, there was another criterion under this family planning target, which required no mass complaints regarding birth control.[134] Notably, the targets of handling mass complaints and maintaining social stability (i.e. Gao's 'social security') themselves had veto power. Apparently, Feng's case had already provoked mass complaints regarding birth control.

The first positive result of society-led social accountability can occur when, in order to prevent their principals from noticing their incompetence or failures to handle these complaints, lower-level authorities actively take remedial action so as to minimise any negative information of their work exposed in the media.[135] As no such remedial action was taken in Feng's case, the second positive outcome was achieved instead – society sought a remedy before higher-level authorities (principals) and tried to invoke sanctions on the lower-level authorities by drawing the principals' attention to their failures.[136] This outcome would also have been possible had remedial action been taken by the lower-level authorities, with which society remained dissatisfied. In this sense, social accountability is reinforced by higher-level State authorities which can hold the responsible State actors to account through a variety of disciplinary measures (i.e. administrative accountability mechanisms).

Distelhorst labelled this type of accountability 'publicity-driven accountability', which bears similarities to 'social accountability' where activism and media coverage can activate State overseeing institutions of 'horizontal accountability'.[137] According

134 Gao (n 102) 135-137.
135 Distelhorst (n 119) 6; Rory Truex, 'Consultative Authoritarianism and Its Limits' (2014) Comparative Political Studies 1, 7.
136 Distelhorst (n 119) 4.
137 See generally Distelhorst (n 119); Guillermo O'Donnell, 'Horizontal Accountability in New Democracies' in Andreas Schedler, Larry Diamond and Marc Plattner (eds), *The Self-restraining State: Power and Accountability in New Democracies* (Lynne Rienner Publishers 1999) 29.

to Distelhorst, publicity-driven accountability emerges from the interaction between a social actor, a lower-level authority (agent) and the authority's superior (principal). Social actors are generally excluded from exercising power over authorities, while the principal can impose vertical control over its agent.[138] The protection of negative information (eg 'agency slippage' or local failings) is what allows this mechanism to function.[139] As Distelhorst asserts,

> To alter the agent's behaviour, social actors threaten or actually seek to publicize agent behavior that might result in sanctions by the principal. This risk of sanction leads to publicity-mitigating behavior by agents, who provide concessions to the social actor rather than risk negative consequences of public exposure.[140]

Given that social stability is of vital importance to China's central government, local governments may face penalties for failing to maintain social stability and to reduce mass complaints.[141] More importantly, negative publicity will undermine public trust in and challenge the legitimacy of China's current political regime, which partially explains why the media have become an effective mechanism for ensuring concessions from the State.[142] However, as will be discussed further in section 7.7.3, the use of the media has certain shortcomings. First, negative publicity may result in the State, which may not appreciate the public critique, countering the use of the (social) media (as a social accountability mechanism). Second, the media may be used in an unjust manner which allows false information to be spread.

To summarise, for the purpose of diminishing government failings and resolving State-society conflict, lower-level authorities actively take remedial actions and make every effort to prevent their principals from learning about their failures. Higher-level authorities, on the other hand, tend to punish their responsible agents and reverse decisions or actions that may harm public trust when negative publicity draws a great deal of public attention.

138 Distelhorst (n 119) 3.
139 ibid 4.
140 ibid 3.
141 ibid 4; Hon Chan and Jie Gao, 'Performance Management in Chinese local governments' (2008) 41 Chinese Law and Government 1, 1.
142 Distelhorst (n 119) 3-4.

In this context, the media plays an indispensable role in holding State actors to account. In numerous cases, the media have helped aggrieved individuals to seek remedies.[143] It is also worth noting that in China, individuals are the main source of information in most of the cases exposed online. Generally, it is individuals, or *netizens* that first post grievances online.[144] Most non-State-owned websites and newspapers and even State-owned media will subsequently report them, if the case attracted or will attract public attention. A common feature of these netizens is that they demand more transparency, accountability and access to information and justice in society. They also have a strong motivation for disseminating information about human rights violations (even though the words 'human rights' may not be explicitly mentioned) and exposing malfeasance in public sectors. By exerting substantial public pressure, these active netizens can to some degree function as watchdogs of public interests. In brief, by disseminating health-related information and exposing unlawful actions and misconduct of State actors online, the attention of large parts of society, the courts, and the governments is likely to be attracted, and responsible State actors are more likely to be held to account.

Although some scholars also identify the media's role in this regard as an external overseeing institution and propose competitive supervision between the media and courts in China,[145] I hesitate to recognise the Chinese media's role as an external overseeing institution that operates parallel to other overseeing institutions such as courts. A major reason is that the media's watchdog role (i.e. investigative journalism) is less endorsed in China,[146] due to the censorship and partially State-dependent nature of the media system. It is less clear whether Chinese journalists will, or indeed wish to take up the responsibility of safeguarding public interest and monitoring or investigating government malfeasance *ex ante*.

As such, I contend that the media still work reactively as a 'social accountability mechanism' for individuals or CSOs to exert *ex post* social accountability. Society can monitor the government's efforts to fulfil its obligations under the right to health

143 Benjamin Liebman, 'The Media and the Courts: Towards Competitive Supervision' (2011) 208 The China Quarterly 833, 840.
144 In China, individuals who are well connected to the Internet and act lively online are termed as netizens. Currently, there is an increasing number of active netizens in China.
145 Liebman (n 143) 847-850.
146 Distelhorst (n 119) 8-10; Tong and Sparks (n 118) 342.

care, mobilise demand for transparency, expose governmental malfeasance, and hold responsible State actors accountable through this mechanism.[147]

7.7.1.2 The role of CSOs

As mentioned earlier, CSOs can act directly or indirectly to mobilise demand for (social) accountability.[148] China's non-governmental organisations, especially patient organisations, are becoming more active and influential in providing external oversight of State actors. My interviews with the Yiyou Charity and BHL China League show that CSOs can aid people living with HBV or HIV/AIDS to claim their health-related rights, to fight discrimination and stigmatisation, and to advocate access to medicines-related policies. In cases of violations, they can hold responsible actors to account through various types of accountability mechanisms. As the example in sections 7.5 and 7.6 illustrate, the Yiyou Charity has helped many HBV carriers to claim their health-related rights through political and administrative accountability mechanisms. By bringing complaints on behalf of individuals, CSOs can demonstrate systematic failures in the health care system to overseeing institutions that have the formal authorities to address failures and remedy grievances. Furthermore, they can also directly hold State actors to account through social accountability mechanisms, which can expose governments' malfeasance and impose pressure on State actors to explain and justify their decisions and actions.

Given their close relationship with right-holders, the role to be played by CSOs in exerting accountability is potentially even more important than that of other overseeing institutions. However, as noted by Alston, there are some institutional obstacles that may hinder the development of the Chinese CSOs. Empirical research indicates that most CSOs working on issues concerning economic and social rights heavily rely on

147 Some scholars in the field of journalism argue that Chinese journalists now use Weibo micro-blogging for investigating reporting, which shows the media's role as watchdog. Some even regard the media as an external overseeing institution that is parallel to courts and propose the idea of 'competitive supervision'. However, since this paper is a preliminary attempt to examine how (the) media ensures accountability for the right to health in China, there is insufficient evidence to suggest that the media functions as the watchdog of public interest. For the time being, it is not clear enough whether Chinese journalists accept the normative role of watchdog journalism and to what extent the Chinese propaganda departments would tolerate this role. Much more needs to be done to understand this active role of the media in ensuring accountability for the right to health in the Chinese context.

148 OHCHR and Center for Economic and Social Rights (n 8) 44.

technical or financial assistance from abroad.[149] Nevertheless, since the enactment of the Law on the Management of Foreign Non-Governmental Organizations in 2017, foreign-based organisations have to register with the Ministry of Public Security in order to operate in China.[150] Further, registration may be revoked and criminal sanctions may be applied if these foreign organisations are found to damage 'national interests' or 'society's interests'.[151] This new Law may greatly restrict the financing and other types of assistance that foreign organisations can provide in China, thus having a negative impact on the groups that work for women's rights, health rights and workers' rights, or other economic and social rights in general.[152]

Both the Yiyou Charity and BHL China League expressed that their lack of funding and personnel largely restricted the development of their organisations. As mentioned in chapter 6, it is important for the State to create an enabling environment to encourage the participation of vulnerable and marginalised groups. However, not many regulations and policies supporting the development of CSOs in China can currently be identified.

7.7.2 State-led social accountability

In addition to the bottom-up approach taken by society, the Chinese government has also launched official mechanisms to establish communication between the State and society, in order to increase their answerability. By taking this top-down approach, the government can encourage the whole society, including vulnerable and marginalised groups in particular, to participate and claim their needs in health-related decision-making processes, thus building consensus and improving the quality of health governance.[153] The case scrutinised below constitutes a good example of a social

149 Scott Wilson, *Tigers Without Teeth: The Pursuit of Justice in Contemporary China* (Rowman & Littlefield 2015) 9-10, 99-100.

150 Law on the Management of Foreign Non-Governmental Organizations (adopted on 28 April 2016, entered into effect on 1 January 2017), art 6 <www.lawinfochina.com/display.aspx?lib=law&id=21963> accessed 28 November 2017. The English version was obtained from the academic database of authority – the pkulaw.

151 ibid, arts 5, 47.

152 UNGA, 'Report of the Special Rapporteur on Extreme Poverty and Human Rights on His Mission to China, Philip Alston' (n 2) para 74.

153 Li Zhang, 'Building Communication Capacity for Good Governance: A Multileveled Analysis' in Zhenglai Deng and Sujian Guo (eds), China's Search for Good Governance (Palgrave Macmilan 2011) 154.

accountability mechanism being facilitated by the State so as to improve the quality of health governance.

Box 7.5: State-led social accountability mechanism for the NHR

Due to the rapid spread of the Internet, health-related problems have achieved a high level of visibility in China. News ranging from the denial of access to health care, high out-of-pocket expenses and protests over medical malpractice are reported in the news media or unveiled by individuals through social media on a daily basis.[154] This leads to higher levels of dissatisfaction within society about the health care system and prompts reform of the current system. To strengthen public support for and to improve the legitimacy of health policy-making without undermining the current political system, the former Ministry of Health established formal participation channels and pioneered its own deliberative governance system during the formulation of the NHR.[155] This innovation triggered animated discussions among various interest groups and, remarkably, featured inclusive public participation. Health care reform inevitably involves a considerable amount of professional knowledge that ordinary people are not familiar with. As such, before the final draft of the new policy was drafted, the government commissioned independent research institutions to design 'an overall conception and framework of the healthcare reform in China'.[156] These independent experts and scholars generally offer a rational perspective from the elite level.[157] However, since they may not have the same experience of being 'kanbingnan, kanbinggui' as grass-roots individuals, the experts and scholars cannot represent the entire population.[158] Therefore, for the purpose of accommodating the needs and demands of all social classes in all regions, the government established an online portal named 'Healthcare Reform Advice and Suggestions' that is open to everyone in China.[159] Any individual or group can freely express their suggestions, comments, or grievances regarding China's health care reform on this platform.[160]

Inviting society to participate in and to express its opinion on health policy-making was unprecedented in China. Individuals of various social backgrounds and holding different views towards health care reform were all encouraged to participate in the process of deliberation, leading to a more transparent, participatory and equal approach to health policy-making.[161] Furthermore, many non-State-owned news websites also initiated similar kinds of portals for soliciting public opinion.

---

154 Alexander Korolev, 'Deliberative Democracy Nationwide? - Evaluating Deliberativeness of Healthcare Reform in China' (2014) Journal of Chinese Political Science 151, 157.
155 ibid; Truex (n 135) 7.
156 Changshan Ma, 'Gonggong Zhengce Hefaxing Gongji Jizhi yu Zouxiang [The Transformation of the Legitimacy Supply Mechanism of Public Policy]' (2012) 2 Faxue Yanjiu [Legal Research] 20, 22.
157 ibid.
158 ibid.
159 ibid.
160 ibid; Korolev (n 154) 161.
161 Ma (n 156) 22.

Although it has been argued that most individuals that actively participated in these online portals were well established members of society, which meant that the portals lacked representativeness,[162] it is still remarkable that both experienced and marginalised groups were engaged in the NHR.[163] In light of the scope and range of public engagement, some scholars regarded the overall process as 'healthcare democracy'.[164]

New information and communication technologies have allowed the Chinese government to employ new participatory techniques. For example, individuals can now voice their opinions regarding the drafting of health policies, lodge complaints and apply for information to be disclosed on the official websites of the NHFPC and the health bureaux at various levels. These new platforms can establish a dynamic dialogue between the State and society, thus promoting the answerability of State actors in the health sector. In short, social accountability mechanisms enable individuals to amplify their voices, to participate in decision-making and even to propose health laws and policies. These mechanisms also strengthen the interaction between the State and society and enable the State to solicit and to receive public input. Ultimately, the State can cultivate a feeling among society that individuals' voice matters and that the government is answerable to their concerns and demands, thus improving public trust in China's health care system.[165] However, it is worth noting that whether, and to what extent the State will take the voice of society into consideration remains unclear – the State is not yet accountable for taking these voices seriously.

7.7.3 Implications and limitations

The cases mentioned in sections 7.7.1 and 7.7.2 illustrate that society has begun to impose external checks and balances on State actors. The 'answerability' for and the 'enforceability' of the right to health care can clearly be strengthened by employing social accountability mechanisms and sometimes by engaging other formal accountability mechanisms (eg administrative accountability mechanisms, as

162 Steven Balla, 'Health System Reform and Political Participation on the Chinese Internet' (2014) 28 China Information 214, 227.
163 Korolev (n 154) 162.
164 Yuanli Liu, 'Reforming China's Health Care: For the People, by the People?' (2009) 373 The Lancet 281, 281-283.
165 Balla (n 162) 218.

mentioned in Feng's case). Nevertheless, some shortcomings have been observed in the implementation of these mechanisms.

First of all, the majority of society-led social accountability initiatives that take place in China are now demand-driven. It can be observed that society-led social accountability pays more attention to providing redress, addressing grievances and punishing wrongdoings *ex post*; only a few social accountability mechanisms aim for *ex ante* prevention, regulating State actors in advance of interferences with the right to health care. In addition, although most incidents that have caught the public's attention or provoked public outcry have been solved effectively – thousands of other incidents remain unsettled. To provide regular external oversight of State actors and to ensure equal access to remedy, it is necessary to establish an institutionalised mechanism that can involve society in both *ex ante* supervision of the governments' conduct and *ex post* redress for their malfeasance. The mechanism should involve, for example, the establishment of an independent overseeing institution to serve as an online ombudsman or watchdog that keeps a close eye on governments' decisions and actions.

Secondly, while empirical data suggests most individuals and CSOs actively pursue publicity in China,[166] the lack of access to information and data, the absence of public awareness of human rights and the incompetence of individuals and CSOs to monitor and review State actors' decisions and actions may undermine society's capacity to hold State actors to account. As mentioned in chapter 6, it is important for the State to create an enabling environment for individuals and CSOs to strengthen their capacity.

Third, social accountability mechanisms rely on informal incentives or sanctions (eg naming and shaming) and thus have a relatively low enforcement capacity. It is possible to push governments to perform their right to health obligations and to hold them to account by generating public pressure. However, as noted by Ma, under China's current non-electoral political system, lower-level officials (agents) are not very enthusiastic about acting on issues that are flagged by society-led social accountability, preferring to be accountable only to their superiors rather than society as well.[167] Basically speaking, the effectiveness of social accountability mechanisms

166 See generally Distelhorst (n 119); Ma (n 111).
167 Ma (n 111) 111-121.

relies largely on higher-level officials (principals) engaging with society and holding their agents to account through a variety of disciplinary measures (administrative accountability mechanisms). For this reason, the willingness and capacity of the principals to discipline their agents is crucial to generating society-led social accountability.

In addition, given that the media constitute a major social accountability mechanism, a media system that can freely (or at least partially) disseminate negative information is an indispensable precondition for exerting social accountability.[168] However, the reality on the ground is that in China certain constraints of censorship from the central government still remain, even though the government's capacity to control negative publicity has been eroded by new information and communication technologies. Without the positive engagement of the government (at least the central government), negative publicity may result in censorship or repression by the State. Considering China's current legal and political context, the State-society synergy is a crucial factor for the success of society-led social accountability.

7.8 Concluding summary

Overall, we see that despite the lack of competitive elections accountability can be applied to the Chinese context to reduce abuses of power, to assure compliance with (right to health) standards and to improve performance. There are a handful of overseeing institutions in China that can provide horizontal oversight of State actors and hold them to account. Within the State, there are also various top-down mechanisms for controlling State actors. In addition, China has established a variety of judicial, quasi-judicial, administrative, political and social accountability mechanisms through which right-holders can complain about and seek remedies for violations of health-related rights (if not the right to health care *per se*). However, as stated above, some shortcomings of these five types of accountability mechanisms have also been identified. Many efforts have to be made to overcome the constraints and to create appropriate accountability mechanisms, recommendations for which are offered in the following paragraphs.

168 Distelhorst (n 119) 8-10; Katrin Voltmer, 'The media, government accountability, and citizen engagement' in Pippa Norris (ed), *Public Sentinel: News Media and Governance Reform* (The World Bank 2010) 154.

Judicial accountability mechanisms are available in China for individuals to claim their health-related rights. However, certain limitations can be observed. First, although several constitutional provisions contain elements of the right to health care, these provisions are not directly applicable in China's domestic courts. Second, it is not possible for domestic courts to provide constitutional review or general review over the constitutionality or legality of health laws, as well as administrative regulations and rules. Rather, only written requests or recommendations can be submitted to the NPCSC for non-judicial review. Third, some elements of the right to health care, when they are reflected in domestic health legislation, are directly applicable in domestic courts. However, most health-related litigations fall within the realm of civil proceedings on the basis of the civil 'rights of life and health', rather than the fundamental (human) right to health. These civil proceedings concern two parties on an equal footing and have little impact on policy or structural change. Therefore, civil proceedings can only exert *ex post* judicial accountability. Furthermore, the outcomes of these litigations seem to have little impact on policy or structural change. Progress was recently made through the 2015 revision of the Administrative Litigation Law, which makes it possible to hold public institutions (and officials) to account both *ex ante* and *ex post*. When right-holders file a complaint against an administrative action, they can also request a judicial review of the legality of the regulatory document on which the alleged administrative action was based. However, domestic courts may still not be able to adjudicate whether a regulatory document is in conformity with constitutional provisions in relation to the right to health care.

In addition, within China there are a few quasi-judicial institutions which have comparable functions to those of NHRIs. However, these quasi-judicial institutions do not provide independent oversight of violations of the right to health care. The existing quasi-judicial mechanisms for holding State actors to account are relatively weak. It is still necessary to establish independent overseeing institutions with a broad mandate to promote and protect the right to health care.

Furthermore, it is possible to exert political accountability in China through the people's congress system. However, the operation of mechanisms for political accountability remains largely rhetoric. Much more work must be done to enhance the practical functioning of the NPC and the NPCSC.

Moreover, administrative supervision within institutions is essential for controlling the performance of State actors. Administrative accountability mechanisms are often associated with disciplinary measures which have a high degree of enforcement, and are therefore very powerful mechanisms for holding responsible State actors to account. However, in practice it is difficult for individuals to use administrative accountability mechanisms to complain about and seek remedies for violations of the right to health care in China, unless the mechanisms are engaged by social accountability mechanisms.

Lastly, and most importantly, this chapter demonstrated that social accountability has become a significant force to advance the right to health care in China. The development of innovative social accountability mechanisms has made it possible for individuals and CSOs, who have traditionally been excluded or marginalised, to participate in health-related decision-making processes, to claim their rights and to hold responsible State actors to account.

From the top down, the State has created formal (social accountability) mechanisms to facilitate the provision of information and to invite society to participate in the processes of health law- and policy-making, thus enabling society to promote the right to health care and shape the nature of the health care system. To a lesser degree, these mechanisms have enhanced the alignment of public preferences with the adoption and implementation of health laws and policies, thus increasing public trust in and support for the health care system. It is also worth noting that the State can and must also have a primary role in this respect, as a requirement of the right to health framework.

From the bottom up, society has actively generated greater accountability by combining social accountability mechanisms with other formal accountability mechanisms, in particular effective top-down mechanisms that allow disciplinary measures to be taken. We see that the (social) media (as a social accountability mechanism), and new and rapid developments thereof, offer great opportunities for engaging the government and other members of society, by amplifying the public's voice and holding responsible State actors to account. The media also empowers society to discipline and restrain State actors in discharging their obligations under the right to health care and allows aggrieved individuals to claim remedies more effectively.

By bringing the malfeasance of State actors to the attention of society and other overseeing institutions, whether as part of the bottom-up or top-down processes, as well as by exerting public pressure, social accountability mechanisms can clearly catalyse judicial, administrative or other forms of sanctions against responsible State actors. On the other hand, as explained earlier, social accountability mechanisms have a relatively low enforcement capacity. With no avenues for sanctions or redress, the transformative value of social accountability processes depends largely on the willingness of other overseeing institutions and State actors to engage with them.[169] To this extent, social accountability may be more effective in China when it is reinforced by other forms of accountability, in particular judicial and administrative accountability. It also deserves noting that without the positive engagement of the government (at least the central government), social accountability mechanisms, in particular negative publicity through the media, would result in censorship or repression by the State. Therefore, the State-society synergy is of vital importance for generating social accountability. Indeed, a State-society synergistic approach to social accountability has the potential to not only discipline State actors but also to foster a more effective and accountable health care system. Eventually, social accountability mechanisms would potentially generate incentives for better performance in the health sector and even for changes in health laws and policies.

In conclusion, China's health care reform and health-related decision-making have for many years been led by health professionals and officials. Individuals, especially vulnerable and marginalised groups, are very often excluded from the debate. Their voices have also rarely been heard in relation to reforms and decision-making by the State.[170] This has created a huge disparity and inequality between people from different social classes in China. The various examples of accountability mechanisms discussed in this chapter have important implications for creating a more accountable health care system in China under the current legal and political system.

169 OHCHR and Center for Economic and Social Rights (n 8) 45.
170 Korolev (2014) 160-163; Changshan Ma (2012) 22.

Chapter 8
Conclusions

8.1 Introduction

The purpose of this study was to explore whether and how accountability could advance the right to health care in light of China's unique political, legal and social background. The reasons for conducting this study were first, that although China ratified the ICESCR in 2001, relatively little (scholarly and practical) attention was paid to the domestic implementation of the right to health care, and second, that violations of this right were identified in reality. Given that China's health care reform is entering into the so-called 'deep-water' zone, it is of vital importance for the Chinese government to investigate how to guarantee everyone equal access to health care. Nevertheless, previous studies have not provided a comprehensive review of China's health-related legislation and policies based on right to health standards.

For these reasons, this study systematically assessed the extent to which China has taken (legislative and policy) measures to give effect to the right to health care within its jurisdiction. The objective of this study was to identify existing shortcomings in China's domestic implementation of the right to health care, and to address the remaining challenges through the lens of accountability. Having done so, this study offers recommendations (section 8.3 below) for Chinese law- and policy-makers for implementing China's obligations of the right to health care through the draft *Basic Health Law* (BHL).

The study synthesised the concepts of the right to health and accountability and integrated them into an analytical framework for 'right to health-based accountability', which can also be applied in relation to other human rights. More specifically, this study provided a constructive right to health-bases accountability model that can be applied to specific health concerns in China as well as in other countries, particularly those with non-electoral regimes. The findings of this study is concluded in section 8.2. Subsequently, section 8.3 offers some recommendations and final remarks.

8.2 Conclusions

Part 1 laid the foundations for the entire study. It delineated the core obligations that States parties undertake to give effect to the right to health care and evaluated the status quo of the legislative and policy measures that China has taken to realise this right at the domestic level.

More specifically, chapter 2 set the stage for the analysis of the implementation of the right to health care in China by answering two seemingly questions: *what does the right to health care mean* and *what does the right to health care entail*? The right to health care is an essential component of the broader right to health framework. In this study, the right to health care was understood as the right to access timely and appropriate health facilities, goods and services that are necessary for the realisation of the highest attainable standard of physical and mental health. The scope of the right to health care extends widely from access to medical care to the provision of essential drugs, to name just a few. States may realise the right to health care progressively, depending on their available resources. However, States also undertake a core obligation to ensure the satisfaction of the minimum essential levels of the right to health, namely essential primary health care.

This study argued that States undertake a variety of core obligations to respect, protect and fulfil the right to health care. Non-compliance with these core obligations would constitute a violation of this right. The core obligations arising from the right to health care encompass: (1) obligations of immediate effect, which are relatively cost-free and can generally be achieved with minimum resource implications; and (2) non-derogable core obligations, which are not subject to resource constraints – States cannot under any circumstances justify their non-compliance with these obligations. Obligations of immediate effect entail that States must guarantee that the right to health care can be enjoyed in a non-discriminatory manner, take steps towards the full realisation of the right, and establish a range of effective, transparent, accessible and independent accountability mechanisms. Non-derogable core obligations encompass the provision of essential medicines, non-discrimination, equitable distribution of health resources and the adoption of a comprehensive and participatory national plan of action. Together with the core obligations, this study selected availability, accessibility, accountability, and participation (AA-AP) as standards for assessing

China's legislative and policy commitments towards the realisation of the right to health care.

Chapter 3 conducted a systematic examination of the legislative measures that China has taken to give effect to the right to health care in its domestic legal system. The Chinese Constitution is silent on the internal effect, direct effect and precedence of international treaties within its legal system, including human rights treaties. It is generally believed that provisions of international human rights treaties cannot be directly applied by Chinese domestic courts. Thus, a prerequisite for invoking the right to health care within China's jurisdiction is that this right be (entirely or partially) transformed into China's domestic legislation through legislative procedures. After conducting a non-exhaustive analysis of the Chinese Constitution and the laws at the national level, this study made the following observations. China has enacted and amended its domestic laws where necessary to comply with its obligations under the right to health care. Both the Chinese Constitution and domestic laws include an explicit reference to non-discrimination and equality. A handful of health-related laws also contain relevant provisions regarding elements of other non-derogable core obligations. In addition, provisions concerning judicial remedies to redress violations of health-related rights were also identified, although they were not entirely equivalent to the right to health care *per se*. Nevertheless, gaps between *de jure* and *de facto* implementation of the right to health care were also discovered. There is no single legal provision that clearly provides for essential primary health care and for essential drugs, which both fall within the scope of core obligations under the right to health care. In addition, the provisions concerning the right to receive medical treatment and financial risk protection remain ambiguous, which may lead to implementation challenges in practice. Furthermore, most laws do not stipulate what kind of essential health care the Chinese government must deliver in order to ensure equal access for all right-holders. Viewed in this light, China's existing legal framework is by and large ill-equipped to regulate the health care system.

Chapter 4 moved from the purely legal approach to evaluate China's policy commitments towards the right to health care. As demonstrated in chapter 4, China has issued a wide range of national health policies over the past decades, and has achieved considerable progress towards universal health coverage (UHC). However, as explained in chapter 4, not all of the State's efforts towards UHC conform with the requirements of its (core) obligations under the right to health care. Chapter 4 thus proposed a refinement of UHC through the reconciliation of core obligations with UHC. Accordingly, a right-based UHC was suggested. This approach to UHC should involve all stakeholders (including vulnerable and marginalised groups in particular) in decision-making that occurs through a transparent and participatory process. The prioritised health needs of vulnerable and marginalised groups should be taken into consideration. In addition, the provision of essential drugs as a non-derogable core obligation under the right to health care should be given top priority when policies are being drafted. Moreover, the principle of non-discrimination requires that protection offered by UHC extends beyond financial discrimination to cover all forms of discriminatory exclusion in access to health care. When considered through this lens, some requirements of the right to health care remain unfulfilled despite China's efforts to achieve UHC. Such requirements include disparities between people with different socio-economic status and between rural and urban areas, where *de facto* discrimination in equal access to health care occurs. The negative impacts of fragmented risk-pooling on portability (i.e. restrictions on the place in which individuals can have their health expenses reimbursed) were identified, including the inefficiency of the whole insurance system as well as inequalities in access to health care for specific members of the population, such as migrant workers (i.e. geographic discrimination). In addition, the lack of an appropriate compensation mechanism for primary health care institutions and the lack of proper pricing-control measures continue to undermine the availability, accessibility and quality of essential medicines. Furthermore, the process for making health-related decisions was not entirely transparent and participatory – no particular attention has been paid to vulnerable and marginalised groups and their prioritised health needs in the policy-making process.

In light of the above, this study chose to address the remaining challenges in China's effective and full realisation of the right to health care through the lens of accountability and explored the extent to which accountability could advance the right to health care in China.

The purpose of part 2 was to set the foundations for the discussion of accountability in the Chinese context. It proposed an analytical framework for right to health-based accountability by answering four questions: (1) who is accountable; (2) for what are these actors accountable; (3) to whom are these actors accountable; and (4) how can these actors be held accountable?

More specifically, chapter 5 distinguished and defined accountability from a human rights perspective. In this study, right to health-based accountability, or human rights-based accountability more generally, was regarded as a dynamic and interactive process in which State actors are obliged to inform right-holders and overseeing institutions about their (past or future) decisions and actions, to explain and justify them and to face positive or negative consequences for them. In case of violations of the right to health, right-holders should have access to judicial or other effective remedies. These aspects together constitute the four building blocks of a constructive accountability process: monitoring, judgment, consequences and remedies. Chapter 5 also identified three elements of (right to health-based) accountability: responsibility, answerability and enforcement. As a particular contribution of the right to health framework to the current debate on accountability, responsibility has the potential to refine the standards for accountable behaviour. Different types of accountability were also analysed in this study, which can be categorised in two ways. First, vertical, horizontal and diagonal types of accountability are categorised on the basis of the nature of the accountable actor's obligation; second, based on the types of overseeing actors, accountability can be further divided into judicial, quasi-judicial, political, administrative and social accountability. The latter classification of accountability was further discussed in chapter 6, together with accountability mechanisms.

Chapter 6 first provided a conceptual clarification between 'accountability' and an 'accountability mechanism'. This study understood accountability mechanisms as the institutional arrangements that facilitate the process of accountability. It then answered the four questions mentioned above. The answer of who is accountable for the right to heath is straightforward: the State itself, as well as public institutions and public officials mandated by the State with responsibilities regarding the realisation of the right to health are accountable (i.e. State actors). In terms of the second question, State actors are accountable for their obligations under the right to health. International human rights law has set out clear standards and principles for respecting, protecting and fulfilling the right to health, encompassing core obligations (including the obligation to establish appropriate accountability mechanisms), obligations of comparable priority, obligations of progressive realisation and some general obligations. Third, State actors are accountable to both right-holders and overseeing institutions (eg courts, national human rights ombudsmen). Furthermore, chapter 6 answered the fourth question by extensively discussing domestic mechanisms for generating judicial, quasi-judicial, political, administrative and social accountability for the implementation of the right to health. Judicial accountability concerns courts' involvement in matters relating to economic, social and cultural rights, the decisions of which can be enforced. Quasi-judicial accountability is mainly generated through independent oversight institutions established by the State, which have a relatively low enforcement capacity compared to that of courts. Political accountability in a narrow sense is generated through periodic elections (i.e. electoral accountability, with relatively low enforcement capacity), while in a broad sense, parliaments can also generate political accountability (i.e. ministerial accountability, with high enforcement capacity). This study analysed administrative accountability in a narrow sense based on internal hierarchical relationships. According to this narrow understanding, administrative accountability is exercised *within* institutions through a chain of command, and thus has a high enforcement capacity. Social accountability is initiated through the actions of individuals and civil society organisations as well as efforts by other actors (eg the media) to support these actions. The role of the media in exerting accountability, either as a social accountability mechanism or as an overseeing institution, was also extensively discussed in chapter 6. This chapter also explored a handful of international supervisory mechanisms and found that international mechanisms have relatively weak enforcement capacity.

Part 3 was based on the hypothesis that accountability could exist in the absence of competitive, free and fair elections and explored whether and how accountability could advance the right to health care in light of China's unique political, legal and social background. Chapter 7 applied the analytical framework for (right to health-based) accountability in the Chinese context to identify linkages between various actors involved in China's health sector and to assess the capacity of overseeing actors to hold accountable actors (i.e. *State actors*) to account via various forms of domestic accountability mechanisms. Overall, although it is not easy to exert the narrow sense of political accountability (electoral accountability) in a non-electoral regime like China, we do see a wide range of accountability mechanisms available for holding State actors to account. Through judicial, quasi-judicial, political, administrative and social accountability mechanisms, right-holders can claim their right to health care (or at least some elements of the right to health care) and seek remedies for violations of this right. These accountability mechanisms, in particular social accountability mechanisms, are to some extent interdependent with one another and can reinforce each other in different ways. Nevertheless, various shortcomings of each type of accountability mechanism were identified.

In general, generating accountability for advancing the right to health care in China has two purposes. The first and most fundamental is to redress violations of the right to health care, such as the *de facto* misuse or abuses of power, or the inequitable distribution of health resources. This amounts to *ex post* accountability. We see that judicial accountability mechanisms, with a high capacity of enforcement, are available in China for individuals to claim their health-related rights. Nevertheless, the availability, quality and other dimensions of the right to health care may still be difficult to advance through claiming rights before domestic courts. It is still difficult, if possible at all, to address systematic failures through judicial accountability mechanisms. Additionally, because of judicial accountability mechanisms are subject to certain restraints, they are often regarded as last resort in China. There are also a handful of quasi-judicial and political accountability mechanisms available to hold responsible State actors to account and to redress violations of the right to health care. However, these mechanisms remain relatively weak in reality and much more work has to be done to improve the well-functioning of these mechanisms. Administrative accountability mechanisms, with a high degree of enforcement, are very powerful mechanisms for providing internal, top-down control of the misuse and abuses of State authority and/or health resources. In practice, when they are engaged with other accountability mechanisms, including social accountability mechanisms in particular, administrative accountability mechanisms would become salient tools for advancing the right to health care in the Chinese context. Social accountability mechanisms can make it possible for the entire society to discipline and restrain State actors in discharging their obligations under the right to health care, and can allow aggrieved right-holders to claim remedies more effectively. Nevertheless, social accountability mechanisms have a relatively low capacity of enforcement. Therefore, these mechanisms would become more effective in China when they are reinforced by other forms of accountability mechanisms. In particular, although social accountability is mostly demand-driven and leads to individual redress, it has the potential to address systematic failure in the health care system when taking a State-society synergistic approach.

The second purpose of accountability is to identify which aspects of law, policy and service delivery are working so they can be repeated, and which aspects should be revised (i.e. *ex ante* accountability). In other words, mechanisms for *ex ante* accountability can identify systematic weakness in controlling abuses of power and assuring compliance with right to health standards and hold State actors to account before a (negative) result occurs in reality. Most existing accountability mechanisms in China focus on *ex post* redress and sanction, with only a few providing for *ex ante* prevention. Under China's current legal system, domestic courts can only provide judicial review of the regulatory document on which an allegedly illegal administrative action was based. The authority to provide non-judicial review of the constitutionality and legality of laws, administrative regulations and rules (political accountability) resides with the Standing Committee of the National People's Congress (NPCSC), but remains largely rhetorical in practice. Right-holders play a very limited role in holding State actors to account *ex ante*. Right-holders can only file a request for judicial review of the regulatory document when they file a complaint against the administrative action or submit a written recommendation to the NPCSC to conduct non-judicial review. Nevertheless, social accountability mechanisms allow society to participate in the process of health-related decision-making and service delivery. This means that the most pressing health needs of the entire population will be taken into consideration in the adoption of health laws and policies, making the health care system more accountable.

In conclusion, concrete (legislative and policy) measures have been taken to progressively realise the right to health care in China. Nevertheless, there is no one-size-fits-all approach; problems remain in China's progress towards the full realisation of this right. Accountability, which gives 'teeth' to human rights, has the potential to address these problems and become a powerful tool for advancing the right to health care within China's unique legal, political and social framework. Although there are still some challenges in achieving the purposes of accountability in the health care system, the various examples of accountability mechanisms discussed in this study have important implications for creating a more accountable health care system in

China. States with similar legal and political settings can also learn from China's experiences.

8.3 Recommendations

In light of the preceding analyses, it can be observed that some structural deficiencies have hampered China's efforts in guaranteeing everyone equal access to health care. The Chinese government has clearly expressed its political will to improve the health of its people. The question then arises of how to address the remaining challenges that undermine the full realisation of the right to health care in reality. This section offers a set of recommendations to address structural shortcomings and to further advance the right to health care in China. In doing so, this section explores the changes, if any, that China's draft BHL could provide in relation to the legislative and policy measures China has taken, as well as the existing accountability mechanisms.

The first and foremost recommendation is to explicitly grant an individual right to health (care) in the draft BHL. As discussed in chapter 3, China's health law system is ill-equipped to regulate the health care system and to provide full protection of the right to health care. Although the Chinese Constitution contains several articles in relation to health and health care, whether these constitutional provisions constitute an explicit reference to the right to health care is still disputed. In addition, constitutional provisions cannot be applied before domestic courts. As it currently stands, constitutional protection of the right to health care occurs rarely, if ever. Furthermore, China's health law system is fragmented in nature; components of the right to health care are protected by separate health-related laws. Most of these laws impose a duty on the State to guarantee equal access to health care without clarifying the consequences for the State, should it fail to do so. Few health-related laws stipulate health care as an entitlement that every individual can demand. This makes it difficult for right-holders to claim their right to health care before the courts and seek redress if State actors fail to discharge their duties. For example, as mentioned in chapter 7, a right-holder can only seek a judicial remedy when a certain health care provider (or health professional) denies his/her access to health care. Yet, it is not possible to seek judicial redress for inequalities and inequity in access to health care on a larger scale. Therefore, it is necessary for the draft BHL to clearly grant everyone the right to health care so that courts can correspondingly provide judicial remedies for systematic failures, which would lead to a greater protection of the right to health care.

The second recommendation concerns the core content of the right to health care that should be defined in the drafting BHL. While most Chinese scholars agree that the BHL should include an article or section in relation to the right to health care, their opinions diverge as to the core content/components of the right to health care that should be embedded in this draft law. For example, Wang argues that the key to establishing a basic health care system is the provision of free basic health care,[1] while Sun and others suggest that the BHL should define the government's responsibility to guarantee universal access to essential health care and medicines regardless of gender, age, religion, social class and financial capacity.[2] In light of the analysis in chapter 4, I argue that the BHL should incorporate the core obligations of the right to health care, which must be fulfilled regardless of China's resource constraints. The BHL should first require the State to ensure access to essential primary health care (including access to essential medicines) that would at least not cause financial hardship, if not be free of charge. Defining essential primary health care should respond to the most pressing health needs of the entire population, with particular attention being paid to vulnerable or marginalised groups. This can be achieved by establishing mechanisms for public participation in all health-related decision-making processes, which is itself also a structural and procedural core obligation. Second, the BHL should articulate structural and procedural (core) obligations, including, *inter alia*, to guarantee non-discriminatory and equal access to the right to health care; to establish effective, transparent, accessible and independent accountability mechanisms; to ensure the equitable distribution of all health facilities, goods and services; and to adopt and implement a national public health strategy and plan of action on the basis of a participatory and transparent process. Clearly, it would be favourable for the BHL to provide for additional obligations or define the scope of health care (or more specifically the availability, accessibility, acceptability and quality of health care to

1 Chengguang Wang, 'Keyi Shixian de Mengxiang: Jianli Puhui Dazhong de Mianfei Jiben Yiliao Fuwu Zhidu [Available Dream: To Establish Universal and Free Basic Medical Service System]' (2017) 5 Yixue yu Faxue [Medicine and Jurisprudence] 1, 1-6.

2 Jing Sun and others, 'Weisheng Lifa de Guoji Jingyan dui Woguo de Qishi [International Experiences and Their Implication for China's Essential Health Law]' (2016) 9 Zhongguo Weisheng Zhengce Yanjiu [Chinese Journal of Health Policy] 66, 66-71.

be provided by the State), but the BHL should at least provide for the core obligations of the right to health care.

The last recommendation sheds light on increasing accountability. As discussed, China's existing accountability mechanisms suffer from some shortcomings. Although the BHL may not be able to address every problem, it can clearly define the responsibilities of various actors in the health sector. China's current legal system does not systematically articulate right to health standards and procedures. If these standards and procedures were to be clearly established under the BHL, it would be easier to hold State actors to account for the right to health.

Furthermore, because individuals cannot directly invoke constitutional provisions in China's domestic courts and there is no law that explicitly provides for the right to health care, it would be favourable for the BHL to explicitly grant individuals a right to health care, as also mentioned in the first recommendation. Including this right would allow right-holders to seek remedies for violations of the right to health care through judicial accountability mechanisms more effectively.

In addition to *ex post* accountability, to address systematic failure or affect policy and structural change the BHL should also strengthen *ex ante* accountability. This could be achieved by granting domestic courts the authority to provide judicial review of the legality of health-related regulations, rules and policies, which extend beyond regulatory documents. Moreover, as the previous paragraph suggests, the BHL should institutionalise public participation (through various accountability mechanisms) in all health-related decision-making processes and in the delivery of health services, thus assuring State actors' compliance with right to health standards and increasing social accountability.

All in all, as the overarching law in the field of health, the draft BHL is expected to define the basic framework and the values that are essential to the health care system, and to stress the State's responsibility to guarantee everyone equal access to health care. This study does not propose to provide a full draft of provisions for inclusion in the BHL, but to offer recommendations for several provisions in light of the preceding analyses.

Box 8.1 Summary of recommendations to be included in the draft BHL
1. Guarantee everyone the right to health (care); allow this to be exercised according to the principles of non-discrimination and equality;
2. Provide essential primary health care (including essential drugs) without the imposition of financial hardship (if not providing them free of charge);
3. Ensure public participation in all health-related decision-making processes, with particular attention being paid to vulnerable and marginalised groups;
4. Ensure the equitable distribution of all health facilities, goods and services;
5. Adopt and implement a national public health strategy and plan of action on the basis of a participatory and transparent process;
6. Clearly define the right to health responsibilities of various actors in the health sector;
7. Oblige the State to establish effective, transparent, accessible and independent accountability mechanisms;
8. Grant domestic courts the authority to provide judicial review of the legality of health-related regulations, rules and policies that extend beyond regulatory documents.

It should be noted, however, that as the core obligations outlined in General Comment 14 have certain limits themselves, much more work has to be done to further develop the core of the right to health care, thus contributing to a clearer understanding of what essential health services package should be provided by States. Furthermore, given the time and financial constraints, the empirical research on the application of accountability mechanisms is still limited. More studies need to be conducted to identify which accountability mechanisms are the most effective ones for redressing violations of the right to health care. Future studies are also necessary for determining how best to monitor, supervise and regulate State actors and to encourage them to act in the broader interest of society towards the full realisation of the right to health care. Ultimately, China has made remarkable progress regarding the right to health (care), and the BHL provides a unique opportunity to make further, fundamental steps towards its full realisation.

Annexes

Annex 1
The OPERA Framework

The OPERA Framework: Outcomes, Policy Efforts, Resources and Assessment[1]

	What Concepts Are We Measuring?	Elements
Measure aggregate levels of right enjoyment	Core obligations: widespread deprivation suggests obligations (eg to reach minimum essential levels of the right to health care) are not being met.	• Packages of services • Essential medicines • (Equal) access
Measure disparities in right enjoyment	Non-discrimination and equality: rights raise concerns about possible discrimination or failure to address disadvantage.	• Gender • Health status • Occupational status (employee/resident) • Origin (rural/urban) • Income (rich/poor)
Measure progress over time	Progressive realisation and non-retrogression: identifying trends in the enjoyment of a right over time indicates whether there is progress or backsliding and whether disparities are growing or reducing.	Same as above
Identify legal and policy commitments	Obligation to take steps: whether the government is taking adequate legislative, judicial, administrative, social and other measures towards the full realisation of the right to health care	• ICESCR and other human rights treaties • Constitution • National law • Administrative directive

1 Center for Economic and Social Rights, 'The OPERA Framework: Assessing Compliance with the Obligation to Fulfill Economic, Social and Cultural Rights' (2012). This table was adapted by the author.

	What Concepts Are We Measuring?	Elements
Examine policy content and implementation	AAAQ - Available, accessible, acceptable, appropriate and of good quality: whether the goods and services needed to fulfil a right are increasingly available, accessible, acceptable and of adequate quality, without discrimination.	• Quality of monitoring and evaluation tool
Analyse policy processes	Participation, transparency, right to a remedy: whether right-holders can actively participate in the design, implementation and oversight of policies and have avenues to hold government to account or seek redress when they are negatively affected by them.	• Parliamentary debate • Participatory decision-making at national level • Litigation
Analyse resource allocation and expenditure	Progressive realisation according to maximum available resources: whether expenditures (planned and actual) in relevant sectors are a transparent, equitable and effective use of available resources.	• Government health expenditure as percentage of THE • Government health expenditure as percentage of government budget • Medium-Term expenditure framework • Allocation primary/secondary/tertiary • Allocation urban/rural • Ring-fenced allocation vulnerable groups
Analyse resource generation	Progressive realisation according to maximum available resources: whether sufficient revenue is being mobilized transparently, equitably and effectively from different sources.	• Government budget as percentage of GDP • Tax income • Insurance fees • Out-of-pocket • Aid
Analyse policy processes	Participation, accountability and transparency: whether the budget process is open and accessible to citizens and whether they have avenues for review of budget decisions or redress.	• Govrnment budget • Government expenditure • Medium-Term expenditure framework

Annex 2
The Evolving Conceptions of '*Weisheng*', '*Yiliao*' and '*Jiankang*'

As discussed in chapter 1, for a proper understanding of the implementation of the right to health care in China, it is necessary to distinguish the different concepts of *weisheng*, *yiliao* and *jiankang*, which will be explained in detail in three sections.

Health and medical care, namely *weisheng* and *yiliao* in Chinese, often appear as a fixed phrase – ***'yiliao weisheng'*** – in Chinese health laws and policies, but convey different meanings. *Yiliao weisheng* generally refers to a set of techniques to preserve ***'jiankang'***, which means to avoid disease and prolong life.

1 Weisheng

The word *weisheng* is currently used as the Chinese translation of various English words, such as hygiene, health or sanitation. Initially, however, it was applied in Chinese cosmology as an expression of 'guarding life' (literally translated from the two characters that comprise the term), referring to a set of techniques that individuals could employ to preserve health, avoid disease and prolong life.[1] In many traditional Chinese medical texts, *weisheng* was more closely related to the so-called ***'yangsheng'*** practices such as diet, meditation and movements. *Yangsheng*, often considered as macrobiotic hygiene, is a different practice from medicine in the Chinese context,[2] but it still falls within the realm of personal health practices. For a long time, *weisheng* has been positioned as a subordinate subject in the research of Chinese medicine.[3]

1 The expression of 'guarding life' can be traced back to the work of Zhuangzi (B.C. 286). Ruth Rogaski, *Hygienic Modernity: Meanings of Health and Disease in Treaty-Port China* (University of California Press 2004) 1, 22, 25.

2 ibid 25.

3 Xinzhong Yu, 'Weisheng Hewei – Zhongguo Jinshi de Weishenegshi Yanjiu [Review on the Study of Sanitary History of China in the Modern Age]' (2011) 3 Shixue Lilun Yanjiu [Historiography Quarterly] 132, 132.

It was not until the late Qing in Guangxu's reign (1875-1908) that *weisheng* began its conceptual evolution.[4] Ruth Rogaski, in her seminal scholarship on the meaning of health in treaty-port China,[5] analysed the shifting conception of *weisheng* from Chinese cosmology to one encompassing 'State power, scientific standards of progress, the cleanliness of bodies, and the fitness of races', which she then termed 'hygienic modernity'.[6] According to Rogaski, the term *weisheng* was mainly used to convey an approach to health led by the State and the laboratory as well as other understandings related to health and disease in the early 20th century.[7]

It was the Japanese physician Nagayo Sensai who, inspired by both the Western ideas of a State-centred public health system and the classical sinology, was the first to choose the word ***'eisei'*** – the Japanese transliteration of *weisheng* – as a translation of the term hygiene, in the 1875 Japanese National Medical Code.[8] In 1872, Nagayo served as a medical observer when he was sent by the Japanese government on an official mission to Europe and the United States of America (USA). During his investigation, he observed that many Western States had established 'a web of engineering, education, policing, and laboratories that linked the health of individual to the health of the nation'. Each State had its own word to describe this system: for example, sanitation in English; *santé* (i.e. health care) in French; and *Sanitäts-wesen* (i.e. sanitary system), öffentliche *Hygiene* (i.e. official hygiene) or *Gesundheitspflege* (i.e. health care) in German.[9] After returning to Japan, Nagayo endeavoured to establish a system similar to the German öffentliche *Medezine* system for the Meiji government and to find an appropriate Japanese name for such a bureau that was responsible for the health of the nation.[10]

In his memoir, Nagayo explained that he had initially failed to grasp the full meaning of such terms as sanitary, health, and *gesundheitspflege* in his study of medical systems in Europe and the USA. It took him some time to comprehend that

4 Hsianglin Lei, 'Moral Community of Weisheng: Contesting Hygiene in Republican China' (2009) 3 (4) East Asian Science, Technology and Society: An International Journal 475, 475, 491.
5 Treaty-port China was the name given to the port cities in China that were opened to foreign trade by the unequal treaties.
6 Rogaski (n 1) 1.
7 ibid 23.
8 ibid 25, 136.
9 ibid 136.
10 ibid 144.

these terms did not simply present a mode of preserving health but also extended beyond this, encompassing the administration of a government and the construction of a society.[11] Nagayo then struggled to find a corresponding Japanese word to describe this medical modernity.

Remarkably, although it is generally believed that the Western word Nagayo intended to translate was hygiene, scholars disagree as to the precise word that he originally wished to translate: the German term *gesundheitspflege* (i.e. health care), or the English term hygiene. While Johnston argued that the original word was *gesundheitspflege,*[12] Tadayasu claimed that the word was hygiene.[13] Irrespective of which term Nagoya originally intended to translate, it can be deduced from his memoir that Nagayo tried to find a corresponding Japanese term that indicated both the public and private approaches to disease prevention.[14] Nevertheless, he found that Japanese words were very often linked too closely to individual practices to guard health, thus failing to convey a public dimension. He also found that there were no Japanese equivalents of the German terms *Sanitäts-wesen* and öffentliche *Hygiene*, which described the government's administration of health.

Inspired by classic Sinology, Nagayo then turned to the Daoist text Zhuangzi for a solution to his translation conundrum and finally found *eisei* to be the most appropriate term to capture the comprehensive nature of his new governmental bureau of health.[15] While acknowledging that the meaning of *eisei* in Sinology was different from the Western concepts he had identified, Nagayo claimed that *eisei* could not only 'refer to the protection of health alone...but instead refers to the particular type of governmental structures that are in charge of protecting the general health of the State's citizens'.[16] Thus, *eisei* conveyed both the traditional concept of guarding (*ei*)

---

11 ibid 143.

12 William Johnston, *The Modern Epidemic: Tuberculosis in Japan* (Harvard University Press 1995) 179. Cited in Rogaski (n 1) 323.

13 Ban Tadayasu, *Tekijuku to Nagayo Sensai, Eiseigaku to Shoko Shishi [The Tekijuku to Nagayo Sensai: Hygienics and the Fragant Pine Memoirs]* (Sogensha 1987) 151-157. Cited in Rogaski (n 1) 323.

14 Rogaski (n 1) 144.

15 ibid 144-145.

16 ibid 136; Shiyong Liu, 'Qingjie, Weisheng yu Baojian – Rizhi Shiqi Taiwan Shehui Gonggong Weisheng Guannian zhi Zhuanbian [Cleanliness, Hygiene and Healthcare - Changing Notions of Public Hygiene in Taiwanese Society during the Japanese Occupation]' (2001) 8 (1) Studies in Taiwanese History 41, 47. Cited in Lei (n 4) 477.

life (*sei*) and also 'a task of defense at the national level.'[17] According to Johnston, it is because the word's first character, ***ei,*** captured a meaning of 'policing or patrolling an area', which was close to the German model of medical police he wished to pursue in Japan that Nagayo consciously chose this term. Rogaski provided another appraisal of the meaning of *ei* that was related to a military guard or fortress designed to protect something important – the life of the citizen and the new Meiji State.[18]

In line with the analysis above, it can be concluded that the term *eisei* (or *weisheng* in Chinese) has three layers: (1) it is a translation of hygiene or *gesundheitspflege*; (2) it points to a particular type of governmental structure that follows the German öffentliche *Medezine* system; and (3) it signals the transition from purely preserving individual health to a special administrative system that is responsible for the health of the entire nation.

The first attempt by the Chinese government to establish a national health administration can be traced back to the Qing dynasty. After Japan's expansion of imperialism in Asia in the 20th century, this new understanding of *eisei* was imported to China as the translation of hygiene. In order to regain its sovereignty, the Qing government was forced to adopt the Japanese model of hygienic modernity and to establish its own *weisheng* bureau in 1905 to carry out its public health responsibilities. Thus, *weisheng* encompassed a new meaning in the Chinese context – 'government scientific control of sanitation, prevention of disease, cleanliness, policing, visual orderliness, and the detection and elimination of germs'.[19] Personal hygiene and public health administration then became architects of civilization and modernity, which Rogashi called 'hygienic modernity'.[20]

Yunlong Fu was the first contemporary Chinese scholar to systematically discuss the meaning of *weisheng*.[21] Fu was sent by the Qing government to learn Japan's new administration of health. Being the head of the Japanese health bureau at that time, Nagayo had a great impact on Fu. It was thus not surprising that in his book, Fu

17 Lei (n 4) 484.
18 Rogaski (n 1) 145; Liu (n 16) 47. Cited in Lei (n 4) 477.
19 Rogaski (n 1) 167
20 ibid; Lei (n 4) 477.
21 Yunlong Fu, *Weisheng Shuo [The Research of Weisheng]* (1889). Cited in Xinzhong Yu, 'Wanqing Weisheng Gainian Yanbian Tanlue [On the Evolution of the Concept of Weisheng in the Later Qing Dynasty]' Journal of Asian History (Dongyangshi Yanjiu) (2006) 915, 926.

completely supported Nagayo's idea.[22] Furthermore, *weisheng* was formally added to the 1915 Chinese dictionary, *Ciyuan*.[23] According to this dictionary, *weisheng* is the science and art of promoting health through the research of the physiological functions of an individual. The study of *weisheng* is mainly based on physiology and medicine, together with physics, chemistry and bacteriology. This study can be further divided into the study of personal hygiene and public health.[24]

However, some contemporary Chinese scholars did not entirely agree with the choice of *weisheng* as the translation of hygiene in the Chinese context.[25] Among them was Chen, Fangzhi, who argued that:

> [t]he Japanese people have rashly translated the word "hygiene" as weisheng xue [lit.: the study of guarding life], which is the origin of the modern Chinese compound weisheng ... To translate "hygiene" into the Chinese language, they should have either used jiankang xue ["study of health"] or baojian xue ["study of preserving health"]. Although the compound baojian has not existed in the past, it would be the ideal choice because the content [of hygiene] is to guard health and not at all to guard life.[26]

Chen observed that the Chinese discourse on *weisheng* was related to the original Western notion of hygiene, but at the same time diverged from it.[27] He asserted that the Chinese discussions on *weisheng* during that period focused mainly on individual practices of hygiene and rarely mentioned the development of a national public health and medical administration system, which was in sharp contrast with Nagayo's intention of translating hygiene as *weisheng*. As quoted above, in his book on the *Study and Administration of Hygiene*, Chen explained that the notion of hygiene was to guard health and not at all to guard life.[28] Accordingly, he made a clear distinction between personal hygiene and public health, and proposed ***'gonggong weisheng'*** (i.e. public health) as the translation of *modern* hygiene.[29] Chen contended the

22 ibid.
23 The Ciyuan is the earliest modern encyclopedic Chinese phrase dictionary.
24 Ciyuan (Commercial Press 1915) 158-159.
25 Lei (n 4) 477.
26 Fangzhi Chen, *Weishengxue yu Weisheng Xingzheng [The Study and Administration of Hygiene]* (Commercial Press 1934) 2. Quoted in Lei (n 4) 477. Lei's translation.
27 Lei (n 4) 484.
28 ibid 477.
29 ibid 478, 484.

use of the term hygiene – new vocabulary in the Chinese context – as requiring a public approach to disease prevention, or *gonggong weisheng,* as he termed it, and excluded the traditional personal *weisheng* practices Chinese people had.[30] Given that many Chinese public health historians adopted Chen's view, contemporary Chinese historical research on modern public health focused mainly on the government's administration of health and the control and prevention of infectious diseases.[31]

Nevertheless, recent research found that *weisheng* in the earlier 20th century concerned far more than guarding health.[32] For example, Lei asserted that the Chinese discourse on *weisheng* includes both the Western notion of hygiene and the Chinese understanding of *weisheng.*[33] He argued that in contemporary China, hygiene not only had to be concerned with providing public health services and constructing a national health system; it was equally important to rebuild the image of the Chinese people. From Lei's perspective, personal hygiene in particular was a key component to fighting the stigmatised image of the Chinese nation at that time,[34] and was thereby helpful in rebuilding a national identity, particularly when the government itself was incapable of advancing the construction of an effective public health system.[35] Lei, accordingly, regarded personal hygiene as the Chinese approach of *weisheng*. He further suggested that the approach of *weisheng*, which centred on 'guarding life', was not limited to the preservation of physical care, but also reflected the new understanding, values and experiences of life at a time when the traditional Chinese medicine and Western microbe theory encountered and struggled with each other.[36] The Chinese approach not only embraced the Western notions of hygiene and microbes but also included such Chinese notions as 'governing the mind', 'mental hygiene' and 'treating illness before it arises', which are notions very closely related to prevention.[37]

30 ibid 478.
31 ibid.
32 ibid 502.
33 ibid 484-502.
34 The stigmatised image of the Chinese nation was often referred to 'John Chairman', or the so-called 'Sickman of East Asia', which was a racist name used to refer to the Chinese and particularly targeted Chinese practices such as foot-binding and opium addiction that were common since the late Qing dynasty.
35 Lei (n 4) 500-501.
36 ibid 480.
37 ibid 481.

Notably, the principle of 'treating illness before it arises', proposed by contemporary Chinese scholar Chen, Guofu was of great importance in the Republican Era (1912-1949). Chen pointed out that a severe challenge with respect to medicine in China was that individuals who got sick could neither afford to visit a doctor or pay for medication. A possible way to solve this problem was to increase the awareness of personal hygiene and indigenous customs that could prevent illness before it arose.[38] Accordingly, Chen argued that the Chinese approach of *weisheng* should focus on preventing people from falling into a state of disease in which they would need medical treatment.[39] Thus, *weisheng* could loosen the connection between individuals' lives and medicine.[40] Seen in this light, Chen's advocacy for personal hygiene was not aimed at counteracting the State's public health measures and national health administration, but rather was due to his belief that personal hygiene, or the Chinese understanding of hygiene, could be expected to solve China's national health care and medicine crises during the Republican period.[41] Based on Chen's statement, Lei further claimed that the Chinese approach of *weisheng* gradually developed as an alternative to that of the medical profession and served as an important tool with which individuals could safeguard their own health. *Weisheng* thus had the potential to decrease individuals' dependence on medicine, which could in turn relieve the heavy burden of medical expenses.[42]

Yu also traced how the concept of *weisheng* shifted from the traditional meaning of 'guarding life' to the modern meaning of hygiene. He pointed out that the traditional meaning of *weisheng*, which had originated in Japan, co-existed with the modern meanings in contemporary China.[43] He stated that, on the one hand, although the contemporary study of *weisheng* reserved the traditional meaning of *yangsheng*, i.e. macrobiotic hygiene, and thus still fell within the ambit of guarding life, its focus shifted from disease to health (1905-1911). *Weisheng* was defined as the science and art of promoting health, thus excluding the meaning of medical care (i.e. *yiliao* in Chinese) from the traditional meaning. On the other hand, given that

38 Guofu Chen, *Weisheng zhi Dao [The Way of Hygiene]* (Zhengzhong Bookstore 1942) 1. Cited in Lei (n 4) 489.
39 ibid.
40 ibid.
41 ibid 489-490.
42 ibid.
43 Yu (n 21) 915.

the administration of *weisheng* included the administration of medical treatment and health providers in general, *yiliao* can still be categorised under *weisheng*, referring to medical administration rather than medical care *per se*.[44] Therefore, although to some extent the concepts of *weisheng* and *yiliao* are still inter-connected, their contours have become clearer.

2 Yiliao

In contrast with the evolving meaning of *weisheng*, the concept of *yiliao* is relatively straightforward, as it clearly refers to medical care. Nevertheless, even though medical care could help preserve individual health, the elements of *yiliao* were excluded in the process of conceptualising *weisheng*.[45] As Yu noted, in contemporary history *weisheng* focused on health rather than on disease; a narrow interpretation of the concept did not encompass medical care and even when interpreted broadly, *weisheng* only included the administration of medical practices.[46]

I agree with Yu that to some extent *weisheng* and *yiliao* overlap with each other (i.e. they both encompass the administration of medical practices), but on a large scale they have different contours. *Weisheng* focuses more on the State's public health measures for preserving health and preventing disease, as well as the administration of the national health system, together with individuals' self-protection. *Weisheng* laws include the Chinese Food Safety Law, the Law on Population and Family Planning, Mental Health (in Chinese: *weisheng*) Law, and the Law on the Prevention and Control of Occupational Diseases. Apparently, the State has an important role to play in implementing these laws. In contrast, *yiliao* is closely related to medical care, in particular medical treatment. *Yiliao* laws concern the responsibilities of medical professionals and the rights of patients. They mainly regulate such issues as informed consent, confidentiality, negligence and liability in relation to medical treatment (eg medical malpractice).

Notably, when it comes to the translation of the phrase *yiliao weisheng*, both the government and academics tend to use the terms health and medical care instead of hygiene and medical care. For example, China's draft national law in the field of

44 ibid 922-948.
45 ibid 921-923.
46 ibid.

health is temporarily entitled ***Jiben Yiliao Weisheng Fa*** (literarily: *Basic Health and Medical Law*). Scholars have proposed different translations for this title, such as basic health law, basic medical and health law or basic medical and health care law. They have commented that this title is not as clear as *Jiben Weisheng Fa* (*Basic Health Law*) or *Weisheng Fa* (*Health Law*).[47] Nevertheless, when the Education, Science, Culture and Public Health Committee of the National People's Congress initiated the drafting of this fundamental health law, it was entitled *Jiben Yiliao Weisheng Fa*, and it would take over five years to restart the whole process so as to change the title. Given that the enactment of this law is currently of considerable importance, the discussion of its title was set aside. In the conclusion of this study, I have discussed, in line with the analysis of the overall study, what should be covered by the law and suggested a desirable title for it.

For the purposes of this research, it is also necessary to explain the transition of *weisheng* from the Chinese translation of hygiene to the translation of health. While the doctrine gradually accepts the phrase *gonggong weisheng* as the Chinese translation of public health (literarily correspond to *gonggong* and *weisheng*), no agreement has been reached regarding the translation of health as *weisheng*.[48] Currently, there is little Chinese literature explaining the transition of the translation. A possible answer may be the growing understanding of the terms hygiene and health globally. According to the current WHO definition, hygiene refers to the 'conditions and practices that help to maintain health and prevent the spread of diseases',[49] while public health is defined as 'the art and science of preventing disease, prolonging life and promoting health through the organized efforts of society'.[50] In this context, the definition of hygiene does not require measures to be taken by the State, while the definition of public health still requires governmental administration. It is thus evident that under the WHO definition, the meaning of *weisheng* in the Chinese context has a broader scope than hygiene.

47 See eg Changqiu Liu, 'Lun "Jiben Yiliao Weisheng Fa" de Mingcheng, Dingwei yu Jibenzhidu [Discussing the Title, Positioning and Structure of the Basic Health and Medical Law]' 2017 (4) Faxue Zazhi [Law Science Magazine] 67, 67.

48 Na Yan, Liyun Chen, '"Weisheng" yu "Gonggong Weisheng" Kao [Textual Research on Health and Public Health]' (2016) 46 (2) Chinese Journal of Medical History 90, 91.

49 Hygiene, the official website of the WHO <www.who.int/topics/hygiene/en/> accessed 28 November 2017.

50 Department of Health, Public Health in England (the Acheson Report) (HMSO 1988).

In contrast, as discussed in chapter 2, health is defined in the 1948 WHO Constitution as 'a state of complete physical, mental and social well-being and not merely the absence of disease or infirmity'.[51] This definition offered by the WHO has long been criticised for being too absolute. More recently, several scholars have argued in favour of a less absolute definition that focuses on the individual's capacity to function adequately in society and to pursue his or her life plans.[52] Nonetheless, the WHO definition is closely related to the Chinese definition of *jiankang*. As mentioned above, the right to health is translated into ***jiankang quan*** in Chinese, where *jiankang* and *quan* correspond to the terms health and right, respectively.

3 JIANKANG

The term *jiankang*, which is now generally used as the translation of health, did not appear in Chinese writings until the 19th century.[53] Although the original source is missing, it is generally believed that this term was created by the Japanese physician Ogata Kōan in 1849 as the transliteration of the Dutch term *gezondheid*. Deeply influenced by the Dutch theory of medicine, Ogata identified ten features of *jiankang* to reflect the continuity of physical stability.[54] The Japanese scholar Fukuzawa Yukichi, inspired by the British scholar John Snow, offered an alternative definition of *jiankang* that was closely related to the British public health theory. Fukuzawa asserted that citizens had the right to attain *jiankang* (i.e. health) and that the government should develop and enact national laws to protect this right.[55] These two contrasting ideas of jiankang were then replaced by Nagayo's theory of *eisei*.

In comparison to the great impact that the theory of *eisei* had on the development of public health theory and on the construction of a national healthcare system, there is not a great deal of research on the study of *jiankang*, not to mention its influence in China. In fact, most Chinese laws and policies regarding, inter alia, the prevention

---

51 Constitution of the World Health Organisation (adopted 22 July 1946, entered into force 7 April 1948) 14 UNTS 185 ('WHO Constitution') preamble.

52 See eg Machteld Huber and others, 'How Should We Define Health' (2011) 343 BMJ, d4163; Brigit Toebes, 'Health and Human Rights: In Searching of the Legal Dimension' (2015) 9 Human Rights & International Legal Discourse 212, 215.

53 Liu (n 16) 44.

54 ibid 45.

55 ibid 46.

and control of infectious and occupational diseases, mental health, family planning and maternal care and the administration of healthcare system, all fall under the ambit of *weisheng* laws and policies; those regarding medical practices fall within the scope *yiliao* laws and policies.[56] Only when it comes to health education or health promotion is the term *jiankang* used. As the right to health is now receiving more attention in China, *jiankang* is currently widely used as the translation of the right to health, which is somewhat similar to Fukuzawa's claim – the right to attain *jiankang* (i.e. health).

As explained in chapter 1, the terminological clarification of these Chinese terms is pivotally important for the choice of key words to be searched for in the Chinese legislation and policies. This search serves as a starting point for assessing the legislative and policy measures China has adopted to discharge its obligations arising from the right to health care.

56 See eg Zhonghua Renmin Gongheguo Weisheng yu Jihua Shengyu Falv Fagui Quanshu [Health and Family Planning Law Collection of the People's Republic of China] (China Legal Publishing House 2016).

Annex 3
Comparison of Chinese Basic Medical Insurance Schemes

Comparison of Chinese basic medical insurance schemes[1]

	UEBMI	URBMI	NRCMS	Urban and Rural Residents BMI - NEW
Launch	1998	2007	2003	2015
Responsible State Organ	MOHRSS	MOHRSS	NHFPC	MOHRSS
Insured population	Urban employees Mandatory	Urban residents Voluntary	Rural residents Voluntary	Piloted in selected cities
Risk-pooling Unit	City Level	City Level	County Level	City Level
Premium paid by	Employer and employee	Government and the individual	Government and the individual	Government and the individual
Premium per person (2015)[2] • Government subsidy • Individual Contribution • Employer contribution	€308 per year • N/A • 2-3% of the payroll • 6-8% of the payroll	€76 per year • €56 • €20 • N/A	€76 per year • €56 • €20 • N/A	Varies according to location

1 Winnie Yip and other, 'Early Appraisal of China's Huge and Complex Health-care Reforms' (2012) 379 The Lancet 833, 835. This table was adapted by the author.

2 ¥7.5 is about €1; See generally <www.mof.gov.cn/zhengwuxinxi/zhengcefabu/201605/t20160506_1978682.htm>; <www.mohrss.gov.cn/gkml/xxgk/201605/t20160506_239541.html> accessed 28 November 2017.

	UEBMI	URBMI	NRCMS	Urban and Rural Residents BMI - NEW
Coverage[3] • Inpatient services • General outpatient services • Outpatient services for catastrophic illnesses	• Covered • Covered • Covered by the IPCD[4]	• Covered • Limited and vary by location • Covered by the IPCD	• Covered • Limited and vary by location • Covered by the IPCD	Varies according to location
Reimbursement rate (2012)[5] • Inpatient • Outpatient	• 75% • Savings account	• 55% • 50%	• 55% • 50%	N/A
Total reimbursement ceiling (2012)[6]	Six times the average salary of urban employees	Six times the disposable income of local urban residents	Eight times the income of local farmers	N/A
Population covered by 2015 (million)[7]	288.93 million	376.89 million	Over 746.7 million	N/A

3 Qingyue Meng and others, 'People's Republic of China: Health System Review' (2015) 5 Health Systems in Transistion 78-81.
4 IPCD: Insurance Programme for Catastrophic Diseases.
5 William Hsiao and others 'Universal Health Coverage: The Case of China' (UNRISD Working Paper No. 2014-15) 17.
6 ibid.
7 Data was derived from the official websites of the Chinese Ministry of Human Resources and Social Security, Human Resources and Social Security 2015 <www.mohrss.gov.cn/SYrlzyhshbzb/dongtaixinwen/buneiyaowen/201605/t20160530_240967.html> accessed 28 November 2017.

List of Instruments

International instruments

Constitution of the World Health Organisation (adopted 22 July 1946, entered into force 7 April 1948) 14 UNTS 185.

Convention on the Elimination of All Forms of Discrimination against Women (adopted 18 December 1979, entered into force 3 September 1981) 1249 UNTS 13.

Convention on the Rights of Persons with Disabilities (adopted 13 December 2006, entered into force 3 May 2008) 2515 UNTS 3.

Convention on the Rights of the Child (adopted 20 November 1989, entered into force 2 September 1990) 1577 UNTS 3.

International Convention on the Elimination of All Forms of Racial Discrimination (adopted 21 December 1965, entered into force 4 January 1969) 660 UNTS 195.

International Convention on the Protection of the Rights of All Migrant Workers and Members of Their Families (adopted 18 December 1990, entered into force 1 July 2003) 2220 UNTS 3.

International Covenant on Civil and Political Rights (adopted 16 December 1966, entered into force 23 March 1976) 999 UNTS 171.

International Covenant on Economic, Social and Cultural Rights (adopted 16 December 1966, entered into force 3 January 1976) 993 UNTS 3.

Optional Protocol to the Convention on the Elimination of All Forms of Discrimination against Women (adopted 15 October 1999, entered into force 22 December 2000) UN Doc A/RES/54/4.

Optional Protocol to the Convention on the Rights of the Child on a Communication Procedure (adopted 19 December 2011, entered into force 14 April 2014) UN Doc A/RES/66/138.

Optional Protocol to the Convention on the Rights of Persons with Disabilities (adopted 13 December 2006, entered into force 3 May 2008) UN Doc A/RES/54/4.

Optional Protocol to the International Covenant on Economic, Social and Cultural Rights (adopted 10 December 2008, entered into force 5 May 2013) UN Doc A/RES/63/117.

Universal Declaration of Human Rights (adopted 10 December 1948) UNGA Res 217 A (III).

Vienna Convention on the Law of Treaties (adopted 23 May 1969, entered into force 27 January 1980) 1155 UNTS 331.

Regional instruments

African Charter on Human and Peoples' Rights (adopted 27 June 1981, entered into force 21 October 1986) 1520 UNTS 217.
American Convention on Human Rights (adopted 22 November 1969, entered into force 18 July 1978) 1144 UNTS 123.
Additional Protocol to the American Convention on Human Rights in the Area of Economic, Social and Cultural Rights (adopted 17 November 1988, entered into force 16 November 1999) OASTS 67.
European Convention for the Protection of Human Rights and Fundamental Freedoms (adopted 4 November 1950, entered into force 3 September 1953, as amended) 213 UNTS 222.
European Social Charter (Revised) (adopted 3 May 1996, entered into force 1 July 1999) ETS 163.

National

Constitutions

Basic Law for the Federal Republic of Germany (1949).
Constitution of October 4, 1958 (1958) (France).
Constitution of the People's Republic of China (1982).
Constitution of the Republic of South Africa (1996).
Constitution of the Kingdom of the Netherlands (2008).

Chinese Legislation

Administrative Procedure Law of 1989 (as amended in 2017).
Civil Procedure Law of the People's Republic of China of 1989 (as amended in 2017).
Drug Administration Law (Revised) of 2001 (as amended in 2015).
Food Safety Law (Revised) of 2015.
Frontier Health and Quarantine Law of 1986 (as amended in 2009).
General Principles of the Civil Law of 1986 (as amended in 2009).
Law on Administrative Reconsideration of 1999 (as amended in 2017).
Law on Blood Donation of 1997.
Law on Licensed Doctors of 1998 (as amended in 2009).
Law on Maternal and Infant Health Care of 1994 (as amended in 2017).
Law on Population and Family Planning of 2001 (as amended in 2015).
Law on Prevention and Treatment of Communicable Diseases (Revised) of 2004 (as amended in 2013).
Law on Prevention of Occupational Diseases of 2001 (as amended in 2017).

Law on Protection of the Rights and Interests of the Elderly (Revised) of 2012 (as amended in 2015).
Law on Regional National Autonomy of 1984 (as amended in 2001).
Law on State Compensation Law of 1994 (as amended in 2012).
Law on the Management of Foreign Non-Governmental Organisations of 2016 (as amended in 2017).
Law on the Procedures of the Conclusion of Treaties of 1990.
Law on the Protection of Disabled Persons (Revised) of 2008.
Law on the Protection of Minors (Revised) of 2006 (as amended in 2012).
Law on the Protection of Women's Rights and Interests of 1992 (as amended in 2005).
Law on the Red Cross Society (Revised) of 2017.
Law on the Territorial Sea and the Contiguous Zone of 1992.
Law on Traditional Chinese Medicine of 2016.
Legislation Law of 2000 (as amended in 2015).
Mental Health Law of 2012.
Organic Law of the National People's Congress of 1982.
Patent Law of 1984 (as amended in 2008).
Social Insurance Law of 2010.
Tort Law of 2009.
Trademark Law of 1982 (as amended in 2013).

Regulations Concerning Consular Privileges and Immunities of 1990.
Regulations Concerning Diplomatic Privileges and Immunities of 1986.
Regulation on Complaint Letters and Visits of 2005.

United Nations Documents

General Comments

United Nations Committee on Economic, Social and Cultural Rights, 'General Comment No. 3: The Nature of State Parties' Obligations (Art.2 Para. 1 of the Covenant)' (14 December 1990) UN Doc E/1991/23.

United Nations Committee on Economic, Social and Cultural Rights, 'General Comment No. 9: The Domestic Application of the Covenant' (3 December 1998) UN Doc E/C12/1998/24.

United Nations Committee on Economic, Social and Cultural Rights, 'General Comment No. 14: The Right to the Highest Attainable Standard of Health (Art. 12 of the Covenant)' (11 August 2000) UN Doc E/C12/2000/4.

United Nations Committee on the Rights of the Child, 'General Comment No. 15: The Right of the Child to the Enjoyment of the Highest Attainable Standard of Health (Art. 24)' (17 April 2013) UN Doc CRC/C/GC/15.

Reports of the Special Rapporteur on the Right to Health

United Nations General Assembly, 'Report of the Special Rapporteur on the Right of Everyone to the Enjoyment of the Highest Attainable Standard of Physical and Mental Health, Paul Hunt' (13 September 2006) UN Doc A/61/338.

United Nations General Assembly, 'Report of the Special Rapporteur on the Right of Everyone to the Enjoyment of the Highest Attainable Standard of Physical and Mental Health, Paul Hunt' (17 Janauary 2007) UN Doc A/HRC/4/28.

United Nations General Assembly, 'Report of the Special Rapporteur on the Right of Everyone to the Enjoyment of the Highest Attainable Standard of Physical and Mental Health, Paul Hunt' (8 August 2007) UN Doc A/62/214.

United Nations General Assembly, 'Report of the Special Rapporteur on the Right of Everyone to the Enjoyment of the Highest Attainable Standard of Physical and Mental Health, Paul Hunt' (31 Janauary 2008) UN Doc A/HRC/7/11.

United Nations General Assembly, 'Report of the Special Rapporteur on the Right of Everyone to the Enjoyment of the Highest Attainable Standard of Physical and Mental Health, Paul Hunt' (11 August 2008) UN Doc A/63/263.

United Nations General Assembly, 'Report of the Special Rapporteur on the Right of Everyone to the Enjoyment of the Highest Attainable Standard of Physical and Mental Health, Anand Grover' (4 July 2011) UN Doc A/HRC/18/37.

United Nations General Assembly, 'Report of the Special Rapporteur on the Right of Everyone to the Enjoyment of the Highest Attainable Standard of Physical and Mental Health, Anand Grover' (1 May 2013) UN Doc A/HRC/23/42.

United Nations General Assembly, 'Report of the Special Rapporteur on the Right of Everyone to the Enjoyment of the Highest Attainable Standard of Physical and Mental Health, Dainius Puras' (5 August 2016) UN Doc A/71/304.

United Nations General Assembly, 'Report of the Special Rapporteur on Extreme Poverty and Human Rights on His Mission to China, Philip Alston' (28 March 2017) UN Doc A/HRC/35/26/Add.2.

United Nations Economic and Social Council, 'Report of the Special Rapporteur on the Right of Everyone to the Enjoyment of the Highest Attainable Standard of Physical and Mental Health, Paul Hunt' (13 February 2003) UN Doc E/CN.4/2003/58.

United Nations Economic and Social Council, 'Economic, Social and Cultural Rights: The Right of Everyone to the Enjoyment of the Highest Attainable Standard of Physical and Mental Health, Report of the Special Rapporteur, Paul Hunt' (16 February 2004) UN Doc E/CN.4/2004/49.

General documents

United Nations Economic and Social Council, 'Summary Record of the Forty-Second Meeting' (6 December 1993) UN Doc E/C.12/1993/SR.42.

United Nations Economic and Social Council, 'Implementation of the International Covenant on Economic, Social and Cultural Rights: Intial Reports submitted by States Parties under Articles 16 and 17 of the Covenant, Addendum, People's Republic of China' (4 March 2004) UN Doc E/1990/5/Add.59.

United Nations Economic and Social Council, 'An Evaluation of the Obligation to Take Steps to the 'Maximum of Available Resources' under an Optional Protocol to the Covenant' (10 May 2007) UN Doc E/C.12/2007/1.

United Nations Economic and Social Council, 'Implementation of the International Covenant on Economic, Social and Cultural Rights: Second Periodic Reports submitted by States Parties under Articles 16 and 17 of the Covenant, China' (6 July 2012) UN Doc E/C.12/CHN/2.

United Nations Committee on Economic, Social and Cultural Rights, 'Provisional Agenda and Annotations: Note by the Secretary-General' (1 September 1993) UN Doc E/C.12/1993/11.

United Nations Committee on Economic, Social and Cultural Rights, 'Twenty-Second Session, Summary Record of the 10th Meeting Held at the Palais Wilson, Geneva' (4 May 2000) UN Doc E/C. 12/2000/SR.10.

List of Tables and Figures

Tables

Figures

Samenvatting

Gezondheid is een belangrijke voorwaarde om een waardig leven te leiden. Tegenwoordig is sprake van een bijna universele onderschrijving van het recht op gezondheid (en het recht op gezondheidszorg als onderdeel daarvan). Ondanks deze groeiende erkenning van het recht op gezondheidszorg blijkt uit empirisch onderzoek dat de tenuitvoerlegging op nationaal niveau van deze norm grotendeels retorisch blijft. Hoewel China bijvoorbeeld het Internationaal Verdrag inzake Economische, Sociale en Culturele Rechten (IVESCR) in 2001 heeft geratificeerd, heeft dit land tot dusverre weinig aandacht besteed aan de implementatie van het recht op gezondheidszorg in de nationale rechtsorde. Schendingen van dit recht zijn dan ook vastgesteld. Aangezien de hervorming van de gezondheidszorg in China de zogenaamde 'diepwaterzone' ingaat, en de realisering van deze plannen nadert, is het van cruciaal belang voor de Chinese overheid om te onderzoeken hoe iedereen gelijke toegang tot gezondheidszorg te garanderen.

Het doel van deze studie is om bestaande tekortkomingen in China's implementatie van het recht op gezondheidszorg te identificeren. Om vervolgens de resterende uitdagingen te onderzoeken vanuit het perspectief van *accountability*, hetgeen ruwweg omschreven kan worden als de 'verantwoordingplicht' van de actoren die verantwoordelijkheid dragen voor het realiseren van het recht op gezondheidszorg. En daaropvolgend aanbevelingen te doen aan Chinese wet- en beleidsmakers voor het implementeren van de Chinese verplichtingen onder het recht op gezondheidszorg door middel van de conceptwet *Basic Health Law* (BHL). De centrale onderzoeksvraag is daarom of en hoe het 'verantwoording afleggen' (*accountability*) het recht op gezondheidszorg kan bevorderen in de context van China's unieke politieke, juridische en sociaal-maatschappelijke omstandigheden. Aldus worden in deze studie twee verschillende concepten gesynthetiseerd: (1) het recht op gezondheid; en (2) *accountability*. Beide concepten worden zo in een analytisch raamwerk, i.e. '*right to health-based accountability*', geïntegreerd. Door zowel theoretische als empirische analyses uit te voeren biedt deze studie voorts een beter begrip van het concept *accountability* en van de verschillende soorten *accountability mechanisms* (verantwoordingsmechanismen) die door staten zouden moeten worden ingesteld. Een concreet doel van deze studie is om een constructief *accountability model* (verantwoordingsmodel) op te stellen dat toegepast kan worden op specifieke gezondheidsproblemen, zowel in China als in andere landen, met name landen met niet-electorale regimes.

Deel 1 legt de basis voor de gehele studie - de implementatie van het recht op gezondheidszorg in China. Het beoordeelt systematisch de mate waarin China (wetgevende en beleidsmatige) maatregelen heeft genomen om het recht op gezondheidszorg uit te voeren binnen zijn rechtsgebied. Door dit te doen identificeert dit deel van het proefschrift de leemtes die bestaan tussen *de jure* en *de facto* implementatie van het recht op gezondheidszorg in China.

Hoofdstuk 2 schets de situatie voor de analyse van de implementatie van het recht op gezondheidszorg in China door twee vragen te beantwoorden: *wat betekent recht op gezondheidszorg,* en *wat houdt dit recht in*? In deze studie wordt het recht op gezondheidszorg gezien als een recht op toegang tot tijdige en passende gezondheidsfaciliteiten, goederen, en diensten die nodig zijn voor een algehele verwezenlijking van een zo goed mogelijke lichamelijke en geestelijke gezondheid. De reikwijdte van het recht op gezondheidszorg strekt zich onder meer uit van toegang tot medische zorg tot het aanbieden van essentiële geneesmiddelen. Staten kunnen het recht op gezondheidszorg geleidelijk realiseren, afhankelijk van hun beschikbare middelen. Deze studie stelt echter dat staten verschillende *core obligations* (kernverplichtingen) hebben om het recht op gezondheidszorg te respecteren, te beschermen, en te verwezenlijken. Deze *core obligations* omvatten enerzijds kernverplichtingen met onmiddellijk effect, die relatief kostenvrij zijn en in het algemeen kunnen worden gerealiseerd met minimale inzet van middelen. Anderzijds zijn er niet-derogeerbare (*non-derogable*) kernverplichtingen; Staten kunnen in geen geval hun niet-naleving van deze verplichtingen rechtvaardigen met een beroep op onvoldoende middelen. Samen met de *core obligations* kiest deze studie *availability* (beschikbaarheid), *accessibility* (toegankelijkheid), *accountability* (verantwoording afleggen) en *participation* (participatie) als standaarden voor het beoordelen van de juridische en beleidsmatige toezeggingen van China met betrekking tot het realiseren van het recht op gezondheidszorg.

Hoofdstuk 3 voert een systematisch onderzoek uit naar de wettelijke maatregelen die China heeft genomen om het recht op gezondheidszorg in zijn nationale rechtssysteem te verwezenlijken. Over het algemeen heeft China waar nodig nationale wetgeving aangenomen of gewijzigd om te voldoen aan zijn verplichtingen onder het recht op gezondheidszorg. Zowel de Chinese grondwet als nationale wetgeving bevatten expliciete verwijzingen naar non-discriminatie en gelijkheid. Een handvol gezondheid gerelateerde wetten bevat ook relevante bepalingen met betrekking tot elementen van andere niet-derogeerbare kernverplichtingen. Daarnaast zijn er bepalingen met betrekking tot rechtsmiddelen om schendingen van gezondheid gerelateerde rechten te herstellen, hoewel deze niet volledig gelijkwaardig zijn aan het recht op gezondheidszorg *per se*. Desalniettemin worden er nog steeds leemtes ontdekt tussen *de jure* en *de facto* implementatie van het recht op gezondheidszorg. Er is geen enkele wettelijke bepaling die duidelijk voorziet in essentiële primaire gezondheidszorg en essentiële geneesmiddelen, twee componenten van de kernverplichtingen van het recht op gezondheidszorg. Daarnaast blijven de bepalingen omtrent het recht op medische behandeling en de bescherming van financiële risico's dubbelzinnig, wat in de praktijk kan leiden tot uitdagingen als het gaat om implementatie. Bovendien benadrukken de meeste wetten niet wat voor soort essentiële gezondheidszorg de Chinese overheid moet leveren om gelijke toegang voor alle rechthebbenden te waarborgen. In dit licht bezien is het bestaande juridische kader in China over het algemeen slecht toegerust om het gezondheidszorgsysteem te reguleren.

Hoofdstuk 4 na bovengenoemde juridische benadering omtrent China's implementatie van het recht op gezondheidszorg richt hoofdstuk 4 zich op een evaluatie van China's beleidsverplichtingen ten aanzien van het recht op gezondheidszorg. China heeft de afgelopen decennia een breed scala aan nationaal gezondheidsbeleid opgesteld, en heeft aanzienlijke vooruitgang geboekt om *Universal Health Coverage* (UHC, universele dekking) van de gezondheidszorg te realiseren. Niet alle inspanningen van de Staat ten aanzien van UHC voldoen echter aan de vereisten van (kern)verplichtingen onder het recht op gezondheidszorg. Hoofdstuk 4 stelt dus een verfijning voor van UHC middels een samenbrengen van de kernverplichtingen met UHC. Deze benadering van UHC, waarbij UHC dus geïnterpreteerd wordt in het licht van de kernverplichtingen onder het recht op gezondheidszorg, vereist dat alle belanghebbenden betrokken worden bij de besluitvorming die plaatsvindt via een transparant en participatief proces. Bovendien moet rekening worden gehouden met de prioritaire gezondheidsbehoeften van kwetsbare en gemarginaliseerde groepen. Daarnaast moet de verstrekking van essentiële geneesmiddelen als niet-derogeerbare kernverplichting onder het recht op gezondheidszorg de hoogste prioriteit genieten bij het opstellen van beleid. Verder vereist het non-discriminatiebeginsel dat de door UHC geboden bescherming verder reikt dan bescherming tegen financiële discriminatie, en alle vormen van discriminatie uitsluit bij de toegang tot gezondheidszorg. Indien het Chinese beleid in dit kader wordt bekeken, dan blijkt dat sommige vereisten van het recht op gezondheidszorg onvervuld blijven ondanks China's inspanningen om UHC realiseren. Dergelijke eisen omvatten ongelijkheden tussen mensen met verschillende sociaaleconomische status en tussen landelijke en stedelijke gebieden, waardoor er dus *de facto* discriminatie bij gelijke toegang tot gezondheidszorg plaatsvindt.

Hoewel er tal van benaderingen zijn, kiest deze studie ervoor om de resterende uitdagingen met betrekking tot China's effectieve en volledige realisatie van het recht op gezondheidszorg door de bril van *accountability* te bekijken en onderzoekt deze studie of de verplichting tot *accountability* de realisatie van het recht op gezondheidszorg in China zou kunnen bevorderen.

Deel 2 van deze studie legt de basis voor de discussie over verantwoording in de Chinese context. **Hoofdstuk 5** onderscheidt en definieert *accountability* vanuit een mensenrechtenperspectief. Een op mensenrechten gebaseerde interpretatie van *accountability* impliceert een dynamisch en interactief proces waarin Staatsactoren en toezichthoudende instellingen verplicht zijn om rechthebbenden te informeren over hun (in het verleden of in de toekomst genomen) beslissingen en acties, om deze uit te leggen en te rechtvaardigen, en om positieve of negatieve gevolgen hiervan te ondervinden. In geval van schending van het recht op gezondheid moeten rechthebbenden toegang hebben tot juridische of andere effectieve rechtsmiddelen. Deze aspecten vormen tezamen de vier bouwstenen van een constructief proces van verantwoording: *monitoring* (controle), *judgment* (beoordeling), *consequences* (gevolgen) en *remedies* (rechtsmiddelen). Dit hoofdstuk identificeert tevens drie elementen van (op recht op gezondheid gebaseerde) verantwoordelijkheid: *responsibility* (verantwoordelijkheid voor de genomen beslissingen en acties), *answerability* (verantwoording afleggen voor deze beslissingen en acties), en *enforcement* (handhaving ter verwezenlijking van het recht op gezondheid). Het eerste onderdeel, namelijk het nemen van verantwoordelijkheid voor genomen beslissingen (*responsibility*), kan bestaande standaarden voor verantwoordelijk gedrag verfijnen en vormt daarmee een belangrijk onderdeel van het juridische kader van het recht op gezondheid. Voorts worden in dit hoofdstuk verschillende typen van *accountability* geanalyseerd, die in twee categorieën kunnen worden ingedeeld: de eerste categorie omvat verticale, horizontale, en diagonale *accountability*. De tweede categorie bestaat uit juridische, semi-juridische, politieke, administratieve en sociaal-maatschappelijke *accountability*.

Hoofdstuk 6 biedt een conceptuele verduidelijking van het verschil tussen de begrippen *accountability* en *accountability mechanism*, en beantwoordt vier vragen: (1) wie is *accountable*; (2) waarvoor zijn deze actoren *accountable*; (3) aan wie zijn deze actoren verantwoording verschuldigd; en (4) hoe kunnen deze actoren aansprakelijk worden gesteld? *Accountable* actoren (1) zijn de Staat zelf, evenals openbare instellingen en openbare functionarissen die door de Staat belast zijn met *accountability* voor de verwezenlijking van het recht op gezondheid (d.w.z. Staatsactoren). Voorts (2) zijn Staatsactoren *accountable* voor hun verplichtingen onder het recht op gezondheidszorg. Het internationale mensenrechten-kader bevat duidelijke normen en beginselen voor het respecteren, beschermen en verwezenlijken van het recht op gezondheid, met inbegrip van kernverplichtingen, verplichtingen van vergelijkbare prioriteit, verplichtingen tot geleidelijke verwezenlijking en enkele algemene verplichtingen. Ten derde zijn Staatsactoren *accountable* zowel richting rechthebbenden als toezichthoudende instellingen (bijvoorbeeld de rechtbank en de nationale ombudsman voor de mensenrechten). Ten vierde kunnen Staatsactoren *accountable* worden gehouden door verschillende *accountability mechanisms*. Hoofdstuk 6 bespreekt uitgebreid de interne mechanismen voor het genereren van *judicial* (gerechtelijke), *quasi-judicial* (quasi-gerechtelijke), *political* (politieke), *administrative* (administratieve) en *social* (sociaal-maatschappelijke) *accountability* voor de implementatie van het recht op gezondheid. Het onderzoekt ook een handvol internationale toezichtmechanismen, en constateert dat internationale mechanismen een relatief zwakke handhavingscapaciteit hebben.

Deel 3 is gebaseerd op de hypothese dat *accountability* kan bestaan in de afwezigheid van competitieve en vrije verkiezingen, en onderzoekt of en hoe de plicht tot verantwoording afleggen het recht op gezondheidszorg zou kunnen bevorderen in het kader van de unieke politieke, juridische en sociaal-maatschappelijke constellatie van China. **Hoofdstuk 7** past het analytische raamwerk van *right to health-based accountability* toe op de Chinese context om aldus verbanden te leggen tussen verschillende actoren die betrokken zijn bij de Chinese gezondheidssector, en om te beoordelen in hoeverre deze actoren in staat zijn om verantwoordelijke actoren (zoals Staatsactoren) ter verantwoording te roepen via verschillende vormen van binnenlandse *accountability mechanisms*. Al met al is het niet gemakkelijk om in een niet-electoraal regime als China *political accountability* uit te oefenen, maar er is wel een breed scala aan *accountability mechanisms* om de Staatsactoren ter verantwoording te roepen. Via juridische, quasi-juridische, politieke, administratieve en sociaal-maatschappelijke verantwoordingsmechanismen kunnen rechthebbenden hun recht op gezondheidszorg (of op zijn minst sommige elementen van het recht op gezondheidszorg) opeisen en remedie zoeken voor schendingen van dit recht. Deze *accountability mechanisms*, met name de sociaal-maatschappelijke verantwoordingsmechanismen, zijn tot op zekere hoogte onderling afhankelijk en kunnen elkaar op verscheidene wijzen versterken.

In het algemeen heeft het genereren van *accountability* voor het bevorderen van het recht op gezondheidszorg in China twee doelen. Het eerste en meest fundamentele doel is om schendingen van het recht op gezondheidszorg te adresseren, wat neerkomt op *ex post* verantwoording. We zien dat juridische *accountability mechanisms* met een hoge handhavingscapaciteit in China aanwezig zijn die individuen in de gelegenheid stellen om hun gezondheid gerelateerde rechten te claimen. Desalniettemin zijn de beschikbaarheid, kwaliteit en andere dimensies van het recht op gezondheidszorg nog steeds moeilijk af te dwingen voor de nationale rechter. Het is nog steeds moeilijk, al dan niet onmogelijk, om systematische tekortkomingen aan te kaarten voor *judicial accountability mechanisms*. Bovendien, vanwege een aantal beperkingen, worden juridische verantwoordingsmechanismen vaak als laatste redmiddel gezien in China. Er is ook een handvol *quasi-judicial* en *political accountability mechanisms* beschikbaar om Staatsactoren ter verantwoording te roepen, en schendingen van het recht op gezondheidszorg recht te zetten. Deze mechanismen blijven in de praktijk echter nog relatief zwak en er moet nog veel werk worden verzet om deze mechanismen goed te laten functioneren. *Administrative accountability mechanisms*, met een hoge mate van handhaving, zijn zeer krachtige mechanismen om een interne, top-down controle uit te oefenen op mogelijke schendingen en het misbruik van Staatsgezag en/of beschikbare middelen in de gezondheidszorg. Indien deze *administrative accountability mechanisms* de interactie zoeken met andere verantwoordingsmechanismen, in het bijzonder *social accountability mechanisms*, kunnen zij belangrijke instrumenten worden ter bevordering van het recht op gezondheidszorg in de Chinese context. *Social accountability mechanisms* zoals de media (e.g. Sino Weibo) maken het voor de hele samenleving mogelijk om Staatsactoren te disciplineren en te dwingen tot het nakomen van hun verplichtingen onder het recht op gezondheidszorg, en kunnen benadeelde rechthebbenden beter in staat stellen verhaal te halen. Niettemin hebben ze een relatief lage handhavingscapaciteit. Daarom worden *social accountability mechanisms* effectiever in China wanneer ze worden versterkt door andere vormen van *accountability mechanisms*. Hoewel *social accountability* vooral vraag-gestuurd is en tot individuele verhaalmogelijkheden leidt, heeft deze vorm van *accountability* in het bijzonder de potentie om systematische tekortkomingen in de gezondheidszorg te adresseren in het streven naar een synergetische Staat-samenleving benadering.

Het tweede doel van *accountability* is om vast te stellen welke aspecten van wetgeving, beleid en dienstverlening goed functioneren, zodat ze kunnen worden herhaald, en welke aspecten herzien moeten worden (dat wil zeggen *ex ante accountability*). Met andere woorden, mechanismen voor *ex ante accountability* kunnen systematische zwakheden identificeren bij het controleren van machtsmisbruik en het waarborgen van naleving van het recht op gezondheid standaarden, en kunnen Staatsactoren ter verantwoording roepen voordat een (negatief) resultaat in de praktijk plaatsvindt. De meeste bestaande *accountability mechanisms* in China zijn gericht op herstel *ex post* en sancties, en slechts enkele bieden *ex ante*-preventie. De rechterlijke macht in China kan alleen rechterlijke toetsing van het regelgevingsdocument bieden als daar een beweerdelijk illegale administratieve handeling op is gebaseerd. De bevoegdheid om niet-rechterlijke toetsing van de grondwettigheid en wettigheid van wetten, bestuurlijke voorschriften en regels (politieke verantwoordelijkheid) uit te oefenen, berust bij het Permanente Comité van het Nationale Volkscongres (NPCSC), maar blijft in de praktijk grotendeels retorisch. Desalniettemin staan *social accountability mechanisms* de samenleving toe om deel te nemen aan het proces van gezondheid gerelateerde besluitvorming en dienstverlening. Dit betekent dat de meest urgente gezondheidsbehoeften van de gehele bevolking in overweging zullen worden genomen bij de goedkeuring van gezondheidswetten en -beleid, waardoor het zorgstelsel meer verantwoording aflegt.

In het licht van de voorgaande analyses kan worden opgemerkt dat een aantal structurele tekortkomingen de inspanningen van de Chinese overheid in de weg hebben gestaan om iedereen gelijke toegang tot gezondheidszorg te garanderen. De Chinese regering heeft duidelijk haar politieke wil kenbaar gemaakt om de gezondheid van haar bevolking te verbeteren. De vraag rijst dan hoe de resterende uitdagingen aangepakt dienen te worden, die de volledige realisatie van het recht op gezondheidszorg in de praktijk ondermijnen. **Hoofdstuk 8** biedt een reeks aanbevelingen om structurele tekortkomingen aan te pakken, en om het recht op gezondheidszorg in China verder te bevorderen.

De eerste en belangrijkste aanbeveling is om expliciet een individueel recht op gezondheid (szorg) te garanderen in de conceptwet BHL. Zoals het er nu uitziet, vindt grondwettelijke toetsing aan het recht op gezondheidszorg zelden of nooit plaats. Het Chinese gezondheidsrechtelijke systeem is gefragmenteerd van aard; componenten van het recht op gezondheidszorg worden beschermd door afzonderlijke gezondheid gerelateerde wetten. De meeste van deze wetten leggen de Staat de plicht op om gelijke toegang tot gezondheidszorg te garanderen zonder de consequenties voor de Staat te verduidelijken, indien hij daarin faalt. Er zijn maar weinig gezondheid gerelateerde wetten die gezondheidszorg erkennen als een recht dat iedereen kan opeisen. Dit maakt het moeilijk voor rechthebbenden om hun recht op gezondheidszorg voor de rechter op te eisen, en schadevergoeding te claimen als overheidsinstanties hun verplichtingen niet nakomen. Daarom is het noodzakelijk dat de conceptwet BHL duidelijk aan iedereen het recht op gezondheidszorg verleent, zodat de juridische instanties rechtsmiddelen kunnen bieden voor systematische schendingen, een benadering die zal leiden tot een betere bescherming van het recht op gezondheidszorg.

De tweede aanbeveling heeft betrekking op de kerninhoud van het recht op gezondheidszorg die in de conceptwet BHL zou moeten worden gedefinieerd. Hoewel de meeste Chinese wetenschappers het erover eens zijn dat de BHL een artikel of sectie moet bevatten met betrekking tot het recht op gezondheidszorg, verschillen zij van mening over de kerninhoud / componenten van het recht op gezondheidszorg die in dit wetsontwerp zouden moeten worden verankerd. Deze studie suggereert dat de BHL die kernverplichtingen van het recht op gezondheidszorg moet opnemen, waaraan voldaan moet worden ongeacht de beperkte middelen van China. Ten eerste dient de BHL de Staat op te leggen om toegang tot essentiële primaire gezondheidszorg (inclusief essentiële geneesmiddelen) te verzekeren. Deze zorg dient zodanig betaalbaar te zijn dat het patiënten geen financiële problemen oplevert, hetzij kosteloos te zijn. Essentiële eerstelijnsgezondheidszorg dient te beantwoorden aan de meest urgente gezondheidsbehoeften van de gehele bevolking, met bijzondere aandacht voor kwetsbare of gemarginaliseerde groepen. Dit kan worden bevorderd door mechanismen in te stellen die voorzien in *public participation* (publieke inspraak) in alle besluitvorming op het gebied van gezondheid, hetgeen eveneens een structurele en procedurele kernverplichting is. Ten tweede moet de BHL structurele en procedurele (kern)verplichtingen formuleren. Het zou voor de BHL gunstig zijn om te voorzien in aanvullende verplichtingen, of de reikwijdte van de gezondheidszorg (of meer specifiek de beschikbaarheid, toegankelijkheid, aanvaardbaarheid en kwaliteit van de gezondheidszorg die door de Staat moet worden verstrekt) te bepalen, maar de BHL moet op zijn minst de kernverplichtingen van het recht op gezondheidszorg omvatten.

De laatste aanbeveling werpt een licht op een toenemende mate van *accountability*. Zoals besproken, lijden de bestaande *accountability mechanisms* in China aan enkele tekortkomingen. Hoewel de BHL misschien niet in staat is om elk probleem aan te pakken, kan het de verantwoordelijkheden van verschillende actoren in de gezondheidssector duidelijk definiëren. Het huidige Chinese juridische systeem geeft niet systematisch uitdrukking aan recht op gezondheidsnormen en -procedures. Als deze normen en procedures duidelijk zouden worden vastgesteld in het kader van de BHL, zou het gemakkelijker zijn om Staatsactoren verantwoordelijk te houden voor het recht op gezondheid. Bovendien kunnen individuen zich niet rechtstreeks beroepen voor de Chinese rechter op grondwettelijke bepalingen, en bestaat er geen wet die expliciet voorziet in het recht op gezondheidszorg; daarom zou het voor de effectiviteit van de BHL positief zijn indien het rechthebbenden expliciet een recht op gezondheidszorg verleent, zodat zij beter in staat worden gesteld rechtsmiddelen te zoeken voor schendingen van het recht op gezondheidszorg. De BHL moet ook de *ex ante accountability* versterken om systematische tekortkomingen aan te pakken of het beleid en structurele veranderingen beïnvloeden. Dit zou kunnen worden bereikt door de rechterlijke macht de bevoegdheid te verlenen rechterlijke toetsing te verrichten van de geldigheid van gezondheid gerelateerde voorschriften, regels en beleidsmaatregelen die verder gaan dan regelgevende documenten. Bovendien zou de BHL de *public participation* (via verschillende *accountability mechanisms*) moeten institutionaliseren in alle besluitvorming op gezondheidsgebied en in de verlening van gezondheidsdiensten, waardoor de naleving door Staatsactoren van het recht op gezondheid en de *social accountability* worden verzekerd.

Al met al zijn er concrete (wettelijke en beleidsmatige) maatregelen genomen om geleidelijk het recht op gezondheidszorg in China te realiseren. Desalniettemin is er geen *one-size-fits-all* benadering; er blijven problemen bestaan in de voortgang die China boekt op weg naar de volledige verwezenlijking van dit recht. *Accountability*, een concept dat mensenrechten kracht bijzet, biedt de mogelijkheid om deze problemen te adresseren en kan een robuust instrument vormen voor het bevorderen van het recht op gezondheidszorg binnen de unieke juridische, politieke en sociaal-maatschappelijke Chinese context. Er zijn nog steeds uitdagingen bij het bereiken van de doelen van *accountabilty* in het gezondheidszorgsysteem. Niettemin hebben de verschillende voorbeelden van *accountability mechanisms* die in deze studie zijn besproken belangrijke implicaties voor het creëren van een meer *accountable* gezondheidszorgsysteem in China. Staten met een vergelijkbare juridische en politieke constellatie kunnen op basis van deze studie leren van China's ervaringen op dit terrein.

Selected Bibliography

Abiiro GA and De Allegri M, 'Universal Health Coverage from Multiple Perspectives: A Synthesis of Conceptual Literature and Global Debates' (2015) 15 BMC International Health and Human Rights 1.

Abrami R, Malesky E and Zheng Y, 'Accountability and Inequality in Single-Party Regimes: A Comparative Analysis of Vietnam and China' <https://wcfia.harvard.edu/files/wcfia/files/abrami_accountability.pdf> accessed 28 November 2017.

Ackerman JM, 'Social Accountability in the Public Sector: A Conceptual Discussion' (2005).

Ahl B, 'Chinese Law and International Treaties' (2009) 39 HKLJ 737.

Alston P and Ryan G, *International Human Rights: The Successor to International Human Rights in Context* (Oxford University Press 2012).

Atela M and Wafula F, 'Mapping Accountability Mechanisms: A Review of In-Country Accountability in Health Systems' (2015).

Aust A, *Modern Treaty Law and Practice* (Cambridge University Press 2007).

Backert LC, 'The Rule of Law, the Chinses Communist Party, and Ideological Campaigns: Sange Daibiao (the "Three Represents"), Socialist Rule of Law, and Modern Chinese Constitutionalism' (2006) 16 Journal of Transnational Law and Contemporary Problems 101.

——, 'Party, People, Government and State: On Constitutional Values and the Legitimacy of the Chinese State-Party Rule of Law System' (2012) 30 Boston University International Law Journal 331.

Backman G and others, 'Health Systems and the Right to Health: An Assessment of 194 Countries' (2008) 372 The Lancet 2047.

Balla SJ, 'Health System Reform and Political Participation on the Chinese Internet' (2014) 28 China Information 214.

Barber S and others, 'The Reform of the Essential Medicines System in China: A Comprehensive Approach to Universal Coverage' (2013) 3 (1) Journal of Global Health 1.

Bertot JC, Jaeger PT and Grimes JM, 'Using ICTs to Create a Culture of Transparency : E-Government and Social Media as Openness and Anti-Corruption Tools for Societies' (2010) 27 Government Information Quarterly 264.

Biddulph S, *The Stability Imperative: Human Rights and Law in China* (UBC Press 2015).

Biddulph S and others, 'Rule of Law with Chinese Characteristics: The Role of Campaigns in Lawmaking' (2012) 34 Law & Policy 373.

Bovens M, 'Analysing and Assessing Accountability: A Conceptual Framework' (2007) 13 European Law Journal 447.

——, 'New Forms of Accountability and EU-Governance' (2007) 5 Comparative European Politics 104.

——, 'Two Concepts of Accountability: Accountability as a Virtue and as a Mechanism' (2010) 33 West European Politics 946.

Braveman P and Gruskin S, 'Defining Equity in Health' (2003) 57 Journal of Epidemiology and Community Health 254.

——, 'Poverty, Equity, Human Rights and Health' in (2003) 81 (7) Bulletin of the World Health Organization 539.

Brinkerhoff D, 'Taking Account of Accountability: A Conceptual Overview and Strategic Options' (US Agency for International Development 2001) 1 <http://1qswp72wn11q9smtq15ccbuo.wpengine.netdna-cdn.com/wp-content/uploads/2011/07/IPC_Taking_Account_of_Accountability.pdf> accessed 28 November 2017.

——, 'Accountability and Health Systems: Overview, Framework, and Strategies' (Partners for Health Reformplus 2003).

——, 'Accountability and Health Systems: Toward Conceptual Clarity and Policy Relevance' (2004) 19 Health Policy and Planning 371.

Burns JP and Zhou Z, 'Performance Management in the Government of the People's Republic of China: Accountability and Control in the Implementation of Public Policy' (2012) 2 OECD Journal on Budgeting 1.

Byrnes A and Renshaw C, 'Within the State' in Daniel Moeckli and others (eds), *International Human Rights Law* (2nd Edn Oxford University Press 2014).

Cai Y, *Collective Resistance in China: Why Popular Protests Succeed or Fail?* (Stanford University Press 2010).

Center for Economic and Social Rights, 'The OPERA Framework: Assessing Compliance with the Obligation to Fulfill Economic, Social and Cultural Rights' 1 <http://cesr.org/downloads/the.opera.framework.pdf> accessed 28 November 2017.

Chan HS and Gao J, 'Performance Management in Chinese local governments' (2008) 41 Chinese Law and Government 1.

Chapman AR, 'Core Obligations Related to the Right to Health' in Audrey R Chapman and Sage Russell (eds), *Core Obligations: Building a Framework for Economic, Social and Cultural Rights* (Intersentia 2002).

——, 'Assessing the Universal Health Coverage Target in the Sustainable Development Goals from a Human Rights Perspective' (2016) 16 BMC International Health and Human Rights 1.

Chapman AR and Russell S, 'Introduction' in Audrey R Chapman and Sage Russell (eds), *Core Obligations: Building a Framework for Economic, Social and Cultural Rights* (Intersentia 2002).

Chen H, 'Jiben Yiliao Fuwu Fazhihua Yanjiu [Research on the Legalization of Basic Medical Services]' (2014) 2 Falv Kexue – Xibei Zhengfa Daxue Xuebao [Science of Law - Journal of Northwest University of Political Science and Law] 73.

Chen PD and Wu D, 'China's Evolution in Progressively Realizing the Right to Health' in in José Zuniga, Stephen P Marks and Lawrence O Gostin (eds), *Advancing the Human Right to Health* (Oxford University Press 2013).

Ciongaru E, The Monistic and Dualistic Theory in European Law <www.ugb.ro/Juridica/Issue1EN/10_Teoria_monista_si_dualista_in_dreptul_europeanCiongaruEN.pdf> accessed 28 November 2017.

Connors and Schmidt M, 'Protection' in Moeckli Daniel and others (eds), *International Human Rights Law* (Oxford University Press 2013).

Coronel S, 'Corruption and the Watchdog Role of the News Media' in Pippa Norris (ed), *Public Sentinel: News Media and Governance Reform* (The World Bank 2010).

Craven MCR, 'The Domestic Application of the International Covenant on Economic, Social and Cultural Rights' (1993) 40 Netherlands International Law Review 367.

Dalton RE, 'National Treaty Law and Practice: United States' in Duncan and others (eds), *National Treaty Law and Practice* (Martinus Nijhoff Publishers 2005).

Daniels N, *Just Health : Meeting Health Needs Fairly* (Cambridge University Press 2008).

Department for International Development, 'Accountability Briefing Note' (2008).

Diamond L, Plattner MF and Schedler A, 'Introduction' in Andreas Schedler, Larry Diamond and Marc F Plattner (eds), *The Self-restraining State: Power and Accountability in New Democracies* (Lynne Rienner Publishers 1999.

Distelhorst G, 'Publicity-Driven Accountability in China: Qualitative and Experimental Evidence' (2012) MIT Political Science Department Research Paper Working Paper 2012-24.

Dubnick MJ, 'Seeking Salvation for Accountability' paper presented at th Annual Meeting of the American Political Science Association (2002) <http://mjdubnick.dubnick.net/papersrw/2002/salv2002.pdf> accessed 28 November 2017.

Forman L and others, 'What Could a Strengthened Right to Health Bring to the Post-2015 Health Development Agenda? Interrogating the Role of Minimum Core Concept in Advancing Essential Global Health Needs' (2013) 13 BMC International Health and Human Rights 1.

——, 'Conceptualising Minimum Core Obligations Under the Right to Health: How Should We Define and Implement the "Morality of the Depths"' (2016) 20

International Journal of Human Rights 531.
——, 'What Do Core Obligations under the Right to Health Bring to Universal Health Coverage' (2016) 18 Health and Human Rights 23.
Forman L and Bomze S, 'International Human Rights Law and the Right to Health: An Overview of Legal Standards and Accountability Mechanisms' in Gunilla Backman (ed) *The Right to Health: Theory and Practice* (Studentlitteratur 2012).
Freeman LP, 'Human Rights, Constructive Accountability and Maternal Mortality in the Dominican Republic: A Commentary' (2003) 82 International Journal of Gynaecology and Obstetrics 111.

Gailmard S, 'Accountability and Principal–Agent Theory' in Mark Bovens, Robert E Goodin and Thomas Schillemans (eds), *The Oxford Handbook of Public Accountability* (Oxford University Press 2014).
Gao J, 'Performance Management in the People's Republic of China During the Market Reform Era: A Case Study of Two Counties in Shaanxi Province' (unpublished PhD dissertation, City University of Hong Kong).
Gao JW and others, 'Shanghaishi 37 suo Yiliao Jigou he 124 wei Huanzhe Yihuanshuangfang Xieshang Jiejue Jiufen Xianzhuang Diaocha Fenxi [Survey and Analysis on Consultation Settlement of 124 Doctor-patient Disputes in 37 Medical Institutions in Shanghai]' in (2011) 15 Zhongguo Yiyuan [Chinese Hospitals] 47.
Goetz AM, 'Introduction' in Anne Marie Goetz and Rob Jenkins (eds), *Reinventing Accountability: Making Democracy Work for Human Development* (Palgrave Macmillan UK 2005).
Gostin LO, *Global Health Law* (Harvard University Press 2014).
Gostin LO and others, Advancing the Right to Health: The Vital Role of Law (WHO 2017).

Han Y, 'Legal Protection of Human Rights in China' in Peter R Baehr and others (eds), *Human Rights: Chinese and Dutch Perspectives* (Martinus Nijhoff Publishers 1996).
Harrington J and Stuttaford M, 'Introduction' in John Harrington and Maria Stuttaford (eds), *Global Health and Human Rights:Legal and Philosophical Perspectives* (Routledge 2010).
Hendriks A, 'The Right to Health in National and International Jurisprudence' (1998) 5 European Journal of Health Law 389.
Ho CS, 'Health Rights at the Juncture between State and Market: The People's Republic of China in Colleen M. Flood and Aeyal Gross (eds), *The Right to Health at the Public/Private Divide: A Global Comparative Study* (Cambridge University Press 2014).

Hogerzeil H, Samson M and Casanova J, 'Ruling for Access: Leading Court Cases in Developing Countries on Access to Essential Medicines as Part of the Fulfilment of the Right to Health' (WHO 2004).

Hogerzeil H and others, 'Is Access to Essential Medicines as Part of the Fulfilment of the Right to Health Enforceable throught the courts?' (2006) 368 The Lancet 305.

Hsiao W and others, Universal Health Coverage: The Case of China (UNRISD Working Paper No. 2014-15) 15.

Hu S, 'Essential Medicine Policy in China: Pros and Cons' (2013) 16 Journal of Medical Economics 289.

Huber M and others, 'How Should We Define Health?' (2011) 343 BMJ <http://www.bmj.com/content/343/bmj.d4163> accessed 28 November 2017.

Hunt P and Backman G, 'Health Systems and the Right to the Highest Attainable Standard of Health' (2008) 10 Health and Human Rights 81.

Hunt P and others, 'Implementation of Economic, Social and Cultural Rights' in Scott Sheeran and Rodley Nigel (eds), *Routledge Handbook of International Human Rights Law* (Routledge 2013).

Jayawickrama N, *The Judicial Application of Human Rights Law: National, Regional and International Jurisprudence* (Cambridge University Press 2002).

Jiao H, 'Lun Zuowei Jiben Quanli de Jiankangquan [The Right to Health as a Fundamental Right]' (2010) 1 Zhongguo Zhengfa Daxue Xuebao [Journal of China University of Political Science and Law] 12.

Kasuya Y and Takahashi Y, 'Streamlining Accountability: Concepts, Subtypes, and Empirical Analyses' 2 <www.ssrn.com/abstract=2493654> accessed 28 November 2017.

Keith L, 'Human Rights Instruments' in Peter Cane and Herbert Kritzer (eds), *The Oxford Handbook of Empirical Legal Research* (Oxford University Press 2010).

Killion UM, 'China's Amended Constitution: Quest for Liberty and Independent Judicial Review' (2005) 4 Washington University Global Studies Law Review 43.

Kinney ED, 'The International Human Right to Health: What Does This Mean for Our Nation and World' (2001) 1457 (34) Indian Law Review 1457.

Kinney ED and Clark BA, 'Provisions for Health and Health Care in the Constitutions of the Countries of the World' (2004) 37 Cornell International Law Journal 285.

Korolev A, 'Deliberative Democracy Nationwide? - Evaluating Deliberativeness of Healthcare Reform in China' (2014) Journal of Chinese Political Science 151.

Lei H, 'Moral Community of Weisheng: Contesting Hygiene in Republican China' (2009) 3 (4) East Asian Science, Technology and Society: An International Journal 475.

Li JZ and Guo S, 'China' in Dinah Shelton (ed), *International Law and Domestic Legal Systems: Incorporation, Transformation, and Persuasion* (Oxford University Press 2011).

Li Y, *The Judicial System and Reform in Post-Mao China: Stumbling Towards Justice* (Routledge 2014).

Li Z, 'The Role of Domestic Courts in the Adjudication of International Human Rights: A Survey of the Practice and Problems in China' In Benedetto Conforti and other (eds), *Enforcing International Human Rights Treaties in Domestic Courts* (Martinus Hijhoff Publishers 1997).

Liang L and Langenbrunner J, The Long March to Universal Coverage: Lessons from China (The World Bank 2013).

Liebman B, 'Watchdog or Demagogue? The Media in the Chinese Legal System' (2005) 105 (1) Columbia Law Review 1.

——, 'The Media and the Courts: Towards Competitive Supervision' (2011) 208 The China Quarterly 833.

Liu C, 'Lun "Jiben Yiliao Weisheng Fa" de Mingcheng, Dingwei yu Jibenzhidu [Discussing the Title, Positioning and Structure of the Basic Health and Medical Law]' 2017 (4) Faxue Zazhi [Law Science Magazine] 67.

Liu X and Qin H, 'Weishengfa Lilun Tixi Goujian de Qianti [Preconditions for the Construction of the Theoretical System of Health Law]' (2015) 4 Xingzhengfa Yanjiu [Research of Administrative Law] 55.

Liu Y, 'Reforming China's Health Care: For the People, by the People?' (2009) 373 The Lancet 281.

Lo VI, 'Towards the Rule of Law: Judicial Lawmaking in China' (2016) 28 Bond Law Review 149.

Ma C, 'Gonggong Zhengce Hefaxing Gongji Jizhi yu Zouxiang [The Transformation of the Legitimacy Supply Mechanism of Public Policy]' (2012) 2 Faxue Yanjiu [Legal Research].

Ma J, 'The Dilemma of Developing Financial Accountability without Election - A Study of China's Recent Budget Reforms' (2009) 68 The Australian Journal Public Administration s62 - s72.

——, 'The Rise of Social Accountability in China' (2012) 71 The Australian Journal of Public Administration 111

MA Z, 'The Structure and Roles of China's Party-State System in Industrial Relations: An Updated Review' (2009) 7 China: An International Journal 370.

Malena C and others, 'Social Accountability: An Introduction to the Concept and Emerging Practice' (Draft paper prepared for the World Bank 2004) 3.

Mao W and Chen W, 'The Zero Mark-up Policy for Essential Medicines at Primary Level Facilities' in Improving Health System Efficiency (WHO 2015) 4.

Marks SP, 'The Emergence and Scope of the Human Right to Health' in José Zuniga, Stephen P Marks and Lawrence O Gostin (eds), *Advancing the Human Right to Health* (Oxford University Press 2013).
Meier BM, 'Global Health Governance and the Contentious Politics of Human Rights: Mainstreaming the Right to Health for Public Health Advancement' (2010) 46 Stanford Journal of International Law 1.
Meng Q and others, 'People's Republic of China: Health System Review' (2015) 5 Health Systems in Transistion.
——, 'Consolidating the Social Health Insurance Schemes in China: Towards an Equitable and Efficient Health System' (2015) 386 The Lancet 1484.
Meng Q and Xu L, 'Monitoring and Evaluating Progress towards Universal Health Coverage in China' (2014) 11 PLOS Medicine 1.
Morris RJ, 'China's Marbury: Qi Yuling v. Chen Xiaoqi - The Once and Future Trial of Both Education & Constitutionalization' (2012) 2 Tsinghua China Law Review 273.
Mulgan R, *Holding Power to Account: Accountability in Modern Democracies* (Palgrave Macmillan UK 2003).

Norris P, 'Watchdog Journalism' in Mark Bovens, Robert E Goodin and Thomas Schillemans (eds), *The Oxford Handbook of Public Accountability* (Oxford University Press 2014).
Nygren-Krug H, 'The Right to Health: From Concept to Practice' in in José Zuniga, Stephen P Marks and Lawrence O Gostin (eds), *Advancing the Human Right to Health* (Oxford University Press 2013).

O'Donnell G, 'Horizontal Accountability in New Democracies' in Andreas Schedler, Larry Diamond and Marc F Plattner (eds), *The Self-restraining State: Power and Accountability in New Democracies* (Lynne Rienner Publishers 1999).
OHCHR, 'The Major Universal Human Rights Instruments and the Mechanisms for Their Implementations' in *Human Rights in the Administration of Justice: A Manual on Human Rights for Judges, Prosecutors and Lawyers* (United Nations Publication 2003).
——, 'Claiming the Millennium Development Goals : A Human Rights Approach' (2008).
OHCHR and Center for Economic and Social Rights, 'Who Will Be Accountable? Human Rights and the Post-2015 Development Agenda' (2013).
OHCHR and International Bar Association, 'Human Rights in the Administration of Justice: A Manual on Human Rights for Judges, Prosecutors and Lawyers' (2003) <http://www.ohchr.org/Documents/Publications/training9Titleen.pdf> accessed 28 November 2017
OHCHR and WHO, 'Factsheet No. 31: The Right to Health' (June 2008).

Ooms G and others , 'Universal Health Coverage Anchored in the Right to Health' (2013) 91 Bull World Health Organ 2.

——, 'Is Universal Health Coverage the Practical Expression of the Right to Health Care' (2014) 14 (3) BMC International Health & Human Rights 1.

Peerenboom R, *China's Long March toward Rule of Law* (Cambridge University Press 2002).

Pelizzo R and Stapenhurst F, *Government Accountability and Legislative Oversight* (Routledge 2014).

Perehudoff K, 'Health, Human Rights and National Constitutions' (WHO 2008).

Potts H, 'Accountability and the Right to the Highest Attainable Standard of Health' (University of Essex Human Rights Centre 2008) <http://repository.essex.ac.uk/9717/1/accountability-right-highest-attainable-standard-health.pdf> accessed 28 November 2017.

——, 'Participation and the Right to the Highest Attainable Standard of Health' (University of Essex 2008) <http://repository.essex.ac.uk/9714/1/participation-right-highest-attainable-standard-health.pdf> accessed 28 November 2017.

Qiu S and MacNaughton G, 'Mechanisms of Accountability for the Realization of the Right to Health in China' (2017) 19 Health and Human Rights Journal 279.

Riedel E, 'The Human Right to Health: Conceptual Foundations' in Andrew Clapham and others (eds), *Realizing the Right to Health* (Rüffer&Rub 2009).

Roberts MJ and others, 'Disaggregating the Universal Health Coverage Cube: Putting Equity in the Picture' (2015) 1 Health Systems & Reform 22.

Rogaski R, *Hygienic Modernity: Meanings of Health and Disease in Treaty-Port China* (University of California Press 2004).

Rumbold B, 'Universal Health Coverage, Priority Setting, and the Human Right to Health' (26 April 2017) The Lancet Viewpoint 1.

San Giorgi M, *The Human Right to Equal Access to Health Care* (Intersentia 2012).

Sandhu PK, 'A Legal Right to Health Care: What Can the United States Learn from Foreign Models of Health Rights Jurisprudence?' (2007) 95 California Law Review 1151.

Schedler A, 'Conceptualizing Accountability' in Andreas Schedler, Larry Diamond and Marc F Plattner (eds), *The Self-restraining State: Power and Accountability in New Democracies* (Lynne Rienner Publishers 1999).

Schoukens P, 'The Right to Access Health Care: Health Care According to International and European Social Security Law Instruments' in Andre den Exter (ed), *International Health Law: Solidarity and Justice in Health Care* (Maklu 2008)

Shi D and others, 'Goujian Woguo Gonggong Weisheng Falv Tixi de Taolun [Discussion on the Construction of China's Public Health Law System)' (2004) 1 Zhongguo Gonggong Weisheng [Chinese Public Health] 80.
Sloss D, 'Treaty Enforcement in Domestic Courts: A Comparative Analysis' in David Sloss (ed), *The Role of Domestic Courts in Treaty Enforcement: A Comparative Study* (Cambridge University Press 2009).
——, 'Domestic Application of Treaties' in Hollis Duncan (ed), *The Oxford Guide to Treaties* (Oxford University Press 2011).
Stuttaford M, 'Methods in Health and Human Rights Research' in Fons Coomans, Fred Grünfeld and Menno Kamminga (eds), *Methods of Human Rights Research* (Intersentia 2009).
Sun J and others, 'Weisheng Lifa de Guoji Jingyan dui Woguo de Qishi [International Experiences and Their Implication for China's Essential Health Law]' (2016) 9 Zhongguo Weisheng Zhengce Yanjiu [Chinese Journal of Health Policy] 66.
Sun P, *Human Rights Protection System in China* (Springer 2014).

Tang S and others, 'Tackling the Challenges to Health Equity in China' (2008) 372 The Lancet 1493.
Teitelbaum JB and Wilensky SE, *Essentials of Health Policy and Law* (Jones and Bartlett 2007).
Theo O, 'Austria and Article 6 of the European Convention on Human Rights' (1990) 1 European Journal of International Law 286.
Tobin J, *The Right to Health in International Law* (Oxford University Press 2012).
Toebes B, *The Right to Health as a Human Right in International Law* (Intersentia/Hart 1999).
——, 'Health and Human Rights: In Searching of the Legal Dimension' (2015) 9 Human Rights & International Legal Discourse 212.
Toebes B and San Giorgi M, 'Dutch Realities: Evaluating Health Care Reform in the Netherlands from a Human Rights Perspective' in Brigit Toebes and others (eds), *The Right to Health: A Multi-Country Study of Law, Policy and Practice* (Springer 2014).
Tong J and Sparks C, 'Investigative Journalism in China Today' (2009) 10 Journalism Studies 337.
Trevaskes S, 'Political Ideology, the Party, and Politicking: Justice System Reform in China' (2011) 37 Modern China 315.
Truex R, 'Consultative Authoritarianism and Its Limits' (2014) Comparative Political Studies 1.
Tsai LL, *Accountability without Democracy : Solidary Groups and Public Goods Provision in Rural China* (Cambridge University Press 2007).
Tyler ET, '"Small Places Close to Home": Toward a Health and Human Rights Strategy for the US' (2013) 15 Health and Human Rights 80.

UNDP, 'Fostering Social Accountability: From Principle to Practice' (2010).
UNDP, Reflecting on Social Accountability: Catalyzing Democratic Governance to Accelerate Progress towards the Millennium Development Goals' (2013).
UNICEF, 'Accountability for Children's Rights: With Special Attention to Social Accountability and Its Potential to Achieve Results and Equity for Children' (2015).

Van Dirk P, 'Domestic Status of Human-Rights Treaties and the Attitude of the Judiciary - The Dutch Case' in Manfred Nowak and others (eds), *Progress in the Spirit of Human Rights* (1988).
Venkatapuram S, 'Health, Vital Goals, and Central Human Capabilities' (2013) 27 Bioethics 271.
Voltmer K, 'The Media, Government Accountability, and Citizen Engagement' in Pippa Norris (ed), *Public Sentinel: News Media and Governance Reform* (The World Bank 2010).

Wang C, 'Lun Yi Baozhang Gongmin Jiankangquan wei Zongzhi Dazao Yiyao Weisheng Fazhi de Jianshi Jichu [Building Solid Foundation of Medicine and Health Care Law – Ruling to Guarantee Citizens' Health Righs]' (2016) 1 Yixue Yu Faxue [Medicine and Jurisprudence] 1.
——, 'Keyi Shixian de Mengxiang: Jianli Puhui Dazhong de Mianfei Jiben Yiliao Fuwu Zhidu [Available Dream: To Establish Universal and Free Basic Medical Service System]' (2017) 5 Yixue yu Faxue [Medicine and Jurisprudence] 1.
Wang DW, 'Right to Health Litigation in Brazil: The Problem and the Institutional Responses' (2015) 15 Human Rights Law Review 617.
Wang L, 'Rengequanfa de Fazhan yu Wanshan - Yi Renge Zunyan de Baohu wei Shijiao [Developing and Improving the Law of Personality - From the Perspective of Human Dignity Protection] (2012) 4 Science of Law 166.
WHO, 'The World Health Report: Primary Health Care: Now More than Ever' (WHO 2008).
WHO, 'The World Health Report: Health Systems Financing – The Path to Universal Coverage' (WHO 2010).
WHO, 'The World Health Report: Research for Universal Health Coverage' (WHO 2013).
WHO, 'Anchoring Universal Health Coverage in the Right to Health: What Difference Would It Make?' (2015).
Wilson S, *Tigers Without Teeth: The Pursuit of Justice in Contemporary China* (Rowman & Littlefield 2015).
Wim M, 'Chinese Practice in UN Treaty Monitoring Bodies: Principled Sovereignty and Slow Appreciation' in Hitoshi Nasu and Ben Saul (eds), *Human Rights in the Asia-Pacific Region: Towards Institution Building* (Routledge 2011).

Wu C, 'Yiliao Renquan zhi Fazhan yu Quanli Tixi [The Development of the Right to Health and its Right System]' (2007) 148 Taiwan Law Review 128.
——, *Zhongguo Weisheng Faxue* [Chinese Health Law] (Pecking Union Medical College Press 2006).

Xu G and Wang J, 'Jichu Yiliao Weisheng Fuwu Yinggai zai Zhongguo Xinyigai zhong Dedao Zhengque Lijie he Quanmian Shishi [Primary Health Care: A Concept to be Fully Understood and Implemented in Current China's Health Care Reform]' (2015) 18 (32) Zhongguo Quanke Yixue [Chinese General Practice] 389.
Xue H and Jin Q, 'International Treaties in the Chinese Domestic Legal System' (2009) 8 (2) Chinese Journal of International Law 299.
Xue H and others, 'National Treaty Law and Practice: China' in Duncan and others (eds), *National Treaty Law and Practice* (Martinus Nijhoff Publishers 2005).

Yamin AE, 'Beyond Compassion : The Central Role of Accountability in Applying a Human Rights Framework to Health' (2008) 10 Health and Human Rights 1.
Yang L, *Renquanfa [Law of Personality]* (China Legal Publishing House 2006).
Yang J, *Informal Payments and Regulations in China's Healthcare System: Red Packets and Institutional Reform* (Palgrave Macmillan 2017).
Yip W and others, 'Early Appraisal of China's Huge and Complex Health-care Reforms' (2012) 379 The Lancet 833.
Yip W and Hsiao W, 'What Drove the Circles of Chinese Health System Reforms' (2015) 1 Health Systems & Reform 52.
Young K, 'The Minimum Core of Economic and Social Rights: A Concept in Search of Content' (2008) Yale Journal of International Law 113.
Yu H, 'Universal Health Insurance Coverage for 1.3 Billion People: What Accounts for China's Success?' (2015) 119 Health Policy 1145.
Yu X, 'Weisheng Hewei – Zhongguo Jinshi de Weishenegshi Yanjiu [Review on the Study of Sanitary History of China in the Modern Age]' (2011) 3 Shixue Lilun Yanjiu [Historiography Quarterly] 132.

Zhang L, 'Building Communication Capacity for Good Governance: A Multileveled Analysis' in Zhenglai Deng and Sujian Guo (eds), *China's Search for Good Governance* (Palgrave Macmilan 2011).
Zhang M, 'The Socialist Legal System with Chinese Characteristics: China's Discourse for the Rule of Law and a Bitter Experience' (2010) 24 Temple University & Comparative Law Journal 1.
Zhang X, 'The Selection Mechanisms of Constitutional Cases' [Xianfa Anjian de Shaixuan Jizhi] Chinese Yearbook of Constitutional Law 2012 [Zhongguo Xianfa Niankan] 98.

Zhang Y, 'The Media's Role in Ensuring Social Accountability for the Right to Health in China' in Marlies Hesselman and others (eds), *Socio-Economic Human Rights in Essential Public Services Provision* (Routledge 2016).
Zhu G, 'Constitutional Review in China: An Unaccomplished Project or a Mirage?' (2010) 43 Suffolk University Law Review 625.
Zhu S, 'Political Parties in China's Judiciary' (2006) 17 Duke Journal of Comparative & International Law 553.
Zuo S, 'Zhijie Shiyong Tiaoyue Wenti Yanjie [Research on the Direct Application of Treaties]' (2008) 3 Legal Research 88.

Curriculum Vitae

Yi Zhang was born in Shanghai (China) in 1987. She obtained her PhD degree *cum laude* from the University of Groningen (May 2018) on a thesis concerning the role of accountability in advancing the right to health care under China's unique legal, political and social background. She currently works as a postdoctoral researcher at the School of Law, Tsinghua University, with a focus on access to medicines. Her research interests include international and domestic health law and policy, medicines regulation, accountability, and health system governance.

Alongside her research, Yi has also been an active member of varoius organisations. She is a member with and the Chinese liaison of the Global Health Law Groningen Research Centre (the Netherlands) and was the editor-in-chief of the Centre's blog. She is also a member of the Netherlands Network for Human Rights Research and a member of the Working Group on Economic, Social and Cultural Rights under this Network. In addition, Yi was the secretary and editorial board member of the Groningen Journal of International Law. Prior to her PhD studies, Yi also worked as a volunteer for UNICEF and participated in activities aimed at HIV/AIDS protection among children and teenagers in different Chinese cities.

Human Rights Research Series

The Netherlands Network of Human Rights Research is aimed at collaboration between human rights researchers in the Netherlands. Its central research theme is the nature and meaning of international standards in the field of human rights, their application and promotion in the national legal order, their interplay with national standards, and the international supervision of such application. The Human Rights Research Series only includes English titles that contribute to a better understanding of the different aspects of human rights.

For previous volumes in the series, please visit http://shr.intersentia.com.

Published titles within the Series:

72. Nelleke Koffeman, Morally Sensitive Issues and Cross-Border Movement in the EU ISBN 978–1-78068–349–2
73. Roland Moerland, The Killing of Death ISBN 978–1-78068–351–5
74. Andrea Broderick, The Long and Winding Road to Disability Equality and Inclusion ISBN 978–1-78068–358–4
75. Christina Peristeridou, The Principle of Legality in European Criminal Law ISBN 978–1–78068–357–7
76. Emilie Kuijt, Humanitarian Assistance and State Sovereignty in International Law ISBN 978–1–78068–366–9
77. Lize R. Glas, The Theory, Potential and Practice of Procedural Dialogue in the European Convention on Human Rights System ISBN 978–1–78068–375–1
78. Paulien de Morree, Rights and Wrongs under the ECHR ISBN 978–1–78068–418–5
79. Malu Beijer, The Limits of Fundamental Rights Protection by the EU ISBN 978–1–78068–455–0
80. Marie Elske Gispen, Human Rights and Drug Control ISBN 978–1–78068–454–3
81. Bart van der Sloot, Privacy as Virtue: Moving Beyond the Individual in the Age of Big Data ISBN 978–1–78068–505–2
82. Mohammad Hadi Zakerhossein, Situation Selection Regime at the International Criminal Court ISBN 978-1-78068-618-9

www.ingramcontent.com/pod-product-compliance
Ingram Content Group UK Ltd.
Pitfield, Milton Keynes, MK11 3LW, UK
UKHW051919100926
8556IPUK00021B/1270

9 781780 686776